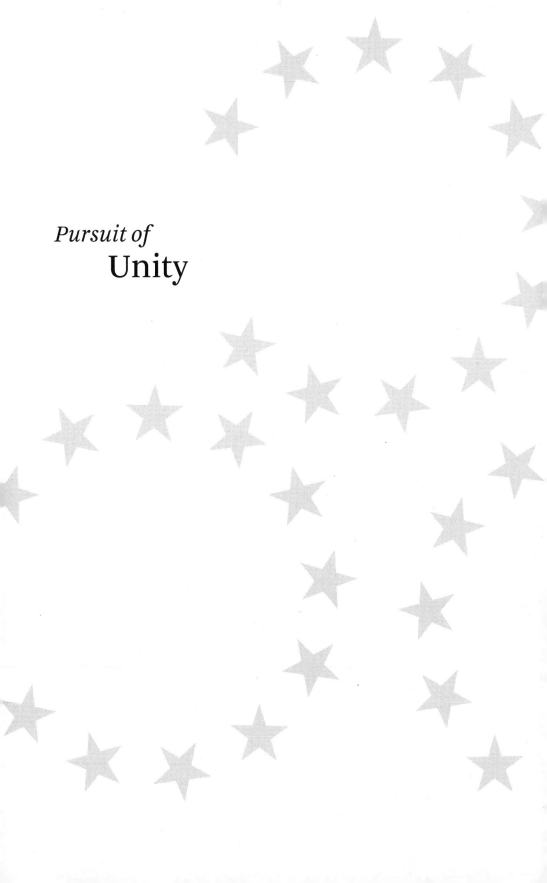

Pursuit of
Unity

THE UNIVERSITY OF NORTH CAROLINA PRESS *Chapel Hill*

Pursuit of Unity

A POLITICAL HISTORY
OF THE AMERICAN SOUTH

Michael Perman

This book was

published with the

assistance of the

Fred W. Morrison

Fund for South-

ern Studies of the

University of North

Carolina Press.

Designed by Courtney Leigh Baker
Set in Arnhem by Keystone Typesetting, Inc.

The paper in this book meets the guidelines for
permanence and durability of the Committee on
Production Guidelines for Book Longevity of the
Council on Library Resources.

The University of North Carolina Press has been a
member of the Green Press Initiative since 2003.

Library of Congress Cataloging-in-Publication Data
Perman, Michael.
Pursuit of unity : a political history of the American South /
Michael Perman.
p. cm.
Includes bibliographical references and index.
ISBN 978-0-8078-3324-7 (cloth: alk. paper)
1. Southern States—Politics and government—19th century.
2. Southern States—Politics and government—20th century.
3. Political culture—Southern States—History—19th
century. 4. Political culture—Southern States—History
—20th century. 5. Political parties—Southern States—
History—19th century. 6. Political parties—Southern
States—History—20th century. I. Title.
F213.P47 2009
306.20975—dc22
2009018545

13 12 11 10 09   5 4 3 2 1

To JOHN HOPE FRANKLIN

(1915–2009), my adviser and mentor,

with GRATITUDE and AFFECTION

CONTENTS

ILLUSTRATIONS AND MAPS

Illustrations

Maps

ACKNOWLEDGMENTS

The idea of a broad-ranging book on the distinctive features of politics in the American South first arose when I was on a year-long fellowship at the Institute for the Humanities at my university, the University of Illinois at Chicago. But it became a reality after Chuck Grench, who had just joined the University of North Carolina Press, asked me in 2002 if I would like to write an overview of the South's political history. The proposed book was to have a wide scope covering the entire span of southern history, in effect, two hundred years. And it was to reach an audience that included academia, yet went beyond it to a more general readership. The book's intended scope and readership were very different from anything I had previously embarked on. And it turned out to be a task that was challenging, but ultimately very gratifying to me. For the book's readers, however, my hope is that the experience will prove rewarding, rather than a task and a challenge, and that they will come away from it with a knowledge of the distinctive kind of politics that has been practiced in the South, along with an understanding of the pivotal, and usually adversarial, role that the southern region has played in America's political history.

In the course of writing this book, I have benefited from the help and advice of a number of people whom I can now thank publicly. First are the three readers of the manuscript when I submitted it to the press. Their reports raised questions, offered suggestions, and pointed out shortcomings, and I am very grateful to them for their thoughtful evaluations. One of them was a political journalist based in the South, whose identity is still unknown to me, but the other two told me who they were, and I was delighted to discover they were Michael Holt of the University of Virginia and Kari Frederickson of the University of Alabama at Tuscaloosa. No wonder these reports proved so valuable.

Because this project was not a specialized academic study, I wanted some reactions to the manuscript in its first iteration from nonspecialists. Two friends, Dale Sorenson and Martha Reese, offered to do this, giving me a lot of their time and providing me with some fine advice and criticism, for which I am in their debt. Later, after the readers' reports, I prevailed upon four other friends, all of them historians, to read a group of three or four chapters each. They gave me both encouragement and perceptive comments, not to mention corrections of some errors. These friends who were so generous with their time and expertise are Jim Roark of Emory University, Les Benedict of Ohio State University, Charles Dew of Williams College, and Rick Fried, my colleague at UIC.

In obtaining illustrations and permission to publish them, I was aided by a number of librarians, but Dale Neighbors at the Library of Virginia and Geoffery Stark in the Special Collections Department of the University of Arkansas at Fayetteville were particularly helpful. Also, Tim Storey of the National Conference of State Legislatures in Denver was so kind as to send me his spreadsheets of state legislative and gubernatorial elections, which were crucial to the creation of map 4 in chapter 15.

At UNC Press, those most involved were, of course, my editor, Chuck Grench, who supervised the entire process with an enthusiasm and persistence that I very much appreciated; Katy O'Brien, his assistant, who made sure I found illustrations and obtained permissions for them; Dorothea Anderson, who, in keeping with the high standards of the press, gave the final version of my manuscript a careful and thoughtful copyediting; and Paula Wald, who managed the editorial process throughout with such great care and skill.

And lastly, for being so very important to me for so many years, I want to thank my children, Ben and Sarah; my brother, David; and my good friend, G. V. Ramanathan.

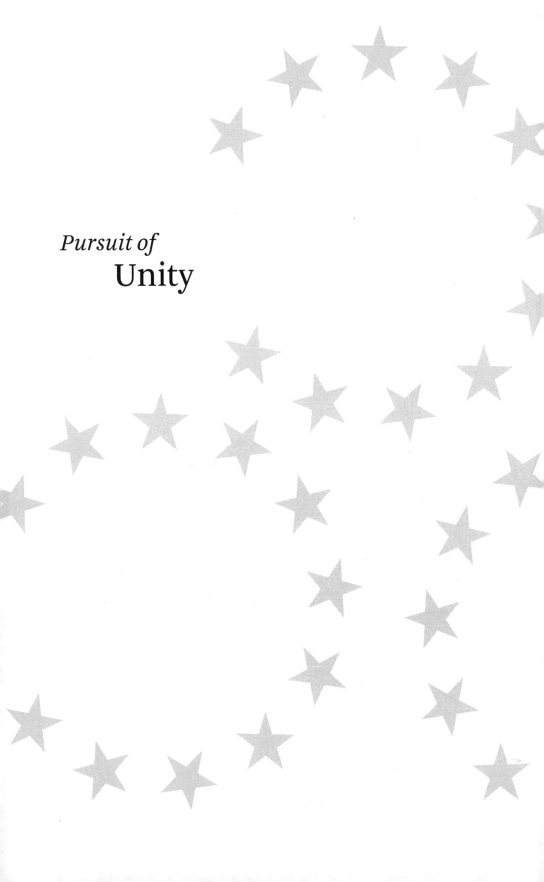

Pursuit of
Unity

Historians have written many, many books about southern politics, and so of course have political scientists. Despite this plethora, or perhaps because of it, no wide-ranging overview tracing the course of southern political history has previously appeared. Yet, like the South's history generally, its political history has possessed distinctive characteristics and patterns that give it coherence and direction. Even though it was just a region within a nation-state, the South has acted, for most of its history, as a self-conscious interest group marshaling its political resources in an ongoing struggle with the rest of the nation.

Over the past generation or so the South has changed a good deal, however, and so has its relationship with the non-South. With the region's economy and society becoming less and less distinctive and its politics also following a parallel course, it is appropriate to look back now to recount and explain the past two hundred years of southern political history and discover why the South took so long to become integrated into the national political system—if indeed that is what the region has just done.

Like most introductions, this one needs to take care of some necessary business before the story begins. The first two items are matters of definition. What is included in the category "the South"? And what does the term "politics" mean and refer to? The other topics are explanatory rather than definitional, and there are two of them as well. One explains the book's overarching theme, as indicated in its title, *Pursuit of Unity*, while the other describes how the book is organized and structured.

BY MANY OBSERVERS and commentators, "the South" has been conceived as an image or idea, an identity, a stereotype that exists in the minds of Americans. It is the antithesis of "the North," and both concepts are laced with distaste and disdain arising from a long history of rivalry and conflict not confined to the four years when they fought each other on the battlefield. But in political history, the definition of "the South" is a good deal more practical and material, namely, the South as a place, a geographic location where a particular form of politics was practiced.

Since states are the primary political entities that define the South, the question is, therefore, What states constitute "the South"?

Unfortunately, there is no official, or even accepted, definition. But all of the existing definitions agree upon one thing at least. Always included in any categorization of the South are the states that made up the Confederacy. These eleven states consist of two groupings. They are the Lower, or Deep, South states of South Carolina, Georgia, Florida, Alabama, Mississippi, Louisiana, and Texas and the Upper South states of Virginia, North Carolina, Tennessee, and Arkansas. These are the states covered by two authoritative studies of the region's politics by political scientists— V. O. Key's classic *Southern Politics* (1949) and Earl and Merle Black's recent study, *The Rise of Southern Republicans* (2002). Further endorsement for this definition of the South as the former Confederate states is that these were the states that disfranchised their black voters by constitutional revision and thereby brought into being the "Solid South" at the turn of the twentieth century. Additionally, these same eleven states composed the membership of the Southern Caucus that was formed in the U.S. Senate after World War II.

Four other definitions have also circulated, but none has acquired the currency of these eleven. Before the Civil War, the South was often defined as the slave states, in contrast to the free states. Usually included as slave states were all those where slavery existed and was legally recognized. This meant that Kentucky, Missouri, Delaware, and Maryland were often included, along with the eleven states of the Confederacy. But this definition was no longer applicable or useful once slavery was abolished after the Civil War. Since that time, three eminent historians of the South—C. Vann Woodward, George B. Tindall, and Numan V. Bartley— have added two others to the eleven Confederate states. They first added Kentucky and then later Oklahoma, in their highly regarded region-wide studies in the authoritative History of the South series. Nevertheless, the U.S. Census has an even broader definition, adding to the eleven Confederate states Delaware, Maryland, West Virginia, and the District of Columbia. But the broadest of all is the U.S. Department of Education's twentieth-century category, which includes all the states with legally segregated school systems, thus adding Kentucky and Missouri and Oklahoma to the list in the Census, for a total of eighteen.

Faced with this variety, the only reasonable conclusion is to restrict the South to the eleven Confederate states. Besides, inclusion of any other states presents problems. Throughout the two hundred years covered in this study, these eleven states (once they have obtained statehood, of

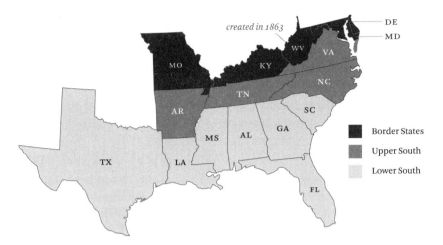

MAP 1. The South. The South consists of the seven Lower South and four Upper South states, the eleven states that seceded from the Union in 1860–61, although Tennessee was occupied by the Union Army in February 1862. The five border states—Missouri, West Virginia, Kentucky, Maryland, and Delaware—are on the South's northern perimeter.

course) have been included in all the definitions. Clearly, they constitute the undisputed core of the region in the nineteenth and twentieth centuries.

ALSO NEEDING DEFINITION is the term "politics." In a study covering two centuries of history in an entire region of eleven states, each with a different political system and governmental arena, it is essential to define the term "politics" strictly, even narrowly. Otherwise, the narrative will lose focus and soon become unmanageable. For example, a political history of the South cannot dwell on politics at the county and municipal level, despite the truistic, and almost banal, claim of Tip O'Neill, the Speaker of the House in the 1990s, that "all politics is local." The political life of the region at all levels and in all its variety cannot be the subject matter of a historical overview like this. Nor should it be, since the purpose of a broad synthesis of this kind is to discover the central issues and themes in the South's political history and then to explain why they arose and how they shaped the role and course of the region within the national political arena. To this end, generalization, rather than detail and variation, is the main concern.

Like the South, the Midwest and New England are regions of the United States. But they have not functioned consistently as politically self-conscious sections, with a history of autonomous, even separatist, organization and action over a long period of time. The South, however, has considered itself a minority at odds with the rest of the country, sometimes even under attack from it. Southern political history has therefore been preoccupied with the region's interaction with the non-South states. And it has been at the national level within the three branches of the federal government that the interests of the South have had to be promoted and protected.

Although Washington has been the focal point of southern politics for most of the past two centuries, it was the interests of the southern states themselves that were being represented and defended there. State politics will therefore feature prominently in the story. But this particular treatment of southern political history is not a compilation of eleven individual state histories. The states will be treated as components of the southern region, not as distinctive entities with their own independent, free-standing political histories.

A HISTORICAL STUDY of this scope and duration has to have an organizing principle or central theme. And it is hard to overlook the fundamental role that political parties have played in the history of the South. Although the parties have changed in form and name and have performed different functions at different times, there is one distinctive characteristic of party politics in the South—the lack of competition between contending parties for almost the entirety of the past two hundred years. As a result, the region has had a history of one-party politics. Either one party has been so dominant that opposition has been completely marginalized or else one party has functioned as the only accepted political organization. The contemporary situation in the South in which there are two viable and competitive parties is therefore not merely unusual—it is an aberration. For most of its history, the two-party system, which is widely seen as a valuable, even essential, feature of American government and politics, has been absent from the South.

The account that follows will trace the region's persistent pursuit of unity. In the process, it will offer explanations for why and when a one-party politics arose, as well as describe its features and how it functioned at both the state and the national levels. But first a few words about what lay behind this preoccupation with unity and what this fear of party competition was all about. Throughout the nineteenth century and most of the twentieth, the white population of the southern states has been deeply concerned about the maintenance of the region's system of race relations.

This system has enabled southern whites to dominate the African American population, both socially and economically.

In the nineteenth century, slavery was the form the system assumed. In the twentieth, it was a system of legal segregation and control over the region's blacks, who were no longer slaves but now U.S. citizens. And for most of these two centuries, the region's system of racial control was questioned and even attacked, usually from outside the South, though not always. In this milieu, the South's political system has functioned as a critical component of the continuous effort to keep organized opposition from becoming a threat, both inside the region and at the national level in Washington. As a result, one-party dominance, or else one-party monopoly, has been the form that politics has assumed in the South. Accompanying this persistent worry about political opposition has been its more affirmative counterpart, the need for unity. Although usually attained, unity has been an objective constantly invoked and pursued in southern politics ever since 1800, when the Republicans and the Virginia Dynasty came to power in the South and the nation.

These ongoing efforts to manage the political system in the interest of southern unity did not, however, go unchallenged. During the first half of the nineteenth century, first the Federalists, though briefly and feebly, and then the Whigs more forcefully, had presented an alternative to the Jeffersonian Republicans and then to the Jacksonian Democrats. But, in the 1850s and during the four years of the Confederacy, opposition faded into insignificance. For a brief time during Reconstruction, a new party, the Republican Party, made two-party politics a real possibility again. But the former Confederates and their allies in the Democratic Party attacked and marginalized their Republican opponents. From the mid-1870s until the end of the century, opposition did exist, most notably the Populists in the 1890s, but it was countered with heavy doses of force and fraud and effectively subdued. The Democrats proceeded to rewrite the region's state constitutions so as to disfranchise the black voters and a large number of whites who formed the base of support for most of the anti-Democratic parties since the Civil War.

With the elimination of all but a few of the black, and most of the poor white, voters, the political system was closed off to organized opposition in the form of independent black politics or any kind of insurgency by disaffected voters, black as well as white. Indeed, the single-party monopoly, the "Solid South," as it became known, was created for the sole purpose of prohibiting opposition. When a serious challenge did arise, in the form of the States' Rights Democrats, or Dixiecrats, in 1948, it came from the right and it endorsed the South's system of racial domination even more vigorously than did the region's all-powerful Democrats. In such a hostile environment, effective electoral opposition and dissent was a virtual impossibility.

THIS ACCOUNT OF the South's pursuit of unity will be organized into five parts. Despite the South's proclivity for one-party politics, its political history was hardly static. Circumstances changed over time and in different ways and thus altered the form and shape of the one-party South. Part 1 covers the period that began with the election of Thomas Jefferson of Virginia to the presidency in 1800 and ended with the South's secession in 1861. During these sixty years, the South experienced an era of one-party dominance. Jefferson's Republican Party dominated the South until the mid-1820s, after which two parties competed within the South for a brief period, as the newly formed Democratic Party of Andrew Jackson faced opposition from the Whigs, also a new party. But soon the Whigs collapsed, leaving the South a one-party region again under the Democrats.

Part 2 covers the South's brief experience as an independent nation under the Confederacy from 1861 to 1865. During these few years, the South did not have to maneuver within a hostile political arena inside the same nation. Freed from this burden, the Confederates experimented with a political system without parties at all, an indication that perhaps southern politicians did not particularly like party competition of any kind.

Part 3 traverses the quarter century or so from the end of the Civil War until disfranchisement around 1900. After their military defeat, the former Confederates resorted again to party, calling themselves Conservatives and then, later, Democrats. But a competitive two-party system did not develop during Reconstruction because the Democrats refused to recognize the legitimacy of their Republican opponents and proceeded instead to drive them from power by whatever means necessary, illegal as well as violent. And this period of one-party hegemony continued until the end of the century.

Part 4 begins at the turn of the twentieth century. The political crisis of the 1890s led to the revival of the Republican opposition and the creation of a new party, the Populists. But this enlarged and emboldened opposition was soon defeated, although not without difficulty. Once their challengers were dispersed, the Democrats confirmed their restored ascendancy by changing the electoral rules drastically and formalizing their dominance with the sanction of law. In effect, a one-party system was declared official and legal. The region referred to itself as the "Solid South," and it remained that way for the next seventy years.

The South's solidity was not, however, unchanging or unchallenged. It reached its zenith over the first thirty years of the twentieth century. But, after the mid-1930s, it began to run into difficulties when opposition from the northern wing of the Democratic Party emerged and gained momentum. For the next three decades, southern Democrats fought a desperate rear-guard action in their region and in the nation, only to meet their Waterloo in the 1960s, a defeat that proved to be decisive and irreversible during the 1970s.

In Part 5, the recent phase of southern political history is examined. It began to emerge in the 1970s, although its form and direction was not evident until a decade or so later. At present, the South is experiencing something quite unfamiliar and unusual. For the first time, there are two parties and they are identifiably different from as well as competitive with each other. Already, the new southern Republican Party and its rival, a redefined and reconstituted Democratic Party, have been in existence for longer than the Whig-Democratic rivalry from 1836 to 1852. It does seem as if the South's political system has changed decisively and that its one-party politics has become, as they say, a thing of the past. Nevertheless, it is still possible that the South might revert to its former self and become a one-party region once again, with the conservative, overwhelmingly white, Republicans replacing the conservative, totally white, Democrats of the Solid South era. Since the southern states have already been designated by many political commentators as "red states," the party's momentum could continue until Republican dominance is the long-term outcome, along with a return to a one-party South.

WE CAN NOW begin to explore politics as it has been practiced and experienced in the South over the past two centuries. And, as we will discover, politics in the South has been strange and unusual—in effect, another "peculiar institution."

PART I.

ONE-PARTY DOMINANCE,

1800–1861

1

A One-Party South

The presidential election of 1800 brought the ten-year-old American republic to the brink of disaster. The vote in the Electoral College was tied,
with the two leading candidates each obtaining 73 votes. According to the
Constitution, which had been adopted twelve years earlier, this meant
that the House of Representatives was now required to resolve the matter.
But the House found this task very difficult to accomplish. It spent an
entire week of bargaining and scheming until, after thirty-five ballots, it
finally produced a winner. This second, or "contingent," election, as it
was then called, was further complicated by the unfortunate fact that the
two rival candidates were from the same party. The decision as to which of
the two Republicans, Thomas Jefferson or Aaron Burr, would become
president lay therefore in the hands of their opponents, the Federalists.
When the Federalists eventually decided to end their unsuccessful efforts
in support of Burr and to switch most of their votes to Jefferson, the
Virginian became the third president, thanks to the hated Federalists.

This closely contested election, with the Federalist, John Adams, receiving just eight votes fewer than the two tied Republicans, produced an
electoral deadlock, which then precipitated a constitutional crisis. Such
a dangerous state of affairs had arisen because the new Constitution's
provisions for choosing a president and a vice president had proven un-
workable. Electors had each been given two votes, the "dual vote" as it
was called, but they were not allowed to rank them. Yet, with the emergence of political parties in the 1790s, it was essential that the vice president be not just the second-largest vote getter but also a member of the
winner's party. This problem had already become evident in 1796 when
John Adams, the Federalist, was elected president and the runner-up,
Jefferson, the preeminent Republican, was elected vice president. Since
this anomaly was not remedied by the time the next election took place,

the federal system stumbled through an electoral process that proved to be prolonged, frustrating, and almost disastrous.

Despite all these shortcomings, the contest in 1800 was one of the pivotal presidential elections in American history. And it was decisive because its consequences transformed the political landscape. In 1804, at the end of Jefferson's first term, the Federalist Party suffered a massive defeat, winning just 14 votes in the Electoral College to the Republicans' 162. The Federalists revived somewhat in Jefferson's second term and in Madison's first, when the ill-conceived Embargo and commercial retaliation against Britain over its interference with American shipping gave the Federalists a political opportunity. But even so, Charles C. Pinckney, of South Carolina, the party's presidential candidate in 1808, could only expand the Federalist electoral vote to 47. And by 1812, the Federalists were reduced to running DeWitt Clinton, a dissident Republican from New York, for president. Four years later, after it had opposed the war with Britain, the party was dead. Its presidential nominee in 1816, Rufus King, received a mere 34 electoral votes to James Monroe's 183, almost all of them coming from Massachusetts, the state where King had spent his childhood. Once the center of Federalism, Massachusetts was now its one remaining outpost.

The Republicans in Power

The rapid decline of the Federalists after the close contest of 1800 and their disappearance as an effective political force sixteen years later meant that the Republicans had attained dominance. In fact, they had become preeminent and were no longer confronted by any organized party opposition. For the South, this was a moment of triumph that it has never again experienced in its history. For the Republican Party was a southern party, and so was its leadership. Jefferson, Madison, and Monroe, all southerners, held the presidency from 1800 until 1824. More than that, they were neighbors living close to each other on their plantations in the foothills of central Virginia. As the rest of the country became increasingly Republican after 1800, it came to resemble the South, which had been solidly Republican even before that critical election. Throughout this quarter century, therefore, the party that dominated the South dominated the nation. The South was in the enviable position of being the majority within the majority party.

The core constituency of the Republicans was located in the South. In the election of 1796, when the newly emerging political parties were first in evidence in a presidential contest, John Adams obtained just two electoral votes in the southern states of Virginia, North Carolina, South Carolina, and Georgia, as well as in the recently admitted states of Kentucky and Tennessee. Meanwhile, Thomas Jefferson received not a single vote north of Pennsylvania. And the picture was almost as bleak for the Federalists in the South's congressional delegations and state assemblies. Between 1790 and 1797, the Federalists sent, on average, just five congressmen from the seaboard southern states of Virginia, the Carolinas, and Georgia, out of a possible total of around thirty-five.

But in the congressional elections of 1798–99, the Federalists managed to cut into the Republicans' southern stronghold by winning a dozen seats from their opponents. The war scare of that year and a concerted effort by Alexander Hamilton, aided by the former president from Virginia, George Washington, accounted for the Federalist success in countering the "Opposition-Faction," which, Hamilton feared, was assuming "so much a Geographical complexion."[1] A year or so later, however, the Republicans surged back, reversing a 63–43 Federalist majority in Congress to generate a 65–41 Republican majority in 1800. And, in the presidential race, Jefferson received 85 percent of the South's electoral vote. Adams, by contrast, obtained 56 of his 65 votes from outside the South, while Jefferson won not a single vote in New England.

The southern origins of the Republican Party are not hard to explain. Long-standing friends from Virginia, James Madison, the leader of the House of Representatives, and Thomas Jefferson, secretary of state until he resigned and returned to Virginia in 1794, were the coordinators of the opposition to the domestic policy initiatives of the Washington administration. Their objections to the government's policies were sharp and deep, and they arose at the outset when Alexander Hamilton, the secretary of the treasury, presented to the First Congress his plans for the new republic's economy. Hamilton's was no modest proposal—but a grand design that envisaged an extensive role for the federal government in shaping public finance and private enterprise. His central idea was to use the public debt of the United States as a device to solidify and empower the new national government and to forge an enduring alliance with its creditors. He also proposed the creation of a national bank. The government's funds would be deposited in the bank and its stock would be payable in government securities, thus making the bank and the government closely connected and interdependent. The third element in Hamilton's plan was his proposal for the government to encourage the growth of manufacturing, so as to enable the United States to produce its own finished goods, a development that would be encouraged by subsidies and a protective tariff.

These measures would create a powerful and active national government, closely allied to financial interests in the northeastern and middle states and to investors and manufacturers who wanted to change the nature and direction of the American economy. To Madison and Jefferson, this agenda was anathema. Both were nationalists who had been eager to strengthen the central government in the 1780s, and they were now playing prominent roles within the governmental structure created in 1787–89. But Hamilton and the Federalist leadership envisioned a system even more powerful and expansive than the two Virginians had imagined. What was more, its effect was to shift resources and benefits toward the northeast and away from the southeast.

The Federalists' blueprint for the fledgling United States at its formative moment was undoubtedly based on Britain's centralized and finance-driven government and its hierarchical society, in a word, the monarchical system that Americans had just recently waged a war to repudiate. Emulation of Britain's system of government and its social order was almost certain to continue the close commercial connections of northeastern shippers and merchants with British interests, which, in turn, would hamper America's ability to break out of its colonial dependence. This unwillingness to sever the ties with Britain that perpetuated America's economic and cultural subservience became problematical when Britain and France went to war in the wake of the French Revolution. The United States became implicated in the hostilities and soon felt compelled to take sides, during the 1790s. Predictably, the Federalists aligned with the British, while the Republicans found themselves siding with the French. Thus, foreign affairs further sharpened the differences already evident between the emergent parties over the vital domestic issues of the early 1790s.

Because Hamilton's policies were presented as interconnected parts of a grand scheme, they were bound to provoke a reaction that a less ambitious set of proposals would almost certainly have prevented. Jefferson and Madison, and others who would join them in opposition to this vision, saw it as antithetical to their own interests and priorities. In the first place, Hamilton's plan was regional and exclusive in its origins and impact. The southern end of the country, and even much of the middle section, would not play a major part in the future shaping of America's political economy. A second objection, stemming from the first, was that the financial and commercial interests were to be the protagonists and beneficiaries. And these were located in the more populous urban areas of the country, in its ports and large towns. By contrast, the countryside, with its farms and plantations and its villages and market towns, where the vast majority of the population lived and worked, was ignored and would soon, it was feared, become subordinated to the cities and their commercialized inhabitants. In direct contrast with Hamilton's vision, Jefferson and Madison, who were plantation owners in the rural South, imagined a very different future. They saw the United States as a nation of industrious and virtuous farmers who fed themselves and were self-sufficient but who were also involved in the marketplace when they sold their surplus produce, even selling abroad if the staple crops were tobacco, rice, or, later, cotton.[2]

A third point of contrast with the Federalists' scenario was the Republican view of the ideal role of government. "A wise and frugal government" was how Jefferson, in his first inaugural address, described a system with few powers and limited resources. And its strength lay, not in its ability to enforce obedience, but in its winning the support of the citizenry. Confronted with Federalist designs for an imposing governmental establishment armed with authority and power, the opposition's response was to prevent these accumulations of energy and responsibility and, in effect, to save the structure created by the Constitution from being expanded and changed beyond recognition.

And, finally, the opposition sought to prevent the Federalists from modeling the United States on Britain. Jefferson detested Britain and found France far more congenial, partly because he had lived there for many years but also because the French had overthrown their own monarchy and embarked on a republican revolution that, initially at least, was similar to America's. In Jefferson's view, the preferred course for the United States was not to model itself on any other nation but instead to act independently and develop a government and an economy that were natural and appropriate for the new republic itself. That is, it should neither emulate nor become entangled with any country, and it should be willing to trade with them all.

The Federalists' initiative was definitive and daring and it aimed to create a prosperous, powerful United States that could very soon take its place among the nation-states of Europe. Attractive though that prospect might have appeared, the means for attaining it opened the Federalists up to a broadly based attack that they proved incapable of repelling. Exclusive and favoring a few regions and interests, expanding the central government beyond what had been feared in 1787–89, and emulating and aligning with its recent British enemy, the Federalist formula was hard to defend. Since a wide swath of opinion felt excluded and was instinctively opposed to the direction in which the Federalists intended to take the country, the Republicans did not really have to develop a proposal of their own. All they had to do was counter and criticize Federalist initiatives. And even when the Republican Party obtained power nationally, it still functioned in an oppositional mode. For its objective, its justification, was simply to restrict and curb the Federalists and their ambitious plans in order to rescue the constitutional system envisaged by the Framers and allow the republic's economy to develop naturally and gradually along primarily agricultural lines.

Federalists in the South

The Republicans' formulation of the issue in the great political struggle of the 1790s resonated deeply in the southern states, leaving little room for opposition to emerge. Despite their brief revival during the war scare of 1798–99, the Federalists proved unable to return to their previous level of support after Jefferson's election in 1800. Instead, they went into a decline in the South more rapid than in any other part of the country. By the end of the Virginian's first term, in fact, the Federalists no longer functioned "as an effective opposition in the South."[3] The extent of the Federalists' collapse was evident in the next presidential election when Jefferson won every electoral vote in the South, with the exception of a few in North Carolina. A year later, in the congressional elections, only four Federalists contended for seats in Virginia, the Carolinas, and Georgia. Two won and two lost, but around forty seats were not even contested. The party's plight was captured by North Carolina's *Wilmington Gazette* in an apocryphal story about two Federalists who met on the street one day. "Federalism begins to look up," remarked one of them. "Very true," replied the other. "Being on its back, it can look no other way."[4]

This precipitous collapse can be explained partly by the success of President Jefferson's first term. And, of course, this hurt the Federalists outside the South too. Not only did Jefferson manage the transition of power from one party to another with great political dexterity, but he also presided over a period of peace and prosperity, after the turbulence of the 1790s. Rather than attacking the Federalists frontally, as his opponents had expected him to do, the politician who had disparaged Federalists as "monarchists" and usurpers proceeded with great caution but also firmness. He reduced the federal debt considerably and repealed the unpopular excise and direct taxes levied by the Federalists. Meanwhile, he pared down the federal civil service and shrank substantially the army and navy, which his predecessors had built up in preparation for war with the French in 1799. Finally, he reserved the patronage positions within his power for Republicans, while removing only a few Federalists, often eliminating not the incumbents themselves, but their offices. After establishing a diminished government manned by Republican loyalists but without giving the Federalists much grounds for opposition, Jefferson capped these achievements with his purchase from the French in 1803 of the vast territory of Louisiana. This initiative cost little ($15 million) but generated enthusiastic support from the Republicans' southern base. It offered to the South the enticing prospect of extensive westward migration, while other regions welcomed the acquisition because it more than doubled the size of the national domain.

For the southern Federalists, there were, however, more specific and local reasons for their party's collapse. In the first place, the South's Federalists proved incapable of expanding their base beyond a few coastal ports and commercial centers. In Georgia, the party was confined to the trading centers of Savannah and Augusta; in South Carolina, to Charleston and a few neighboring parishes; in North Carolina, to the port of Wilmington and the commercial area around Fayetteville; and in Virginia, to urban areas such as Richmond, Norfolk, and Alexandria and along the eastern shore. Outside these enclaves, where merchants and bankers were the party's main supporters, Federalists generated very little enthusiasm. Nor did they attempt to expand the party into the rural areas of the South where the region's economic life and its population were mainly to be found.

And this propensity highlighted the second problem with southern Federalists. Men who aligned themselves with the party were invariably well-off and status-conscious members of the social and economic elite who did not relish getting involved in organizing the party or campaigning among the voters. Consequently, they did not confer with each other as election time approached in order to coordinate and plan their activities. Instead, they acted as individuals in announcing their candidacies, frequently waiting until late in the campaign. The inevitable result was that more than one candidate often ran for the same office, and, of course, none had any plans to electioneer and get out the vote. A notable exception occurred in Charleston, where Federalist tickets for city elections and house-to-house canvassing were not unknown after 1800.

The party's elitism and the location of its base in the coastal cities prevented it from taking advantage of the popular issues that percolated through southern politics during the early nineteenth century dealing with legislative reapportionment, constitutional revision, and judicial reform. These demands came from the rapidly growing numbers of settlers in the western sections of each state, who wanted greater representation in the legislature and increased participation as voters. Only in Virginia were some Federalists in the west actively involved in this contest. In the 1810s, Charles Fenton Mercer of Loudoun County, in northern Virginia, who had become the leading Federalist in the state, tried to create a Federalist beachhead in the democratizing western counties by proposing a public system of primary education. But his objective in proposing this plan was to control, rather than elevate and liberate, "the idle, worthless, ignorant and corrupt mass of the population."[5] With attitudes like these, Mercer presented the Republicans with sufficient ammunition to expose the initiative's motives and thus defeat it. In South Carolina, on the other hand, the Republicans precluded any Federalist attempt to broaden the party's base by securing their dominance over the state through the "Settlement of 1808." This arrangement reapportioned the legislature and vastly increased its power to appoint state and local officials, thereby giving the Republican-dominated assembly overwhelming control of state government for years to come.

Out of touch with each other and with the voters, the southern Federalists were also disconnected from their counterparts elsewhere. Conspicuous by their absence were the southern representatives at the quadrennial meetings to select a presidential candidate. On each occasion, the party notables gathered together, usually in New York, and produced a ticket with a southerner on it. This had quickly become the custom since the Washington-Adams ticket in 1792. It acknowledged a widely perceived reality that the vice presidential position was supposed to balance the ticket and that there existed only two elements that needed to be balanced, that is, the two regions, the South and the Northeast. And this regional division of the American polity was not lost on the Republicans either, because they too aligned their tickets regionally. At any rate, the Federalists selected Charles Cotesworth Pinckney of South Carolina and Rufus King of New York to run in 1804 and again in 1808. Pinckney and King ran again in 1816, though in the reverse order this time, with King heading the ticket. The only exception was 1812, when the nominees were DeWitt Clinton of New York, a Republican who opposed the war with Britain, and Jared Ingersoll of Pennsylvania.

Even though a southern candidate was usually selected and southern Federalists were specifically invited to attend the meeting of party leaders in 1804 and 1808, no official delegates showed up. On one occasion, in 1808, John Rutledge Jr. of South Carolina happened to be in New York at the time of the meeting, so he attended, albeit on the spur of the moment. Otherwise, the listless and marginalized southern Federalists simply accepted the sop that was thrown them by their colleagues to the north but did nothing with it. Their region was lost to the Federalist Party, and the only possible reason to have a southern candidate on the ticket was that, without it, the party's unrepresentativeness would be completely exposed. Even so, the party's insistence on putting Charles C. Pinckney, the southerner, at the head of the party's presidential slate on two occasions is puzzling. The first time, the party did it in hope of competing directly with Jefferson the Virginian, but by 1808 its stake in the South had diminished so much that it made little sense. Of course, it is possible that the party's national leaders were quite unaware of how weak their party had become south of the reliable border state of Maryland.

Never more than a small minority after Jefferson's first term, the southern Federalists had to become active and organized if they were to be competitive. But, unable and unwilling to expand their membership and electoral base, they had just two alternatives available. They could either wait for the unchallenged Republicans to divide, which seemed quite possible in 1808 when supporters of James Monroe contested the succession of James Madison to the presidency. Or they could hope for an issue to arise that might draw support away from the Republicans. And the failure of the unwise Embargo policy and the drift to war with Britain offered such a possibility between 1806 and 1812. But the Monroe split was smothered by the Republicans, and the conflict with Britain did not affect the farmers of the South as much as it did the commercial and shipping interests of New England. So the Federalists' Micawber-like hope that something would "turn up" to help them revive their prospects did not materialize. The party remained a presence, but not a force, in southern politics.

Meanwhile, the Republicans' grip on the South became more complete. Rather surprisingly, however, they did not develop much of a party organization. As a leading historian of the Jeffersonian Republicans concluded, "Formal party machinery was less fully developed there than in New England or in the middle states."[6] For the party was so dominant in the South that it did not need to build a party structure to choose candidates and mobilize voters. By contrast, in those states outside the South where the party faced competition, it was compelled to organize. And the greater the threat, the more developed the party's machinery became. Therefore, New England Republicans were better organized than those in Pennsylvania and New York. Also contributing to party development was the need to conduct elections at the state level. If there were few state-wide elections, or none at all, then there was no compulsion to create an apparatus for coordinating the party above and beyond the local level. And in the southern states, the selection of governors and state officials was invariably the responsibility of the legislature, while presidential electors were usually chosen either by the assembly or through elections in each congressional district. In the states to the north, where there was more party competition and where statewide elections were more common, machinery for making nominations and coordinating campaigns was established in one of three ways—through caucuses of the party's state legislators, through committees consisting of the party's leaders and officeholders, or even, in several of the smaller states, through gatherings with such broad participation that they could almost be considered conventions.

Without coordination at the state level, Republican activists were left to their own devices in local races. Men who wished to run for election to local and district offices would put themselves forward with little or no consultation, relying on an announcement in the newspaper or the circulation of notices or handbills informing voters of their candidacy. Sometimes this form of self-nomination was supplemented by the endorsement of friends of the candidate, who bestowed on him the authority of their social or political reputations. Local leaders might even select a candidate and place his name before the voters through printed declarations in newspapers or the printing of announcements. This kind of informality in generating Republican candidates for office was not characteristic of the rest of the country, where the practice of self-nomination was rejected as behavior unbecoming for a gentleman. But in the South, the acceptance of self-promotion did not end with the announcement of a candidate's own eagerness to be elected, for candidates also engaged in electioneering and traveled out among the voters to solicit their support. Usually, however, campaigning was undertaken on behalf of candidates by party officials and through distribution of campaign literature rather than by the candidate himself speaking on the stump.

Surprisingly perhaps, campaigning was very common in the South. In the more recently settled states of Kentucky and Tennessee, it could become raucous and rowdy, with politicians courting voters with flattery and appeals to their emotions, all the while plying them with food and drink. But candidates felt compelled to campaign, even though many found it distasteful and time consuming. William Brockenbrough, a Republican who came from an established Virginia family, was successful in his effort to get elected to the state assembly in 1801. "Two months before the Election were almost exclusively appropriated to electioneering," he complained. "I traversed every part of the Country, and became acquainted with almost the whole of the people." But he often discovered that "Grog, strong Grog was to them of much more Consequence than giving their Votes for this or that man. These persons I generally neglected, having determined not to gain my Election by such means, and I succeeded, for I believe I did not spend two Dollars during the two Months, in which I canvassed."[7] Brockenbrough was clearly pleased with himself for resisting the lures of treating and pandering to voters.

But no matter how reluctant a candidate might be, the informality of the nominating process and the lack of organized backing required candidates to take an active and personal role in securing their own election. This assertiveness contrasted with the passivity of the Federalists. Although neither party developed statewide party machinery, the Republicans, it seemed, were prepared to involve themselves in the electoral process to the benefit of both the individual candidate and the party itself.

The Virginia Dynasty

In a region conspicuous for its undeveloped party machinery, there arose a political organization during these decades unlike any other in American political history, either before or since. The Virginia Dynasty controlled the presidency from 1800 to 1824, an entire generation. Jefferson, Madison, and Monroe each spent eight years in what became, quite unexpectedly but very rapidly, the nation's most important and most visible public office. A position that the Framers considered largely ceremonial and above politics became, as early as Washington's second term, intensely contested and political. Once they gained possession of the presidency in 1801, the Virginians decided immediately to devise a scheme to keep it under the control of the Republican Party they had created. If they could deny the Federalists access to the power and patronage of the office for long enough, the opposition party would be so weakened that it would simply wither away.

The making of a president went through two phases. The nominating procedure, which occurred at the national level, was followed by the election itself, which took place in the states, where presidential electors were chosen. These electors then cast their ballots for a particular candidate. Amazingly, neither part of the process was given any specificity by the Constitution, yet further evidence of how little weight the Framers gave to an office that they regarded as the executor of the laws of Congress and unlikely to exert much power or act independently of the more important legislative branch. There was simply no specific provision at all for how presidential candidacies were to emerge or for how the nominees, once selected, were to be elected to office. Yet this procedure could not be left to chance, despite the Framers' oversight. As the elections of 1796 and, even more frightening, 1800–1801 had demonstrated, failure to close these gaps could be fatal.

The most glaring omission in the nominating procedure was the lack of discrimination in the listing of candidates between the office of president and that of vice president. To rectify this defect, which had produced the calamitous tie between Jefferson and Burr, the Republicans in Congress proposed a constitutional amendment that would list candidates according to the office they sought. As the Federalists realized immediately, this would produce a ticket for both offices arranged by the parties. Although this remedy would solve the problem at hand, it would, in practical terms, ensure victory for the majority Republicans in the contests for both offices. The party that was out of office would be prevented from interfering in the event of a tie by backing the lesser of the two evils, as the Federalists had been able to do in 1800, or from obtaining the vice presidency as the runner-up in the balloting. Possessing more votes, the party in power would win both offices. Nevertheless, after extensive debate and despite solid Federalist opposition, the Twelfth Amendment to the Constitution obtained a clear two-thirds majority in the Senate, though barely in the House. It was then ratified in 1804 by all the states, save the Federalist strongholds of Massachusetts, Connecticut, and Delaware.

As had been the practice in 1800, the selection of the Republican nominees was to be arranged by the party's delegation in Congress, which would meet as a party caucus for this purpose. The aim was to create a ticket that was regionally balanced. A southerner, from Virginia each time, was selected for president, and a northerner, invariably from New York, as had been the case in 1800, was chosen for the second spot. This would provide the necessary regional balance, but the nominee for the second office was to be a politician who, unlike Burr, had no aspirations for the presidency and would be content to play second fiddle. The size of the Virginia delegation in Congress and the influence of the Virginia leaders within the party virtually guaranteed the success of the scheme. But skillful and tenacious maneuvering and cajoling were still required if the Virginians' aims were to be realized.

Besides the congressional caucus, the other base on which this system rested was located in Virginia itself. Members of the Electoral College, who, according to the Constitution, actually chose the president and vice president, were themselves to be selected by each state. But, remarkably, the Framers did not specify how and by whom this was to be done. And two hundred years later, this process is still not specified in the document itself, since no amendments to rectify this omission have been adopted. Even more amazing, the Electoral College itself, which was created for the sole purpose of filtering and diluting the vote of the people, still exists. In a nation that, in the twenty-first century, considers itself democratic, this is an oddity, to say the least.

In the two decades following the ratification of the Twelfth Amendment in 1804, three methods for selecting the members of the Electoral College were experimented with, and individual states went back and forth, choosing their electors one way and then later changing to another. One way was for state legislatures to choose the electors. Another was to hold elections in each congressional district at which electors would be chosen. And the third method provided for statewide elections to select electors, usually referred to as the "general ticket" system. Most southern states operated at one time or another under the legislative system; few opted for the "general ticket" formula. Under the legislature and the district methods, the electors would probably be split between the parties, whereas the "general ticket" ensured that the winning party would obtain them all. In 1800, in order to maneuver for advantage in the upcoming election, several states had considered changing their method of selecting electors. One of them was Virginia, which shifted from the district to the "general ticket" method of holding a single statewide election. At the time, this method was in operation in just three states, Pennsylvania, New Hampshire, and Georgia. And there was only a wafer-thin majority in the assembly favoring the change in Virginia. But the consequences were to prove enormous. For Virginia's ability to deliver the largest bloc of electors as a unit for the Republican presidential ticket gave the state immense leverage in the Electoral College.

Winning a statewide election required management, however. Without an effective state organization, the Republican Party in Virginia could not have turned its unmatched quota of twenty or so electors into a quadrennial series of solid votes in the college. Yet, in defiance of the apparent

Thomas Ritchie. The editor of the *Richmond Enquirer*, 1804–45, Ritchie was the leading figure in the Richmond Junto. Throughout his long public life, first within the Republican Party and then as a Democrat, he played an extremely influential role nationally as well as in Virginia. Library of Virginia.

southern pattern, or style, of minimal electoral cohesion and machinery within both parties, the Virginia Republicans created a formidable apparatus. A caucus of the party's state legislators and other respected notables chose a standing central committee located in the capital, Richmond, and then established and selected the members of committees in each county. Overseeing the whole process was an informal group of well-connected and often kin-related men, numbering among them several Nicholases, Barbours, and Wirts, some of whom were also members of the central committee. Known as the Richmond Junto, this informal group gathered around Thomas Ritchie, the editor of the *Richmond Enquirer*, which was the mouthpiece of the Republican Party and the publisher of its official information and propaganda. This centralized network coordinated the elections throughout the state and also ensured continuity of membership. As a result, valuable experience and loyalty was forged at the head of the party's electoral machinery.

The impressive system created by the Virginia Republicans was quite out of character in a region whose politics was the least organized and competitive in the entire country. But nowhere else was a concerted effort made to control the presidency in the interests of a tight-knit and powerful political class. An extraordinary group of talented politicians lived in the state, and they had led the opposition to the plans of the Federalist administration, headed by George Washington, for shaping the new system of government. In the process, they had initiated the formation of an opposition party. The Virginia Dynasty that resulted was based, not only on Virginia's size and its pool of presidential contenders, but also on its preeminence within the party ever since its founding. Also contributing to Virginia's influence were its close connections with the states of Kentucky and Tennessee in the west, since both were, in a real sense, extensions of the commonwealth, having been settled from the outset by Virginians migrating across the Appalachians.

These natural assets were thus forged into a system to control the presidency. At the federal level, the Virginians took advantage of the Twelfth Amendment to create a party ticket. It was chosen by the Republican congressional caucus, where Virginia's influence was decisive for installing Jefferson or Madison or Monroe in the presidential slot and then choosing a New Yorker of little influence or advanced age as the running mate. The succession to the presidency was also kept out of the electoral arena by an unofficial mechanism whereby the man the president chose as his secretary of state became the automatic successor, once the incumbent decided to leave office. This decision became an automatic ritual, since Madison, Monroe, and John Quincy Adams were groomed for the highest office by first being appointed secretary of state. In 1824, however, the mechanism broke down completely because the election had to be decided in the House of Representatives, where one of the candidates, Henry Clay, threw his support to John Quincy Adams, who thereby became president. Because President Adams had then appointed Clay as his secretary of state, the charge was immediately made that he had received the post traditionally assigned to the heir apparent as a reward. Adams's opponents who supported Andrew Jackson proceeded to denounce it as "a corrupt bargain."

Virginia's dominance was also bolstered by the policy adopted by Jefferson and his successors to deny national office to the leading Federalists, thus keeping them out of the cabinet and other influential and visible posts. This tactic prevented them from building and reorganizing their party, while it also restricted their ability to develop a personal following in the country that could shape them into presidential contenders. Once control of the nomination process was secured, Virginia's state organization went into operation to choose a solid bloc of presidential electors on the "general ticket" system. The system the Virginians created produced its intended outcome in the five presidential elections following the Republicans' victory in 1801. The first time the system was tested it actually functioned brilliantly. In 1804, Jefferson was returned with an electoral vote of 162–14, along with a new vice president, George Clinton of New York.

Continued Republican ascendancy was not, however, a certainty. Dissatisfaction and disagreement arose within the party and led to challenges in each of the presidential elections after 1804. The first challenge originated within Virginia itself, and it led to a dispute over the succession at its very first trial in 1808, as Jefferson prepared to leave public life for his bucolic retreat at Monticello. When the Republicans had gained control of the executive branch, they became the governing party and no longer the opposition. Yet the principles and perspectives of the party were forged for the purpose of curbing the exercise and expansion of governmental power. So, once they began to administer the government, questions soon arose about the growth of executive power and federal authority, for which the Republicans themselves were responsible. The first to warn of these dangers was the eccentric and flamboyant Virginian, Congressman John Randolph of Roanoke, who raised his high-pitched voice to challenge Jefferson in 1806 over two actions he had taken that looked suspiciously Federalist in character. Particularly worrisome to Randolph was his fellow congressmen's apparent unawareness that, in giving the president what he wanted, they were complying with his wishes and power, rather than upholding party principles.

The episodes that precipitated Randolph's attack were, first, the administration's secret negotiations with France to purchase West Florida and, second, its unwarranted capitulation to the demands for compensation from the purchasers of the Yazoo lands in a corrupt deal that the government of Georgia had later been forced to rescind. Neither West Florida nor the Yazoo claims were major lapses from party doctrine, but Randolph wanted to sound the alarm before it was too late. And, besides, he was determined to keep the presidential succession out of the hands of James Madison, whom he and many others in the party considered by this time to be too much of a nationalist. And, of course, Madison was the secretary of state who was involved in the highly questionable Florida landgrab, even though to a far lesser degree than Randolph imagined. Jefferson responded to Randolph's confrontational attack by having him deprived of his chairmanship of the powerful Ways and Means Committee, the basis of his influence in Congress. Undeterred, Randolph and a significant number of conservative Republicans continued their criticism of the administration by challenging Jefferson's methods of retaliating against Britain for its interference with American shipping in the Atlantic.

These conservatives criticized his efforts to build up the country's army and navy and his general embargo against foreign trade, chiefly because of the powers that both policies gave to the executive branch.

By 1808, the attempt by its conservative wing to return the Republican Party to its fundamental principles took the form of a movement to deny Madison the succession. James Monroe, who had voted against the proposed federal constitution in Virginia's ratifying convention of 1788, seemed a more reliable keeper of the party's conscience than Madison, and, besides, he was also untainted by service in the cabinet. To head off Madison's nomination by the party's congressional caucus, Monroe's supporters called a meeting at the state capitol in Richmond to develop momentum for their candidate among the state's legislators. They calculated that, if they could defeat Madison in Virginia, Monroe's chances would be increased considerably, convincing evidence in itself for Virginia's centrality in the making of Republican presidents. But the Monroe campaign's failure to persuade a majority of the state legislators to support its candidate put an end to this subversive maneuver intended to bypass the caucus and generate the nomination inside Virginia itself. The party caucus in Washington proceeded to vote for Madison, even though the New York and Virginia delegations did not attend. And that nomination stood unchallenged, backed as it was by the Virginia legislators as well. Although Monroe's name remained in the ring, the candidate himself was very reluctant about challenging the party hierarchy and his two fellow Virginians, Jefferson and Madison. By the time of the election, his candidacy had become so problematic that he obtained not a single electoral vote.

The conservative Republicans, often referred to as "Old Republicans," had failed in their challenge to the emergent Virginia system. But they nevertheless maintained their opposition in Congress to what they considered the centralizing tendencies of the party's leadership. Its core of support came, ironically, from Virginia, where kinsmen and friends of Randolph, like Littleton Tazewell and Benjamin Watkins Leigh, were the leading figures. This support also included Nathaniel Macon of North Carolina and a group of Georgians headed by Senator William H. Crawford and William Wyatt Bibb. Although this was a discernible group of some size, the members proved unable to sustain the visibility they had enjoyed during the last years of Jefferson's presidency and the brief challenge they had mounted behind Monroe.

The main reason for this decline was that the Madison presidency was consumed by preparations for war and then by fighting the war itself, and these preoccupations over war and peace prevented an alignment of the Old Republicans against the administration on the defining principles of Republicanism. Instead, issues of national defense overshadowed criticisms of executive power. Because Madison acted reluctantly in dealing with the British threat and tried to avoid war, as his predecessor had done, the conservatives found themselves supporting him against his critics, the War Hawks, who demanded confrontation with Britain and warlike action. Then, when war was declared and embarked upon, the South's solid support made opposition difficult, even if the conservatives had felt inclined to join the Federalists and a body of northern Republicans in voting against hostilities. Only three southern Republicans (Randolph and two of his closest followers) voted against war in the House; none at all in the Senate opposed it.

In wartime, the powers of government are bound to increase. By voting for war, conservative southern Republicans all but abandoned their faltering efforts to keep the party true to its Jeffersonian doctrines. Nevertheless, they had one final chance to register their protest against creeping Hamiltonianism when the Madison administration submitted a comprehensive plan for developing the nation's economic infrastructure in the aftermath of a war that had revealed its structural weakness and lack of development. Introduced into Congress by Henry Clay and John C. Calhoun, two young Republicans from the South who had entered public life when the Republican Party was ascendant, the plan consisted of three measures. They were, first, a protective tariff to encourage the emergence of a manufacturing sector; second, a national bank to replace Hamilton's first bank, which Congress had considered unconstitutional, refusing to renew its charter in 1811; and, finally, a federally financed program of internal improvements in the form of roads and canals, the "bonus bill."

The tariff met with some opposition in the House, but none in the Senate. More southerners opposed the proposal in the House than supported it, though the objections to it were based, not on principle and constitutional considerations, but on a lack of local interest in manufacturing. The bank encountered even less resistance. The votes showed that the South was heavily in favor. After all, Madison, a southerner himself, who had considered both a national bank and a protective tariff to be unconstitutional a few years earlier, now supported both measures. The need for economic development had assumed precedence, and evidently most southern congressmen concurred. But on the bonus bill, Madison demurred at the last moment, concluding rather arbitrarily that there were still limits to what the Constitution allowed.

Unlike Madison, however, those southerners who voted against the bill did so because of their district's lack of interest in, or need for, roads and canals. Only a few of the votes against the measure were cast by southerners with constitutional scruples, such as North Carolina's Senator Macon, as well as some of the Virginians in the House, like Randolph and Philip Barbour, who both delivered long speeches emphasizing the constitutional objections.[8] As the Republican administration began to espouse Hamiltonian policies for national economic development, most southerners adapted to this change of direction by the party they had always dominated. Nevertheless, the South still supplied the bulk of the dissenters, who urged the party not to abandon its creed. And they still came mainly from Virginia. But, in a surprising reversal, the true believers from Virginia would soon be lined up in opposition to Monroe's administration because it was not conservative enough. Among them would be Thomas Ritchie and the Richmond Junto, once the linchpin of the Virginia system that had managed the Republican Party and kept it in power.

Opposition within Virginia itself to the Republicans' straying from the party's "limited government" doctrines was not the only source of resistance to Virginia's hegemony within the party. A second challenge arose outside Virginia, and predictably it was an attempt to curb the power of the commonwealth of Virginia through its control of the party's system for nominating presidential candidates. Not surprisingly, New York was the primary antagonist. The other part of the Virginia–New York axis on which the Republican Party was built, the Empire State was no longer willing to play the supporting role it had been assigned. By 1820, its population had grown to the point where the state was entitled to a larger congressional delegation than Virginia's and therefore more presidential electors as well. Well before then, however, New York's Republicans had figured out that the Virginians' fixing of the presidential ticket with a token New Yorker in the second slot was certain to keep them forever subordinate and deprive them of the presidency. So, in 1808, at the first opportunity, they balked. They stayed away from the party's congressional caucus, as the backers of Monroe had done, and then they made an overture to the Federalists to join them in running George Clinton for president, a Republican and the sitting vice president. The Federalists rejected the offer, preferring to keep their party intact and nominate their own ticket, thereby avoiding the indignity of becoming the tail to the Republicans' kite.

Four years later, in May 1812, New York Republicans again refused to attend the caucus and instead took a leaf out of the Virginians' book by having the New York legislature nominate DeWitt Clinton. Interestingly, the legislatures in Virginia and Pennsylvania had already done the same thing by meeting early and proposing Madison's reelection. This initiative forced the congressional caucus to accept what was virtually a fait accompli. After selecting Clinton, the New Yorkers proposed, as they had in 1808, that the Federalists back their dissident candidacy—a Clinton as before but not the same one. With their numbers dwindling and the party almost certain to oppose the impending war with Britain, the Federalists preferred not to reveal their hand, but to wait, in the hope that, first, a peace party might emerge and, then, that other Republican legislatures might oppose the Madison candidacy. Also, DeWitt Clinton did not want to alienate his party by aligning openly with the Federalists. Instead, he issued an address stating that he was simply trying to counter the "Virginia influence" and have New York's rightful claims to the presidency recognized, along with those of the northern commercial and shipping interests that the dominant South had continually ignored. Eventually, the Federalists decided to back DeWitt Clinton, but they did not campaign openly for him. They also disguised their identity by calling themselves the Peace Party. The result of all this rather puzzling and complicated maneuvering was, as might be expected, Madison's reelection. Still, DeWitt Clinton did contribute New York's and New Jersey's electoral votes to the Federalists' total of 47 four years earlier.

Frustration at Virginia's domination was not confined to Republicans. Federalists lashed out at the state's stranglehold on national politics. In December 1814, as the war with Britain entered its final stage, a convention of Federalists met in Hartford, Connecticut, and recommended a series of constitutional amendments as conditions for New England's deeply aggrieved Federalists to stay in the Union. Angered by the war itself, as well as by the Republican majority's treatment of New England commerce and shipping, the Federalists proposed seven amendments to the U.S. Constitution. Most of them restricted Congress's authority to declare war and interfere with shipping and foreign commerce, but three were clearly aimed at the South—and at the Virginia system in particular. One of them eliminated the three-fifths clause and based representation on "free inhabitants" only, an obvious attempt to reduce the number of House members from the slave states. Another required a two-thirds majority for the admission of new states, so as to make it more difficult for the Republicans to increase their support by adding sympathetic new states. And the third amendment prohibited second terms for presidents and also forbade those who came "from the same state two terms in succession," an undisguised effort to uproot Virginia's mechanism for controlling the presidency.

If there were still any doubts about the Hartford convention's anti-southern animus, its report referred to the insidious role of a particular state that had combined with others to obtain "the controul of public affairs in perpetual succession." As a result, "men of exceptional merit" were denied public office merely "for want of adherence to the executive creed."[9] But the end of the war and the convention's threat to secede meant that the amendments were never given the time of day. Indeed, the Federalist Party was widely condemned for its association with opposition to the war and its murmurings about breaking up the Union. Consequently, the Federalists proved utterly incapable of checking the Virginia system. Only the Republicans themselves could change it.

As the Virginians' lock on the presidency entered its sixteenth year, Republicans outside the state pondered how they could prevent the coronation of James Monroe as the fourth president from Virginia, the third since 1800. This time, the focus of opposition was located not in New York but in the South and West. And the figure on whom the dissidents set their hopes was William H. Crawford of Georgia, a conservative Republican who had aligned with the likes of Randolph and Macon and who was currently secretary of the treasury. But Crawford was unwilling to challenge Monroe directly, and his backers feared dividing the party for the sake of a nomination that Crawford might reject. All the same, the opposition was now widespread, and Monroe was justifiably concerned that the caucus vote might go against him. In effect, the Virginia game was up.

Even though the Federalists' congressional delegation was now reduced to a corporal's guard of 34 votes from three New England states, which was incapable of stopping a nominee once he had been selected, the nomination system itself had broken down. Obedience to the will of Virginia and respect for the caucus as a legitimate device for selecting the Republican nominee had both evaporated. And Monroe himself acknowledged that this was so. When he selected his cabinet, he purposefully excluded Virginians and chose, not a southerner as secretary of state, but John Quincy Adams of Massachusetts. Had he selected a Virginian, he told Jefferson in a letter of February 1817, he would have angered "the whole country, north of the Delaware, immediately," and all of the states south of the Potomac would have added their protest soon after. "My wish," he admitted with his customary understatement, "is to prevent such a combination, the ill effect of which would be so sensibly felt, on so many important public interests."[10]

The omission of Virginia from his cabinet did not cause Monroe any regret or disappointment, nor did his choice of an Adams from New England as his likely successor. Rather, both were indications that the Virginia system of maintaining tight control on the presidency was no longer necessary for the survival of the Republican Party. For the Republicans had succeeded in their mission. They had eliminated the Federalists, whom Jefferson had once described, in a remarkable outburst of vitriol, as an "Anglican monarchical aristocratical party whose avowed object is to draw over us the substance, as they have already done the forms, of the British government."[11] The Federalist Party had tried to impose on the new republic a system of energetic and splendid government that the Constitution had never contemplated. And the Republicans had beaten back these attempts and finally eliminated the party itself. After preserving the constitutional order from Federalist perversion and subversion and saving the country itself from British invasion, the Republicans were now the only existing party. Thus, they represented the nation, not just a part of it.

With the Republicans' triumph, the new republic's political system had reached a turning point. The Virginia Dynasty was no longer needed to discipline and control the Republican Party. Also no longer needed was the Republican Party itself. In an elective, representative republic such as the United States, parties and factions were considered anomalous, even dangerous, because they created strife and division. Only in a monarchy, where the king and his ministers needed to be reined in, were parties regarded as indispensable for maintaining balance and equilibrium. That is how the founding generation understood the function of parties. Consequently, the Era of Good Feelings during Monroe's first term was welcomed as the successful outcome of the struggle to purge the incipient monarchical system introduced into the new republic by the Federalists. According to this theory of political parties, the Republicans would presumably wither away as well, not just the Federalists. With no political or constitutional need for parties, there was no reason for them to exist. Perhaps the days of parties and party competition in the United States were numbered.

The Missouri Crisis, 1819–1821

The confidence and calm, the "good feelings," of the late 1810s did not last long. Two domestic events occurred in 1819 that disrupted the equanimity of the nation's political class. In the summer, a financial panic was set in motion by the forceful efforts of the Second Bank of the United States to control the speculative boom of the postwar years by requiring state banks to repay their loans in specie, that is, in gold or silver, not in paper. The turmoil that followed saved the bank itself but sent the economy into a tailspin, precipitating a depression that lasted into the next decade. A few months earlier, in February, the House of Representatives had taken up the application of the territory of Missouri for admission to the Union. Much to everyone's surprise, this innocuous request precipitated another crisis. Both crises had far-reaching political repercussions that will become apparent in the next chapter. But the Missouri Crisis had an especially decisive impact on the course of southern political history.

The Missouri Territory was carved out of lands that were part of the Louisiana Purchase. Indeed, it was the first territory within the Louisiana Purchase, besides Louisiana itself, to apply for statehood. And, presumably, slavery's prior existence in the French possession would be acknowledged in the case of Missouri, as it had been in Louisiana's own territorial and statehood legislation in 1803 and 1812. But a Republican congressman from New York, James Tallmadge, who was affiliated with the DeWitt Clinton faction, proposed an amendment to the Missouri enabling bill. This amendment contained two clauses. The first forbade the introduction of more slaves into the territory, and the second required that those born later, after the state was admitted, be freed when they reached the age of twenty-five. This provision did not affect the 10,000 slaves already living in Missouri who were to remain slaves for life; it dealt only with additions to the slave population through in-migration or birth. All the same, slavery would end when the last of the existing slaves died and with the freeing of those reaching age twenty-five. Obviously, Tallmadge's amendment was a proposal for gradual abolition, even though there would be slaves in Missouri for many years after statehood, even as late as the 1870s.

The amendment was passed on two occasions by the House, but each time the Senate voted it down. In the initial House vote, southerners opposed the proviso almost unanimously, 66–1 on the first clause and 64–2 on the second, the three dissenting votes coming from the border states of Delaware and Maryland. Gradual emancipation, even if it took more than fifty years, was evidently anathema to southern congressmen.[12] Soon after the second House vote on the amendment's two provisions, the term of the Fifteenth Congress expired.

When the new Congress convened the following year, several months

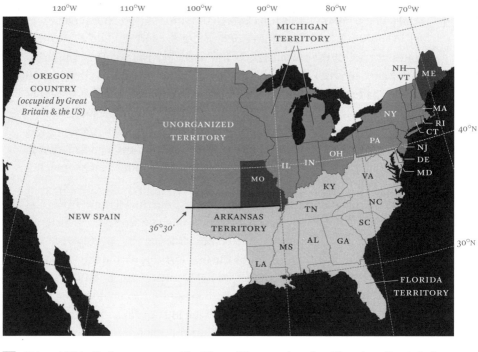

MAP 2. The Missouri Compromise, 1820. After a long dispute in Congress lasting two years, Missouri entered the Union in 1821 as part of a deal between slaveholding states and free states. Maine was admitted as a free state to offset Missouri, which came in as a slave state. A line drawn at latitude 36°30′ prohibited slavery in the areas north of the line and allowed slavery, but did not guarantee it, below the line.

States established by the Missouri Compromise

States and territories where slavery was *permitted*

States and territories where slavery was *prohibited*

of vigorous and inconclusive debate over the Tallmadge amendment ensued until a compromise proposal was developed. It consisted of three parts. First, Missouri would be admitted as a slave state without the Tallmadge proviso. Second, Maine would be admitted as a free state. And third, slavery would be prohibited in future territories within the Louisiana Purchase north of 36°30′. In an attempt to hasten passage of the legislation, the Senate decided to vote on the entire package. It passed, with southerners voting 20–2 in favor of the compromise and northerners voting 18–4 against, a clearly sectional vote. The House, however, opted to vote on each part separately. The parts dealing with statehood for Missouri and Maine were approved with predictably sectional votes. But, on the part that involved compromise, the 36°30′ restriction, the South was only narrowly in favor, 39–37. The border states of Delaware, Maryland, and Kentucky were strongly supportive, 16–2, while the rest of the

South was in favor by a close margin of 19–17. But Virginia, an Upper South state and the heart of the resistance, was strongly opposed, 18–4.[13] The southern vote was split because the 36°30′ restriction measure was offered by the South as a concession to the North, in exchange for acceptance of Missouri as a slave state without the gradual abolition required by Tallmadge's amendment. And many southerners evidently refused to endorse it, fearing that this was an unwarranted concession. As Thomas Ritchie, a leader of the Virginia resistance, saw it, "Shall we surrender so much of this region, that was nobly won by the councils of Jefferson, and paid for out of a common treasury?" Answering his own question, he responded, "If we yield now, beware—they will ride us forever."[14]

But this hard-won settlement of the issue was jeopardized in 1821 when Missouri was about to take its seat in Congress. The state came to Congress seeking admission with a constitution that contained a prohibition against free Negroes entering the state. As was to be expected, northerners responded by trying to deny Missouri admission. Each side accused the other of bad faith, but, after a lengthy and even more angry debate than a year earlier, a second compromise was forged. Citizens of all states were to be allowed to enter Missouri without restriction, though the compromise purposely avoided deciding whether free blacks were citizens, since this was a matter to be determined at the state level and most previous decisions had actually been negative.

This protracted struggle over the admission of Missouri as a slave state was now resolved, but its implications were devastating. Differences between the North and the South before 1819 had centered on economic interests, namely, the commercial and shipping interests of the northeastern states and the export agriculture of the southeastern states. And this was accentuated by the rivalry between the regions in the contest for national political power, with their respective strongholds located in Massachusetts and Virginia. The question of slavery had arisen from time to time in Congress in the years since the constitutional convention in Philadelphia, when it had been a subject of much discussion. But a general understanding prevailed among the founding generation that it should not be allowed to become a source of contention. Moreover, everyone assumed that if accommodated and uncontested slavery would either cease over time to be a problem or gradually die out.

By the 1810s, northerners felt confident that slavery was in retreat. The gradual abolition of slavery in the northern states after Independence, the termination of the slave trade in 1808, and the growing economic problems in the tobacco-growing states of Maryland and Virginia all seemed to indicate this trend. Furthermore, southerners themselves had frequently expressed misgivings about slavery, none more so than Thomas Jefferson himself, and dozens of antislavery societies had sprung up in the border states in the early nineteenth century. Meanwhile, the southerners had acquiesced in the ending of the Atlantic slave trade as well as in the exclusion of slavery from the northwestern territories by the Northwest Ordinance of 1787, which had been drafted by Jefferson.

This complacency was shattered by the bitter and protracted Missouri Crisis, which lasted for two years. Southerners discovered that northern feelings about slavery were no longer just sentiments but were beliefs held strongly and asserted forcefully. And, in turn, northerners encountered a southern commitment to slavery that was surprisingly vehement and unyielding. The positions that each side took during the months of debate over Missouri were not, however, as advanced or as schematic as they would later become. Northern congressmen criticized slavery for its deleterious economic and social impact on the region and its white inhabitants, rather than for its effect on the slaves. And southerners parried these charges by pointing out slavery's success as a labor system and as a way of organizing society. But they did not go so far as to suggest that slavery was a moral system and "a positive good," as they would later on. Although the content of the debates could be considered moderate, the speeches were declaimed with such unexpected ferocity and stridency that the crisis warranted Jefferson's celebrated analogy likening it to "a fire-bell in the night [that] awakened me with terror."[15]

The slavery question, which had been kept in the wings ever since the founding, was now on stage and a matter of public discussion. And the argument that ensued was vigorous and uninhibited. Even more alarming, the southerners had taken an extreme position in defense of slavery. Although they still voiced some ambivalence about the desirability of the institution, they had nevertheless insisted that slavery was to be considered permanent in America. Any attempt to end it in the future by freeing as-yet-unborn slaves had to be resisted. And this applied to territories not yet part of the United States where gradual abolition would not harm or threaten the institution in those states where it already existed. Tallmadge's amendment was anathema to the South, which rose up in fury and voted it down with complete unanimity in the 1820 vote, an astonishing 98–0 on the combined, or joint, ballot of both houses. By accepting the 36°30' ban on slavery in the Louisiana Purchase north of Missouri's southern border, southerners were prepared to give up access to most of the territory within the Purchase, in exchange for gaining Missouri as a state in which slavery was guaranteed permanence. Below that 36°30′ line, however, slavery was more likely to expand than above it, though the extent of its expansion was unpredictable. The southern vote on the 36°30′ line had been close, but, remarkably, southerners had abandoned most of the Louisiana Purchase in exchange for keeping slavery unrestricted in Missouri.

Future territorial gains were not, however, the South's primary concern in 1819–21. Instead, the region's political leaders had ensured that gradual abolition was out of the question as a mechanism for eliminating slavery. A moment of truth had arrived more than a decade before abolitionism had become an organized movement. As Jefferson realized, "A geographical line, coinciding with a marked principle, moral and political, once conceived and held up to the angry passions of men, will never be obliterated; and every new irritation will mark it deeper and deeper."[16] Regrettable though this might be, neither Jefferson nor any other southern leader intervened to advise their region against taking such an intractable stance. In effect, the Missouri Compromise was a compromise to appease the South for taking an uncompromising position.

It is not known precisely why James Tallmadge introduced his amendment to the Missouri enabling bill. But it seems quite likely that the New Yorker's initiative was a continuation of the running sectional battle against Virginia and the southern states because of their decades of domination of the Republican Party. With the elimination of the Federalists as the opposition party by the late 1810s, the Republicans' need to maintain party loyalty and discipline declined. As a result, northerners' frustration with the South's political influence as well as with its economically and socially deleterious system of slavery burst out of its party confines. Judging by the response to Tallmadge's proposal, this demand for redress was close to the political surface. The crisis indicated that, without disciplined national parties to restrain them, sectional interests might well break loose. Maybe parties should not be allowed to wither away. Instead, a new system of parties might be able to keep these sectional interests and ambitions in check. The attempt would soon be made.

2

A Two-Party South

WHIGS AND DEMOCRATS

"Rush then to the polls, ride, walk, or swim to reach them, and let your song of triumph be *Jackson* and our *Country* forever."[1] Heeding the exhortation of the *Baton Rouge Gazette*, voters in the southern states showed up at the polling places in 1828 and cast their ballots overwhelmingly for Andrew Jackson for president.[2] The Tennessean carried the entire electoral vote of every southern state except Maryland, which split 6–5 in favor of John Quincy Adams. In the popular vote, Jackson won twice as many votes as his opponents. Tennessee, Georgia, Alabama, and Mississippi supported him almost unanimously, while North Carolina and Virginia voted massively for him. He even carried Henry Clay's Kentucky.[3]

Four years later, in 1832, Jackson swept the South again, and, as before, he won with enormous popular majorities, ranging from 75 percent in Virginia to just shy of 100 percent in Georgia and Mississippi. Because his opponent this time was Clay himself, he lost Kentucky and, as in 1828, he split the vote in Maryland, 5–3. But besides these two states and closely contested Louisiana, Jackson carried all but a dozen counties in the South.[4] The South was again united, as it had been since the mid-1790s, except for a brief moment in 1824 when several competing presidential candidates, namely Henry Clay, John C. Calhoun, Andrew Jackson, and William H. Crawford, had divided up the southern vote.

To those 350,000 southerners who voted for him in 1828, Jackson was known as the victor in the brief military engagement in 1815 known as the Battle of New Orleans, as a large slaveholder from Tennessee, and as a successful fighter of Indians in the southwestern territories of Alabama and Mississippi. He was also perceived as a rough-hewn outsider uncorrupted by the respectable social and political world of Washington, and he had been deprived of the presidency in 1824 by a "corrupt bargain" between political insiders, despite winning more popular and electoral votes than any other candidate. Some of these perceived characteristics, perhaps all of them together, generated an enormous response from southerners, especially when compared with his leading opponent in 1824 and 1828, John Quincy Adams, the son of the despised Federalist president, John Adams, whom Jefferson had defeated in 1800.

What the slaveholding Indian fighter would do once in the White House, however, was not absolutely certain, but his attractiveness to southerners was obvious. Jackson's appeal extended to voters who lived across the Appalachian Mountains, not only in the southern part of what was called the West, but also in other newly settled northern areas like Ohio, Indiana, and Illinois, which went strongly for Jackson. All the same, the heart of Jackson's great popularity and electoral support lay in the South. In the 1832 election, when his primary opponent was another southerner, Henry Clay from the border state of Kentucky, the region's voters rejected Clay overwhelmingly. The South was clearly Jackson country.

Southerners were not just supportive of Jackson himself in 1828. They were also voting for the party that had been constructed around his candidacy. Because the administration of John Quincy Adams was committed to a program of national initiatives that looked very similar to Hamilton's vision of the early 1790s, supporters of Andrew Jackson in 1824 had been determined to defeat the neo-Federalist from Massachusetts. Since the Republican Party had split into rival factions formed around three or four of its leading men, the moment had arrived when it needed to be redefined and restructured. To Jackson's closest advisers, this meant reorganizing the party around Jackson's candidacy and along the lines of the original Republican Party, created in the 1790s by Jefferson and Madison in opposition to the Federalists headed by Hamilton.

The upshot was the formation of the Democratic Party, which carried Jackson to victory in 1828 and again four years later. The primary instigator of this move was Martin Van Buren, a practical politician from New York who had already created an organization of his own, the Albany Regency, that had enabled him to control his state's Republican Party. He was also a true believer in the vintage Jeffersonian principles of minimal government and state rights, who was appalled at President Adams's plans to build a system of nationally sponsored and financed roads and canals and even a national university. In January 1827, Van Buren explained his plans to Thomas Ritchie, the influential editor of the *Richmond Enquirer* and the leader of the Richmond Junto that had been so vital to Virginia's recently eclipsed presidential dynasty. And he invited Ritchie to play a major part in realizing his objectives.[5]

Van Buren's strategy consisted of three elements. First, an electoral organization had to be created with sufficient scope and discipline to head off Adams and elect Jackson to the presidency denied him in 1824. To this end, Jackson's personal popularity and his following was to be converted and organized into a political party. Second, "and what is of still greater importance," in Van Buren's view, was "the *substantial reorganization of the old Republican party*." And this goal was to be achieved by reviving the alliance at the heart of Jefferson's original Republican Party between "the planters of the South and the plain republicans of the North." Reunited by means of the New York–Virginia axis, which Jefferson had forged, the Republicans would obtain sufficient strength to drive out the Adams administration and its backers, the aristocratic elite and the commercial and manufacturing interests, with their neo-Federalist ambitions for expanding the reach and influence of the central government.

The third component of Van Buren's strategy was his hope that the resulting alliance between the sections could contain the divisive and threatening controversy that had erupted earlier in the Missouri Crisis. For Van Buren feared that, "if the old ["party feelings"] are suppressed, prejudices between free and slave holding states will inevitably take their place." In effect, national parties were necessary, "by producing counteracting feelings" to prevent sectional differences from becoming the focus of political debate and electoral activity. Even though parties were inherently divisive, they were needed to keep the country together by smothering the more destructive sectional allegiances and sentiments.

The importance of creating a national party in order to offset sectional divisions was also evident from Van Buren's journey to the South in December 1826 to met with John C. Calhoun, then emerging as a leading advocate and defender of the South's interests. At the time of the visit, Calhoun was the sitting vice president in the Adams administration, though the position was becoming increasingly uncomfortable for him. Van Buren's purpose was to gain his support for Jackson's bid for the presidency, a request that Calhoun readily agreed to. In fact, Calhoun's backing for Jackson was considered so crucial that he was offered the second position on the ticket. And so he simply continued in the vice presidency through two vastly dissimilar administrations. The revived and reorganized Republican Party that Van Buren envisaged was intended to protect the country from two imminent dangers, Federalism and sectionalism. The creation of the Democratic Party as a vehicle for Andrew Jackson's bid for the presidency was therefore just one component of a critical mission to change the nation's political course and save the foundering republic from the forces that threatened it.

In the 1828 election, Van Buren's hopes for both a successful Jackson candidacy and a reorganized national Republican Party were realized. And for two terms thereafter, Andrew Jackson occupied the presidency and his party ran the federal government. Nevertheless, as Van Buren had anticipated, the Democratic Party stimulated the emergence of a rival political organization that developed support throughout the nation, even within Jackson's stronghold in the South.

A System of National Parties

In the immediate aftermath of their defeat in 1828, Adams, Clay, and the National Republicans kept a low profile. They hoped that President Jackson, who was relatively unfamiliar with the government and politics of Washington, would falter. If that happened, his diverse coalition, organized around his own reputation and some vague declarations about his political sentiments, would fall apart once he had to make policy and govern. But, to their surprise and regret, Jackson took hold of the government and began to consolidate power in the executive branch. He used the patronage as spoils for his loyal supporters. He asserted control over the talented and ambitious members of his cabinet. He took firm action toward carrying out his popular election pledge to remove the remaining Indian peoples from the Atlantic states. And he started using the veto power to defeat major legislation, as in the Maysville Road bill veto, thus setting limits on federal aid for internal improvements. His decision to veto the bill to renew the charter of the Second Bank of the United States provided final proof of Jackson's ambitions to strengthen the presidency at the expense of Congress.

In the minds of his opponents, led by Henry Clay, the indictment of General Jackson for "executive usurpation" and the depiction of him as "King Andrew the First" raised a fundamental question about the kind of government Americans had opted for in 1787. And on that issue Henry Clay waged the campaign of 1832, only to discover that the electorate saw Jackson as the defender of a federal government with restricted powers from powerful economic and social interests that Clay and his forces were believed to represent. So the electorate preferred to reward Jackson with a second term, giving him a 219–49 victory in the Electoral College and increasing his popular vote, while simultaneously augmenting the Democrats' lopsided majority in Congress.

Despite this miscalculation in 1832, the opposition's prospects brightened considerably during Jackson's second term. The president continued to act in ways that confirmed the worries of the opposition and enabled it to extend its support into the South, the Jacksonian heartland. Three developments in particular brought this about. After the 1832 election, Jackson's war against the Second Bank of the United States moved from avowals of intent to provocative and unprecedented deeds. To destroy the bank, Jackson needed to veto the bill for its recharter and then force it to cease operations by removing the government's funds that were deposited there. So constitutionally questionable was this move that two secretaries of the treasury refused to do Jackson's bidding. Finally, his friend, Roger B. Taney, complied, an act of personal loyalty that was rewarded later with the chief justiceship of the Supreme Court. Meanwhile, the opposition's initial argument for renewing the bank's charter on economic grounds had been replaced by the constitutional and political charge of "executive usurpation." "The whigs of the present day," Clay asserted confidently in an 1834 Senate speech, "are opposing executive encroachment, and a most alarming extension of executive power and prerogative."[6]

Jackson's high-handedness and impetuosity were also evident in his handling of the concurrent crisis in South Carolina, where the state's political leadership, spurred on by John C. Calhoun, who had served as Jackson's vice president during his first term, was refusing to enforce U.S. tariff regulations on imported goods. Jackson tried to appease the Carolinians' fears about the excessive rates of the tariffs of 1828 and 1832 by reducing them in 1833. But the president was still causing unease and hostility because he insisted that Congress enact legislation to enforce the tariff, called by its opponents the "force bill," and he threatened to march troops into the Palmetto State to collect the customs duties and put down resistance to federal authority. Although most southerners did not endorse South Carolina's action or its advocacy of the right to nullify federal laws, many were incensed by Jackson's aggressiveness and his apparent contempt for their region and its interests. The result was a further weakening of support for Jackson, especially in the South.

But the third, and most critical, development in Jackson's second term that spurred the formation of organized opposition was King Andrew's selection of his successor. The choice of Martin Van Buren first as Jackson's vice president for his second term and then as his heir apparent in 1836 was perceived, not only as a reintroduction of the Virginia system for passing down the succession to handpicked favorites, but also as a threatening move on substantive grounds as well. First of all, Van Buren was considered the epitome of the party operative because of the Albany machine he had created in New York and his management and coordination of the Jacksonian organization nationally. Moreover, his loyalty to Jackson and his party had secured him the party's nomination. He was therefore the exponent and beneficiary of that discipline and loyalty intrinsic to the Jacksonian approach to politics that so irked those who left to join the opposition. And second, Van Buren was a northerner whose ascendancy represented the transfer of the Jacksonian coalition from the control of the South where it had originated. His ascendancy worried southerners further because leadership was taken from a sympathetic slaveholder who had helped clear vast swaths of southern territory of its Indian inhabitants, both before his election and then once he became president, through his vigorous implementation of Indian removal. Making matters worse for southerners, and no doubt for many northerners too, was the scandalous behavior of the Democrats' vice presidential choice, Senator Richard M. Johnson of Kentucky, who lived openly with his mulatto mistress and their two children.

By the 1836 election, the opposition to Jackson's "usurpation" had organized itself in Congress and established bases of support in most states. During the congressional elections of 1834, his opponents had campaigned as Whigs, giving themselves a name and a rallying cry, both as the opponents of executive tyranny like their revolutionary predecessors and also as their heirs in the ongoing struggle to preserve the legacy of 1776. Valuable as they undoubtedly were, these achievements could guarantee neither a coordinated national campaign nor a party platform based on much besides opposition to Jackson and his surrogate, Van Buren. Men who became Whigs ran the gamut—from supporters of Henry Clay's program of federally sponsored economic development, which he called "the American System," at one extreme, to state rights advocates who fell just short of Calhoun's doctrine of nullification, at the other. Predictably, they agreed on very little.

Indeed, so fragmented was the incipient party that its leaders decided to acknowledge political reality in the presidential contest of 1836 by allowing several regional candidacies already in formation to stand in for a single national nominee. Accordingly, there were three Whig candidates. William Henry Harrison, an Indian-fighting general and U.S. senator from Ohio, became the candidate of the new western states. Daniel Webster ran as the choice of little more than Massachusetts and several other states in New England after many of the Atlantic coast states drifted to Harrison when Pennsylvania's Whigs refused to endorse the New Englander. And in the South, revulsion at Van Buren coalesced around Senator Hugh Lawson White, a Tennessee friend of Old Hickory and a loyal Jacksonian in Congress, who nevertheless balked at the selection of the northerner, Van Buren, as his successor.

Even though the three-candidate strategy revealed the deficiencies of the Whigs as a cohesive national party, it was nevertheless a politically shrewd arrangement. It prevented regional differences from undercutting identification with the Whigs, while making it still possible to deny the Democrat a victory in the Electoral College. Indeed, the outcome was reasonably gratifying. As expected, Van Buren won, but the Whigs collected 124 electoral votes to Van Buren's 170 and won almost half of the popular vote, a clear improvement over 1832. Webster carried Massachusetts; White won Tennessee and Georgia and lost narrowly in North Carolina, Mississippi, and Louisiana; and Harrison won seven states—three border states and two in the Midwest, along with New Jersey and Vermont. The results were very encouraging, but the Whigs still seemed far from becoming a national party possessing both an organization and a program.

Four years later, however, the Whigs achieved a stunning victory that changed the political landscape and made the party a competitive national force. They captured the presidency with William Henry Harrison and won control of both houses of Congress as well as a large number of state governments. Two parties now competed nationwide and would continue to do so for the next decade or so. How had the Whigs been able to transform an improving but still quite uncertain situation in 1836 into a dramatic success by 1840? The events and circumstances of those intervening four years contributed significantly to their triumph. No sooner had Martin Van Buren entered the White House than an economic crisis erupted, triggered by the Panic of 1837. The panic and the ensuing recession were brought on, so it was widely believed, by the anti-inflationary measures that Jackson had taken to curb the speculative boom in land and finance. This speculation had been fueled by the destruction of the Second Bank and by the loosening of restrictions on credit that resulted. Faced by this disaster, Van Buren's only real proposal for dealing with it was the creation of an "Independent Treasury" to separate the government's financial activities completely from the state and private banks. This was the last campaign in the Jacksonians' war against the national bank. But it offered nothing to alleviate the economic instability and hardship that the Democrats' impulsive and ill-considered deflation had precipitated. Offering no remedy for a crisis that he himself (he had been, after all, vice president at the time) and his own party had created, Van Buren was quickly pilloried as inept and callous.

This leadership vacuum provided the Whigs with a rare opportunity, which they seized eagerly. In contrast to the Democrats' clinging to the dogmas of Jacksonian laissez-faire and their relentless hostility to banks and banking, the Whigs formulated a clear alternative. Not just a remedy for the current crisis, the Whig program amounted to a distinctive and divergent approach to the role of the national government in the economy. And this provided the Whigs with an agenda capable of giving the party an identity that was clearer and more substantive than merely opposition to Jackson and "executive usurpation."

The Whig approach was based primarily on Henry Clay's American system of federal aid to economic development through internal improvements (mainly transportation, such as canals and roads), tariff protection for domestic manufacturing, and public land sales to encourage frontier settlement and generate revenue for subsidizing the proposed transportation improvements. Although the protective tariff was no longer a live issue and neither was the national bank, which his system had initially included, Clay's approach was still distinctive. The Whigs were eager to encourage economic development, and they were not hostile to the primary institutions such as banks that would facilitate it. As an indication of this intent, the party, led by Clay, had been trying to pass a bill during the previous Congress to redistribute the surplus from federal land sales to the states for use in internal improvement projects, a form of federal subsidy for state-supervised economic development. Thus the Whigs offered an activist and programmatic approach to the central issue of governance in the Jacksonian era. With the economic crisis in the front of voters' minds in the 1840 election, the choice was clear, and the Whigs benefited handsomely from their successful framing of the main issue.

The contest of 1840 was therefore a defining election. It marked the arrival of the Whigs as a national party and, as a result, the emergence of a stable, competitive system of political parties for the first time in American history. It is curious to note, therefore, that this election has usually been dismissed as shallow and inconsequential. After all, how could an electoral contest be taken seriously when one side appealed to voters to support its nominee because he was a man of the people whose life experience could be summed up in the slogan "a log cabin and hard cider" and who ran on a ticket made memorable by a silly jingle, "Tippecanoe and Tyler too"? The wealthy New York Whig, Philip Hone, commented wittily in his diary that "there was rhyme, but no reason to it."[7] Also contributing to this verdict was the very nature and style of the campaign. The managers of Jackson's campaigns had already introduced the parades and carnivals, the slogans and ballyhoo, that were new to this era of greater popular participation and a more democratic politics. But in 1840, the Whigs, who were thought to be more respectable and responsible, stooped low and pandered to the masses by giving them processions, pole raisings, and soapbox oratory. From another perspective, however, they simply beat the Democrats at their own game.

The Whig Party in the South

The similarity of campaign tactics did not mean, however, that the parties were interchangeable or that they each stood for little besides mindless slogans. Rather, the Whigs had adapted to the new circumstances that gave rise to new methods of campaigning. By the 1830s, the electorate had expanded significantly, since almost all adult males were now enfranchised. Only Rhode Island, Virginia, and Louisiana retained a property qualification. Although eight states still required that a voter be a taxpayer, this was a restriction that proved in practice to be quite minimal and that excluded only a small number of voters. And all of these voters were eligible to vote in presidential elections because the rules governing the selection of electors had gradually become uniform. By 1836, South Carolina was the only state in which the legislature still chose its electors. Everywhere else, the general ticket system was in force, which meant that electors were chosen by voters who went to the polls to cast ballots for them. Voting for president was therefore much more inclusive, as restrictions on eligibility were removed and more voters participated directly in presidential elections. This increase in voter participation proceeded incrementally in the 1820s and 1830s, but between 1836 and 1840 there occurred a massive increase in turnout. About 1.5 million votes were cast in the 1836 election. In 1840, that number soared to around 2.4 million, an increase of about 60 percent. Even more significant, the turnout of eligible voters rose from 57.8 percent to an enormous 80.2 percent in 1840.

No doubt, much of that increase has to be attributed to the successful methods of getting out the vote that were now being employed. Parades and slogans did make elections more exciting. But both parties were engaging in the hoopla, thereby doubling the electoral effort. And that in turn drew out even more participants. The parties were competing for voters' attention and support. And, of course, the parties differed, not just in their rhetoric and slogans, but in the policies they proposed for dealing with the economic crisis, as well as in the characteristics and tone they projected. Rather than demonstrating how trivial politics had become with the emergence of a mass electorate, the 1840 election showed how engaged and mobilized a large electorate could become if the parties competed for votes and also offered different agendas. The system of electoral politics that had been emerging since 1828 had reached fruition, with parties competing vigorously across the nation and voters turning out in unprecedented numbers on election day.

Naturally, the impact on the South of these national developments was far-reaching. In a region where opposition to Jackson and the Democrats had been nonexistent in 1824, 1828, and 1832, the Whig candidate in 1840 managed to carry all of the South except Arkansas, Alabama, South Carolina, and Virginia. And this meant that, as usual, the South backed the winning candidate in a presidential election. But even more meaningful, there now existed in the South, hitherto a solidly one-party region, a viable, even competitive, opposition. The Whig Party was not confined merely to a few states or to a small group of marginalized enclaves, as had been the case with the Federalists. Instead, it presented a challenge to the Democrats in states throughout the region.

This transformed system emerged in the late 1830s, and it continued until the early 1850s, when the Whig Party collapsed. During this period of roughly fifteen years, political life in the South became remarkably different from what it had been previously. Yet, rather than becoming the norm in the political history of the region, this brief episode of competitive party politics turned out to be quite unusual. In fact, it proved to be an aberration. For a brief moment of roughly fifteen years' duration, the South experienced competitive two-party politics. And then it vanished, never to appear again for well over a century. The historian Charles S. Sydnor captured the anomalousness of the late 1830s and the 1840s over the entire course of southern political history when he wrote in 1948: "The formation of the Whig party early in Jackson's second administration introduced the only thoroughgoing two-party period in all Southern history."[8] After the demise of the Whigs in the wake of the 1852 presidential election, the southern states would experience brief flurries of region-wide party competition, but these episodes never developed into a stable or enduring pattern of partisan conflict that could approximate a system. Some parts of the region did experience longer periods of party competition, notably in the Upper South, but these developments failed to spread throughout the section as a whole. They indicated the possibility of what might have become general and normal, but the potential was never realized.

The South's brief experience, its flirtation perhaps, with competitive party politics during what has been called the "Second Party System" from the 1820s to the 1850s can also be viewed from a national perspective. Soon after its emergence, the Democratic Party had developed strong support beyond its initial base in the Southeast and Southwest and, to some extent, in the Northwest. Similarly, its rival, the Whig Party, developed from its base in the National Republican campaigns of John Quincy Adams in 1824 and 1828 and expanded into the border states, the Northwest, and the South by about 1840. These two major parties were therefore national in scope, and so the nation too experienced competitive party politics for the first time in its history. As Richard P. McCormick noted, "The two new parties were balanced and competitive in every region," and thus "two parties that were truly national in their dimensions had arisen."[9]

To those who still feared that political parties were, by definition, divisive and dangerous, the existence of two national parties was not necessarily welcome. But political parties that were national in scope and able to bridge regional differences and tie the nation together were surely beneficial in a polity and society so loosely integrated as was the United States in its early years. Political institutions of national scope would strengthen the nation-state by supplementing the quite limited coordinating mechanisms that the federal Constitution had provided.

Whatever hopes might have been placed in the unifying potential of national political parties were very soon dashed, however. For the Whig Party proved unable to establish organizational roots and voter support sufficient to sustain itself throughout the nation. By 1850, it was clearly in difficulty, and a few years later it collapsed, leaving the Democratic Party as the only party. Moreover, even the Democrats' claims to be a national party were, by the late 1850s, quite debatable, since it was now dominated by the South. The party of Jackson did, however, manage to reestablish its national credentials, but only much later, by the 1870s, in fact. But the Whigs did not. As an organized political party, they had disappeared from the political scene altogether by 1856.

The brevity of this era of competitive national parties is evidence of its ineffectiveness at overcoming the serious political divisions already apparent in the Early Republic. The Whigs and Democrats had originated in different regions of the country, and those regional origins had colored their identities. Even though they became national in scope, they could not overcome, or repudiate, their regional affinity and image. Yet transcending the geographic divisions in the country was an objective of the parties, and even a major justification for them. If they could not achieve this aim, their national purpose was lost. And, in fact, the demise of the Whigs in the early 1850s and the disintegration of the Democrats by the late 1850s were brought about by the resurgence of those same regional differences it had been one of their purposes to pacify or resolve. As Richard P. McCormick observed, the party system of the Whigs and Democrats "could survive only if the regional feelings that had so largely shaped its being were obliterated."[10] Because they could not eliminate, or even contain, these regional divisions, McCormick went so far as to suggest that the system was "curiously contrived," even " 'artificial.' "[11] In retrospect, this short-lived attempt to create national parties so as to offset and break down sectional divisions that were so deep-seated as to be impervious to external political pressure does seem overly hopeful.

Earlier, as the two national parties began to take shape during the 1830s, the greatest uncertainty was whether the Whig Party could create a viable presence in the South. As we have seen, Jackson swept the region in 1828 and 1832, making it seem unlikely that an opposition party might arise. In addition, the precedent of the Federalists' inability to expand their support after the Republicans came to power nationally in 1800 was not at all encouraging. Despite this depressing outlook, opposition to the Democrats did develop in the South and in the nation as a whole. And it arose so rapidly that as early as 1840 the Whigs were able to carry both the nation and the South in that year's presidential election.

The Whigs had developed policies and a party identity that were recognizably distinct from the Democrats. As might be expected, these features and characteristics appealed to different kinds of voters with contrasting interests. In the South, Whigs drew their strength from the more commercialized parts of the region, the cities and ports, which were deeply involved in trade and banking and dealt with markets and financial networks beyond the immediate locality. In other words, they attracted economic groups that were participating in the emerging market economy. A generation or so earlier, most of these areas were centers of Federalism. But now the economy was changing dramatically, and these merchants and bankers were larger in number and playing a greater role in the economy of the region and of the nation. And, of course, they were deeply disturbed by the Jacksonians' animus against banks and by the financial turmoil they had precipitated in the late 1830s. These economic groups tended also to be prosperous and respectable, the well-to-do and the pillars of the community, who valued law and order and respect for the authority of the better sorts. Needless to say, they were worried by the economic conflict generated by Jackson's campaigns against the "money power" and the economic establishment, as well as by his party's identification with the values and interests of the "common man," the "bone and sinew of the republic," as Jackson called these middling sorts as well as urban and rural laborers. By contrast, the Whigs tended to attract support from the wealthy and the respectable classes. But a party of the elite was doomed in a system of mass parties, unless its base of support could be broadened considerably.

In the South, support for the Whigs was to be found in two locations that provided the large blocs of voters that were essential to the party's viability. And these enabled the party to expand beyond the urban, commercial centers that had defined, and fatally restricted, the Federalists. The most important sector of southern agriculture in a region overwhelmingly agricultural and rural was the cash-crop plantation system. These plantations were located in the low-lying rich soils of the black belt, so-called because its earth was dark in color, and coincidentally so was the skin of the large slave labor force that was forced to work these lands. An extensive H-shaped region within the South, the black belt spread west from the Atlantic coast of Virginia, the Carolinas, and Georgia, across the central portions of Georgia, Alabama, and Mississippi, and then halted its westward movement at the Mississippi River. At this point, the black belt extended north and south on both sides of the river from Memphis in the north down to the port of New Orleans. The residents of these three black belt areas of the South—the coastal Tidewater, the inland black belt, and the Mississippi Delta and Valley—were wealthy slaveholders, producing export crops of cotton, rice, sugar, and tobacco, and, like the urban merchants and bankers, they too were involved in commerce and in distant markets. Most of them aligned with the Whigs.

But there were major exceptions. In the coastal areas of Virginia and North Carolina and in all of South Carolina, plantation owners stayed Democratic. Indeed, South Carolina remained an overwhelmingly Democratic state throughout the antebellum decades. But the Whigs began to generate considerable support in the western foothills and mountain sections of the Upper South states of Virginia and North Carolina, where small farms rather than plantations were the norm. The two geographic regions of west and east diverged on other grounds too, which proved to be decisive in determining party allegiance. The western areas of Virginia and North Carolina and also eastern Tennessee needed internal improvements to overcome their remoteness by connecting them, through roads or railroads, with the more settled parts of each state, as well as with areas beyond the state itself to the west and north. These mountainous areas were also engaged in a battle with the east over expanding the suffrage and increasing their own representation in the legislature, and this further confirmed the emerging alignment between the rival parties. A pressing need for economic development and a preexisting struggle for political influence produced intrastate rivalries in these Upper South states that ran counter to the general trend within the region as a whole. In the rest of the South, wealthy planters and merchants generally voted Whig rather than Democratic, while food-producing small farmers, who were somewhat isolated in the up-country and made their living outside the market system, continued to back the party of Andrew Jackson.[12]

The Whigs also enjoyed considerable support in states that would benefit from another of the party's economic proposals, a protective tariff. In two states in particular, an economic interest engaged in processing raw material or in manufacturing needed a high tariff to protect it from foreign competitors. The first was the hemp-producing, central portion of Kentucky. Not surprisingly, the home state of Henry Clay had generated a significant opposition to Jackson and the Democrats in the early 1830s, well before most other southern states. And it consisted of two elements. These were the exporting hemp growers in the central bluegrass region of the state and the small nonslaveholding farmers who predominated in the mountainous eastern part, far from the more settled and developed areas.

Another, and less likely, center of Whiggery was the Lower South state of Louisiana. To the sugar planters of South Louisiana, a protective tariff was of great importance, since they refined the raw cane and then sold it abroad, where they had to compete with Caribbean and South American producers. With their large slave plantations and great wealth, the sugar planters dominated the politics of parishes such as St. Landry, Ascension, St. Martin, and St. Mary that were located west of the Mississippi River and along the Gulf Coast. As a result, South Louisiana became the stronghold of the Whig Party. Also providing considerable support for the Whigs was the heavily populated city of New Orleans, the state's capital and the South's largest port. The city's commercial and financial leaders were Whigs, as was that segment of its population that was Anglophone. Unlike the French-speaking and Catholic sugar planters in South Louisiana, the Francophone, or Creole, inhabitants of New Orleans tended toward the Democrats, as did the antitariff and English-speaking small farmers and cotton planters in the rest of the state. This South Louisiana–New Orleans axis, based on similar economic interests and social status, provided the Whigs with sufficient prestige and influence and enough voters to enable them to maintain a slim majority in the state from the mid-1830s to the mid-1840s, only to decline thereafter.[13]

The Whigs' rise to prominence as a party of national scope that was able to compete with the Democrats in almost all the states was based primarily on their economic priorities and approaches. In a society undergoing settlement and development at a time when manufacturing and industrialization were just emerging, economic issues surely demanded attention throughout the nation. Moreover, the approaches to economic development taken by the Whigs and the Democrats were sufficiently distinctive to justify and sustain them as separate party organizations. But if this divergence on policy began to dissolve or if other concerns arose to push aside economic issues, then the national party system of Whigs and Democrats might come under siege.

John C. Calhoun's Search for Southern Unity

The emergence of political parties during the 1830s was not universally welcomed, however. And no one was more fearful about the implications of this new phenomenon in the country's political life than John C. Calhoun. The South Carolinian worried that the electoral process was being changed fundamentally from the local and personal style of politics that had existed at the beginning of the nineteenth century. In those days, voters knew the candidates and participated directly in choosing their representatives. But now the parties were coordinated and organized across the nation. They had created electoral machinery run by men skilled in the "vicious arts" of electioneering and had built party structures controlled by managers and cliques that selected candidates.[14] Even though nostalgic, Calhoun's lament at the disappearance of an earlier face-to-face political world was shared by many in the new age of parties. Most Whigs in particular rejected the "party dictation" that they saw prevalent within the Democratic machinery forged by Jackson and Van Buren and their party managers. And these Whigs hoped their own party would be able to resist, not just Jackson's "executive usurpation," but his "party dictation" as well.

Calhoun, however, went much further in his critique of organized parties and formulated a distinctive theory of American government as a way of countering the dangerous effects of party. At the same time, the political notions and constitutional devices that he proposed could defend the South from its increasingly vocal and powerful enemies. Calhoun's political maneuvers acted as a foil, a counterpoise, to the growing influence of national parties in the South. Rather than a blessing to the region, parties were a curse, and Calhoun endeavored to weaken and undermine them.

Alongside his criticism of the new parties for destroying the direct and personal politics of the early nineteenth century, Calhoun opposed them for three other reasons. First, they were now national institutions whose primary objective was control of the presidency, an office that had become elective by the 1830s through statewide general ticket elections, rather than appointed by state legislators, as had earlier been the case. Second, the introduction of the spoils system by Andrew Jackson had made the presidency a source of patronage and a lure for "a great, a powerful and mercenary corp[s] of office-holders, office-seekers and expectants" who were "destitute of principle and patriotism" and drawn to politics solely to obtain office.[15] Possessing the ability to bestow patronage, parties were certain to become permanent.

And this led to the third of Calhoun's objections to the new parties. When one of them won the presidency, that party became automatically a national majority with the power to enforce its will. This was the very eventuality Madison had feared in the 1780s. In his theory of the multiplicity of factions and interests, Madison had offered a formula for avoiding such a dangerous outcome. But once national majorities arose and were given cohesion and form by a party, Calhoun worried that the fate of minorities, whether based on regions or interests, was sealed. And it has to be remembered that Calhoun was, above all else, a southerner for whom the Union was a guarantee of protection for his region. Throughout his long political career, he saw himself as a leader of the South, and by the 1830s, *the* leader, whose responsibility was to ensure that the United States did not falter in its obligations to its member states.

John C. Calhoun is quite possibly the most intriguing politician in American history. What makes him so interesting is not merely his centrality in national politics in the first half of the nineteenth century but also the many contradictions at the heart of his public career and political personality. He was a formidably powerful force in the national government, holding most of the highest offices throughout his forty-year career. Yet, ultimately, he was a resolute sectionalist and defender of the South. Calhoun was one of the most original of American political thinkers and is often linked with James Madison for his formal disquisitions on representative government and on the U.S. federal system in particular. Like Madison, the South Carolinian was a practicing politician, and a very active one at that, giving lengthy and compelling speeches, organizing political support, and playing the political game with zest. Calhoun was an avowed conservative. "My object is to preserve. I am thoroughly conservative in my politics," he once proclaimed categorically.[16] Yet, invariably, he took extreme positions in defense of his native region, forcing the issue, drawing lines in the sand beyond which he and the South would not yield, and provoking turmoil and crisis as his preferred mode of operation. And, finally, Calhoun's frequent claim that he was motivated only by principle and a disinterested love for the South was offset by his evident ambition and thirst for power and eminence, above all for the presidency.

Because of these contradictory facets of his political course and character, the Carolina slaveholder evoked contrasting, but rarely calm or unbiased, reactions among his contemporaries. Some admired, even venerated, him; others despised and denounced him. Upon his death, the *New Orleans Bee* eulogized him as "the statesman, the orator and patriot, the purest and most upright of all the public men of the age." But his longtime political foe, Thomas Ritchie, the former head of the Richmond Junto, dismissed him contemptuously, remarking that "Mr. Calhoun is for agitation, agitation."[17] Whether praised or hated, Calhoun was a force to be reckoned with. He was the great rival of Henry Clay, the leader of the Whig Party, who, unlike Calhoun, believed that conciliation, rather than confrontation, was the most fruitful way of dealing with sectional disagreement. Clay's approach was to mock the Carolinian in order to undermine his reputation and influence. In a Senate debate on the Second Bank in 1841, the Kentuckian parodied his opponent's meeting with President Tyler to get him to veto the bill under discussion: "There, I say, I can imagine stood the Senator from South Carolina, care-worn, with furrowed brow, haggard, and intensely gazing, looking as if he were dissecting the last and newest abstraction which sprang from metaphysician's brain, and muttering to himself, in half-uttered sounds, 'This is indeed a real crisis.' "[18]

Clay's depiction of the physical features of John "Crisis" Calhoun, as the *Richmond Whig* once named him, was astute, though scornful. For the Carolinian's looks were distinctive and also formidable. By the 1840s, his gray hair hung long and somewhat disheveled down the side of his head, and his eyes were penetrating. Mathew Brady photographed Calhoun just months before his death and was struck by his gaze. "Calhoun's eye was

John C. Calhoun. This photograph was taken by Mathew Brady in 1850, just a few months before the senator from South Carolina died at the age of sixty-eight after almost a half century in politics. It captures Calhoun's piercing eyes, which Brady found so remarkable. Library of Congress, Prints and Photographs Division.

startling, and almost hypnotized me," he recalled. Mesmerizing, but also forbidding and cold, Calhoun appeared to most as a walking abstraction with little affect or feeling. The most frequently quoted description of him came from Harriet Martineau, a well-known British writer, who, after they met in 1835, called him "a cast-iron man, who looks as if he had never been born and never could be extinguished."[19] This daunting figure took upon himself the task of protecting the South during the 1830s and 1840s, by confronting its enemies, taking firm, unyielding stands, and creating an atmosphere of almost perpetual crisis.

Calhoun's political course from his election to Congress in 1811 until his death in 1850 has seemed tortuous and inconsistent, lacking pattern and coherence. But actually, there seem to have been four phases, during each of which he adopted a different tactic or maneuver in order to protect the South while simultaneously advancing his own ambitions.[20]

In the first phase, from 1811 until the 1820s, Calhoun was a nationalist and an advocate of a physically strengthened Union. He was one of the young War Hawks, along with Henry Clay, who urged war with Britain in 1812. After its conclusion, he became secretary of war under Monroe, from 1816 to 1824, and he pressed urgently for the consolidation and strengthening of the nation, by means of a national bank, a grand system of internal improvements to "conquer space" and "bind the republic together," a strong military, and even a protective tariff. By playing an active role in a growing, energized United States, the South would, in Calhoun's Hamiltonian view, derive significant benefits.

In the mid-1820s, the South Carolinian moved suddenly in a very different direction as he embarked on his second phase. He realized that the South was now in danger, as Congress seemed intent on raising the tariff to protective levels, which would play havoc with the South's reliance on imports in exchange for its exported cash crops. To counter the tariff, Calhoun devised the constitutional remedy of nullification, the right of a state to veto a federal law that it considered seriously harmful to its welfare. There followed a series of confrontations with the federal government over the collection of import duties in the port of Charleston. Although hard to believe, Calhoun was actually the nation's vice president when he urged his state to nullify the federal tariff law. The contest lasted, on and off, from 1828 to 1833. Eventually, after President Jackson threatened to enforce the law by sending troops into the state in 1832 and after a compromise tariff was steered through Congress by Henry Clay and enacted in 1833, South Carolina backed down. As for Calhoun, he had already been replaced by Van Buren as Jackson's vice president in 1832.

Although never implemented, the idea of nullification persisted as both a conceivable remedy for southern grievances in the future and a symbol of resistance. But, as a mechanism sanctioned by the Constitution, it was implausible because it rested on the assumption that a single state could override the national government. Indeed, many southern opponents of Calhoun's doctrine, and of the nullification movement itself, argued that it was reckless and extreme. Moreover, most believed that secession, not nullification, was the only ultimate remedy available and that Calhoun had acted prematurely and irresponsibly in raising that perilous possibility. Calhoun's resistance they admired, but they distanced themselves from his dangerous doctrine. They also disagreed with his efforts between 1832 and 1838 to organize supporters of southern defiance and nullification into a third political force, which he hoped could function as a balance wheel between the Whigs and Democrats, with the two major parties forced to compete for the unaligned southerners.

The third phase of Calhoun's career began in 1838 with his decision to return to the Democratic Party. By this time, the threat to slavery that had first become evident in the Missouri debates of 1819–21 had grown because of the emergence in the 1830s of a movement to abolish slavery, even though its support was quite limited. And southerners in Congress were having to deal with public petitions favoring abolition in the District of Columbia and with abolitionists' use of the U.S. mails to distribute their subversive literature. To both of these threats, the southerners, led by Calhoun, responded immoderately. They pressed Congress to table and never discuss abolitionist petitions (this prohibition was derided as "the gag rule" by its opponents). And they urged Congress, though ultimately without success, to prohibit the U.S. Post Office from handling abolitionist pamphlets. From his position in the Senate, where he would serve from 1832 until his death in 1850, Calhoun tried to push the Democrats toward increased reliance on the South and greater identification with its interests. Because of his fundamental distrust of the national mass parties, he put no faith in the Democrats but was using them to protect the South and its well-being.

In 1844, however, Calhoun's ultimate objective became apparent. He readily accepted President John Tyler's offer of the post of secretary of state, since he shared the Virginian's determination to annex Texas. Both men sought the annexation of a state that was almost certain to be slave. Tyler saw the issue as a springboard to mount a campaign to retain the presidency in 1844 through a personal third party, based primarily on support from his native South. Calhoun's hidden agenda was rather different. He conceived of Texas annexation as an offensive maneuver to create a southern party separate from the Whigs and the Democrats. And so Secretary Calhoun presented the case for annexation as provocatively as he could. Annexation, he announced, was intended to benefit the South, and therefore southern congressmen should endorse it overwhelmingly. Hearing this justification, northerners in both of the major parties would react angrily, so Calhoun predicted, and would proceed to read the southerners out, thereby creating the basis for a separate southern party. When the annexation of Texas was eventually approved by Congress after the 1844 election, it took the form of a joint resolution, not a treaty, and the vote was party-based rather than sectional. So Calhoun's devious strategy was frustrated, since the Texas issue did not split the parties internally along sectional lines.[21]

After serving briefly in Tyler's Whig administration, the South Carolinian broke completely with the Democrats in order to continue his desperate pursuit of an exclusively sectional party. With this objective in mind, Calhoun entered the fourth, and final, phase of his political career. For the remainder of the 1840s, after the war against Mexico heightened sectional tensions over the expansion of slavery, Calhoun took a series of initiatives to rally and coordinate the South politically. The first was the Southern

Address of 1849, which pressed for southern unity on the "grand and vital question" of the maintenance of slavery. "Instead of placing it above all others, [this issue] has been made subordinate," the address insisted, "not only to mere questions of policy, but to the preservation of party ties and ensuring party success." Yet only 48 of the South's 124 congressmen were prepared to endorse the move and consider making southern unity a priority over their existing party affiliations. Calhoun's second initiative was the calling of a southern convention in Nashville in 1850 to organize a united southern front prepared to oppose the settlement of differences between the sections, later called the Compromise of 1850. The convention met, but attendance was disappointing, with most of the South's political leaders expressing considerable wariness about the risks of organized southern action outside the major parties.

On his deathbed, Calhoun proposed yet another constitutional remedy for the South's plight as a besieged minority. Like his earlier proposal for a state veto over hostile national legislation through nullification, Calhoun now formulated another constitutional device that would institutionalize a regional, or sectional, veto. On the assumption that two rival, antagonistic interests existed that were permanent constituent parts of the nation, Calhoun's mechanism would recognize the "concurrent majority" as well as the numerical majority. Thus, both majorities would be recognized and therefore be allowed to coexist. Although the "concurrent" majority, which was actually a numerical *minority*, could not command the power and recognition which the numerical *majority* enjoyed because of its greater number of votes, the smaller entity, that is, the slaveholding South, could not simply be ignored forever. The governmental system, Calhoun insisted, had therefore to provide permanent mechanisms for the expression of the minority's will and interests. To supplement the device of the "concurrent majority," Calhoun proposed a "dual presidency," with a northerner and a southerner holding the office simultaneously. Ingenious and resourceful though it was, Calhoun's two-part mechanism generated little support. Indeed, constitutional change of this magnitude was even less attainable than a change in the attitude of most southern politicians toward the existing political parties.

The campaign waged by Calhoun and his band of followers throughout the South was a running battle against the national parties that had recently emerged in American politics. Although it failed to generate broad support, one particular state, Calhoun's own South Carolina, had managed to exclude parties and operate outside the party system of Whigs and Democrats. In the Palmetto State there was no opposition party, since the state was united, just like Calhoun wanted the South to be. The state's congressmen all affiliated with the Democratic Party, and its internal politics remained undisturbed by party competition. There were no state-wide elections, since the general assembly selected presidential electors as well as all executive and judicial officers, even down to the local level. Officeholding was still based on the possession of substantial property, but, surprisingly, universal suffrage had been instituted as early as 1810. Two years earlier, the underrepresented up-country section of the state had obtained additional legislators through the constitutional settlement of 1808. This settlement had ended several decades of conflict between the state's growing up-country districts and the low-country. It consisted of a set of concessions to propitiate and include the slave-owning planters of the up-country, but it left the coastal gentry still very much in control of a state in which the majority of the population were slaves. More overtly than any other state, South Carolina's politics were hierarchical and oligarchical. In fact, unlike any other state, it lacked political parties altogether in the 1830s and 1840s when competing parties became the national norm.[22]

During these two decades, John C. Calhoun dominated his state's politics as the leading nullifier in the early 1830s and as U.S. senator thereafter. His powerful and looming presence further consolidated the state's unity and its repudiation of parties. At the national level, Calhoun's unceasing combativeness proved unsettling and troublesome, even though he failed in his persistent attempts to destabilize, or even topple, the system of national parties. After all, the political division of the nation along sectional lines, toward which Calhoun worked and struggled, was the great threat that national parties were intended to prevent.

3

A One-Party South Again

DEMOCRATIC ASCENDANCY

Success for the system of national parties depended upon its ability to manage the contentious sectional interests. But the pressures on the system neither dissipated nor diminished. Instead, they battered it continuously until midcentury. By the decade of the 1850s, the parties as well as the nation itself were in dire peril.

Sectional Issues in National Politics

Even while the Democratic Party and the Whig Party were still in their formative stages, the sectional dispute had taken a new and unanticipated turn. And the emergence of a movement for the immediate abolition of slavery was the cause. Though few in numbers, the abolitionists took an uncompromising and radical stand against slavery, and they quickly made abolition of the institution a public issue. In 1835, they mounted a petition drive demanding that Congress abolish slavery in the District of Columbia, which was governed directly by the national legislature itself. Southern congressmen responded forcefully by insisting that these petitions be tabled, thereby preventing the target of these demands, the institution of slavery, from being discussed in Congress. Enacted with the aid of votes from northerners, the "gag rule" was sustained from 1836 until its repeal in 1844. Simultaneously, southern congressmen pressured Congress to pass legislation prohibiting the U.S. Post Office from handling abolitionist pamphlets and broadsides. Although President Jackson and his postmaster general, Amos Kendall, endorsed it enthusiastically, the measure failed to pass in Congress.

In the ensuing decade or so, however, the slavery question proved impossible to suppress. By the mid-1840s, the focus of attention in the debate shifted to areas that, surprisingly, were located outside the territorial limits of the United States. Removing the issue beyond the nation's borders might perhaps have been expected to relax the tension and anxiety. But it did not. Ironically, the matter became more problematic and more urgent than earlier when slavery inside the country itself had been the preoccupation. This renewed agitation around the slavery question arose from demands to expand the nation's frontiers to include large areas in the Southwest by acquiring land currently in the possession of Mexico. The ensuing furor propelled the issue to the center of American politics. It began in 1844, with President John Tyler's provocative move to annex the independent Republic of Texas, which had formerly been a province of Mexico until it broke away after a seven-month war in 1836. Since Texas was rapidly being settled by an influx of slaveholding Americans, who now dominated the new republic's politics, its annexation guaranteed the addition of at least one slave state, and possibly several if the enormous territory were divided up. Tyler's annexation efforts were thwarted by the Senate's rejection of the treaty he had negotiated with the Republic of Texas. Refusing to be foiled in his determination to add another slave state, Tyler resorted to a subterfuge. Three days before he left office, he signed a resolution of annexation and sent it to the Texas government to be approved, which, after some debate, was soon accomplished.

Meanwhile, the prospect of further expansion produced a frenzy of excitement. The 1844 presidential election pitted an ardent expansionist, James K. Polk of Tennessee, against Henry Clay, in what would be Clay's third and last bid for the presidency. Although Polk won by a slim majority of 38,000 votes, he considered his victory a mandate for acquiring more land and extending the boundaries of the United States. The lands he sought were the Oregon territory, which was jointly administered by Britain and the United States, as well as California and the vast territories west of the Rio Grande, which were all part of Mexico. Acquisition of these two massive areas had been the central issue in the campaign, and President Polk wasted no time in trying to seize them. After finalizing the annexation of Texas, he added the territory of Oregon below the 49th parallel, although he had vowed in his election campaign to get all the land as far north as the latitude of 54°40', even if that meant going to war with Britain. Still not satisfied and still spoiling for a fight, Polk next provoked a war with Mexico. The acquisition of the lower portion of Oregon and the conflict with Mexico were both approved by a majority of northerners, although they were far less enthusiastic about the latter. The South fully expected to be the main beneficiary from the annexation of Texas and a victory over Mexico, since the territory that was anticipated from these two landgrabs lay due west of the slaveholding states. The southerners' expectations proved to be overly optimistic, however. Texas was certain to be a slave state, but the status of lands gained from Mexico was far less clear because Mexico had previously outlawed slavery. Over the future of these Mexican territories, a dispute erupted whose outcome was unpredictable and, as it turned out, disastrous.

Even before the military campaign against Mexico was concluded, northerners in Congress vowed their determination to keep slavery out of any territories the United States acquired as part of the spoils of war. The Wilmot Proviso was a rider attached by David Wilmot, a Pennsylvania Democrat, to Polk's request for appropriations to bring the war to a conclusion and negotiate a peace treaty. It required Congress to ban slavery from any lands obtained from Mexico. Initiated by northern Democrats who were frustrated at the domination of their party by Polk and his southern followers, the Wilmot Proviso was also supported by many northern Whigs who had opposed this war of conquest, even though a mere sixteen in both houses had been prepared to vote against appropriating the funds to commence it. But the fierce reaction in the South to the proviso's federal ban on slavery's expansion persuaded the Whigs that a better approach was to insist that no territory at all be obtained from Mexico. That way, the vexatious problem would be removed altogether. Indeed, a large number of southerners already believed that nothing was to be gained from insisting that slavery be permitted. John C. Calhoun himself had even opposed the war because he feared that its consequences would hurt the South, since very little, if any, of the southwestern desert would be hospitable to slavery. And most Whigs in the South concurred. Alexander H. Stephens of Georgia spoke for them when he asked the House in June 1846 "if this is to be a *war for conquest*, and whether this is the object for which it is to be waged. If so I protest against that part of it."[1]

Despite the opposition of most northern, and many southern, Whigs, vast amounts of land were acquired by the United States after its victory, consisting of the future states of New Mexico, Arizona, Nevada, and Utah, as well as the massive territory of California, an area even larger than Texas, extending down the Pacific coast from the southern boundary of Oregon to the Mexican border. Naturally enough, the stakes in the ensuing dispute over the disposition of the Mexican Cession were enormous. But more significant was the turn that the sectional issue had now taken.

Attention now shifted from the abolitionists' initial focus on slavery within the United States where it already existed to slavery in territories beyond its current borders where it did not yet exist but might sometime in the future. This speculative twist to the dispute in the aftermath of the

Alexander H. Stephens. This portrait by Mathew Brady was probably taken in the late 1860s after the war. "Little Alec," as Stephens was known, was a small and very sickly man who nevertheless had a long public career from the 1840s until the early 1880s. In the antebellum decades, he was a leading southern congressman, first as a Whig and then as a Democrat. He was also the vice president of the Confederacy, although he remained in Georgia for most of the war. Library of Congress, Prints and Photographs Division.

War against Mexico was supplemented by the increasing emphasis on the *right* of slaveholders to take their slaves into these new territories, rather than on their *ability* to do so. Even if slavery could not be transplanted and made to flourish in these unsettled lands, the South insisted that the *right* of American citizens to take their slaves there had to be acknowledged and guaranteed. Because the Wilmot Proviso called on the national government to ban slavery from the Mexican Cession, southerners countered with the demand for federal protection of slavery there. Federal nonintervention, or neutrality, was no longer sufficient. Rather, respect for southern rights and equal treatment were deemed essential in the dangerously escalating sectional struggle.

Party Differences Disappear

The War against Mexico enabled the United States to increase its size by one-fourth. At the same time, this newly acquired land brought the sectional dispute to a head and almost certainly hastened the breakup of the Union. Quick to recognize the serious danger that the nation's lust for land had created, party leaders in Congress tried to bring the problem under control. At the forefront of this move was Henry Clay, whose Whig Party had opposed both the conduct of the war and the acquisition of territory. Clay hoped to revive his party's fortunes as well as boost his own reputation as "The Great Compromiser" after his exploits in 1821 and 1833 in the Missouri and nullification crises. To this end, he brought together a set of proposals for adjudicating the problem of slavery in the Mexican territories and for settling several other unresolved sectional issues. The eventual outcome of Clay's initiative was the Compromise of 1850. But it would be managed and brought to completion, not by the Kentucky Whig, but by an Illinois Democrat, Stephen A. Douglas.

Reluctantly yielding to Democratic pressure to combine his half-dozen measures into a single, or omnibus, bill, Clay found it impossible to rally a majority of senators in favor of its passage. The bill was defeated in July 1850, just a few weeks after the sudden death of the Whig president, Zachary Taylor. A new president, Millard Fillmore, and a new floor manager, Stephen Douglas, returned to Clay's initial preference for presenting the plan's components as separate bills. This alternative approach proved successful, since each measure passed both houses and became law in September 1850. The trouble was that each bill relied upon a sectional majority, or near majority, for passage. As Michael Holt, the historian of the Whig Party, concluded, "Sectional divisions over slavery helped blur party differences."[2] In the final version of the Compromise of 1850, California was to be admitted as a free state, while slavery's status in the territories of New Mexico and Utah was to be left unrestricted, with Congress neither prohibiting nor protecting it. The disputed boundary between Texas and New Mexico was settled in the latter's favor, for which Texas was compensated with $10 million to help pay off the state's debt. The slave trade was abolished in the District of Columbia and, in return, the South was placated with a more stringent federal law to enforce the return of fugitive slaves.

This seemingly felicitous outcome was hailed by President Fillmore as "a final settlement" of the outstanding sectional differences. But Fillmore's optimism was unwarranted, since the Compromise, which was no compromise at all but a series of sectional votes, also proved to be neither a settlement nor final. There were many in both sections who still hoped it might be. But some felt otherwise, and the most immediate and dramatic manifestation of this sentiment appeared in the South in a political convulsion that has sometimes been described as the "First Secession Crisis."

The crisis had its origins in earlier efforts by Calhoun and his followers to unite the South through the formation of a southern party. Gravely ill and fearful that the newly elected Whig administration of Zachary Taylor would favor the North in its plans for resolving the territorial issues arising from the Mexican War, Calhoun took action to attain his long-cherished goal of uniting the South. In December 1848, he convened a caucus of southern congressmen and then issued his "Address to the People of the Southern States," in which he denounced northern aggression against slavery and urged southerners to unite in a sectional party. But just 69 of the region's 124 congressmen attended the initial caucus, and only 48 of these signed the Southern Address. Since the creation of a southern party was premised on the breakup of the national parties, the failure of all the southern Whigs except two to put section above party and sign the Southern Address was a major setback. Nevertheless, Calhoun persisted. For there was mounting concern, especially in the states of the Lower South, about the substantial support in Washington and the northern states for the Wilmot Proviso and its proposed ban on slavery in the Mexican territories.

Encouraged that "the South is more united, than I ever knew it to be, and more bold and decided," Calhoun issued a call, supported by some of Mississippi's leading politicians, for delegates from the southern states to meet in Nashville in June 1850.[3] Once again, however, the response was disappointing. The delegation from Calhoun's own state consisted of sixteen influential politicians, but, outside South Carolina, less significance was attached to the movement. The border states stayed away, as did North Carolina and Louisiana, while many participating states sent only a few delegates. Evidently, the movement in Washington toward some kind of intersectional settlement made an organized southern response less vital and urgent than Calhoun had assumed. Meanwhile, the ability of the national parties to hold the sections together and adjust their differences seemed to warrant their continued existence, rather than their dissolution in order to form a southern party. Nevertheless, Calhoun's convictions about the South's need to act independently and as a unit had repercussions beyond the abortive Nashville convention and his own death a few months before it met. As his political enemy, Thomas Hart Benton of Missouri, warned the Senate the day after Calhoun died, "He is not dead, sir—he is not dead. There may be no vitality in his body, but there is in his doctrines."[4]

Between 1850 and 1852, four states in the Lower South (Georgia, Mississippi, Alabama, and South Carolina) took steps toward creating southern unity around the issue of secession, rather than by creating a southern party as Calhoun had preferred. In Georgia, Mississippi, and Alabama, southern extremists had lost faith in the ability of the federal government and the national parties to protect slavery. Even while the Compromise was still being debated, Southern Rights factions in Georgia and Mississippi mounted campaigns to call a state convention to consider secession. And they succeeded, first, because fear that Congress would not protect slavery in the Mexican territories was widespread, especially in view of its determination to admit California as a free state. And, second, the governors of both states, George Towns and John Quitman, were themselves Southern Rights Democrats, and they actively supported the movement for a convention. Alabama's governor, Henry W. Collier, was less sympathetic, anticipating that so drastic and precipitate a course was almost certain to generate significant opposition within his state.

Although very real, the crisis did not unfold in the secessionists' favor. In Georgia, the Unionist forces consisted of the vast majority of the state's Whigs who had supported the Compromise, along with the nonslaveholding Jacksonian nationalists of the hill country who resented the black belt planters who dominated the Democratic Party. Together, they inflicted a massive defeat on the Southern Rights men, whom they depicted as reckless disunionists. Winning 240 seats to their opponents' 23, the Unionists controlled the ensuing convention and snuffed out secession. After winning such a decisive victory, the Unionists decided quite understandably to forge their coalition into a party that could win control of the state in the 1851 elections. Howell Cobb, the Speaker of the House in 1849–50 and a pro-Compromise Democrat, was the Union Party's candidate for governor, while Alexander Stephens and Robert Toombs, both of them experienced Whig congressmen, were the leaders of the coalition's Whig majority.

The Union Party proceeded to sweep the state and congressional elections. Cobb was elected governor with 60 percent of the vote, and the Unionists took six of the eight congressional seats. They controlled both houses of the assembly overwhelmingly and proceeded to select Toombs for the Senate seat. This triumph was especially important for the Whigs. It improved their declining prospects, which had been fading ever since their brief ascendancy in the state from 1843 to 1847. And their identification with the Union Party offset the political liabilities they had incurred because of their affiliation with the antiexpansionist, and increasingly antislavery, northern Whigs. Indeed, Stephens and Toombs hoped that a Union Party could be forged in other southern states as well as in the rest of the nation to replace the Whig Party, which was collapsing under the pressure of its increasingly divergent northern and southern wings.

Meanwhile, in Mississippi and Alabama, a similar pattern of events unfolded. A pro-Compromise Unionist coalition dominated the convention to consider disunion in Mississippi. After voting it down, 72–17, the Unionists denounced secession as "utterly unsanctioned by the Federal Constitution" and proceeded to organize for the upcoming elections. They ran Henry S. Foote for governor, who then defeated the secessionist candidate, Jefferson Davis, the replacement for John Quitman, who had decided to withdraw from the race. The pro-Compromise Unionists then won overwhelming control of the state legislature, along with three of the four congressional seats. Since the Whigs had never come close to winning in Mississippi's legislative or congressional elections during the 1840s, the formation of an interparty coalition gave them unprecedented influence in the state. Watching the fate of the disunion conventions in Georgia and Mississippi, Alabama's Southern Rights men decided not to risk likely defeat by calling a convention to consider secession but to focus instead on state and congressional elections in 1851. They were defeated, all the same. With a Democratic U.S. senator, Jeremiah Clemens, as the Unionist candidate for governor and with the state's more numerous Whigs playing a larger role in the Union Party than in Mississippi, the Union coalition repeated the resounding success of its neighboring states to the east and west. In all three, an electoral majority composed of black belt Whigs and hill country Democrats formed the basis of the new Union Party.

Watching these developments very closely, the South Carolinians proceeded to take action, despite the evident collapse of the secession movements elsewhere in the Lower South. In July 1851, the state legislature voted overwhelmingly to call a convention to consider secession. The body was dominated by men who wanted their state to secede. Meanwhile, the legislature also chose a small delegation of fourteen (two from each congressional district) to attend a congress of southern states, should a region-wide initiative become possible. When the convention met in spring 1852, it passed an ordinance asserting the right of a state to secede but refused to provide for the state's secession on its own. Instead, the convention decided to wait until other southern states were ready to join the eager Carolinians.

Governed by its all-powerful legislature and dominated by slave-owning planters from all parts of the state, South Carolina presented a united front in defense of slavery not replicated in the rest of the South. Since the state's political leadership had come to believe by 1850 that slavery could not be protected adequately inside the Union, the only question was how and when South Carolina should secede—either on its own when it was ready to do so or in cooperation with other slave states when enough of them were prepared to leave? In 1850, the Carolinians waited for others to join them. Ten years later, they would act alone and expect the others to follow.

Secession had been averted. But the sudden and extraordinary success of the Unionist coalitions in the Lower South indicated that far-reaching political developments of another kind were about to surface. Since new issues and new alignments had emerged and threatened to overwhelm the existing parties, the future of the Whig Party in the southern states was unpredictable. But the Democrats' prospects were not that certain either. Surprisingly, southern politics after 1851 assumed a shape and direction that was very different from what might have been expected. Instead of setting a trend toward an enduring alignment around the competing issues of union and disunion, the turbulence of 1850–52 precipitated even greater instability and regrouping over the following decade. In fact, the system of two national parties would shatter, and nothing so orderly would take its place.

The crushing of the Southern Rights remedy of secession meant that disunion was no longer an option for countering the northern threat. Yet, if disunion was out of the question, then union was the only alternative. Since the outstanding issues in the Mexican territories, along with ending of the slave trade in the District of Columbia and a tougher fugitive slave law, were all adjusted in the 1850 negotiations, it could be argued that there was no reason anymore to oppose the Compromise. Indeed, the Unionists in Georgia had made it clear that, despite its flaws, they considered the Compromise "a permanent adjustment of this sectional controversy" that had been reached in "a spirit of mutual concession." Their "Georgia Platform," formulated in the state convention of 1850, which had voted down secession, stipulated the conditions under which the state would resist "a disruption of every tie which binds her to the Union." Georgia's ties to the Union would be broken only if Congress took any action hostile to slavery in the District of Columbia or on any other federal property; if it prohibited slave sales across state lines (that is, the interstate slave trade); if it refused to admit any new slave state; if it excluded slavery from Utah or New Mexico; or if it repealed or modified the new fugitive slave law. Passed with only 19 votes opposed, this declaration obviously reassured as well as curbed Georgia's Southern Rights group, while its firmness and specificity also commended it to the other Unionist-controlled states in the Lower South, Alabama and Mississippi. Thus, the Compromise of 1850 was law and its legitimacy was sanctioned at the state level, though under specified conditions. With secession rejected and union under the Compromise accepted, both positions were no longer in contention. In effect, they were no longer live issues capable of aligning two rival parties.

On organizational grounds too, the potential union/disunion alignment of 1850–52 possessed no staying power. In the first place, no other states regrouped into similar parties, even though it was sometimes debated. In solidly Democratic Arkansas and Texas, secession was never proposed, perhaps because such a contentious issue was almost certain to cause dissension within the ascendant Democratic Party. On the other hand, in states where the Whigs were dominant or closely competitive (such as North Carolina, Louisiana, and Tennessee), the Democrats could not propose secession, even if they had wanted to, without risking serious opposition from the rival party.

A second obstacle presented itself within the three Lower South states themselves (Georgia, Mississippi, and Alabama) in the form of the Democratic Party. Once the Unionists had won power, they found their Democratic colleagues in the coalition maneuvering to return to the party from which they had recently strayed. These disloyal Democrats worried that their own party, which provided a national connection and an organizational base in the South, would come under the control of their Southern Rights rivals if they delayed their own return. And so they began to flock back to the Democratic Party. And, finally, the southern Unionists' likely allies in the North soon proved incompatible and unreliable. Southern Whigs were hoping to broaden their base and their appeal by becoming a Union party. But northern Whigs opposed the Compromise, while their position on slavery and its expansion was also at odds with their southern colleagues. Taking a pro-union position when that stance depended on an alliance with northern Whigs was therefore fundamentally problematic. And alliance with untrustworthy northern Whigs was even less attractive to Democrats in the Union Party. As the southern Whigs themselves soon found out (when their party backed Winfield Scott for president in 1852 rather than their preferred candidate, the pro-Compromise Millard Fillmore), the national party was a congenitally unreliable ally.

The South's Whigs hoped that union as an issue and the Union Party as an organization might redefine and revitalize their own party. But their expectations soon evaporated. At the very moment when southern Whigs were discovering that this new initiative was proving elusive, they were also experiencing considerable difficulty retaining two of the traditional issues that, at the state level, had given their party a political identity and differentiated it from the Democrats.

In the 1830s, the Whig Party's primary justification as an alternative to the Democrats had been its distinctive stand on economic questions. The party favored government promotion of economic development, in sharp contrast with the Democrats' preference for laissez-faire and their aversion to government activism. During the 1840s, however, the Democrats' position began to shift, as the demand for improved transportation and more reliable and accessible banking institutions mounted.

The Democrats' embrace of Whig economic principles was particularly evident in North Carolina. After the 1854 state election, the *Charlotte Western Democrat* observed approvingly that "the subject of Internal Improvements was fully discussed; both parties are committed to a liberal policy." As a result, the Democratic candidate for governor proceeded to win the election, despite his own and his party's previous hostility to state aid to railroads. After a decade or so of vigorous resistance, the Democrats had had to submit to the pressure to connect the western parts of the state to its eastern ports, thereby preventing crops grown in the upcountry from being carried by out-of-state shippers. Recognition of the need to create transportation links throughout the state meant that, by the mid-1850s, the legislature was "running wild about Railroads," so the president of the Raleigh and Gaston Railroad once noted, adding that logrolling rather than partisanship was now shaping the votes on each project. And the same was true with banks. North Carolina had just two before 1848, but over the next decade the number increased to thirty.[5]

In Louisiana too, the Democrats changed course and accepted Whig economic policies in the early 1850s. Although the state's constitution of 1845 institutionalized the Democrats' laissez-faire beliefs and their hostility to banks and concentrations of capital, these provisions generated considerable opposition among the commercial classes of New Orleans and among interests eager for economic development. Taking advantage of their control of the legislature in 1852, the Whigs proposed calling a constitutional convention to remove the burdensome restrictions on business activities and on the granting of state aid, as well as to make the state's electoral system more democratic. The outcome was a convention with a Whig majority, which voted to allow free banking under general incorporation laws, to raise the state's absurdly low debt ceiling from $100,000 to $8 million, to remove restrictions on the life of corporations, and to overturn the prohibition on the state's purchase of stock in corporations, thereby allowing it to aid internal improvements projects. And these specific changes were evidently approved by the Democrats, because the convention completed its business in a mere twenty-seven days and then voted solidly in favor of the new constitution, with only eight delegates opposed.[6]

Louisiana's 1852 constitution included another significant feature—an increase in the people's role in government, through making judges elective and basing representation in both houses of the legislature on total population. The Whigs had proposed these changes to indicate that their party was as democratic as their opponents, who had generally been the advocates of broader suffrage and representation. On both of these issues, the convention delegates of each party were in considerable agreement. Although the Whigs could not claim sole responsibility for the changes, their shift of position on the issue had made enactment of these reforms possible. But, to their great dismay, the 1852 constitution that the Whigs had shaped did not result in their dominance of the state's politics for the ensuing decade as they had hoped. The Whigs' success in getting the Democrats to agree to greater state involvement in the economy and their own shift toward increased democratization meant that the Whig Party had forfeited its defining issue—the demand for revision of the 1845 constitution, which had been framed by their Democratic opponents.

The second of the two issues that had differentiated Whigs from Democrats during the Age of Jackson was democratization, specifically broader suffrage and fairer representation. In general, the Whigs were on the conservative end of this contest, fending off the Democrats' pressure for greater inclusion and participation. For example, in North Carolina, between 1848 and 1854, the Whigs found themselves under constant pressure to support expansion of the suffrage. In the 1848 gubernatorial election, the Democratic candidate, David S. Reid, had raised the issue of "equal suffrage" by calling for an end to the requirement that voters for the state senate own fifty acres of land, a property test that no longer applied to the house. For the next six years, the Whigs resisted what they considered a dangerous leveling tendency. But this antidemocratic stance began to hurt them electorally, and so they shifted position and embraced equal suffrage in 1854. Indeed, by the early 1850s, the Whig Party throughout the South had accepted universal male suffrage.

The issue of equal representation was usually less volatile and had, for the most part, been resolved to the satisfaction of the up-country Democrats. But in Virginia it was still a live issue that was eventually settled in the constitutional convention of 1850–51, after rankling for two decades since the previous constitutional revision in 1829–30. In this instance, the Whigs, with their primary source of support in the underdeveloped and underrepresented western areas of the state, were the proponents of fairer representation and also of broader suffrage. Once the 1850–51 convention assembled, the western delegates threatened to secede from Virginia if their demands were not met, while the dominant easterners, who were mainly Democrats, feared that concession of greater representation to the western Whigs would reduce their political power and maybe expose their property in slaves to unfriendly legislation. After a standoff lasting more than three months, the slave-owning Tidewater and Southside agreed to an apportionment based on white population alone ("the white basis," as opposed to the existing "mixed" basis, which included property as well as population). As a result, westerners obtained a majority in the house while easterners still controlled the senate. In addition, the convention agreed to an unrestricted white male suffrage, while offsetting this western gain with concessions to the easterners on the taxing of their slaves.

Even though the Whigs had achieved their objective in Virginia, the upshot was not a boost to the party's prospects. For they had lost an issue that had energized the party's supporters and given it definition by contrast with its Democratic rival. And in virtually every southern state, settlement of the voting and representation issue, along with the concurrence of both parties on the need for government encouragement of internal improvements, mainly in transportation and banking, gave voters little incentive to support the Whigs anymore. The party had little to offer at the state level, while its appeal to southern voters as a national party was receding rapidly. With the ground cut from under them, the Whigs collapsed, leaving the Democrats dominant, as the party more sympathetic and reliable on the question of fundamental concern to most southerners —defense of the region's economic and social interest in slavery.

The Southern Whigs Disappear

One issue on which the two parties might have differed still needs to be considered. And this was the question of how best to protect and defend the South. Since both parties were national, they were unavoidably implicated in the intensifying controversy in Congress over the influence of slavery on the country's government and economy. The South's political leaders did not, however, question the institution of slavery itself or its continued existence and preservation. For the centrality of slavery in the southern economy and in its social and racial order was agreed upon. By the 1840s, there was little or no debate about this within the political elite, even though its members worried about the reliability of nonslaveholders.

The commitment of the region's political leadership to the institution of slavery was not at all surprising, since slave owners dominated state government. The majority of legislators in the southern states were owners of slaves. By contrast, slaveholders were a minority of between one-fourth to one-third of the population. They were therefore substantially overrepresented in the state legislatures. In North Carolina in 1850, 25.6 percent of the state's white families owned slaves, and just 3.1 percent of them were planters who, by definition, owned over twenty slaves. Yet 81.2 percent of the state legislators that year owned slaves and 36.1 percent were planters.[7] A similar pattern prevailed in Georgia, where 36.9 percent of the state's white families owned slaves and 5.7 percent were planters. Yet 69.7 percent of the state's legislators were slave owners in 1850 (over 80 percent by another historian's estimation) and 29.8 percent of them were planters. In another Lower South state, Alabama, 34.2 percent of white families owned slaves, yet 66.4 percent of the legislators in 1850 were slave owners. And the corresponding proportions for planters were 5.5 percent of the white population and 33.6 percent of the legislators.[8]

In effect, the southern legislatures contained clear majorities of slaveholders. In five of them, over two-thirds of the members owned slaves. Meanwhile, the incidence of large slave owners, or planters, among the legislators was even more disproportionate to the population at large, ranging from five times to twelve times greater.[9] These statistics do not take into account elected officials at the national level (U.S. senators and representatives) or elected governors and appointed executive officers at the state level, all of whose wealth and slaveholdings were almost certain to be considerably greater than those of the legislators, because these men held major offices that required greater recognition and prominence.

Slavery was therefore at the center of southern political life by 1850, if not several decades before. What was at issue, however, was not its existence and viability but its protection. How best to protect and defend slavery became the dominant issue in the region's politics at both the national and the state level. And the possibility of slavery in the territories was now the compelling question, not the existence of slavery in the states. In this dispute about slavery in the territories beyond and outside the slave states, the great issue became therefore the defense of slavery and slaveholding, not just as a southern interest, but as a southern right that the rest of the country had to recognize.

The dispute began with the debate over Texas annexation in 1844. It gained momentum with the controversy over the territories in the Mexican Cession and the disposition of them through the Wilmot Proviso and the Compromise of 1850. And it led finally, during the mid-1850s, to the dispute over the expansion of slavery into the lands of the Louisiana Purchase, which was precipitated by the Kansas-Nebraska Act, followed by the conflict inside Kansas itself. Throughout this sequence of events, the South's Whigs and Democrats engaged in an increasingly shrill and fateful contest to determine which party was the more vigorous and vociferous defender of the region. And the audience they were appealing to and trying to convince was, of course, the southern electorate. Ironically, therefore, the two national parties found themselves dragged into a dispute to decide which of them was the more southern and therefore the more sectional. As Marc Kruman observed about the two parties in antebellum North Carolina, "State party competition exacerbated sectional tensions, while national party ties mitigated them."[10] By the mid-1850s, however, those "national party ties" were all but broken in most of the South.

In this ongoing contest, the Whigs were at a disadvantage, and ultimately they lost the struggle. But there had been successes. As early as the presidential contests of 1836 and 1840, they had been able to convince most southern voters that Whig candidates for president would be safer for the South than Martin Van Buren. And eight years later, their own presidential candidate, Zachary Taylor, a slaveholder from Louisiana who owned more than one hundred slaves, was deemed more reliable than the Democrats' Lewis Cass. These exceptions aside, however, the Whigs' credentials as protectors of the South generally fell short.

In this battle to win the confidence of southern voters, the disadvantages faced by the southern Whigs can be attributed to three elements. First, their ties to the Union were essential and fundamental, unlike those of the Democrats. The Whig Party's identity and its agenda were national in focus because its activist and integrated economic program, Henry Clay's American System, required centralized direction. Also, its advocacy of cultural homogeneity and assimilation presumed a national cultural unity and norm. By contrast, the Democrats' laissez-faire approach to economic policy and their corresponding tolerance of social and cultural differences led them to espouse policies that encouraged decentralization and heterogeneity. Southern regional interests were therefore more readily accommodated by the Democrats.

A second, and related, problem for the Whigs was that they invariably found themselves responding to the initiatives of the Democrats and their claims to be the party better able to protect the South. Time after

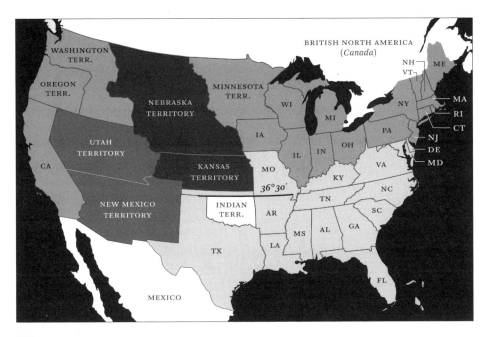

Free state or territory

Slave state or territory

Opened to slavery
by principle of popular
sovereignty, Compromise
of 1850

Opened to slavery by
principle of popular sovereignty, Kansas-Nebraska
Act of 1854

MAP 3. The Kansas-Nebraska Act, 1854. This map dramatizes the extent of the area opened up to the possible entry of slavery by Stephen A. Douglas's proposal. It included the remainder of the Louisiana Purchase (the territories of Nebraska and Kansas). With the 36°30′ line nullified by the act, settlers in these two vast territories had the authority, under popular sovereignty, to vote to extend slavery above the line, where it had previously been prohibited. The upshot was the destabilizing of the Whig and Democratic parties and the formation of an "Anti-Nebraska" coalition, which soon developed into the northern, antislavery Republican Party.

time, the Democrats would discover dangers and problems facing the South, and they would then rally their party and the voters to face down and ward off the threat. For the most part, the Whigs did not look for impending dangers or perceived insults but were rather more circumspect before sounding the alarm, by which time the Democrats had seized the initiative. A leading Whig from North Carolina, Kenneth Rayner, offered a perceptive observation along these lines in December 1856, several years after the Whigs' demise: "The Democratic party seems determined for political purposes, to keep up an endless agitation, on the subject of slavery. Just as soon as one slavery difficulty is settled, they reopen the agitation in some other shape. And any Southern man who may then dare oppose such policy, will be *tabooed* as an abolitionist." He then offered a most astute insight: "The true interest of a slave-holding community is a defensive one. The moral sense of the Christian world and of a large portion of our country, is against us, in regard to slavery. We can't afford to be aggressive. We are in a minority." For the previous fifteen years, Rayner had been warning that "sectional politics and reckless slavery agitation" were detrimental to the South and likely to be destructive of the Union, an admonition that southern Democrats never took seriously. For they were convinced that attack was the best form of defense.[11]

At critical moments in the slavery agitation of the 1840s and early 1850s, southern Whigs took positions that were unionist and accommodating because they believed these were more beneficial to the region. They urged a policy of "no territory" during the Mexican War in order to preclude a struggle afterward to determine whether the acquired lands should be open to slavery. Southern Whigs supported the Compromise of 1850 after it was enacted and urged that it be considered a settlement of the problems, mainly relating to slavery, between the sections. And they supported the Kansas-Nebraska bill, believing that popular sovereignty might not be harmful to the South. But, in each instance, the region's Democrats heightened the tension by denouncing these conciliatory and unassertive positions as dangerous to the South and its fundamental interests. It made no difference that the Whigs' approach might seem more reliable. Once their stance was denounced by the Democrats as submissive and a betrayal of the South, the Whigs were inevitably forced onto the defensive for being insufficiently alert and aggressive. Invariably, impulse trumped caution.

Finally, and most important, southern Whigs belonged to a national party whose northern wing was far less friendly to the South than were northern Democrats. Northern Whigs were, for the most part, antislavery, and they tended to be hostile on moral grounds that allowed for little bargaining or conciliation. Most northern Whigs were unwilling to treat the Compromise of 1850 as a settlement, and they later opposed the Kansas-Nebraska Act because it allowed slavery to expand north of 36°30′, the line to which it had been restricted by the Missouri Compromise. A majority joined the anti-Nebraska coalition, which was emerging in response to the act's repeal of the Missouri Compromise, a move that finally dissolved the Whig Party. But the need to cooperate with the party's northern wing made the southern Whigs' task extremely difficult. Not only was it hard for southerners to agree with the northerners, but the very fact of their being in the same party as the antislavery northerners undermined the Whigs' credibility as dependable defenders of the South.

As the Whig Party went into terminal decline, Alexander H. Stephens urged his colleagues in 1854 to form a new opposition party. "The truth is the southern Whigs must strike out a lead for themselves. They cannot afford either for their own sake or that of the country to fall into the ranks of either of the great national parties as they are now organized and constituted."[12] Just one year later, however, the Georgia congressman had to eat his own words when he threw in his lot with the Democrats, as did many other southern Whigs. By contrast, those who tried to follow Stephens's earlier advice found themselves searching in vain for a viable new party.

For a brief moment, however, the dreams of these Whigs for a new anti-Democratic organization seemed about to come true. As if by request, a party emerged in 1854 within the South, and outside it too, possessing many of the ingredients that the Whigs in transit were looking for. The American Party, or Know-Nothings, as its critics preferred to label it, had arisen, almost overnight, as a national organization equipped with voter support as well as electoral machinery. In its values and sentiments, the American Party was also national because the issue around which it formed was nativism, specifically an intense fear that the large influx of foreign, overwhelmingly Irish and therefore overwhelmingly Roman Catholic, immigrants in the late 1840s was posing a threat to America's social order and its ethnic and religious character. Since an abiding concern about the nation's identity and the conformity of its values was a fundamental tenet of Whig political thought, the American Party's platform possessed considerable appeal.

But the Whigs' compatibility with the Know-Nothings had serious limits. First of all, the party originated as a secret society with hundreds of lodges, which met behind closed doors and swore not to divulge the business of their meetings. Its detractors seized on this, referring to the party as the "Know-Nothings" because its members were purportedly required to swear, "I know nothing," when asked about their society. Although some Whigs were Masons who could understand a need for vows of secrecy, most were not. And this secretiveness struck them as devious and conspiratorial and therefore inimical to the values of harmony and homogeneity they espoused. A second difficulty arose from the extremism of the American Party's attitudes toward foreigners. Many of the Whigs were avowedly nativist and fearful of the growing foreign population, but the American Party's policies, insisting that public office be restricted to native-born citizens and that the naturalization period be extended from five to twenty-five years, seemed to most Whigs to be hostile and draconian. And, finally, the Know-Nothings' nativism lacked resonance and immediacy in the southern states where foreigners were a small minority—never more than 10 percent—and Catholics were scarce outside a few cities, such as New Orleans, Charleston, and Mobile, and the French-speaking areas of South Louisiana. Moreover, neither foreigners nor Catholics posed a serious threat and consequently were not enough of a problem or issue on which to form an enduring political party.

Nevertheless, most of the South's Whigs affiliated with the American Party in the hope that their organization might provide a temporary refuge, making it possible for individual Whig politicians to stay in the public arena and run for office and for their party to reconstitute itself and somehow reemerge. To Alexander Stephens, developments along these lines in his own state of Georgia struck him as contemptible. "The old Whig party is about to be sold out to the Know Nothings," he declared angrily in April 1855.[13] And the results of the state elections held later that year confirmed his misgivings as the American Party candidates, aided by their Whig associates, went down to defeat. The party's candidates for governor lost all but one of the eight races they contested, Kentucky being the lone exception. Democrats won majorities in all of the South's state legislatures, except in another border state, Tennessee. In the congressional elections a year later, however, the Know-Nothings did better. They won twenty-seven of seventy-three seats they contested, eight more than the Whigs had won in 1853, four of them coming from the solidly Democratic states of Alabama (two seats), Mississippi, and Texas. Twenty-two of the twenty-seven successful Know-Nothings were former Whigs, which suggested that the American Party was not isolated and might yet survive.

This possibility soon evaporated, however, when the American Party itself disintegrated as a national movement during the following year. At its national convention in Philadelphia in 1856, the party broke into two hostile wings, North American and South American. And it broke apart over the twelfth section of the party's 1856 platform. Pledging "to abide by and maintain the existing laws upon the subject of slavery, as a final and cohesive settlement," and asserting that Congress "ought not to legislate upon the subject in the territories," the twelfth section was clearly a southern victory. But, the following year, the northerners walked out of the national convention after failing to get the objectionable section removed. Most joined the emerging northern, antislavery Republican Party, while the South Americans nominated Millard Fillmore for president. As a national party, the American Party was finished, collapsing as rapidly as it had arisen.

The significance of the 1856 election was even greater, however. For two national parties were annihilated that year, not just one. The Whig Party also disappeared altogether after 1856, as the prospect of reviving it, or even sustaining it, either through the American Party or through the candidacy of the last Whig president, Millard Fillmore, vanished. Fillmore won a mere eight electoral votes and carried but one state that might possibly be called southern, Maryland. As a result, the American Party was replaced as the opponent of the Democratic Party by the northern Republican Party.

Thus, the sectional party envisaged by Calhoun, which was to replace one of the national parties, or play off both of them, came into being in the North, not in his beloved South. He would have been horrified. A southern party might have protected the South; a northern one certainly would not.

One-Party Politics Returns

In the 1856 presidential election, the Republicans carried eleven of the sixteen northern states. The new party's remarkable showing recast the South's political world. For the region now faced an imminent threat, and it had to decide how to respond. Previously, the question in the South had been how best to defend its interests within the Union. After 1856, the issue became whether the region was better protected inside the Union or out of it. Secession as a desirable course of action moved to the center of southern politics, becoming the fulcrum around which debate swirled and politicians organized campaigns between 1856 and the showdown in the winter of 1860–61.

Deliberations to determine the future course for the southern states had to take place within the Democratic Party, the only remaining national political organization in the South and also the overwhelmingly dominant one in the region. The Democrats' opponents were in no position to take the initiative, having failed during the past two years either to raise a new issue capable of countering the persistent slavery agitation or to create a new national party committed to maintaining the South's ties to the Union. Lacking an issue of their own choosing and a national party to promote it, the non-Democratic political forces were loose fragments without coherence or cohesion. Not surprisingly, they usually referred to themselves simply as "the Opposition."

The Opposition was especially marginalized after 1856 in Lower South states such as Mississippi, Alabama, Georgia, Louisiana, Texas, and, of course, South Carolina, most of them with large slave populations where the Whigs had failed to develop much of a presence or had lost what influence they had by the late 1840s. Two states in this category, Georgia and Louisiana, where the Opposition was quite active, serve to illustrate the group's limitations and its quandary. In Georgia, the American Party and the Whigs worked together in the 1857 gubernatorial election and did quite well behind their candidate, the state's finest campaign orator, Benjamin H. Hill. Hill lost a close race, with 45 percent of the vote, to the Democrat, Joseph E. Brown. But Brown's party won three-quarters of the state's counties, carried six out of eight congressional seats, and racked up two-thirds majorities in both houses of the legislature. Running against the Democrats but offering no substantive issues of its own, the Opposition was reduced to criticizing the Buchanan administration for its bungling of the Kansas question as well as the southern Democrats for their inadequate defense of the region.

These deficiencies became even more evident two years later when the American Party, now calling itself "the Opposition," once again challenged Joseph E. Brown, who was by now an experienced and popular governor. Brown swamped Warren Aiken, the Opposition candidate, with 60 percent of the vote. Because the Democrats dominated the discussion of both state and national issues, the Opposition found that it had no other way of making itself heard than to adopt the extremist southern position of insisting that Congress actively protect slavery in Kansas and other territories. In effect, it found itself "forced into a pro-slavery shouting match that [it] simply could not win."[14] Yet the Opposition was the latest incarnation of the Whig Party and the American Party in Georgia, both of which had, of course, espoused the Union and the Compromise of 1850 rather than southern rights.

In Louisiana, the city of New Orleans, with its large Irish population, provided the nativist Americans with an enemy to fight and an electoral base among the non-Irish majority, from which they and their ex-Whig comrades could build support to challenge the state's Democrats. But, as in Georgia, the only debate over the state's future that mattered was taking place inside the Democratic Party. Unlike the party in Georgia, however, which was becoming increasingly hard-line and secessionist, the party in Louisiana was under the control of Senator John Slidell, who supported President Buchanan and his approach to the critical Kansas problem. However, Slidell had long been opposed by Pierre Soulé, his rival for control of the party. Since Slidell was taking a moderate, unionist stance, Soulé's wing felt compelled to adopt an opposing position, so they embraced an extreme southern rights posture, insisting on federal protection of slavery in the territories. In the 1857 state and congressional elections, the American Party ran candidates who collaborated with the anti-Slidell Democrats led by Soulé, and these candidates were often proponents of southern rights.

In the 1859 governor's race, the two factions, now calling themselves Old Line Democrats and New Liners, ran competing candidates. Soulé's New Liners appealed for support from the Whig Party and the American Party, as well as from Democrats, and they worked out fusion tickets with members of the American Party for a number of offices, including governor. These hybrid arrangements were then labeled the "Opposition." This collaboration meant that the nationalist Whigs and Americans had again aligned with southern rights extremists. But neither group benefited much from their coalition, since the pro-Slidell, Old Line Democratic nominee for governor, Thomas O. Moore, swept the state, defeating Andrew S. Herron, the Opposition candidate, with over 62 percent of the vote and carrying forty-six of the state's forty-eight parishes. The Democrats won overwhelmingly in the legislative (79–36) and congressional (three out of four districts) races as well.[15]

By 1860, every state in the Lower South had lost all semblance of party competition, just like Georgia and Louisiana. The remnants of the Whig Party and the American Party that had functioned as the Opposition had resorted to whatever tactic and policy position seemed likely to win them votes and so had been revealed as merely opportunistic and utterly unreliable. Predictably, the Democrats had shattered them and were now in the ascendancy. But in the Upper South states of Tennessee, Virginia, and North Carolina, the political world after 1856 looked rather different. And this difference would persist through the presidential election of 1860 and into the secession crisis that followed in its wake.

All three Upper South states possessed several common characteristics that encouraged a vibrant and coherent opposition, even though the anti-Democratic parties at the national level had foundered. The economic interests and the need for development of the northwest sections of Virginia and North Carolina and the eastern part of Tennessee were very different, as we have already seen, from the concerns of the plantation-dominated lowlands and foothills of these states. Their political parties had reflected this long-standing division, with Whigs strongly represented in the west and the Democrats in the east. (Since Tennessee was located beyond the mountains, it was the eastern part of the state that favored development and was Whig, by contrast with the plantation areas in the west, which were Democratic). Contributing further to the maintenance of an organized opposition to southern rights separatism was the proximity of these states to their northern neighbors across the Ohio River, linking their economies and generating commercial exchange and cultural and social connections.

At the same time, however, all three, but especially Virginia and North Carolina, were slave societies. In North Carolina, 29.1 percent of white families owned slaves, a percentage similar to Alabama's 35.1 percent and Louisiana's 31.0 percent. Furthermore, the sheer number of slave owners was greater in the Old North State than in each of the Lower South states except Georgia.[16] Similarly, Virginia had a slave population numbering 430,000, which was larger than any other southern state. Most of it was located in Piedmont and Tidewater, where slaves constituted 49 percent and 41 percent of the total population, respectively, with an additional 4 percent and 8 percent of the population consisting of free Negroes. Another 62,000 slaves could be found in the western region of the state.[17] Slavery was therefore a matter of vital concern in these two states. Offsetting this compatibility with the Lower South were, however, economic connections with the North that were stronger as well as internal economic and political divisions that were more entrenched than in the states farther south.

In Virginia's state elections of 1859, the Opposition, which was little more than a revived Whig Party, ran a well-organized campaign. It lost the governorship, though by a narrow margin, capturing 48 percent of the vote and winning the usually Democratic Piedmont and Southwest regions. With William L. Goggin, a former Whig and four-term congressman, as its nominee, the Opposition criticized the extravagance and corruption of the Buchanan administration, reaffirmed the Compromise of 1850 (a Whiggish pro-Union stance), and assailed the state's Democrats for their extremist policies that had failed to protect slavery and the South adequately. Admittedly, the Democrats selected a poor campaigner, John Letcher, whose record on slavery was compromised by his earlier public endorsement of a plan for gradual emancipation, the Ruffner Pamphlet of 1847. And they were also weakened by the ongoing feud between the factions of Henry Wise, governor from 1855 to 1859, and the Young Chivalry, based among the eastern planters and headed by Senator Robert M. T. Hunter, a former Calhounite. But still, the Opposition was a real political force.

Opposition to the Democrats was also viable in North Carolina after the Whig Party reorganized itself and reemerged with political strength in 1859 and 1860. The state elections in 1858 had revealed how marginal the American Party had become and how misplaced had been Whig hopes that its broader nativist appeal would stimulate more voter interest than their own party was capable of generating. Because the American Party candidate for governor had still won over 40 percent of the vote in 1858, despite his being a former Democrat for whom the Americans had demonstrated little enthusiasm, a significant amount of anti-Democratic sentiment persisted in the state and could be mobilized.

What the anti-Democratic forces needed was better organization and appealing issues. Luckily, a group of leading Whigs took the initiative to supply both. By running Whig candidates in the 1859 congressional elections on a platform attacking the extravagance and corruption of the Buchanan administration, the party won four of the five races it contested. A year later, Whigs unveiled an issue in the state campaign that further revitalized their party. Their promise to tax slave property ad valorem appealed strongly to voters, especially nonslaveholders, who resented the tax break that slave owners enjoyed because the taxes on their chattels were based on an assessment below their market value. Like the issue of "equal suffrage" that had benefited the Whigs in the early 1850s, "equal taxation" appealed to voters as a fair and just policy. And it certainly stimulated the Whig vote, because the gubernatorial candidate, John Pool, who was himself a Whig, increased the opposition vote to 47.2 percent in 1860, running best in formerly Whig counties. Whig leaders now predicted a bright future for their party.[18] But North Carolina was an exception. Everywhere else, the Whigs had disbanded, and the South was once again a one-party region dominated by the Democrats.

The Secession Crisis

This resurgence of opposition to the Democratic Party in the Upper South was occurring just when the region was embarked upon the critical presidential campaign of 1860. The political trajectory in the Upper South went in one direction—toward some degree of party competition. In the Lower South, many more state polities were moving in the opposite direction—toward one-party domination, with organized dissent not just minimal but also incoherent and chaotic.

If the state party systems of the Upper and Lower South were diverging, the same was also true of the Democratic Party itself. By 1860, southern Democrats were quite aware that the Republicans would do even better than in the presidential contest of 1856. Therefore, they had to determine how they would respond if, as seemed likely, an antislavery and exclusively northern party gained control of the presidency, and perhaps even of Congress. But no coordinated plan existed. Instead, the party in each southern state contained a divergence of opinion that boiled down to two general approaches for protecting slavery and the region's interests. The first assumed that slavery and the interests of the South could only be protected outside the Union, though many advocates of secession did not think the election of a Republican president was sufficient cause, or the right time, to leave. The second group assumed that the Union still offered better, but by no means guaranteed, protection. Some were prepared to abandon this position, however, should the federal government take any action that threatened the security of the South and slavery.

Since they needed the southern states to move actively and overtly in order to sever relations with the United States, the advocates of secession had to seize the initiative and force the issue. And they increased the pressure in three arenas in the aftermath of the portentous 1856 presidential election. The first of these was the territory of Kansas. The struggle to control Kansas in its territorial stage had preoccupied the nation between 1855 and 1858. For Kansas became, in effect, the laboratory for experimenting with popular sovereignty, the new formula for dealing with slavery in the territories. Popular sovereignty stipulated that the people of a territory were to decide whether it should be a free or a slave state, a seemingly evenhanded formula, which southerners initially supported. In practice, however, they soon realized that, if slaveholders were uncertain whether their slave property would be legal and safe in Kansas, they would be unwilling to risk going there. And if slaveholders refused to migrate to Kansas, the territory would be lost to slavery at the outset because there would be too few voters to approve a slave state and too few slaveholders living there to justify it. Therefore, southern congressmen began to demand that slavery be protected by the federal government during the territorial stage when the area was being settled.

But Stephen Douglas, the proponent of popular sovereignty, regarded prior approval of slavery as tantamount to loading the deck and perverting the doctrine. When asked his position on the question by Abraham Lincoln in their unprecedented debates during the Illinois senatorial contest of 1858, Douglas reaffirmed his position that "the people of a

Territory have the lawful means to admit it or exclude it as they please." But southern rights extremists were adamant that Congress guarantee slavery in the territories from the outset. Since the territories were "the common property" of all the states, a constitutional doctrine first advanced by Calhoun in 1837, they argued that the local interests of every state had to be recognized there. Those who were determined to force the issue even further so as to precipitate a breakup of the Union insisted that Congress draw up a slave code for the territories and embody it in federal legislation.

Congress was therefore the second arena where the advocates of secession tried to force the issue. And the link with Kansas was again in evidence. On the ground in Kansas, the slave-state faction had managed, by rather devious methods, to produce a constitution that endorsed slavery. Drawn up at a constitutional convention in the little settlement of Lecompton, the constitution caused a furor in Washington after its submission. The Buchanan administration decided to endorse it and admit Kansas with a proslavery constitution. Douglas, the leading contender for the Democratic nomination, denounced the Lecompton constitution as a perversion of popular sovereignty because of its fraudulent origins in a convention which was boycotted by the free-state forces after its election had been rigged by the slave-state faction. With the prospect of a fatal split within the Democratic Party, the secessionists grasped at this auspicious opportunity to break up the only remaining national party and the last political connection between the South and the rest of the nation. So they encouraged Buchanan in his effort to appease the South with the Lecompton constitution, a course of action that was certain to divide the Democratic Party, to which most southerners belonged. By 1859, the imbroglio over the Lecompton constitution had ruined Douglas's attempt to settle the territorial issue through the mechanism of popular sovereignty and had also damaged his prospects for the Democratic nomination in 1860. The Kansas issue had shattered the Democratic Party.

The Democrats' disastrous split over Kansas and Lecompton had a bitterly ironic outcome for the South. In 1852, before the Kansas-Nebraska Act had caused a furor in the North and before the Whigs had collapsed and then exited from the political scene, the Democratic Party was balanced sectionally, with a reasonable degree of parity between its northern and southern wings. In 1852, the Democratic delegation in the House consisted of ninety-two from the free states and sixty-seven from the slave states. Six years later, however, the proportion had been reversed, as thirty-one northern Democrats found themselves outnumbered by sixty-nine southerners. And in the Senate, too, a corporal's guard of twelve northerners was confronted by a phalanx of twenty-seven southerners.[19]

During these six pivotal years when the Kansas imbroglio played havoc with the new party system, the Democrats had become a sectional southern party, while the Republicans, a sectional northern party, had replaced the Whigs. Ever since the founding of the Democratic Party under Jackson, the southern wing had been extremely influential. During its first decade, the South had been the base on which the party was built. Then, in the 1840s, it was able to pressure the party to endorse its priorities and protect its interests, even though not always in the majority. The southerners' numerical preponderance in the Democratic Party in the mid-1850s was doubly ironic. First, the party in which the southerners were now ascendant could no longer claim to be national either in its composition or in its identity. And, second, the Democrats' electoral prospects were seriously diminished at the national level. In effect, the South had achieved ascendancy in a party that was disintegrating.

The scene now shifted to the third arena, to Charleston, South Carolina's major city and the location for the Democratic national convention in 1860. The center of "red-hot" secessionism, Charleston was about as disastrous a choice as could be imagined for a gathering whose purpose was to cool the party down and then harmonize and unify it behind an acceptable presidential candidate. Indeed, the southern state delegations were in no mood to talk and negotiate. They saw this as a moment of reckoning when the northerners would have to "put up or shut up." So they came to the convention with a set of conditions for their support of Douglas that they knew he could not possibly accept. First adopted by Alabama and then approved by the Democratic Party in the other Lower South states, the South's demands amounted to a federal pledge to protect slavery in the territories and to enact a territorial slave code. The Douglas delegates managed to defeat the attempt, led by Alabama's leading secessionist, William Lowndes Yancey, to insert these demands into the party platform. Instead, they replaced them with an endorsement of popular sovereignty, the vote dividing closely on free-state/slave-state lines, 165–138.

As they had promised if their demands were rebuffed, fifty Lower South delegates walked out immediately. The remaining delegates were unable to produce the required two-thirds majority to nominate Douglas, because the chair of the convention ruled that this two-thirds applied to the original body, not just those who were still present in the hall. So the remainder agreed to adjourn and meet again in Baltimore, where they would later nominate Douglas. Before leaving Charleston, Yancey fired up his supporters with a speech in the courthouse square, concluding with a call for three cheers "for an Independent Southern Republic." Secession from the Democratic convention was to be the precursor to secession from the Union.

Besides the reconvened Democratic convention, which chose Douglas as its nominee, three other party conventions gathered in the long, politically hot summer of 1860. The Democrats split into two camps, with Douglas as one nominee and the sitting vice president, John C. Breckinridge, as the other. Breckinridge was chosen by a convention of the seceders at Charleston after they had seceded once again, this time from the reconvened Democratic convention in Baltimore. When they reassembled after their second walkout, they were joined by delegations from the Upper South and some northern proslavery Democrats. Meanwhile, the Republicans met in Chicago and selected as their nominee Abraham Lincoln, from Douglas's home state of Illinois. Party leaders believed Lincoln could carry one of the three crucial midwestern states, along with Pennsylvania, and so give the Republicans the victory that had eluded them in 1856. He was chosen over New York's senator, William Henry Seward, who was considered more radical toward slavery and the South than Lincoln. And, finally, a fourth major candidate emerged, John Bell of Tennessee, who was the standard-bearer of a hastily assembled organization calling itself the Constitutional Union Party. Bell was a well-regarded and experienced Whig from an Upper South state, who, it was hoped, could mobilize former Whigs in both sections and capture the political middle ground between Lincoln and Breckinridge, the rival sectional candidates.

Reduced to its essentials, the contest became a referendum on federal policy toward the territories, the central and defining element in each candidate's platform. Lincoln endorsed "free soil," specifically federal exclusion of slavery from the territories. Breckinridge's position was the reverse—federal protection of slavery in the territories, in effect, "slave soil." Douglas, naturally, espoused the "popular sovereignty" formula of federal nonintervention and letting the people of each territory decide. Finally, Bell advocated restoration of the Missouri Compromise provision that excluded slavery from territories located above the 36°30′ line but allowed it below that dividing line. Therefore, the election was not fought over the future of slavery in the states where it already existed, at least not directly so. Rather, the question at issue was what to do with slavery in the territories where it did not yet exist. So, the expansion of slavery as a future issue, and not the existence of slavery as a current problem, lay at the heart of the decisive 1860 election.

Although the contestants were taking up positions on slavery's prospects in regions beyond the current borders of the United States, the issue was nevertheless neither remote nor lacking in urgency. Whether these lands became free or slave would determine, not just the future of slavery, but the future characteristics of America and its society and economy. The Republicans' insistence on "free soil" and the nonextension of slavery threatened the South with a barrier of states on its western borders that would contain slavery and prevent its expansion. And if slavery could not expand, it would soon die out, so it was claimed, because it needed new land to replace the depleted soils that cotton cultivation generated. Nonextension would lead inexorably, in the opinion of the Republicans, to slavery's "ultimate extinction." Similarly, northern free states were faced with encirclement by slavery if it were allowed into the western territories. And the result would be the demotion of free labor and the idea of individual freedom to an embattled, and quite likely subordinate, position in American life. In this contest for control of the western territories by the two competing interests of free labor and slavery, represented by the rival doctrines of "free soil" and "slave soil," the future of the United States as a nation of either free states or slave states was ultimately at stake. And the "popular sovereignty" and "36°30'" proposals of Douglas and Bell were simply mechanisms for delaying the final decision about this all-or-nothing struggle.

In this critical election to determine the future course and character of the American republic, the four candidates embodied four theories, each one believed by its advocates to be compatible with the Constitution, for dealing with slavery in lands not yet organized into states in the Union. And the electorate was being asked to choose the formula it preferred, presumably aware that the winning doctrine and the winning candidate in this four-way contest would not be the choice of a majority of the voters. When the ballots were counted, the victorious theory and candidate was Lincoln, the Republican advocate of "free soil." He received just 39 percent of the popular vote, although he carried the electoral vote decisively.

The election could also be seen as two separate contests, rather than a four-way fight among candidates representing four parties and four constitutional formulae. These two contests took place in the northern states, where Lincoln was pitted against Douglas, and in the southern states, where Breckinridge was competing with Bell. Lincoln was not on the ballot in ten of the slaveholding states and received only 4 percent of the vote in the five Upper South and border states where he was eligible. Douglas also ran poorly in the South, gaining only 12 percent of the popular vote there. On the other hand, Bell did very well in the southern contest, for he won three states (Kentucky, Tennessee, and Virginia). Breckinridge's popular vote in the South was actually less than that of Bell and Douglas combined, although his tally in the Electoral College was impressive because he won eleven states in the South (including Maryland and Delaware in the border) to Bell's three and Douglas's one (Missouri). Even more convincing was Lincoln's sweep of the North, where he won a commanding electoral total of 180 votes. No matter that the election was more complicated than usual and that the issue was not a straightforward vote on whether slavery should be abolished or not. Its meaning was glaringly obvious to most southerners, particularly the slaveholders among them. Their enemies had seized control of the national government.

To the advocates of secession, Republican control of the presidency presented an immediate threat to the South, which had to be met with immediate secession. Waiting for some overt act on Lincoln's part before resorting to secession was dangerous, so the secessionists warned, because the new administration was certain to move against the South and slavery from the moment it entered office. Employing the extensive federal patronage at his disposal, President Lincoln would build a Republican Party in the southern states. "It would not be long before they would have a party formed against us," Congressman Milledge Bonham of South Carolina predicted on 5 November 1860.[20] Once Lincoln "places among us his Judges, District Attorneys, Marshals, Post Masters, Custom House officers, etc., etc.," warned Governor Joseph E. Brown of Georgia, he would "destroy our moral powers, and prepare us to tolerate . . . a Republican ticket, in most states of the South in 1864."[21] In October, even before Lincoln was elected, the South's preeminent secessionist, William Lowndes Yancey, told an audience at the Cooper Union in New York that "the abolitionists and black republicans . . . will build up an abolition party in every Southern state—there is no doubt of it."[22] Unless the South left the Union right away, it would be exposed to the hostile influence within its midst of a Republican administration determined to create an opposition party there.

But what kinds of southerners would be willing to serve in a Republican administration? The secessionists suggested three sources of support. First, those who were at all times eager to obtain public offices for ignoble pecuniary reasons. Second, northerners who were ready to move south to promote the antisouthern, antislavery goals of the Republican Party, some of whom might well be abolitionists. And third, though less often mentioned, those southerners who themselves had no financial stake in slaveholding and who resented the slave owners who did. At all events, the creation by the Republicans of an opposition party whose aim was to subvert slavery was proclaimed by the secessionists as the dire and imminent threat that made secession the only conceivable recourse.

Since all but a few of the southern states had become free of an organized opposition party ever since the demise of the Whigs, why stay in the Union, where a hostile Republican Party was almost certain to challenge the political unity the region had managed to achieve? The only way to keep the South united and to escape from the immediate danger of a hostile opposition party was therefore to leave and form a separate confederacy.

"No division of opinion. All for immediate secession." This was the report of Edmund Ruffin, the Virginia secessionist and agricultural reformer, during a visit to Charleston soon after the election.[23] South Carolina's governor, William H. Gist, had already contacted most of the southern governors to discover whether their states were prepared to secede if Lincoln were elected. The governors of Alabama, Mississippi, Florida, and Georgia had replied affirmatively, but Louisiana, and especially North Carolina, expressed reluctance. This time, South Carolina's secessionists vowed to precipitate secession by taking the lead, rather than by waiting helplessly for others to act collectively and simultaneously as they had done in 1852. As Christopher Memminger, a South Carolinian and future Confederate secretary of the treasury, had insisted in late November, "Our great point is to move the other Southern States before there is any recoil."[24] Lincoln's election, with its accompanying threat of a Republican opposition in the South, provided sufficient cause for them to move ahead without delay.

On 20 December, just three days after it had convened, South Carolina's secession convention decided to leave the Union by a remarkable vote of 169–0. During January 1861, the six other states in the Lower South, including Texas, followed the vanguard state of South Carolina. After that burst of activity, there was a lull for three months while the Upper South states debated whether to secede. And none of them did so until April and May when Virginia, Arkansas, Tennessee, and North Carolina resolved their dilemma after President Lincoln called up 75,000 militia troops in response to the firing on Fort Sumter on 12 April. Just as there had been two election contests in 1860 within a dividing Union, there were two convention movements in the winter of 1860–61 within a seceding South.

In the Lower South, conventions to consider secession were called astonishingly quickly, and elections for delegates followed in rapid succession. The preponderance of those elected were immediate secessionists, but they were offset by others who favored secession only if accompanied by other states. This cooperationist position sometimes arose out of a belief that southerners were creating an embryonic nation, not merely a cluster of separate states each acting on its own. But for most who urged cooperation, their tactic was intended to achieve a more effective secession that required deeper deliberation and also interstate collaboration, rather than separate state action that might be impulsive. At the farthest end of the cooperationist spectrum was a small minority who opposed secession altogether and advocated delay in the hope that secessionist sentiment would cool off or that some external development would intervene to bring secession to a halt. For the most part, however, the Lower South's conventions were secessionist in their thrust and objective. But there was a distinction in tactics between the majority, whose secessionism was unconditional (the immediatists), and the remaining delegates, whose stance was conditional (the cooperationists).

In the secession conventions of South Carolina, Alabama, Mississippi, and Florida, the overwhelming majority were immediatists, and they showed their strength in lopsided votes to secede. At an earlier stage in the conventions' deliberations, the cooperationists had tried to stall the rush to leave by demanding that the final decision be submitted for ratification by the electorate. But this delaying tactic was voted down as well, though by closer margins than the vote to secede itself. By late January, when the conventions in Georgia and Louisiana were meeting, the cooperationist position had become less viable, because, with four states already out of the Union, cooperating with other states now meant joining them in seceding, not in staying. Therefore, as one Louisianan predicted, "Cooperation is dead."[25]

The momentum was clearly with the immediatists. Since four states had already seceded, Georgia's cooperationists, who, on 18 January, had numbered 130 in a vote to call a convention of southern states rather than secede, dropped to 89 when the vote to secede was taken the next day. And in Louisiana, where there had initially been 50 cooperationists among the 150 delegates, only 17 votes were cast against secession on 26 January. Six days later, Texas voted 166–8 to secede. By this point, 1 February 1861, seven states had left the Union, a sufficient number to justify calling a meeting to form a Confederate government in Montgomery on 4 February. Two weeks later, Jefferson Davis was sworn in as provisional president.

But the Upper South states of Tennessee, Virginia, North Carolina, and also Arkansas, still hesitated. Deeply involved in slave owning yet tied economically to the adjacent northern states and containing organized political opposition as well, the option of secession was less attractive and more easily resisted. Although long dominated by the Conway-Johnson Dynasty, which had controlled the Democratic Party since the days of Andrew Jackson, Arkansas experienced a political convulsion in the late 1850s when the nonslaveholding northwestern hill country, led by Thomas C. Hindman, challenged the Dynasty's control of the Democratic Party. Once in power, the victorious faction began to resist the move toward secession. As a result, opposition to secession was so rife within the Arkansas legislature that the attempt to call a convention was beaten back.

Meanwhile, Virginia held an election that produced a convention, but its members were heavily unionist, with only an estimated thirty to fifty delegates favoring secession. In Tennessee, voters went to the polls and decided against calling a convention. In the vote to select delegates just in case the state needed to take action of some kind, Tennessee's voters produced a body whose membership, if it had actually convened, would have been thoroughly unionist. In the meantime, the Arkansas legislature reconsidered, and on 18 February an election to call a convention was held, but more delegates were elected as unionists than as secessionists. In late January, North Carolina's assembly had yielded to Governor John Ellis's pressure for a convention, but the voters rejected the call by a slim margin and, at the same time, chose 81 unionist delegates, who would have dominated the 120-man body, had it assembled.

The Upper South states were therefore strongly unionist in sentiment. Nevertheless, like secessionism in the Lower South, there were two aspects to their unionism, one unconditional and the other conditional. Most were probably opposed to leaving the Union, while others were waiting to see whether the northern states would offer acceptable concessions or whether a convention of border states, such as the planned meeting in Kentucky in May, could work out adequate and acceptable terms for the protection of slavery. In Virginia, unconditional unionism was to be found in the northwest, where the Republican Party had even made its presence felt in the 1860 election and where a separatist movement arose during the war that resulted in the creation of the state of West Virginia.

When the secession convention met in Richmond, it remained in session for the entire month of February. During this long wait, the convention took two affirmative votes—that its decision on secession should be ratified by popular vote and that slave property should be taxed ad valorem—before it finally got around to voting on secession. On the day of Lincoln's inauguration, the vote to secede was defeated, 88–45. The convention then adjourned to await further developments in Washington.

When those developments resulted in the Confederates' bombardment of Fort Sumter on 12 April and Lincoln's call-up of 75,000 troops immediately afterward, the Virginia convention reassembled. The delegates decided in favor of secession by a vote of 88 to 55, and the state's voters approved the verdict overwhelmingly by 128,884 to 32,314. Virginia's decision to secede was replicated in the other three reluctant states. Surrounded by a Union government mobilizing for war and a Confederate government newly formed and resolved to defend slavery, these four states had no other choice. They could not abandon their seven slaveholding compatriots. And besides, the critical question of whether the South and slavery were more secure in the Union than outside it had now been answered, and answered decisively.

PART II.

NO-PARTY POLITICS,

1861–1865

4

Politics without Parties

THE CONFEDERACY

The South did not secede as a unit. Instead, individual states left the Union one by one. Although they acted separately, the six Lower South states that had seceded by the end of January 1861 wasted little time before creating their own central government. In just over a month, the provisional Congress of forty-three members, rising to fifty when Texas seceded on 1 February, adopted a provisional constitution, chose a president and vice president, and then wrote and approved a permanent constitution. Within six weeks, it had been ratified by the seven states that had already seceded. In effect, this multitasking legislature functioned as an electoral college, a constitutional convention, and a legislature when it created a governmental system for the new nation-state. If the speed with which it operated left no doubt about the earnestness of the movement for southern independence, then the constitution it produced revealed a good deal about the nature and purpose of the Confederacy under construction. Given the opportunity to frame its own government, what kind of government did the southern slaveholders choose?

A categorical answer to that question came from the new president, Jefferson Davis, in his inaugural address a year later. "The Constitution framed by our fathers is that of these Confederate States," he announced.[1] In its essential features and even in most of its language, the Confederate Constitution was a replica of the U.S. Constitution. Indeed, this wholesale adoption of the American frame of government was self-conscious and purposeful, since the seceding states were leaving primarily because the rest of the nation had failed to uphold the strictures of the federal Constitution. The South was therefore loyal to the Constitution and to the legacy of the Revolution. Like the colonists, who had left the British Empire in 1776 because the British were not enforcing their own constitutional sanctions and protections, the southerners felt compelled to withdraw from the Union because the North was betraying the U.S. Constitution. Secession was therefore a conservative, legitimizing movement and not a rebellion or a revolution. The similarity of the two constitutions has led many historians to argue that the Confederates were merely disappointed Americans who were forced reluctantly to secede. In that case, they probably possessed only a minimal sense of a separate national identity when they began to set up a government of their own. Rather than creating a new nation, they were trying merely to form an independent and separate version of the old one.

The Confederate Constitution

At first glance, the similarities between the two governmental frameworks are overwhelmingly obvious. But there were differences that indicated the Confederates' determination to avoid some of the problems they had encountered previously and to forge a polity that was both distinctive and better. This is what Davis was referring to in his inaugural when, in the preceding sentence to the one quoted earlier, he admitted: "We have changed the constituent parts, but not the system of government." And it is possible that the provisional Congress might have gone even further, had it not been under such pressure not only to create a government very quickly but to include in it only a few changes for fear of scaring off the Upper South states, which were expressing considerable unease about joining this unknown and unproven Confederacy. All the same, there were a number of changes. Some might have been anticipated, but others indicate a determination to begin anew.

Those alterations in the U.S. Constitution that were to be expected dealt primarily with slavery. The Confederate Congress was forbidden to pass any law "denying or impairing the right of property in negro slaves," and it was required to protect slavery in any territories acquired by the new government. The provisional Congress debated a proposal to reopen the Atlantic slave trade, another to prohibit the admission to the Confederacy of any free state, and yet another to repeal the three-fifths clause and thus make a slave equivalent to a whole person for purposes of representation. The federal Constitution's ban on the slave trade was sustained, and so was the three-fifths clause, though by a narrow vote of four states to three. However, free states could be admitted with the approval of two-thirds of both houses. Evidently, the more thoroughgoing and radical secessionists, like Robert Barnwell Rhett, who headed the twelve-man committee charged with drafting the new constitution, had to yield some of their pet projects. But they suffered a clear defeat in their attempt to be consistent and ideologically sound by getting the right of secession recognized and included. Although secessionists claimed the right of secession under the U.S. Constitution, their colleagues were evidently unwilling to legitimize a course of action that could dissolve the Confederacy.

A similarly mixed record was compiled on the powers of the central government, even though southerners had insistently favored their restriction when they were dealing with the federal government. On the one hand, the federal government was more restricted. The powers given to Congress were merely "delegated by the states" rather than "granted," language that conferred less authority on the central legislature than the 1787 document had bestowed. The preamble was rewritten as "We, the people of the Confederate States, each State acting in its sovereign and independent character." And, finally, the states, not Congress, were to initiate amendments to the Confederate Constitution, while Congress's involvement in the amending process was eliminated altogether. These concessions to the states were accompanied by elimination of the "general welfare" clause, which had provided an opening for expansion of central authority under the old regime. This possibility was shut off further by specific restrictions on Congress's legislative jurisdiction. The Confederate Congress was prohibited from enacting protective tariffs or providing aid for internal improvements, except rivers and harbors. These provisions were welcomed wholeheartedly by Alexander Stephens, who had been a member of the committee that had drafted the revised constitution, because they would prevent the promotion of "one branch of industry to the prejudice of another" and avoid the "extravagance and profligacy that existed under the old government."[2] To limit even further Congress's proclivity to spend, a two-thirds vote was required to approve any appropriation other than those initiated by the president.

Offsetting these limitations on the power of the central government, especially the legislative branch, the constitution makers of 1861 increased its scope and authority in several ways. They accorded to Confederate legislation the authority and status of "supreme law" and also retained the U.S. Constitution's "necessary and proper" clause, often referred to disparagingly as the "elastic clause." Meanwhile, the preamble stated that the purpose of the constitution was "to form a permanent federal government" whose durability was ensured by the document's repudiation of nullification and the right of secession. A judicial branch was also created with features that suggested it might possess even greater jurisdiction than in the U.S. Constitution. A tribunal was to be established to settle claims against the central government, and a supreme court was proposed, consisting of the district judges of each state. Under legislation passed by the provisional Congress in March 1861, the court's powers of judicial review were broader than those provided in the United States' Judiciary Act of 1789. But curiously, the framers' evident intentions for the supreme court had little impact, because the Confederacy never even managed to establish the court during its four years of existence.

The most powerful branch of the new Confederate system was the presidency. Here, the Confederate constitution makers were at their most innovative. The president's term was to last for six years and to be nonrenewable. Measures that the president proposed for raising revenue required only a plurality to pass, whereas Congress's own appropriation bills had to have a two-thirds vote for approval. The president was also given an "item veto," enabling him to exclude specific provisions of an appropriation without having to veto the entire bill, a power that twentieth-century American presidents have all wished they possessed. Members of the Confederate president's cabinet could go to Congress and participate in debate on the floor of either house on measures within their own department's jurisdiction. And the president could dismiss cabinet officials and members of the diplomatic corps for any reason he chose. But all other executive appointees could only be removed for cause, that is, for "dishonesty, incapacity, inefficiency, misconduct or neglect of duty."

The general thrust of these novel features of the Confederate presidency was to strengthen the office and enable its holder to interact with Congress. At the same time, some of these innovations had a rather different purpose. The nonrenewable term and the limitation on presidential control of subcabinet appointees were intended to eliminate the primary breeding grounds for the creation of permanent political parties and the executive patronage that nourished and sustained them. By preventing the president from using the offices at his disposal to reward political supporters, the Confederates were choking, at its source, the spoils system that Andrew Jackson had introduced. When the prohibitions against Congress's ability to enact protective tariffs and schemes of internal improvements were added to these severe restrictions on executive patronage, all possibility of building party organizations through the distribution of government largesse and offices to grateful supporters had, it was hoped, been forestalled, if not eliminated.

The power of party was also curbed by restricting the president to one term only. Because he no longer needed to get himself reelected, he would not need to build political support and create a party organization for that purpose. As a result, the president could be independent of party, even above it. Moreover, he could then govern disinterestedly, with the public good as his overriding concern. A president above party, a "patriot president" like Washington, was the ideal in the minds of the Confederates as they fashioned the head of state of their new nation. And this image of President Washington was definitely what Jefferson Davis had in mind when he planned his two inaugurations, in April 1861 as provisional president and a year later as permanent president. In 1861, he rode to the capitol in Montgomery in a carriage drawn by six gray horses, just as Washington had done in April 1789. And the ceremony in 1862 that took place in the new capital of Richmond took place on 22 February, Washington's birthday, and Davis delivered his address as the first president of the Confederacy standing on the capitol steps, right next to the statue of the first president of the United States.

Besides serving as the model president for this new nation, Washington was invoked by the Confederates as an inveterate opponent of political parties. The leaders of the Revolutionary generation had considered political parties dangerous and divisive, and quite unnecessary in fact, so they had made no mention of them in the constitution they wrote. But fierce political rivalries had broken out during Washington's two administrations, and they quickly formed into organized factions. Fearful that they might endanger the republic, Washington had devoted most of his famous farewell address to inveighing against "the baneful effects of the spirit of party." Although Washington's advice seemed to have been heeded during the Early Republic, the political environment changed during the second quarter of the nineteenth century, when organized parties arose and competed to win nationwide electoral majorities. And the result, as Washington had feared, was the division of the country and its eventual disintegration.

As the victims of these unfortunate developments, the Confederates vowed never to allow parties and regional majorities to break up their experiment in nation building. Rather, they were determined that the original intent of the framers be realized in the Confederacy. Indeed, a return to the initial ideal of a polity without parties, not just the creation and maintenance of a separate national existence, was the objective of the Confederacy. As Davis proclaimed in his 1862 inaugural, "The tyranny of an unbridled majority, the most odious and least responsible form of despotism, has denied us both the right and the remedy [to defend ourselves as a minority]. Therefore we are in arms to renew such sacrifices as our fathers made to the holy cause of constitutional liberty."[3] By making a few changes in the federal Constitution, the Confederates felt confident they could realize the ideal of unity and liberty that the Framers of the U.S. Constitution had hoped for. Rather than simply emulating them by adopting their frame of government, the southerners were improving it and thus ensuring its ultimate success—and their own independence as well.

The Confederacy's Political System

The Confederates' discouragement of political parties was no doubt understandable in time of war. Indeed, historians have often assumed that the need for wartime unity made parties seem undesirable and even dangerous, and so the Confederacy tried to curb and suppress them. But the Confederacy's animus against parties preceded the outbreak of hostilities. The Confederate constitution had been written and adopted before the war began. And it omitted any mention of parties, while it created a governmental structure that was intended to stifle them. Actually, the Confederates went even further than merely restricting party activity, for they wanted to outlaw or ban political parties altogether. This intention preceded the war, and their decision against parties was then sustained throughout it, regardless of its impact on the war effort. Parties were intrinsically injurious, so they believed, and they intended to prove that republics were better off without them, just as the Framers of the U.S. Constitution had contended.

The South's experience during the 1850s left its political leaders thoroughly jaded about the usefulness of parties. Most of them had been actively involved either in the Democratic Party or in the Whig Party because they had hoped that the identification of their region with both of the national parties would force each of them to heed, and respond to, the interests of the South. In turn, the South would be viewed as a national entity and not as a separate section with discrete interests and aberrant values. These party politicians, or "party men," were persuaded that involvement in, and identification with, national electoral organizations was more beneficial than the course proposed initially by Calhoun and later by the secessionists. Both the Calhounites and the secessionists argued that the South should shun these national institutions because they divided and weakened the region and should work instead toward creating a regional political force that could unify and consolidate the South.

When the Whigs collapsed in the early 1850s, the South could no longer bargain with each party or play off one against the other. Rather, the region was left tied to one of them, the Democrats, who had become identified with, and under the influence of, the South. Meanwhile, within the South itself, efforts to generate an opposition party in place of the Whigs, who remained viable in only three states (Virginia, North Carolina, and Louisiana), soon proved unavailing. The hopes they had placed in the national parties had been dashed.

But worse was to come when the Republican Party emerged as the alternative major party. For it was not a national party in fact, but a sectional, northern one. When the Republicans won control of the presidency in 1860, the much-feared "tyranny of the majority," the "despotism of numbers," had arrived. Parties could protect the South no more. Accordingly, the focus of southern politics veered sharply toward what was considered the only remaining remedy, secession.

Once the South had seceded from the Union and had begun to form a new government, parties could have reemerged around new issues and allegiances. The most salient of these was, of course, the stance that politicians had taken on the most momentous decision in southern history—whether or not to secede. It would have been quite understandable if the advocates of secession had formed a party through which they could control the government they had made possible, while at the same time excluding and proscribing those who had opposed secession or been reluctant to embark on it. A secessionist party claiming a mandate to govern the nation they themselves had created could have rallied support and carried elections against an opposition consisting of antisecessionists, whether unionists, conditional unionists, or cooperationists. For none of these groups deserved to hold power in a new nation whose inception they had resisted. A second basis for party organization was past party allegiance. Most of the politicians who were experienced and likely to be leading figures in the Confederacy had all been either Democrats or Whigs during the 1840s and even into the 1850s. And party labels and identities, along with continuing party rivalries and party competitiveness in a number of states, were not entirely extinguished with the transition to a new governmental system in 1861.

Yet the leaders of the Confederacy in formation made no real effort to resuscitate past party allegiances, or to continue the very recent differences over secession, as the basis for a new party system. Rather, they did everything possible to prevent any such thing from happening. As the provisional Congress was adjourning on 17 February 1862, a year after it had first assembled, its president, Howell Cobb of Georgia, a leading Democrat who had been Speaker of the House, 1849–50, and secretary of the treasury in the Buchanan administration, gave a farewell speech to the members in which he congratulated them on their harmonious proceedings: "In our common danger there should be no division. The spirit of party has never shown itself for an instant in your deliberations, and I would that it should be the good fortune of each successive presiding officer in the closing scene of every Congress to be able to bear the testimony I publicly give to the honor of this body."[4]

Although Cobb was disingenuous about the complete absence of party spirit in the provisional Congress, there is no denying the decrease in partisanship and organized factions there. More important was his clear intent in the speech, which was to proclaim, as a basic feature of the Confederacy, its repudiation of political parties. And this imperative was evident in the public speeches of the Confederacy's leading officials, none more stridently so than the vice president, Alexander Stephens, who had been a major national party politician in the 1840s as a Whig and in the 1850s as a Democrat. In his controversial "Cornerstone" speech of March 1861, he denounced party. His assertion that "the cornerstone of the Confederacy" rested on racial supremacy rather than slavery earned him a reprimand from President Davis because it undermined the president's own insistence that the Confederate cause rested, not on race or slavery, but on state rights and the right of secession. Quite acceptable, however, was Stephens's admonition to his audience in Savannah that "if we become divided—if schisms arise—if dissensions spring up—if factions are engendered—if party spirit, nourished by unholy personal ambition, shall rear its hydra head, I have no good prophesy for you."[5] This determination to eviscerate party was evident in more practical ways when the president appointed his cabinet. Instead of trying to balance it with representatives of both the secessionist and cooperationist elements, he indicated very publicly that the secretaries would be selected according to the state they came from and that each state would obtain one post.

Since the Confederacy was a new government, the number of appointments that needed to be made was enormous. To that large total in the civilian sector was added the fresh supply of officers required to lead a Confederate army that was being built from scratch. And, again, Davis tried to appoint according to criteria other than party. When in July 1861 he was charged by the governor of Tennessee, Isham G. Harris, with assigning military commissions to men of a particular party affiliation, Davis responded curtly. He "regard[ed] all good and true men *now*, as belonging to the *one party* of the South in which *all* are loyal and *all* are equally entitled to recognition and honor."[6] Since almost all candidates for civilian or military office had an identifiable political past of some kind, it was hard to claim that parties had been ignored altogether in these decisions. And one political group in particular had justifiable cause to grumble.

The secessionists insisted that, since they had brought the Confederacy into being, they should be put in charge of its government. But the counterargument was that, if the government were to be solidly based and widely supported, a broad array of interests had to be given recognition and influence. Most obviously, the Upper South and those who had resisted secession had to be included and given good reason to support the cause. To outraged secessionists, like Howell Cobb's brother, Thomas, it was becoming apparent as early as spring 1861 that "the best claim to distinction under the existing regime seems to be either to have opposed secession or have done nothing for it."[7] Frustrating though it was, an appointments policy that rewarded former secessionists and Democrats, just like Davis himself, would have weakened support for the Confederacy and also jeopardized the campaign to exclude parties.

The seriousness of the Confederates' antiparty intentions was clear for all to see in the elections of November 1861. These were the first elections to be held in the Confederacy because the provisional government of February 1861 had been appointed, not elected. Delegates from each state had been sent to Montgomery by their state secession conventions to write a constitution. This body of appointed delegates, who would vote as state units, not individuals, had produced both the provisional and the permanent constitutions and, as we have seen, had appointed the provisional president and vice president before reconstituting itself as the provisional Congress. Throughout this process, there were no parties and, often, not even a contest.

The continuation of Davis and Stephens in the offices to which they had been appointed in March was achieved, not by an election, but by an unopposed ratification procedure. The rule proposed by Congress required simply that presidential electors be chosen by state legislators or by voters. But there were to be no conventions to nominate the Davis-Stephens ticket, nor any other rival ticket for that matter. So there was no opposition, and therefore no campaigns, no rallies, no speeches—in effect, none of the ruckus and hoopla of the presidential canvass as it had been practiced during the Jacksonian era and thereafter. Because there was no contest, turnout was minimal and election day eerily quiet.

The only note of dissension to disturb the harmony of this ratification election was some questioning of Stephens's suitability, either because he had opposed secession or because his presence precluded the possibility of any representation from the Upper South. The diminutive and frail "Little Alec" soon proved to be a disastrous choice because he simply withdrew in disgust from participation in the Davis administration, whose centralizing policies he deplored. But his presence on the ticket was testimony to the Confederates' deep desire to harmonize the polity and preclude the possibility of parties. For Stephens's cooperationism and his earlier affiliation with the Whig Party balanced Davis's past Democratic allegiance and advocacy of secession. As Don Fehrenbacher noticed, harmony was further enhanced by the coincidence that the two men's first names coincided with Thomas Jefferson and Alexander Hamilton, thereby suggesting a belated reconciliation between the leaders of the first political factions, or parties, that President Washington had warned against. This imagined reconciliation degenerated into hostility, tinged with irony, during the war, since Davis's un-Jeffersonian nationalist and consolidationist policies were opposed vehemently by Stephens's unyielding adherence to state rights localism and constitutional liberty, hardly Hamiltonian doctrines.

The harmony and serenity of the presidential election were also evident in voting for Congress. Because there were no parties, the nominating conventions, which had become a feature of American politics since the 1830s, were unnecessary. Instead, candidates simply announced their availability and interest, just as they had done in the 1810s and 1820s. Sometimes this practice resulted in as many as a half-dozen candidates in the field. And sometimes potential challengers refused to run because they feared that opposition would be viewed negatively as divisive and factional, or even self-serving and unpatriotic. Only in North Carolina, where parties were still viable, were nominating conventions or meetings called, but even then in only a few districts.

With candidates running as individuals rather than as representatives of a party, there was no need for organized campaigning or for raising divisive issues. Instead, voters were urged to support the better man, the candidate with superior qualifications. And, according to the *Richmond Whig*, the political situation demanded "grave, sensible earnest men, [who] have the talent and manliness to meet it."[8] Thus aspirants for Congress stressed their own virtues and experience, as well as their loyalty to the Confederacy and their support for the war effort. The specifics of how they would contribute to the success of the Confederacy or what policies they would advocate if elected were both downplayed. With so little to engage and stimulate voters, it was no surprise that throughout the Confederacy so few showed up on election day. In fact, less than half the usual presecession percentage of the electorate turned out in 1861.[9]

This apparent apathy did not alarm Confederate politicians, however. Rather, it encouraged them because it showed that unity and harmony prevailed. An aroused and active electorate, on the other hand, would have been a warning that parties were at work, stirring up the voters and creating dissension. Confederate hostility to parties was presented both as an attack on the contentiousness that parties fomented and as a reform of the corruption and favoritism that partisan patronage produced. But there was another aspect to the antiparty campaign—an elitist distaste for parties as organizations. The primary objective of parties was to increase popular participation in politics and government and to encourage the kind of campaigning among, and appealing to, the masses that many in the planter class had earlier considered insufferable and demeaning. Thus, the purification and reform of politics, by removing parties and the abuses they had engendered, was a reaction to the democratization of the political system in the 1830s and after. The sentiments of a leading Georgia politician, Eugenius A. Nisbet, were typical. After once telling Alexander Stephens that a broad franchise was an "impracticable dream," he revealed his own fears of what would happen to the Confederacy if it allowed democratic politics to reemerge. Among the disastrous results, as Nisbet explained contemptuously, would be "a licentious press, ignorance among the large voting masses, the revival of old party animosities, and a low grade representation in our legislatures state and national."[10] To be antiparty was, invariably, to be antidemocratic as well.

The way elections were conducted in 1861 had all the characteristics of the preparty era from 1800 to the Era of Good Feelings during Monroe's presidency. In those days, respectable, leading men announced for office. They asked voters to support them because of their qualities of character and ability. And they never needed to resort to organizing election campaigns or appealing to the masses because only the propertied were able to vote. This idealized version of the preparty era fueled the imagination of the Confederates and provided them with the vision of a politics, not only without parties, but with extremely limited popular interest and participation.

Lacking parties, Confederate politics also lacked organization and structure. And this quickly became a feature of public life in the Confederacy, which was evident from the way the Confederate Congress conducted its business. Congressmen ran for election as individuals and, once they arrived in Richmond, they functioned that way as legislators.

According to the most authoritative analysis of the voting behavior of the Confederate Congress, "Lawmaking was every man for himself, for Congress was an amorphous body in which it seemed that almost every atom behaved according to its own rules."[11] Contributing to this atomization was the absence of two elements that would have structured the actions of the congressmen. First, there were no party caucuses or meetings and no party leadership on the floor to line up and coordinate votes for roll calls on measures before either house. Even the chairs of standing committees in the House and Senate acted independently and did not function as leaders on whom even President Davis could rely to mobilize votes for his legislation. And, second, Davis himself was very hesitant about organizing votes in support of his own measures and initiatives, for fear that he would appear to be creating an administration party. Besides, he firmly believed that his role as president was to stay above party and that his responsibility as head of the new nation was to protect it from the taint and strife of parties.

Without these organizational constraints, the majorities and minorities that formed on each measure simply dissolved after the votes were taken. They then reconstituted themselves differently for the next roll call. There seemed, in fact, to be little continuity or pattern to the voting behavior of Confederate congressmen. Accordingly, voting blocs were barely discernible, and factions of like-minded congressmen never arose. Since "disorganized" is a judgmental term, it would be better to describe Confederate politics as "unorganized."

The Confederate Congress's unorganized politics did not, however, result in torpor or paralysis. And it certainly did not produce deadlock with the executive branch, which would have prevented the president from obtaining the appropriations and powers he needed to prosecute the war and govern the new nation. "President Davis had his way with Congress," concluded his most recent biographer, William J. Cooper Jr., who considered him "a vigorous and potent chief executive." Moreover, "Congress never stymied him on a critical matter."[12]

This was remarkable, since Jefferson Davis, as chief executive of an embryonic nation-state, was demanding swift action and unprecedented authority to create a government and to forge and equip a military system, both of them from the ground up. The government built railroads where necessary and established an executive board to supervise their operation. Because it was a massive purchaser of war-related goods, the government also had a controlling influence over the industries that produced them and therefore over the labor force that worked in them. Furthermore, it became a manufacturer itself, building ships for the navy, operating mines to excavate phosphate, and constructing factories to manufacture gunpowder. And, of course, the government introduced conscription, declared martial law, and forcibly impressed civilians' property and crops— even their slaves. Achieving these successes certainly required cajoling and negotiation, but Davis could not complain about a "do-nothing" Confederate Congress or obstructionist legislators. Sometimes the votes were very close. He was forced to wield the veto on thirty-nine occasions and was overridden only once. All told, the record of legislative achievement was impressive, especially since the southern political class had been schooled to be suspicious of central governments and had been reared on a steady diet of state rights and personal autonomy.

Davis's ability to forge legislative majorities in favor of his proposals was facilitated by two assets he could count on. The first was his embodiment of the cause of Confederate independence. Depicting himself as the "patriot president" who represented the entire country, not just a portion of it or a political party within it, Jefferson Davis was asking Congress to provide him the means for winning a war and ensuring the survival of the Confederacy. For congressmen to deny him the powers and the resources that the country needed in a time of crisis and danger would have run the risk of being labeled unpatriotic or factious. Since it was Davis who took the initiative and presented his plans, Congress's responsibility was either to limit what he asked for or to reduce what he requested. But outright refusal seemed too risky and even unwarranted. Invariably, Congress was reacting instead of taking the lead in making a recommendation or presenting programs of its own. This presidential activism was just what the Confederate Constitution had provided for.

The second of Davis's assets was the lack of an organized opposition within Congress. Although most of the president's initiatives were controversial and even intrinsically objectionable to southern legislators with their obsessions about limited government, Congress never developed anything approaching an effective opposition. In their study of the Confederate Congress, Thomas B. Alexander and Richard E. Beringer could not find even a minuscule group of congressmen who voted consistently in opposition to the president. They had assumed that at least a small knot of diehard recalcitrants had to have existed, and they examined the votes that Davis won by two-thirds majorities to see if the small minorities of one-third of the members who voted against him contained a cluster of consistent opponents. But even here, only an individual or two emerged as, in effect, perpetual losers. Not even a group of a half-dozen or so known Davis-haters got together to vent their anger and disdain over the course of several votes.

In the four sessions of the First Congress, one representative, Lewis M. Ayer of South Carolina, and one senator, Williamson Oldham of Texas, "were for a single session in the minority more often than not" in those roll calls that carried strongly with two-thirds of the vote. And, in the two sessions of the Second Congress, there was no evidence whatever of a minority bloc, since not a single senator was "preponderantly in the minority status" and only three representatives were "in the minority barely more than half the time."[13] With so few congressmen voting against the administration on anything like a regular basis, opposition became peripatetic, incoherent, and unorganized—yet another symptom of the Confederates' political preferences and priorities.

This remarkably fragmented, even atomized, politics gave rise to a cacophony of criticism of the president. Acting and speaking separately, congressmen berated the administration for its shortcomings and failures. Perceiving him as the embodiment of the executive branch, Jefferson Davis himself rather than his policies became the target, as the legislators' attacks became increasingly personal. "Davis' supreme imbecility has well nigh undone us," complained Laurence Keitt (pronounced "Kit"), a secessionist congressman from South Carolina, in June 1862. "You cannot find a more signal failure in history."[14] Davis's own vice president even weighed in, calling him "weak and vacillating, timid, petulant, peevish, obstinate, but not firm."[15] Had Davis been evaluating Alexander Stephens, instead of the other way around, it is quite likely that he would have used the very same language to describe him. But no one hated Davis more than Senator Louis Wigfall of Texas, who once recommended to a public meeting that "Jeff Davis ought to be hung in Richmond."[16]

Many of Davis's critics, like Robert Toombs of Georgia, Mississippi's Henry S. Foote, or Louis Wigfall, were men with tempestuous and mercurial temperaments, who would resort to personal invective at the slightest provocation. But their kind of unbridled behavior was encouraged by the lack of organization and constraint in the Confederacy's politics. And it was contagious. Others of a more restrained and cautious disposition were affected, and they too engaged in the ad hominem, anti-Davis rhetoric. For they were all confronted by the same dilemma. They found themselves unorganized and powerless in a politics that disavowed parties and denounced opposition as factious. Yet the elements of the electoral and governmental system that had given rise to parties were still very much in evidence in the Confederacy. Congressmen competed in elections and sought public office, all the while repudiating parties and political ambition. Meanwhile, Davis possessed immense power and dispensed large amounts of patronage, but members of Congress could neither share in this nor organize to oppose him. This discrepancy, and the frustration it generated, produced a shrill and rancorous response. Not surprisingly, "a persistent contentiousness characterized public life" in the Confederacy, as George C. Rable has observed.[17]

The failure of the opposition to cohere and organize itself has led some historians to conclude that the absence of parties was a liability for the Confederacy. Because parties enable individual politicians to coordinate their actions as well as provide a means for channeling and moderating their views and policy positions, they help to forge agreement on issues and party platforms. Such an outcome would undoubtedly have been beneficial to the Davis administration's discordant and contentious opponents. Moreover, it would have contributed to an improved political climate. But an organized and cohesive opposition would not have been welcomed by President Davis. Opposition that was "personal and factional" may have been "difficult to deal with," as James M. McPherson once surmised, but it was far less powerful and threatening.[18] Indeed, to suggest otherwise would seem counterintuitive. Why would Davis have wished for a coordinated and powerful opposition party? On the other hand, of course, he would have benefited if he had been able to avail himself of the assets and discipline of a political party. Yet even without a party of his own, Davis usually got what he wanted and was able to defeat by his veto what he opposed. Although he might have gained by having a party of his own to mobilize his supporters, he would probably have lost on balance because a presidential party would almost certainly have provoked coordination and cohesion among his scattered and ineffective opponents.

Although President Davis had little to gain from the introduction of organized parties, their existence would have improved the Confederate polity itself. Elections would have been more competitive, voter participation would have increased, and policy issues would have edged out personal rancor and bickering. In addition, parties would have become the instruments for linking politics at the Confederate level with the states. As it was, however, these two political arenas and jurisdictions, each possessing elements of sovereignty, were left uncoordinated with each other. Contributing further to the estrangement between the states and the central government was the habit of the Confederate Congress of holding its sessions in secret and thereby preventing the outside world from learning what was going on there. Partly, this was a wartime precaution (though the Congress in Washington seemed to be quite unconcerned that the enemy might discover what it was doing) and partly a result of the worry about divisions within the polity and the emergence of parties. Lacking information about the actions taken and the matters discussed in the Confederate legislature, politicians and voters were deprived of the information essential to form parties.

Although parties might have given structure to the politics of the Confederacy and improved the contentious political climate, it is far from clear that the administration needed to create a party organization. Had the Davis administration been confronted by opposition to the war itself, the need might have presented itself. Things were different in the North, where the Democrats questioned the wisdom and necessity of the war and pressed for a negotiated peace. Within the Confederate Congress, no such opposition arose. Davis's measures for prosecuting the war, in particular conscription, impressment, and suspension of habeas corpus, were roundly criticized. But the need to fight and win the war was questioned only marginally. When a peace party did emerge in one of the states, in North Carolina to be precise, in the 1864 elections, its leaders were at pains to deny that they intended to rejoin the Union but sought only a negotiated peace to be worked out by the Confederacy. Besides, this was merely a local initiative, not a challenge to the central government's war policies. The Confederacy was not being threatened politically from within. Therefore, Davis did not have to face the kind of resistance that confronted Lincoln. As long as he was able to obtain the means to prosecute the war and thereby preserve Confederate independence, he did not need to resort to further organization of his support beyond what he was already managing to do quite adequately.

Interesting though these speculations may be, they do not alter the fundamental reality within the new southern nation. The Confederates intended to create a political system without political parties, just as the federal Constitution had envisaged. It mattered little that parties might have benefited the administration, or its opponents, or both. Parties were considered intrinsically undesirable and unhealthy. And the nation-state that the Confederates were constructing presented the opportunity to start afresh and avoid the mistaken predilection for parties of the Jacksonian era.

In a very real sense, the Confederate experiment was a moment of truth. The South's planter class and its allies had been able to control the government of the United States during the quarter century after the Revolution. But thereafter, with the emergence of a mass electorate and the rise of political parties to mobilize those millions of voters, the South's leadership had lost its struggle to remain in the ascendancy. Even though the region's politicians had been actively involved in the hurly-burly of the new style of campaigning and sloganeering and even though the rate of participation in elections by southern voters rose to levels as high as anywhere in the country, the new system of parties seemed to have worked, not just to their temporary disadvantage, but to their eventual defeat. Of course, it is not necessarily true that the southerners would have been better off in the 1830s and 1840s without parties. Evidently, they thought the Framers might have been right about the dangers of parties. A serious attempt to manage without them was, therefore, an experiment worth trying.

In 1861, they vowed to exclude political parties from the Confederacy. Elections would be conducted as they had been at the turn of the century, when men of reputation made themselves available for public office and sought the endorsement of their constituents, whose number was limited to property holders and taxpayers. Southern unity and security, it was believed, were jeopardized by competitive party politics and the raucous involvement in public life of the masses. So the Confederacy turned away from them. This change of course proved to be pivotal. For the South's political leadership would continue, though with varying degrees of success, to reject the idea of competitive political parties and to curb popular participation in elections after the defeat of the Confederacy, and even beyond—for about a hundred years, in fact.

PART III.

ONE-PARTY HEGEMONY,

1865–1901

5

Party Politics under Assault

RECONSTRUCTION

By 1865, the Union had won the war and, in the process, freed the slaves. Both were massive accomplishments. They settled the issues of secession and slavery, which had generated the conflict between the North and the South as well as the war that ensued. But winning the peace after a protracted, destructive war and two hundred years of slavery presented an enormous challenge. As Frederick Douglass, the abolitionist and former slave, had warned back in November 1862, "The work before us is nothing less than a radical revolution in all the modes of thought which have flourished under the blighting slave system." In effect, "the work does not end with the abolition of slavery but only begins."[1]

At the very least, the North would have to introduce further changes into the South after the war, not only to protect the slaves' freedom and independence but also to create and sustain loyal governments there. And federal intervention was almost certain to be resisted by the former Confederates. So the struggle for control of the South would continue. This time, however, it would be fought, not on the battlefield, but in the legislatures and the polling stations of the southern states.

The North's Terms

The struggle over the postwar peace took place initially in Washington and not in the South. After the main Confederate military force, the Army of Northern Virginia, surrendered at Appomattox Courthouse in April 1865, peace terms had to be drawn up by the Union government. The initiative was quickly taken by the newly installed president, Andrew Johnson, who had succeeded Abraham Lincoln after his assassination, on 15 April, at the very moment of his great triumph in winning the war. Like all negotiators of postwar settlements, Johnson had a choice in dealing with his defeated opponent. He could pursue a course of conciliation, assuming that good relations with the enemy were more likely to emerge as a result of magnanimity and cooperation. Or he could use coercion, on the premise that the enemy had to be dealt with firmly, and even punished, in order to produce a sense of finality and submission that confirmed the actuality of military defeat. Johnson chose conciliation.

As military governor of Tennessee from 1862 to 1864, he had taken a firm stand toward the rebels within his home state, announcing on numerous occasions that "treason must be made odious and traitors punished." But Andrew Johnson was a white southerner. Despite being an opponent of secession, he nevertheless identified instinctively with his native region. He also calculated that his wisest course politically was to follow Lincoln's example and continue his wartime initiatives to reconcile with the South and draw it back into the Union on "silken threads." As Johnson once told a Democratic senator, his policy was "everywhere to stimulate the loyalty of the South themselves, and make it the spring of loyal conduct and proper legislation rather than to impose upon them laws and conditions by external force."[2]

Accordingly, the president introduced a set of policies intended to accomplish these ends. In April, he appointed a provisional governor in every southern state, each of whom had invariably been an opponent of secession in 1861 or a wartime Unionist. Each provisional governor was to call a constitutional convention to ratify the Thirteenth Amendment ending slavery and to nullify the state's secession ordinance. Then congressmen would be elected, as well as a new governor and a state legislature. Those who had taken an oath of loyalty or, if leaders of the rebellion, had applied for and been granted a personal pardon by the president would make up the eligible electorate. After complying with these requirements, the region's congressmen would be seated and each state would be readmitted to the Union.

Instead of producing loyalty and cooperation in response to the generous terms offered by the president, Johnson's policy of "restoration," as he called it, gave the former Confederates sufficient latitude to balk at the terms he required them to meet. When this happened, Johnson did not adjust his approach so as to put pressure on the southerners to comply. Rather, he stood by his initial proposal, even though it had failed to produce the desired effect of repentance and collaboration. Since the Republican majority in Congress could not possibly overlook such recalcitrance, they denied the southern states readmission and then proceeded to challenge the president for control of postwar federal policy toward the South.

The Republicans' attempt to reformulate the terms for southern readmission proved difficult, even perilous, for the party and the nation. First of all, President Johnson refused to acknowledge that his plan had proven inadequate. Adamant that his approach had been wise, he refused to adapt to political reality in the South or to recognize the Republicans' worries about admitting a delegation of unreconciled former Confederates into Congress. Instead, he fought every attempt by the Republican majority to produce, and then implement, an alternative set of terms.

A second problem the Republicans had to deal with was their own difficulty in agreeing upon a formula for readmission to replace the president's. The more moderate element in the party favored a conciliatory approach that was still firmer than Johnson's clearly insufficient and overly conciliatory policy. But the party's radicals were convinced that only a vigorous, even coercive, course would induce the former Confederates to change their behavior. A considerably more forceful and far-reaching policy was essential, so the radicals believed, to ensure protection for the vulnerable former slaves, the "freedmen" as they were called, and also to curb the political influence of the former slave owners and leaders of the rebellion who were returning to power in the South under Johnson's plan. Because Johnson indicated that he would veto any legislation that imposed additional demands on the South, the Republicans had to resolve their differences, or else every proposal they introduced would be defeated with the help of the watchful and united Democratic opposition.

In early 1866, the Republicans introduced a civil rights bill defining African Americans as citizens and guaranteeing federal protection of citizens' legal and civil rights. Johnson responded truculently with a veto and an accompanying message denouncing the bill's provisions. Realizing that the president was unlikely to cooperate, the Republicans struggled over the next few months to devise alternative terms for readmission. Eventually, they proposed an amendment to the Constitution, which later, after it was adopted, became the Fourteenth Amendment. This measure incorporated the civil rights provisions of the Civil Rights Act, which was eventually passed over Johnson's veto. It then provided a formula for a limited black suffrage. But, most important, the amendment prohibited the Confederacy's political leaders from holding office, that is, it kept them out of power. As expected, Johnson opposed these additional requirements. Quite unexpected, however, was his decision to make the Republicans' plan the issue in the congressional elections of 1866. Not only did he take to the hustings but he also formed his own political organization, the National Union Party, to run candidates against the Republicans. Then, after his reckless attempt failed and the Republicans were returned to Congress in increased numbers, he recommended to the southern legislatures that they reject the new terms by refusing to ratify the amendment. This they proceeded to do, overwhelmingly.

The Republicans had now to come up with another set of terms. The Military Reconstruction Act of 1867 was their answer, and this was the piece of legislation after which the Reconstruction period was named. Because Johnson vetoed this law as well as three others that the Republicans drew up to protect the original plan from his constant interference and obstruction, there were actually four Reconstruction Acts. The Republicans' initial proposal in 1867 was formulated and introduced by Thaddeus Stevens of Pennsylvania, the leading and most insistent of the radicals in the House. He and most other radical Republicans were convinced that the former Confederates should not be allowed to return to Congress until their hostility had cooled down and significant political changes had been implemented within the South. Only a period of government under U.S. military supervision would allow the necessary developments to emerge and become established. In Stevens's opinion, "The whole fabric of southern society *must* be changed, and never can it be done if this opportunity is lost. . . . How can republican institutions, free schools, free social intercourse exist in a mingled community of nabobs and serfs? If the South is ever to be made a safe republic let her lands be cultivated by the toil of the owners or the free labor of intelligent citizens."[3]

Most Republicans probably agreed with Stevens's vision of a transformed South, but they found his proposal for military occupation too extreme and risky, and they proceeded to gut his plan for long-term military rule by inserting a procedure for readmitting the South rather than keeping it out. Their amendments to the bill created a new southern electorate consisting primarily of African Americans. These voters would form the basis of a Republican party in the South, and they would elect new governments run by officials who were not ex-Confederates, since the old leadership would be denied the vote and prohibited from holding office. In all probability, the newly created electorate would send a delegation of Republicans to Congress.

Less extreme than Stevens's initial proposal, the law that resulted was still radical in many respects. It enfranchised the former slaves within two years of their emancipation, a course of action never even considered by other slave societies in the Americas, such as Brazil, Cuba, and the British

"We Accept the Situation," *Harper's Weekly*, 13 April 1867. Passage of the Reconstruction Act of March 1867 put the former Confederate states under military rule and mandated the election of new state governments, with the recently emancipated slaves now voting and the Republican Party likely to win control. Since their struggle to avoid the North's terms for reunion had ended in failure, the ex-Confederates admitted very reluctantly that they accepted the situation. Also accepting the situation were African American men, like the young Union soldier in this cartoon by Thomas Nast who was beside himself with delight about the news and the vote he now possessed. The hollowness of the South's lip service is apparent in the posture and grimace of the resentful "Ex C.S.A." soldier. Library of Congress, Prints and Photographs Division.

West Indies, that abolished slavery in the mid-nineteenth century. Also radical was the creation of a new political system in the South, with a previously nonexistent Republican Party being formed almost overnight and catapulted into power. Radical too was the sidelining of the men who had dominated the politics and government of the region before the war. Most of them were members, or allies, of the slaveholding elite and leaders of the Confederacy, and they were now banned from participation in public life. A last radical feature was the role of the military. The region's ten unrestored states were to be divided into five military districts, with a U.S. general as the ultimate authority in each of them. The military was to supervise the process of registration and the subsequent elections, as well as remain to garrison the South until it was reconstructed politically and readmitted to Congress.

When the South returned to Congress in June 1868, the terrible uncertainty that had lasted three long years seemed to be over. The region had been reconstructed and was now under the control of Republican administrations in the states. Equally important, the Republicans had managed to emerge from their bitter and dangerous struggle with Andrew Johnson still in control of Congress. The party's power was further in evidence in 1868 when the Republican nominee, Ulysses S. Grant, was elected president. Admittedly, three southern states (Virginia, Mississippi, and Texas) had been unable to participate because they had not yet completed the procedure for readmission. And two others (Louisiana and Georgia) had voted for Grant's Democratic opponent, Horatio Seymour of New York, a southern sympathizer during the war. Not as auspicious a beginning as hoped perhaps—but still the South had been reorganized under new leadership and readmitted to Congress. And so the nation was finally reunited.

The South's Response

The creation of Republican-controlled state governments marked the successful culmination of the struggle over Reconstruction policy, but the reconstruction of southern politics and society depended upon the ability of these governments to stay in power long enough to bring about the necessary political and economic changes. Their longevity was, however, far from assured.

These governments had come into existence only because the former Confederates' desperate attempt to thwart Congress had been beaten back and defeated. In fact, from the very outset, in 1865, when President Johnson had taken the initiative with his conciliatory "restoration" plan, the southern leadership had been uncooperative and contentious. Despite Johnson's mild terms and his hope that the South's leaders would respond positively to his search for evidence of loyalty and accommodation, they had refused to comply. They had balked at ratifying the Thirteenth Amendment, which abolished slavery, and at nullifying their ordinances of secession. They had pressed Johnson to allow them to organize state militias, an attempt to coerce black laborers by an armed force similar to the slave patrol. In some states, the legislature had promulgated "black codes" to reduce the freedmen to a status akin to that of the free Negroes under the slave regime, only to have the U.S. military annul them. And, in the fall 1865 elections, they had sent men with sterling Confederate records to Congress. The selection of Alexander Stephens as one of Georgia's senators caused even Johnson to complain helplessly that "there seems, in many of the elections something like defiance, which is all out of place at this juncture."[4]

Had the ex-Confederates taken advantage of Johnson's leniency by accepting his terms, they would have made the Republicans' task of preventing their readmission very difficult, perhaps impossible. But their squandering of this opportunity did not seem to chasten them, for they persisted in refusing to comply. Over the next few months, as Congress developed its own set of requirements in 1866 in the form of the Fourteenth Amendment, the noncompliance of the former Confederates became out-and-out rejection. In the summer and fall of 1866, Johnson's strategy of creating the National Union Party in support of his own policy and ambitions and then campaigning against Congress's alternative proposal went down to a humiliating defeat. Yet the southern leadership made its own predicament even worse by rejecting the amendment brazenly, with barely a vote in favor. In Louisiana, not a single legislator cast a ballot to ratify. And in the remaining nine states, the amendment that Congress required for readmission received only 33 votes.

Confronted with the defeat of Johnson and the Democrats, why didn't the southerners face political reality? Why didn't they recognize the need for expediency and, by accepting the amendment, avoid worse terms? Although such a course made political sense, most southerners considered it the height of folly. They chose resistance instead and refused to submit to terms they considered unacceptable. By rejecting the amendment, ex-Confederates hoped to force the Republicans to resort to even more radical schemes that would anger the moderates and result in the breakup of the party. As a Georgia newspaper saw the situation in early 1867, the Republican Party had "arrived at the crisis of its fate, in which advance is perilous but retrogression ruin."[5] More radical and extreme measures from the Republicans, accompanied by growing frustration at the endless delay in reuniting the country, was likely to provoke a reaction among the northern electorate whose "sober second thought" would result in the repudiation of the Republican Party at the next election.

At the same time, submission to Congress's terms was actually no solution, because compliance served only to reveal the South's vulnerability. As Governor James L. Orr of South Carolina observed: "Our true policy . . . is to assent to no further conditions that are tendered by our conquerors." Great risk was involved in consenting, because "the more palpably our submission to the laws and constitution of the United States and our acquiescence in the disastrous termination of the war is manifested the more exacting, tyrannical and humiliating to us become their demands."[6] Acceptance of Congress's terms was therefore tantamount to submission. Besides being degrading, such willing compliance with these terms invited further demands. Orr's counterpart in North Carolina, Jonathan Worth, was even more insistent that the region's honor was involved, not just its political weakness. Employing an analogy from slavery, he insisted that "no generous man ought to expect us to hasten to the whipping post and invite the lash in advance of condemnation." Several months earlier, Worth had also likened consent to servility when he observed, "If we are to be degraded, we will retain some self-esteem by not making it self-abasement."[7]

Calculating that compliance could wring no political benefit but only elicit contempt from their Republican enemies, the former Confederates opted for continued noncooperation in the expectation that impatient public opinion in the North, or destructive factional conflict within the Republican Party, would frustrate its attempts to make the terms for the South more radical. So they concluded that they should not acquiesce but wait instead for the Republican Party to break up or be repudiated at the polls. The assumption behind this strategy of "masterly inactivity," as many of them began to refer to it, was stated very clearly by Benjamin F. Perry, an antisecessionist from the up-country of South Carolina, who had been Johnson's choice for provisional governor in 1865. In a letter to the *New York Herald* in September 1866, he acknowledged that he did "not believe the Radical leaders ever expected [the amendment] to be adopted," because "nothing will satisfy them but universal negro suffrage and the disfranchisement of all prominent Southern men, who do not act with them in carrying out their nefarious purposes. Their object is to establish the permanent rule of the Radical party, secure the next presidential election, and exclude Northern Democrats, as well as Southern men, from all influence in government."[8] And Perry was quite correct. This was exactly what the Republican Party had to ensure. His predictions were confirmed when a few months later the Republicans passed the Reconstruction Act. Evidently, Perry was speaking for the South's political establishment, because the former Confederates were virtually unanimous in their decision to reject Congress's proposed amendment, regardless of the short-term consequences.

This remarkably solid consensus had emerged without any organization. There was no southern political high command or coordinating committee, not even much collaboration, except through personal correspondence or opinion pieces in the newspapers that were written and submitted by individuals. Continued noncompliance seemed, under the circumstances, to be appropriate and necessary to all but a few. For their policy of inactivity was proving to be masterly. In fact, they were already in control of the situation, since the former Confederates held power in the South, where incumbency and control really mattered. Under Johnson's plan, they had been elected to the governorships and legislatures of the southern states in the fall of 1865, and they were still in office in spring 1867.

Although these former leaders of the Confederacy had almost no influence over Congress and had to deal with the U.S. Army and the Freedmen's Bureau in their efforts to keep their recently emancipated labor force under control, they were nevertheless the duly elected officials of the region's state governments. Moreover, their hold on political power was directly threatened by the proposed Fourteenth Amendment's third clause disqualifying supporters of the Confederacy from holding office. And they knew, as Governor Perry pointed out, that their own removal from power in the South and their exclusion from Congress were vital to the national Republicans' continued ascendancy. Consequently, nothing was to be gained from agreeing to the halfway measures that many of their Republican adversaries considered insufficient. Noncompliance ensured that they would continue to be in control in the South, and it might bring them further benefit if their inactivity caused the Republican Party political difficulties.

In an attempt at finality, the Republican congressmen presented their second set of terms in the form of a mandatory statute, rather than as a constitutional amendment that the South would be asked to ratify and therefore approve voluntarily. Throughout the process of introducing and enacting this piece of legislation, the party had managed to stay intact and muster enough votes to pass the law over the predictable veto from President Johnson. Now the law of the land, the Reconstruction Act was nevertheless so unprecedented and so complex that the prospect of the Supreme Court declaring it unconstitutional was quite real. The southerners therefore could look to the Supreme Court for deliverance—and also to the president, who, as commander in chief, was responsible for implementing the new military law.

But the statute itself actually offered the former Confederates several opportunities to obstruct, and even halt, its operation within the South. In the formation of new governments based on universal suffrage, which was the goal of the Reconstruction Act, elections were to be held in each state and a new constitution was to be produced and ratified. In this process, opponents could participate in the voting and win control of the offices and of the constitutional convention, even though this might prove difficult because officeholders under the Confederacy were banned by the act from voting as well as from officeholding. Nevertheless, the entire project could still be frustrated by its opponents at the very end when the vote to ratify the new constitution came around. Because the law required a majority of the registered voters to participate, the rank and file of the opposition, but not its disfranchised leaders, could of course register and then abstain in the ratification vote. Without a new constitution, a state could not be readmitted. In Alabama, the first state to submit its constitution to the electorate, opponents of Reconstruction were urged to stay away, with the result that less than a majority of the eligible voters participated. The resisters' success was short-lived, however, because the Republicans moved immediately to enact a new Reconstruction law requiring that only a majority of the vote cast would ensure ratification. And it passed over the inevitable presidential veto.

With this frontal attack thwarted, the former Confederates' three-year resistance to Congress's desperate efforts to produce a viable set of terms came to an end. They were thrown out of power in their own states and replaced by Republicans whose primary support came from the votes of enfranchised former slaves. Now the ex-Confederates had to concentrate their attention and resentment on state politics, not on Congress. But this had been their main concern, all along. For control of their state governments, which they had retained ever since Johnson's plan had enabled them to return to power in 1865, was the heart of the matter in 1868, as it had been ever since the end of the war. Readmission to Congress was far less important than controlling their states and thus holding onto political power where it most mattered, in the South itself.

Illegitimacy and Insurgency in the Reconstructed South

The Republican Party that was catapulted into power in the election of 1868 had no prior history in the southern states, except in western Virginia. It was brought into existence by the four Reconstruction Acts of 1867–68, and its formation was supervised by U.S. military officers, who were responsible for registering the new voters. The party's membership was drawn from three sources, but each of these elicited scorn from the former Confederates and from the South's political class in general.

First, there were northern whites, often Union soldiers who remained in the South to work with the Freedmen's Bureau or to embark on a new livelihood there. This group also included civilians who came south during and after the war to participate in the rebuilding of the war-torn region as teachers, farmers, and entrepreneurs or as public officials and political activists. A second group consisted of southern white men who had opposed, or been lukewarm in their support of, the Confederacy. Many of them saw in the new party an opportunity to modernize and democratize the South, in effect transforming it into a new South. Other white southerners who joined the Republicans were politicians who, for various reasons, calculated that they themselves and the region would benefit if the Republican Party succeeded. And, finally, African Americans, both the freedmen and those previously free, were confirmed Republicans, knowing that their own future and that of their race was tied closely to the party that had emancipated most of them and that alone could protect them and advance their prospects.

Unfortunately, all three groups were, in a very real sense, outsiders and therefore anathema to most white southerners, who wasted no time before launching vitriolic attacks against them. They dismissed the northerners as rejects from their own society, "carpetbaggers" who came south with no assets and belongings, save what could be carried in a suitcase, or carpetbag. Northerners in North Carolina's constitutional convention of 1868 were dismissed by the state's leading newspaper as "men without character or talent, unknown to the people, unaccustomed to public life and know[ing] little of Constitution-making than so many wild Arabs. . . . They came as adventurers to *make gain*."[9] The native whites who affiliated with a party that was alien to the South and had been imposed from outside were denounced as "scalawags," renegades of no account or worth who were traitors to their race and region. Even though many of these "scalawags" were politicians who had figured prominently in southern politics previously, such as Joseph E. Brown, the former governor of Georgia, or James L. Alcorn, a Mississippi congressman before the war, they were still treated with suspicion and contempt. And, of course, blacks were vilified just as they had always been, except that their role and influence in the party were now wildly exaggerated so as to damn Republicanism as equivalent to "Negro rule." A mere 15 blacks sat in North Carolina's 1868 constitutional convention, out of a total of 133 members, yet the body was denigrated by one newspaper as "an Ethiopian minstrelsy, Ham radicalism in its glory," containing "baboons, monkeys, mules, . . . and other jackasses."[10]

Nonsensical as these disparaging slanders were, they were an essential element in a deadly serious campaign of vilification aimed at the fledgling Republican Party. By ridiculing the leaders and showing how dependent their party was on the votes of illiterate and ignorant blacks, who just three years earlier had been slaves, the opponents of Reconstruction intended to dismiss the Republican Party as grotesque, incompetent, alien, and essentially illegitimate. Obtaining legitimacy is critically important if an elected government is to earn the respect and gain the allegiance of the citizenry. Without it, government lacks authority and is unable to obtain the consent and support of the governed. Because of its suspect origins and membership, the Republican Party started out with its claims for acceptance and legitimacy fundamentally contested. Somehow, the party had to acquire legitimacy or it would not be able to govern. The opposition knew this full well and was determined to prevent the Republicans from being accepted as a legitimate political force within the South. In December 1867, on the eve of the Republicans' ascendancy in South Carolina and in every other southern state, the *Charleston Mercury* proclaimed, with grim confidence, that white southerners "are not *ruled* by any governments they do not recognize as legitimate over them. . . . The white race of the South have only to will the rule of the South: and there is no power on this continent, which can prevent it."[11]

Therefore, immediately upon taking control of the executive mansions and statehouses of the former Confederacy in the spring and summer of 1868, the Republicans had to decide how they could gain acceptance and establish their legitimacy. At a moment when southern politics was being transformed by the creation of a new, alternative political party based on the votes of former slaves, the Republicans might have developed into an alliance of the poor and propertyless among both whites and blacks, who together could bring about substantial economic and social change. A segment of the party wanted to seize the opportunity to move it in a radical direction and make it an instrument for bringing about major changes in the region. But these advocates of a radical Republicanism were outvoted by the more cautious and moderate in the new party, who insisted that securing acceptance and respect was essential to the party's survival.

Convincing evidence of the party's moderation and its desire not to alienate respectable white southerners was revealed in the actions of the Republican-dominated constitutional conventions that had met during 1868. They had written into the constitutional framework of the states a number of features that promoted greater civic participation and expanded governmental activism and responsibility. But they had refused to entertain such contentious proposals as the redistribution of land or the continued proscription of Confederates through denying them the vote and office. Rather, the state constitutions insisted on equal rights before the law; eliminated property restrictions on officeholding; abolished imprisonment for debt and provided relief for debtors; encouraged economic development through the offer of state financial aid; and required government to provide public services and institutions, chiefly a system of public education, which almost all southern states currently lacked. Most important initially was the decision to restore the vote to the former Confederates, who had been denied it by the Reconstruction Act, for it meant that the Republicans' electoral prospects would be seriously diminished. Moreover, the Republican Party would now have to appeal to its opponents, who had usually called themselves Conservatives since 1865, not just to get them to approve and accept their party as legitimate but actually to win their votes.

To this end, the Republicans began to court former Confederates, or Conservatives, and offer them appointments. Some were prominent like the former governor, Joseph E. Brown, who was appointed chief justice of the Georgia Supreme Court. But hundreds of other lesser men were beneficiaries of Republican largesse. The consequences of this overture were particularly evident in Brown's Georgia. In an attempt to win Conservative favor and support, Republican legislators collaborated with the Conservatives in 1869 to expel their twenty-five black colleagues, on the grounds that they had been granted the vote but not the right to hold office. This effort to reduce the visibility and influence of blacks within the new party and, at the same time, to elevate well-known whites in an attempt to identify it as respectable, and therefore legitimate, was invidious. One of the expelled African Americans, Tunis Campbell, denounced the scheme of "seeking to make the Republican Party of Georgia *Respectable* by Puting White Men in office. That cry of puting men forward who can command the confidence of the People is all Bosh," he said. "I understand it all."[12]

The Republican administration in each state also hoped to gain credibility by establishing public hospitals, orphanages, and asylums, as well as statewide systems of public education for all children, black and white. But the Republicans pinned their greatest hopes for gaining legitimacy on the promotion of railroads. After the war, railroads were believed to be the key to southern economic revival. They were expected to stimulate economic development and usher in a new South. A North Carolinian told his state's Republican governor that "the party that first completes the Internal Improvement System of the state without regard to cost will hold the reins of power here for years to come."[13] Believing that the entrepreneurial and financial elite could be won over by policies to promote railroad projects and that countless other economic interests would be grateful beneficiaries of an expanded system of rail transportation, the Republicans rushed to enact these kinds of measures as a "win-win" proposition. Mississippi's Republican paper, the *Jackson Pilot*, was convinced that railroad legislation "will prove to the thinking people that the great Republican party is one of progress, of energy, of principles, founded upon good, sound common sense."[14]

Eagerly, the Republican legislatures passed general railway laws and then offered their support to individual companies, not through direct subsidies but by endorsing the bonds with which the promoters expected to raise the large amounts of capital needed to build railroads. The backing of the state's credit and reputation made the roads' bonds attractive to investors, and, in return, the state acquired a lien on these companies' assets. In their enthusiasm, the states granted their aid far too generously and indiscriminately. When most of the companies ran into financial difficulties a few years later, either because they overextended themselves or because they were simply mismanaged, the state governments were left holding the railroad companies' debts, as well as a whole lot of uncompleted railroad track. The impact on the party was devastating. Rather than proving their competence and their ability to bring prosperity to the region, this initiative damaged the Republicans' reputation irretrievably, while saddling the states with millions of dollars in debt. Even though the Conservatives had approved of state aid to railroads and many of their supporters had invested in them, they now took political advantage of the Republicans' embarrassment, flaying them relentlessly for their irresponsibility, their incompetence, and their squandering of the public credit and honor.

The collapse of the centerpiece of the Republicans' quest for respectability and legitimacy seemed to demonstrate what the opposition had claimed all along. A political party based on the votes of blacks, most of whom had just been released from slavery, was simply unfit to govern. It mattered little that some politically respectable whites affiliated with the party or that it made conciliatory gestures in its appointments and in its policies. The Republican Party was considered an intrinsically alien and illegitimate institution.

The opposition's contempt had been abundantly clear even earlier in its willingness to resort to violence in order to undermine and cripple the Republican usurpers. From the outset, the Conservatives employed violence as a political instrument. And they justified it, because they were not simply engaged in a partisan electoral contest with the Republicans but were overthrowing a regime imposed on the South from outside. The Republicans were not an indigenous southern organization but were viewed as occupiers, the political arm of a garrison in the South sustained since 1868 by 20,000 U.S. soldiers. The defeat of the Republicans was essential, but the real objective was something larger. It was the ending of Reconstruction, a program and a regime that had been imposed on the South. As Benjamin H. Hill, a former Confederate senator from Georgia, proclaimed in 1873, "The first thing to be done is to secure Home Government for Home Affairs."[15] Local control, not just an occasional electoral success, was the goal.

In the aftermath of emancipation, violence had been endemic in the plantation areas. Mostly it arose from anger and frustration on the part of owners against their former slaves because they no longer had control over them. Smarting over the humiliation of their military defeat, they were in a foul mood and lashed out at the freed slaves as they left the farms where they had previously lived and worked, in search of new homes and prospects. No more a master's valuable property, the former slaves were now at the mercy of the entire white population. The incidents of physical abuse were legion, as blacks were assaulted, mutilated, and murdered. Usually these assaults were the actions of individuals, but quite often whites ganged up to threaten or injure ex-slaves. The observation of one freedman that "Nigger's life cheap now" was frighteningly perceptive and accurate. The constant flow of reports to northern newspapers recounting incidents of violence against blacks had contributed significantly to the decision of the Republican-controlled Congress in December 1865 that the South was unrepentant and quite unready to be readmitted.

By 1868, when the new state governments headed by the Republican Party took office, organizations committed to violence existed throughout the region. Although usually referred to as the Ku Klux Klan, these armed groups were not part of a coordinated, centralized structure but functioned quite loosely, arising and operating independently in different places. But, as Eric Foner has observed, "the unity of purpose and common ties of these local organizations makes it possible to generalize about their goals and impact."[16] The Klan was an armed force whose purpose was to intimidate and commit violence against supporters and officials of the Republican Party, against black laborers on the plantations and farms, and against anyone, whether black or white, who challenged white supremacy. A state legislative committee in Tennessee charged with

"This Is a White Man's Government," *Harper's Weekly*, 5 September 1868. In this cartoon,
Thomas Nast captured the spirit of the Democratic Party as it tried to reclaim its prewar
position in national politics. Uniting around the dogma of "white supremacy" and opposition to Reconstruction, symbolized by the African American pinned to the ground, the
national Democrats consisted, in Nast's view, of three primary components. The central
element was the white South, depicted here brandishing a knife with "The Lost Cause"
written on it. To the right of the Confederate South were the financial and commercial
interests of the Northeast, New York especially, and, to the left, the immigrants, mainly
Irish, who provided the votes for the Democratic bosses and their political machines that
controlled the northern cities. Library of Congress, Prints and Photographs Division.

vestigating the Klan in 1868 reported that "there is an eternal hatred existing against all men that voted the Republican ticket, or who belong to the Loyal League [formed in the South to mobilize African Americans politically], or [are] engaged in teaching schools, and giving instruction to the humbler class of their fellow men."[17] Although no single branch or cell of the Klan operated within all three of these arenas of civic life, it is evident that its objective was the restoration of the political, economic, and social control previously enjoyed by whites. And it was Reconstruction, the federal government's policy, which had created a hostile and subversive regime, that was to blame for their loss of control.

Although these bodies of armed men, often consisting of demobilized Confederate foot soldiers and cavalrymen, had been active earlier, it was not until the 1868 presidential election that they played a significant role in electoral politics. Having lost control of their state governments during the summer of that year, they calculated that a Democratic victory in the national contest could bring an end to Reconstruction. Accordingly, the Klan instigated a campaign of violence intended to intimidate and, on occasion, kill Republican leaders, while creating a feeling of fear and helplessness among the party's voters. An Arkansas congressman, James M. Hinds, was murdered, as were three members of South Carolina's legislature and several others who had served in state constitutional conventions. In Georgia and Louisiana, the violence and intimidation were bloodcurdling. According to the congressional committee examining the Klan in 1870–71, over a thousand people were killed in Louisiana during the 1868 presidential election. In Caddo parish, in the northwest part of the state, which had been carried by a 2,987 Republican majority in the state election earlier in 1868, Ulysses S. Grant, the Republican candidate, received just one vote in November's presidential contest. In the village of Camilla, in southwest Georgia, 400 armed whites attacked a Republican meeting and then scoured the countryside in search of blacks, notching up more than a score of dead or wounded victims. And in eleven of the state's black-majority counties, not a single vote was cast for Grant, as a result of the reign of terror.[18] Predictably, General Grant carried neither state.

During the next few years, armed resistance broke out again, located primarily though not entirely in the foothills, or piedmont, in the upcountry of most states. In these areas, the proportion of blacks to whites was relatively equal, and, therefore, Klan pressure on a critical number of black voters or Republican officials could swing the state to the Conservatives. Besides threatening the party's electoral prospects, violence against

Republicans also challenged the party's authority and its ability to govern. A party that could not protect the citizenry, or even its own supporters, could not count on their loyalty and allegiance. As Dr. John Winsmith, one of the Klan's white victims in South Carolina, noted angrily, "I consider a government which does not protect its citizens a failure."[19] But protection was difficult to provide because it required the mobilization of the state militia, which was composed primarily, if not entirely in some states, of African Americans. A remedy of this kind was thought likely to provoke even further violence, leading perhaps to the race war that southern whites dreaded. So Republican governors were reluctant to act. Governors in the Lower South, like William H. Smith of Alabama and James L. Alcorn of Mississippi, were particularly stymied because they had little support among whites and their state militias consisted overwhelmingly of black troops.

Only in Arkansas and, to some extent, in Texas were Republican governors successful in putting down disorder, because both Powell Clayton and Edmund J. Davis moved quickly and forcefully against the Klan. Clayton, for example, managed to create a state militia composed of separate black and white regiments that then arrested scores of Klan suspects. In ten Arkansas counties martial law was declared, and, after a few months, the Klan had been virtually eliminated. In North Carolina, on the other hand, Governor William W. Holden had less success because he delayed too long before acting and then brought in white troops from outside the state. After suspending the local civil courts, he proceeded to arrest a number of Klansmen and put them on trial before a military commission. The Conservatives responded with outrage, accusing him of despotism by denying citizens their habeas corpus rights, a cynical cry that rallied the Conservatives to defeat the Republicans in the legislative election in 1870. Once in control of the assembly, they proceeded to impeach Holden and remove him from office. The violence threatened the Republicans' supporters with physical harm, but it also presented their party with an insoluble dilemma. Taking coercive action might undermine its efforts to be accepted, while it also revealed the party's seeming inability to govern by popular consent. At the same time, inaction exposed them to the charge that they were weak and could not govern at all.

The threat to Reconstruction posed by the Klan's campaign of violence and terror was formidable. The attacks undermined the Republican Party's ability to win votes and limited its ability to govern. In elections held in 1870, the Republicans lost in North Carolina, Georgia, and Alabama. In each case, the demoralizing and intimidating impact of violence played a crucial role. But even in South Carolina, where the Republicans managed to hold on, violence was rife, especially in a band of up-country counties where an armed white resistance had arisen, whipped up by a widespread fear that a predominantly black state militia was being formed. By September 1870, the state's chief constable, John B. Hubbard, reported to Governor Robert K. Scott that "a complete organization exists from the Savannah river to Chester, a distance of nearly two-hundred miles in length, and that its object is to intimidate Republican voters on Election day and if necessary murder leading Republicans."[20] A year later, a black Republican from South Carolina told the congressional committee investigating the Klan that the party in the up-country was "scattered and beaten and run out." In Union County, the situation was dire, he reported, because "they have no leaders up there—no leaders."[21] The Klan had done its work.

Alarmed that its vital and hard-won initiative to reconstruct the South was in danger of collapse, Congress took action in 1870–71. Three measures were passed, giving the federal government power to protect citizens' right to vote, to appoint federal officials to supervise elections, and to criminalize conspiracies like the Ku Klux Klan that aimed to deprive people of their political rights. The Democrats and many Republicans had opposed these measures as an excessive expansion of federal authority, but Amos T. Akerman, the new attorney general and a Republican from Georgia, was convinced that "extraordinary means" were needed to suppress the armed insurgency. "These combinations amount to war and cannot be effectively crushed on any other theory."[22] So Akerman embarked on an offensive in the South, instructing federal legal officers in North Carolina and Mississippi to arrest Klansmen and bring them to trial. In South Carolina, habeas corpus was suspended in the up-country and hundreds of suspects were rounded up by federal troops. The ensuing trials during the winter of 1871–72, especially some dramatic courtroom confrontations in Columbia, focused public attention on Klan violence. But, in the end, few of the perpetrators were convicted and sentenced to jail terms, while thousands of them fled the state to avoid arrest.[23] Nevertheless, the national offensive against the Klan insurgency did contribute significantly to its cessation of operations in 1872. Political violence in the Reconstruction South had not been eliminated, however. For it reappeared, a year or so later, in a different but virulent and shamelessly overt form.

Regime Change in the Reconstruction South

The Klan's activities had inflicted political damage on the Republican Party at a critical moment when it was first becoming organized and gaining control over the South's state governments. In North Carolina, Alabama, Georgia, and South Carolina, Klan intimidation and terrorism had been particularly effective in weakening and destabilizing the party. But, with the exception of Georgia, where the Republicans never regained power after 1870, the party was able to rebound and regain these governorships at the next election. South Carolina's black constituency was large enough to be able to maintain the party's control over both the legislative and the executive branches, despite the violence and lawlessness created by the Klansmen. The Klan insurrection did not actually topple Republican administrations, but it weakened them and exposed the limits of their ability to protect their supporters. Their credibility as viable governments was challenged frontally. And, without credibility, legitimacy is hard to obtain from a skeptical and insecure electorate.

Although the Klan was not solely responsible, the Republicans had lost control of several states by 1873. In 1870, Tennessee and Virginia, along with Georgia, had fallen to the opposition, which was beginning to identify itself as Democrat, not Conservative. And they would be joined by Texas in 1873 and Arkansas early in 1874. Meanwhile, Alabama and North Carolina teetered on the verge of a Democratic resumption of power until 1874. In most of these states, white voters were in the majority and therefore the Republicans needed to win over a large number of them to be able to survive at the polls. But whenever a serious split developed within Republican ranks, as happened in Virginia, Tennessee, and Arkansas, the chances of the Republicans holding onto power were further diminished. Provoking and then exploiting divisions among the Republicans was a frequent maneuver of the opponents of Reconstruction. Because they never conceded legitimacy to the Republican Party, the Democrats constantly cajoled and bribed its members in order to foment dissension, in the hope that they could pry loose a faction and induce it to bolt from the Republicans and ally with the Democrats. These cynical schemes were often successful in building coalitions of bolting Republicans and Democrats, which were then able to defeat the regular Republicans on election day.

The Republicans' difficulties mounted after the collapse of their railroad promotions and the rising state indebtedness that ensued. Their troubles were compounded by opposition from white taxpayers, who, with encouragement from the Democratic Party, protested the costs of providing the public schools and other public services introduced by the Republicans. By the mid-1870s, the new Republican administrations were under assault, less from destructive violence this time but from the setbacks to their own policy initiatives and the opposition they provoked among disgruntled voters.

The southern Republicans' mounting problems and their waning electoral prospects were aggravated by developments outside the South. The financial panic that hit the stock market in 1873 produced an economic downturn that soon worsened into a depression, which continued for the rest of the decade. Since the Republicans were in power nationally, they were punished for the depression in the congressional elections of 1874. As a result, the Democrats eliminated the Republicans' 110-seat majority in the House and also won many governorships in the North as well as in Texas, Arkansas, and even Alabama in the South. In the wake of the panic, concerns about the national currency and about labor discontent and agitation preoccupied the national government, leaving Reconstruction very much a matter of secondary concern.

With the nation's attention turned elsewhere and with the Republicans' hold on the southern states slipping away, the opponents of Reconstruction vowed to deliver the coup de grâce to Republican rule—and therefore to Reconstruction itself. By early 1874, Republicans retained power in just five states—Mississippi, Louisiana, Alabama, Florida, and South Carolina, all of them in the Lower South. In these states, with their black electoral majorities or near majorities, state campaigns based on race were an invitation to disaster, and so the Conservatives had never considered them seriously. As the *Charleston Daily News* had warned as late as 1873, "Any policy which contemplates the arraying of whites against blacks at the polls, must fail, and will deserve to fail. Fortunately, there is little likelihood that so wild a project will be seriously submitted to the public."[24] But the danger of identifying the parties along racial lines seemed a risk worth taking, now that the Republicans were on the run. A race-based election campaign could succeed, if it aroused white voters and drew them to the polls in vastly increased numbers or if blacks could be dissuaded from voting by the threat of violence or the actual experience of it. Could not a campaign to restore white supremacy and demonstrate white power increase white turnout as well as discourage black voting? Race was, after all, the essential difference between the two Reconstruction parties, and so elections that focused on the racial identity of each party would openly acknowledge what had, until then, been generally understood but downplayed.

A race-based campaign had already proven viable in the Democrats' gubernatorial election of 1873 in Virginia. A leading figure in General James L. Kemper's successful "white line" campaign, Nathaniel B. Meade, explained the strategy: "To save the state, we must make the issue *White and Black*[,] race against race and the canvass red hot."[25] Policy differences between the parties were irrelevant. The objective was to differentiate the parties on racial grounds only, so that "white supremacy" or "Negro rule" were the clear alternatives. Faced with this choice, every voter would vote according to what he saw in the mirror on the morning of election day. To sharpen the contrast between the two parties, Virginia's Conservatives no longer disguised their essential identity or expressed a desire to appeal to independents or former Whigs. They now referred to themselves as Democrats, and they ran a "straight-out" Democratic campaign, with race as the defining issue. The mask was off and the color line was drawn.

The campaigns between 1874 and 1876 in the Lower South states still under Republican control were quite possibly the ugliest in American history. But this display of racial violence did not signify a reemergence of the Klan, which had pretty much disbanded in 1872. The renewed violence of the mid-1870s was very different in form and purpose. Even though units of Confederate veterans participated again, along with countless angry white men, their activities were organized for purely political purposes—to intimidate and overawe black voters so that they would not turn out to vote for the Republicans. These displays of force were carried out openly, in broad daylight, whereas the Klansmen wore hoods and operated under cover of darkness. Most significant of all, their activities were encouraged and coordinated by officials of the Democratic Party, or at least in conjunction with them, and always at the highest level.

This systematic mobilization of violence was intended to demoralize black voters and fatally undermine the Republican Party. At an early stage in the Democrats' "white line" campaign in Alabama in 1874, the party's state chairman, Walter L. Bragg, reported that the plan seemed to be working well. "The spirit of our people is roused to the highest pitch that will admit of control—the negroes sink down before it as if stricken with awe—and the white men who have been using the negroes [that is, the Republican leaders] show by their conduct that they feel that 'Othello's occupation is gone.'"[26]

Although the campaign in Alabama was not as relentlessly systematic as in three other Deep South states, the pattern was similar. Paramilitary units or organized bands were formed at the instigation of the Democratic Party. Calling themselves Red Shirts in South Carolina, Rifle Clubs in Mississippi, and the White League in Louisiana, they spread fear and terror among the Republicans, especially among blacks. They paraded at regular intervals through the African American sections of the small towns in the rural, black-majority areas, intimidating the residents and inciting racial confrontations. During the election campaign itself, whites would provoke a public racial incident, and, after the brawl or riot that ensued, white men would scour the nearby countryside in search of blacks to beat up and kill. In Eutaw, Alabama, in 1874, in Clinton, Mississippi, in 1875, and in Hamburg and Ellenton, South Carolina, in 1876, riots of this kind broke out, resulting in the deaths of dozens of blacks. Throughout the election campaigns, when Republican meetings or joint appearances with Democratic candidates were held, detachments of Confederates on horseback, dressed in their ghostly gray uniforms, appeared and arrayed themselves behind the platform, clicking the triggers on their rifles. Finally, on election day, whites, often armed, swarmed around polling stations, intimidating Republican voters and sometimes seizing the party's ballot boxes. In Mississippi, Governor Adelbert Ames, a transplanted New Englander and former Union general, declared bitterly on election day in 1875 that "the reports which come to me almost hourly are truly sickening."[27]

In Louisiana, the assault on the Republican Party and its black supporters was of a different order of magnitude. Beginning in 1873, the Democratic Party initiated a paramilitary campaign to undermine the Republicans at the local level, within the parishes they controlled. Launching what was essentially an insurrection at the grass roots, members of the state's White League attacked parish government buildings and assaulted Republican officials over the course of the next two years. The massacre in cold blood of more than a hundred African American men, women, and children at the Grant Parish courthouse in Colfax, where they had fled for sanctuary in the face of marauding armed whites, was the worst of the violent confrontations that resulted from this campaign. The loss of life at Colfax in April 1873 was probably greater than in any other racial incident in American history. But it was followed a year later by another frightful incident at Coushatta in Red River Parish, where a group of leading Republican officials was seized by a mob and murdered, in effect destroying the party by eliminating its leadership. And, finally, a month after Coushatta, thousands of men from the White League took control of the city hall in New Orleans and were repelled only after federal troops were sent in and fought them on Canal Street in the so-called Battle of Liberty Place. As a result of this two-year campaign by armed bands, encouraged by the Democratic Party, the Republican Party in Louisiana was effectively demolished. The election of 1876 simply confirmed what the Democrats had already achieved by means of targeted assassinations and overwhelming violence.

The dismantling of the last remaining outposts of Republican control by systematic political violence prompts three observations about the abnormal politics of the Reconstruction South. First, the attempt to intimidate blacks into not voting did not really succeed. Amazingly, Republicans continued to vote and refused to be cowed. The Republican total in Mississippi was only slightly less in 1875 than it had been in 1873, while half of the state's counties increased their vote for the Republicans. In South Carolina and Alabama, the statewide Republican vote actually grew by a few thousand during the decisive "white line" campaigns. But the Democrats' victories were attributable mainly to the dramatic expansion of the total Democratic vote. In Alabama, for example, the Democratic vote increased by 26,000, and in South Carolina it grew by about 15,000. Although the Republican vote in some black counties dropped precipitously, African Americans in each state turned out in numbers that demonstrated their courage and their determination to vote, despite the enormous personal risk. Although the violence failed to intimidate blacks into wholesale withdrawal from the polls, the prospect of victory generated by their party's use of violence gave the whites a thrill sufficiently exhilarating to drive them to the polls.

The second observation is that the violence in these campaigns was intended to ensure Democratic success in the upcoming elections rather than to prevent the elections from taking place altogether. Lawless and utterly undemocratic means were employed to secure the desired outcome, which was to win a lawful, democratic election. The architects of the Mississippi Plan in 1875 instructed the Rifle Clubs to "carry the election peaceably if we can, forcibly if we must." Evidently, the Democrats' intention was to deploy violent and illegal methods in order to win, but not at the expense of the legitimacy of an election. Rather than overthrow the entire process, they wanted to seize power violently but within the accepted electoral procedures.

The implications of the third, and final, observation reach beyond the Deep South campaigns and into the nature of the Reconstruction political system itself. The Republican Party was so stigmatized that any means were deemed acceptable to defeat it. Admittedly, the most drastic method was rejected—the exclusive use of violence without even the inconvenience of an election. All the same, the Republican Party was, from the outset, an alien presence in the South as far as the Democrats were concerned. It was composed of "carpetbagger" and "scalawag" whites and recently freed blacks; it was grounded in the unnatural suffrage of inferior Africans; and it had been imposed on the South by political interests from outside that were solely responsible for its existence and that then sustained it. Alien, unnatural, and imposed, the Republicans' presence in the South was impugned by the opponents of Reconstruction as illegitimate. Competing with such a party in electoral contests as if the situation were normal was therefore unimaginable for most of those in the anti-Reconstruction party. Since their rival was illegitimate and its right to hold office and assume power had been rejected from the outset, the political system itself was under siege.

The Republican Party was, after all, the raison d'être of the political system established in the South by Congress's Reconstruction laws. Therefore, its ejection from power did not mean that the Democrats had simply won an election and would stay in office until the next one. No, the Republicans had been driven out. Their defeat meant that they would not return to compete in the next election. For Reconstruction itself, not just the Republican Party, had been overthrown. The Democratic takeover, which the Democrats themselves often referred to as "redemption," has to be understood as more than the postelection transfer of governmental power from one party to another. It was a regime change.

6

Achieving Democratic Hegemony

THE 1880S

Because its potential was thwarted, Reconstruction has recently been described as "an unfinished revolution." But the Democrats' offensive that ended Reconstruction in the mid-1870s and "redeemed" the South could be considered "an unfinished counterrevolution." The Democrats succeeded in overthrowing the Reconstruction governments controlled by the Republicans, but they did not destroy the infrastructure that created and supported those governments. The Republican Party, and the African American voters who provided its electoral base, still remained. Ejected from power, the Republicans continued nevertheless to function as an electoral force within the political system. But, as far as the Democrats were concerned, the Republicans were still alien and unnatural, essentially "unsouthern."

When the Democrats returned to power in 1877, they could have completed the counterrevolution by moving decisively to repeal the state laws and constitutional provisions that guaranteed the civil and political rights of African Americans. Many black leaders feared that this was exactly what they would do. Instead, General Wade Hampton, who had just been elected governor of South Carolina in the violent "Red Shirt" campaign of 1876, exemplified the cynical course taken by most of the region's Democrats when he reassured his state's black citizens that "we propose to protect you and give you all your rights."[1]

Having regained political control, the Democrats decided not to jeopardize their recent success by stripping African Americans of their protected rights and thereby risk renewed federal intervention in southern affairs. Besides, the Democrats needed repose after the agitation of the "white line" campaigns. No doubt they also anticipated that, as landlords and employers who had been restored to control of southern government, the region's traditional rulers could persuade, or even coerce, African American voters. So black southerners continued to vote.

But they did not vote as the Democrats hoped they would. Although paternalistic whites might delude themselves, it made no sense for blacks to support the party of white supremacy. As long as the Democrats identified themselves as the white man's party, blacks were compelled to vote for their Republican opponents. Since drawing the "white line" had been essential to overthrowing Reconstruction, southern political parties would continue to be organized along racial lines. The Democrats disparaged the opposition party as unsouthern and illegitimate and regarded the voters who were its predominant source of support as unworthy and unthinking. As the Democrats resorted increasingly to fraud and manipulation in order to subvert or destroy black men's votes, the normal rules of party competition seemed irrelevant. An illegitimate opposition and its captive, unqualified supporters could be taken care of, fittingly and appropriately, by methods that were illegal.

This fundamental reality shaped southern politics in the 1880s and 1890s. Only one party was deemed legitimate, so the Democrats' hold on power had to be maintained at all costs. The Republican Party and any other parties that might arise were to be treated as threats to the South and its white population. Because all whites were to be herded together into "the white man's party," the Democrats had managed to design what C. Vann Woodward has called "a Procrustean one-party system." Regardless of whether they were too long or too short, the mythological giant, Procrustes, had forced his victims to fit into his bed by either stretching them or lopping off their limbs. Similarly, all whites, whatever their class or occupation, were to be forced into the Democrats' white supremacist bed. With only one legitimate party, and with that one party defined by its racial composition and identity, southern politics remained abnormal and distorted. Under these conditions, the political system was extremely unstable—even volatile.

Some historians have speculated that a more rational and normal politics was attainable. The quarter century after Reconstruction, they suggest, was a period of flux, a time of transition, a moment when alternatives were possible. If these possibilities had been seized the South might have moved toward a politics organized around questions other than race. What happened instead was that economic or social and cultural issues were subordinated to racial identity, because the Democrats clung to race as their mainstay and would not let go. For them, the aftermath of

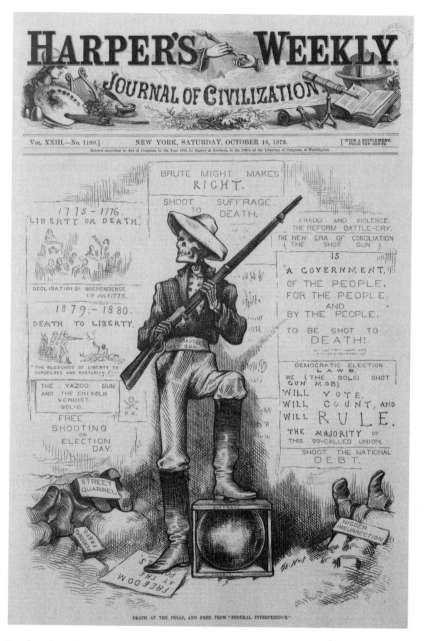

"Death at the Polls, and Free from 'Federal Interference,'" *Harper's Weekly*, 18 October 1879. Another of Thomas Nast's hard-hitting cartoons demonizing the white South, this one represents the Democratic Party as a skeletal Confederate soldier who is armed with what his belt describes as a "Solid Southern Shot Gun." He is making sure that no black voter gets to cast a vote for the Republicans. On the wall behind the grim soldier are posters proclaiming, "Brute Might Makes Right," "Shoot Suffrage to Death," "1775–1776, Liberty or Death," "1879–1880, Death to Liberty," and others with similarly threatening slogans. Library of Congress, Prints and Photographs Division.

Reconstruction was not a period of possible change but a time of danger. The dangerous instability that resulted from the overthrow of the Republican governments had to be countered and brought under control. To paraphrase the injunction issued by the leaders of the Mississippi Plan in 1875, the Democrats would keep control, legally if they could, fraudulently if they must!

The Southern Democrats in Power

The political world that the resurgent Democrats dominated seemed to be straightforward and obvious. Their own party had delivered the South, or "redeemed" it, as they preferred to say, from Reconstruction and "Radical Rule." Their opponent was the party of northern-imposed Reconstruction and of black people. What could be more simple? Yet the politics of the late-nineteenth-century South was convoluted and utterly perplexing—so baffling and confusing that voters' heads began to spin. In Vann Woodward's view, "The average Southerner retreated into some form of political nihilism," and "The region lapsed into a period of political torpor more stultifying, perhaps, than any in its long history."[2]

With their return to power in the mid-1870s, the Democrats began immediately to impose their own priorities and principles on southern state governments. They enacted a battery of laws giving landlords almost total control over the crops produced and rents paid by their tenants and sharecroppers. Then they rewrote the region's state constitutions so as to minimize the powers of government, prohibit state aid for railroads and other development projects, and reduce drastically the allowable rate of taxation. Finally, they scaled down, or repudiated, the debts incurred by their states during Reconstruction. After putting state government in a straitjacket, the Democrats presided over administrations whose policies were, by any standard, lean and mean. Retrenchment was their watchword, and it meant inactive, low-cost government, providing few public services and raising negligible amounts of revenue through taxation. In the words of George F. Drew, Florida's governor in the late 1880s, the maxim of these Democratic administrations was: "Spend nothing unless absolutely necessary."[3]

Rather than regretting their inability to provide social services and economic development, the Democrats considered it an achievement. The party's leaders embarked on a crusade against the extravagance of their Republican predecessors, eagerly pursuing policies that reduced the responsibilities and costs of government severely. Low-cost government hurt the disadvantaged most, however, as expenditures on public schools dried up, public health and social services went unfunded, and state institutions such as hospitals, asylums, and prisons languished. While the common folk and the needy were ignored, the tax structure was manipulated to benefit railroads, utilities, and manufacturers, through favorable assessments of their taxable property or exemptions from taxation, or both. Despite their claim to protect all taxpayers by reducing expenditures and tax rates, the Democrats were actually favoring one economic group at the expense of the rest. These Democratic governments let down the majority of taxpayers yet again when, in the early 1880s, almost every southern state discovered that its often long-serving treasurers had been embezzling public funds for years. The amounts may not have been large but, as a proportion of the states' paltry budgets, they were considerable. So much for the Democrats' boast that, unlike the Republicans, they were purveyors of good, clean, honest government.[4]

The Democrats' partiality for minimal government was not just ideological; it was pragmatic too. The Democratic Party was a broad coalition of discordant interests and factions, which unless carefully managed would compete with each other for influence and threaten the party's fragile unity. Opposition to Reconstruction had brought them all into the same party. But now, with virtually all the region's whites joined together in that one party, the differences between them would come to the surface and threaten its unity. The basic cleavages were between town and country and between New South industrializers and the more traditional planters of the black belts. But divisions also existed between up-country farmers in the white-majority counties and large planters in counties with sizable black majorities, between those who would honor the state's debt and those who would repudiate it, and between hard-money contractionists and soft-money inflationists—not to mention differences over such issues as fence laws, interest rates, railroad freight rates, and funding public schools.

These numerous sources of potential conflict were certain to be stirred up by policies that actively promoted particular interests or programs. By taking few initiatives and spending little money, the Democrats lessened the risk that rivalries would emerge. Inaction and inertia were safe. As a party newspaper in North Carolina observed in the run-up to an election, "It would be hazardous for the Democratic party to raise any new issue that might divide the whites."[5] Heeding this warning, the Democrats identified their party with retrenchment to please taxpayers; with minimal government to appeal to traditional Democrats; and, of course, with white supremacy, on which all real southerners could agree.

This three-pronged strategy of low taxes, inactive government, and white supremacy proved an effective formula for keeping the party in office. Even so, the Democrats had their work cut out to keep dissent under control and prevent blocs and factions within their own ranks from being lured away to join a new party. Too many major issues and problems confronted the South in the late nineteenth century. And they would not go away, especially when the party in power refused to respond to them. The region's desperate lack of currency led to cries for inflation and paper money, leading to the emergence of the Greenback Party in the late 1870s and early 1880s. A decade later, widespread discontent among farmers produced the People's Party. By suppressing dissent and rivalry within their own party, the Democrats created the conditions under which rival parties emerged to deal with these fundamental issues. And one of them, the People's Party, would eventually present a challenge to the Democrats far more dangerous than any internal disputes might have become.

While new parties arose intermittently to challenge the Democrats, the Republicans maintained an ongoing presence in the post-Reconstruction South. In two Upper South states, Tennessee and North Carolina, they posed a constant threat to the Democrats, establishing a base among white farmers in the mountain and Piedmont areas, most of whom had been Unionists during the Civil War. In the Lower South, Republican strength was located in the plantation districts where African Americans were numerous. Even so, Republicanism was weak in Mississippi and Georgia and almost nonexistent in South Carolina. The reason was simple. The Democrats had developed an array of tactics for reducing the Republican vote during Reconstruction, and they continued to hone these techniques thereafter. They used violence and intimidation less frequently, concentrating their attention instead on electoral laws and the ballot box itself.

The Democrats employed a variety of devices to diminish the Republican vote. One tactic was to redraw electoral districts so as to disperse black votes throughout white-majority districts and consolidate the remaining black vote into one, perhaps two, congressional seats. Through similar gerrymandering schemes, they also diluted the black vote for the state legislature. Other legislation guaranteed Democrats a majority on the county boards that supervised elections, enabling them to control the polling places. As a result, election judges could mislead and frustrate Republican voters. Since these judges also oversaw the ballot boxes, they seized the opportunity to destroy or lose boxes or else stuff them with ballots marked for Democratic candidates. As a Virginia Democrat, William L. Royall, admitted, his party had passed the Anderson-McCormick Act in 1884 "so that the officers of election, if so inclined, could stuff the ballot boxes and . . . make any returns that were desired."[6] The Democrats also enacted state laws that made registration more complicated by, for example, setting early deadlines well before the election was to take place and adding arcane requirements for marking the ballot. Some states passed laws requiring multiple ballot boxes so as to confuse the voter about where his ballot was supposed to be deposited. South Carolina's eight-box law of 1881 was so effective that it reduced the Republican vote by two-thirds.[7] Aimed at the Democrats' opponents, who were usually Republicans but could be third parties, these election regulations were targeted specifically at African American voters, who were generally poor and/or illiterate.

Besides confusing their opponents' voters, the Democrats constantly meddled and interfered with the Republican Party's leaders and officials. Since white Democrats would be outpolled in every election in the plantation areas where black voters were in the majority, Democrats could only win if they managed to reduce the black vote by means of these kinds of electoral devices and schemes. But that was often not enough. They supplemented it with another tactic from Reconstruction days—fusion. Arrangements would be made with Republicans to back Democratic candidates in exchange for some lesser offices for blacks. Through agreements to fuse their tickets in this way, the Republican majority was tamed, whites gained control of the significant offices, and blacks were left with a modicum of patronage, but little else. Fusion often occurred at the state level too. Democrats in Congress would direct federal patronage to black Republicans in their state in exchange for agreement to support state or local Democratic candidates. Fusion kept Republican leadership out of the hands of whites in the party and appeared to empower blacks. As a leading white Republican in Mississippi complained, the Democrats "keep up negro rule in the Rep party, in order that fear of negro rule in the state may keep white men in the Dem party."[8]

Fusion was a convoluted and devious strategy. Democrats were negotiating with black Republicans and running them for office so that they could manage the voters in black-majority counties. At the same time, white Democratic voters denounced Republicans because they encouraged black voting and officeholding. The hypocrisy sometimes infuriated Democrats. "If Democrats do what they have persistently abused and condemned Republicans for doing, how can they hope to escape just censure?" demanded angry Democrats in the North Carolina house in the 1876–77 session after their party had just voted to install a group of black county magistrates. This deviousness was "inconsistent with the principles and purposes of the party."[9]

Completely contradictory behavior like this was but one aspect of a dilemma the Democrats had created for themselves. Unwilling to treat the Republican Party and its hundreds of thousands of black supporters as a legitimate element in the political system, the Democrats resorted to manipulating it in their own interest. They reduced the black vote and restricted its free operation, while also using black votes to pad Democratic totals. And they manipulated the Republican Party to ensure their own control in black counties, all the while demonizing that very same party as a threat to white supremacy, and therefore to Democratic hegemony.

In effect, the Democrats needed the Republican Party to keep their own voters in line by inducing a fear of black assertiveness. Without opposition, it would be hard to keep the Democratic Party from breaking up. Yet they could not allow the Republicans to become too strong because they might then win elections. Thoroughly baffling to their supporters, the Democrats also proved endlessly frustrating to their opponents. Had they decided to compete with the Republicans in the normal electoral process, the Democrats would have had to recognize the legitimacy of black voting and of the Republican Party, thereby running the risk of losing. But that possibility was unthinkable because "Negro domination" was too awful to contemplate. Far better to talk endlessly about it and use the threat of it as a partisan weapon.

The Democrats' plan for keeping the Republicans viable but ineffective ran into still further complications. First, white politicians in the Republican Party attempted, during the 1880s, to make their organization "respectable" by broadening its appeal to white voters. As a result, two factions emerged, the "Lily Whites" and the "Black and Tans." As these factions struggled for position and patronage, southern Republicanism was kept agitated and weakened. The Lily Whites argued that the party should disassociate itself from Reconstruction and blacks and should instead take clear positions on economic questions like the protective tariff and the currency shortage. Since the prospect of a redirected and revitalized Republican Party was alarming to the Democrats, more meddling in Republican Party affairs was required. They kept the factional and racial conflict among Republicans virulent by aiding and encouraging the Black and Tan faction, which favored keeping the party biracial by not ignoring its black base.

Another difficulty for the Democrats was that the continued viability of southern Republicanism meant continued northern involvement in the region's politics. In the 1880s and beyond, federal patronage in the South was channeled through the state Republican parties, sustaining them and providing inducements for many politicians to work with them. In states where the party was weak, it became "little more than a brokerage firm for federal patronage."[10] The national Republican Party tried to build up its outposts in the southern states, using strategies that varied from time to time according to circumstances in the South itself and depending on which Republican was president. As part of his policy of withdrawing U.S. troops from the South in 1877, President Rutherford B. Hayes had tried to create a new alternative to the ascendant southern Democrats by forming an alliance with former Whigs and businessmen. He hoped that eventually this group would abandon the planter-dominated and traditionalist Democratic Party and become the core of a modernizing and industrializing party in the South, affiliated with the Republicans and opposed to the Democrats.

When this improbable scenario failed to materialize, Hayes's successors, James A. Garfield and Chester A. Arthur, attempted to revive the existing Republican organizations in the South by supporting independent parties that were springing up in the region. No matter what these bolters stood for, they received patronage and presidential encouragement and were urged to collaborate with the local Republicans. President Arthur explained his strategy in 1881, soon after he had assumed the presidency upon Garfield's assassination. "I have made up my mind that a permanently defeated Republican party is of little value [in the South]," he announced, "and that if any respectable body of men wages war on the Bourbon Democracy, with reasonable prospects of success, it should be sustained."[11]

On occasion, breakaway factions did form coalitions with the Republicans. But these incompatible combinations were not much of a threat because they required financially conservative and fiscally respectable Republicans to collaborate with disloyal, bolting Democrats. Usually, these bolters were either Greenbackers who advocated inflation and an increase in the money supply or they were opponents of their state's oppressive debt who wanted to repudiate or readjust it. These former Democrats were also quite likely to be white supremacists who felt uncomfortable aligning themselves with the southern Republicans and their black supporters. Unable to reach agreement on substantive issues, bolting independents and their Republican allies were invariably reduced to campaigning together on purely pragmatic terms, either simply as anti-Democrats or as proponents of election reform whose demand for "a free ballot and a fair count" was a rallying cry but not a policy. Predictably, these discordant coalitions, little more than marriages of convenience, failed to arouse voter interest and fell prey to Democratic skulduggery. And so they rarely lasted beyond a single election.

The Challenge of the Virginia Readjusters

The Democrats encountered serious opposition on two occasions before the end of the century. The first occurred in the late 1870s and early 1880s, and the second occurred exactly a decade later. Both revealed the degree of discontent among ordinary southerners as the Democrats pulled the region in a conservative direction supportive of the economic and social status quo.

The first surge of opposition arose in the late 1870s when the national Greenback-Labor Party made inroads into the southern electorate. The party arose from the widespread anger over the shortage of available currency and the resulting financial stringency, its high interest rates and low wages. Forming alliances with the Republicans enabled the Greenbackers to create and lead a broad-ranging anti-Democratic front in state elections, beginning in 1878. These campaigns fared especially well in Alabama, Arkansas, and Texas in 1880. They continued to be an electoral force, drawing between 30 and 40 percent of the vote during the next two or three years.

In Tennessee and Virginia, the opposition was more powerful. The pivotal issue in both states was not monetary reform but reduction of the state debt. After their return to power during the 1870s, the Democrats in most southern states scaled down or repudiated the debt incurred by the Republican governments during Reconstruction. But in some states, particularly Tennessee and Virginia, a formidable conservative faction refused to risk harming the state's fiscal reputation by failing to honor its financial obligations. In Tennessee, the fight over the debt split the Democrats into two strident and combative camps, the State Credit and the Low Tax factions. They made the disastrous mistake of running separate tickets in 1880, allowing the Republicans to win the state. For the next decade or so, the Republicans, with their solid base among white farmers and wartime Unionists in East Tennessee, remained competitive in state elections.

A more spectacular upset occurred in Virginia because the dispute led to the formation of a new party that went on to win control of the state,

William Mahone. Although it might be hard to imagine from his dress and demeanor in this photograph, Mahone had been both a tough Confederate general and a successful railroad entrepreneur before he joined the Readjuster Party in the 1870s. Clearly the most prominent Readjuster, he was elected to the U.S. Senate in 1879. This undated photograph was probably taken in the mid-1870s, when he became involved in Readjuster politics. Library of Virginia.

obtaining a majority of the legislature in 1879 and the governorship from 1881 to 1883. The Readjuster movement came into existence in the mid-1870s when Virginia was mired in a deep crisis. In 1871, the Democratic-controlled assembly, in collaboration with an overly sympathetic Republican governor, Gilbert Walker, had committed the state to funding its huge prewar debt in 6 percent bonds that could be used to pay taxes. Once taxes were paid with these bonds, or coupons, cash receipts plummeted, resulting in enormous budget deficits. The party leadership insisted that the state's credit had to be upheld at all costs. In 1877, the governor, James L. Kemper, a celebrated Confederate general, asserted unequivocally that "no Commonwealth can flourish while its credit is in a state of prostration or dishonor."[12]

Rather than scaling down the state's massive and increasingly valueless debt, the Funders, as Kemper's faction of the party called itself, insisted that paying off its creditors in full was the primary obligation of the state, to which all its other responsibilities had to be subordinated.

As a result, social services were slashed. Dissatisfaction turned to anger when the Funders decided to divert the school fund and close about half of the public schools by the 1878–79 academic year in order to pay off the debt. Discontent was further inflamed because the Funders had already made payment of the school tax a prerequisite for voting.

The Funders' program provoked a widespread revolt whose origins lay in the southwestern and Shenandoah Valley regions of the state where white farmers were its main supporters and also in the Southside and Tidewater where black tenants and small farmers were numerous. But the Readjusters' support was not entirely rural, since laborers in the cities as well as merchants and well-to-do urban dwellers were also alarmed at the extremely restrictive fiscal priorities of the Funders.

The independent Readjuster Party that resulted was led by a number of experienced politicians and lively campaign orators. But none was more vital to the party's growth and success than William Mahone. Weighing less than a hundred pounds and sporting a full beard that extended down to his chest, Mahone had been a major general and one of Lee's most trusted divisional commanders in the Army of Northern Virginia. After the defeat of the Confederacy, he became the leading railroad owner and developer in Virginia. He created a consolidated network of Virginia railroads, fanning out from Norfolk and capable of preventing railroads based in the North, chiefly the Baltimore and Ohio, from getting control of the state's railroad system. He had achieved his objectives by cultivating extensive political connections within the Democratic Party and among the various independent factions and parties that had existed briefly during the decade of Reconstruction.

When his railroad system went bankrupt in the wake of the 1873 panic and the ensuing depression, Mahone got involved with the movement to end the state's bankruptcy by readjusting the debt and saving the schools. "This twaddle about the honor of the state . . . is sheer nonsense," he once remarked, when compared to the "robery of the school fund."[13] He played the leading role in forming the Readjuster Party, and when the party won control of the state legislature in 1879 he was elected to the U.S. Senate. As shrewd a politician as he had been a builder of railroad systems, he seized the main chance in Washington when he decided to break the partisan tie in the Senate by siding with the thirty-nine Republicans, thereby giving them control. In return, Mahone and the Readjusters were awarded the federal patronage in Virginia, a gift from the incoming Garfield administration, which was backing them against the Democrats.

In possession of 2,000 federal positions and President Garfield's endorsement, the Readjusters entered the 1881 state elections with great confidence, after increasing their support substantially since 1879 by forming an alliance with the Republicans, especially their African American voters. With thirteen black Republicans giving the Readjusters control of the legislature in 1879 and with African Americans providing the major component of the Readjuster vote (they made up 40 percent of Virginia's electorate), the party included policies of concern to blacks in its platform and promised them influence and offices once elected.

Although readjustment of the debt was still the primary objective, the Readjusters' 1881 campaign stressed other issues as well. The party committed itself to securing equal suffrage and equality before the law, while Mahone himself pledged that "a free and priceless ballot" was of central importance. The complaints from blacks about the reintroduction of the whipping post to punish petty larceny were to be satisfied by its abolition. The public schools were to be maintained and given adequate public funding, while payment of the school tax was no longer to be a prerequisite for voting. Taxation was to be levied fairly, which meant that the minimal taxes of railroads and other corporations were to be raised and the tax rate for farmers was to be reduced. To appeal to urban workers, the party promised a mechanics' lien law, protecting workers from their creditors, and also advocated a federal protective tariff to aid manufacturing in the South. To their credit, the Readjusters implemented almost all of these campaign promises after they won control of the governorship and the assembly in 1881, while they also passed the Riddleburger Act of 1882, which readjusted the state debt.

In his inaugural address, William E. Cameron, the Readjuster governor, announced proudly that Virginia "furnishes a grave upon her soil for the vexed question of [the] color line in politics." To this end, "the laws of Virginia guarantee equal protection and privilege to every citizen [and] all departments of the government shall execute the spirit and letter of these laws."[14] On this controversial question of black rights and representation, the Readjusters' record was also impressive. African Americans were appointed in considerable numbers to public positions at the federal and state levels. Other blacks secured offices that were elective by running successfully as Readjusters at the state and local levels.

In many municipalities, Readjusters won the mayor's office and the city council, as happened in Petersburg, the state's largest black-majority city and the hometown of both Mahone and Cameron. Once they were in control of Petersburg, the Readjusters enacted a series of reform ordinances and then moved forcefully to rectify the school system's failure thus far to appoint a single black teacher. Although blacks did not advocate mixed schools, attended by both black and white students, they did insist on the appointment of "colored teachers for colored schools." In response, one-fourth of the city's white teachers were dismissed, and their places were taken by blacks. Other municipalities where the Readjusters were already in power followed suit, and the number of African American teachers and principals in the state tripled between 1879 and 1883. Meanwhile, the state assembly passed legislation requiring equal pay for teachers of both races.[15]

The Funders were determined to reverse these dangerous developments and defeat the Readjusters before they became established and powerful. Unfortunately, the Readjusters provided them with the one issue that was sure to succeed, "Negro domination." To the leaders of the "white man's party," any political party that was dependent on black votes and was responsive to black demands was, by definition, "dominated" by blacks. And no white man worthy of the name should affiliate with such a party. So the Funders laid the groundwork for their offensive in the months before the election of 1883. What they still lacked, however, was a shocking episode or event to dramatize the threat of "black domination" over whites.

In May 1883, an episode likely to provoke white panic presented itself to the Funders. With Governor Cameron's encouragement, the Readjusters had appointed two black men to the school board in Richmond, the state capital and a city with a white majority. The very idea that black men, even though only two out of the nine board members, should be in positions of authority and power over white children and schoolteachers, most of whom were female, conjured up all sorts of racial fears and fantasies. Funders denounced the appointments as too awful to tolerate.

Then, in November, just days before the election, a street brawl between black and white men in Danville, a Readjuster-controlled city in the foothills close to the North Carolina border, resulted in the deaths of four African Americans. Although blacks were the victims, this incident was depicted by the Funder press as the "Danville Riot," proof that the streets were not safe when a black-dominated party ran a southern city. The Funders published provocative circulars announcing: "War Declared between the Races" and "WHAT COALITION RULE MEANS." The choice in the election was presented in dramatic terms: "Are you going to vote with the whites, or niggers, this time?"[16] Fearful of being identified with blacks, a sufficient number of whites, especially in the southwestern counties, deserted the Readjusters on election day to give back the state to the "white man's party." That was all it took to reverse the 1881 election result and destroy the Readjuster Party.

Whether organized around the issue of currency expansion or debt repudiation, the independent campaigns of the early 1880s were countered vigorously. But none posed as great a threat as the Readjusters, who actually gained control of state government in Virginia. They proceeded to implement economic and social policies that were much needed, as well as changes in race relations that were unprecedented in the post-Reconstruction South. The Democrats' response was swift and overwhelming. A racial incident and an appeal to white solidarity, and it was all over. As the defender of the region's racial order, the hegemonic Democratic Party could not tolerate dissent or division. A decade later, another and more threatening insurgency arose. This time, the Democrats' insistence on regional unity would have consequences even more decisive and devastating.

7

Eliminating the Opposition

THE 1890S

In the late 1880s, farmers in the South and the Far West rose up in protest against their desperate economic conditions. Their economic distress was compounded by an alarming decline in their social status and self esteem, as America became increasingly industrialized and urban. The farmers were frustrated because they found themselves trapped in a system of agricultural production that was impoverishing them. They were especially hard hit in the South, where the constant need to produce cotton to pay off debts incurred under the exploitative crop-lien system was proving disastrous. With farmers tied to cotton and with cotton functioning as currency in the cash-poor South, the result was overproduction and therefore constantly falling prices. From this cycle of deprivation there seemed to be no escape. So southern farmers flocked to join the new agricultural organization, the Farmers' Alliance, which arose in western Texas in the early 1880s. The alliance offered sons of the soil a mechanism for mobilizing their own resources to challenge the bankers, supply merchants, land speculators, and railroads, which were the most visible agents of the financial and economic system that exploited them.

By 1890, 852,000 farmers had joined the alliance, as it spread eastward through the region. Enthusiasm was so great that one organizer in North Carolina marveled that "the farmers seem like unto fruit—you can gather them by a gentle shake of the bush."[1] The country dwellers who signed up so eagerly were neither well-to-do planters nor impoverished sharecroppers but rather the small farmers and tenants in between. Most of them lived outside the black belts and in the more recently settled areas of the up-country and the foothills.[2] Since most owned property and actively engaged in buying supplies and marketing their crops, these farmers participated in the existing financial and business economy. They were not, however, pastoral primitives who longed to return to a bygone era, nor was their protest, as one of them insisted, "a retrograde movement . . . to hog and hominy."[3]

Nevertheless, critics of the protesting farmers often saw them as nostalgic and hostile to the modern world. This image was colored by the alliance's emphasis on cooperation and community, in contrast to the competition and individualism intrinsic to industrializing America. Alliance members considered cooperation essential—among the farmers themselves as well as with other working people, especially urban laborers—as a means of empowering the exploited masses against their richer and more powerful opponents. To enable farmers to buy their provisions and supplies from each other and cut out the middleman, the alliance organized cooperative stores and warehouses. Later, the alliance rallied behind a proposal to create what it called a sub-treasury system, through which the federal government would lend money to farmers based on the cotton they stored in warehouses until prices rose.

While the alliance developed practical proposals to enable farmers to gain control over their purchasing and marketing, it also drew up a radical program for government action to deal with the current problems arising from money, land, labor, and transportation. Adopted at its convention in Cleburne, Texas, in 1886, the "Cleburne Demands" insisted on, first, a flexible currency through the unlimited coinage of gold and silver; second, recognition by the states of cooperatives and also labor and farmer unions; third, the freeing up of land for settlement but the taxing of land bought for speculation; fourth, protection for laborers through a mechanics' lien law and statutes requiring laborers to be paid on time and in cash; and, fifth, increased state taxation of railroads and their regulation by a federal railroad commission. Many of these ideas were also circulating among other protest organizations, like the Knights of Labor. As its membership soared into the millions, the alliance realized that it possessed a voting power that could be used to pressure candidates for public office to endorse its programs.

So irresistible was the alliance's influence that hundreds of candidates for state and congressional office in 1890 assented to the "Alliance yardstick." And most of them won. Alliance-backed majorities were sent to the legislatures of Georgia, North Carolina, Alabama, Florida, and Tennessee; six governors and more than fifty congressmen identified themselves as Farmers' Alliance candidates. Almost all of these men were Democrats, and once elected they found it difficult to act independently of their party leaders' priorities. Moreover, the alliance's numerous proposals were not prioritized, leaving sympathetic legislators with no agenda or idea about how to proceed. Meanwhile, several of the items—such as proposals to reform the currency, create an interstate railroad commission, and introduce the sub-treasury (which was urged very forcefully in 1890 as the most distinctive alliance measure)—were federal, rather than state, matters. Finally, many candidates had responded favorably to the alliance's list of demands just to obtain the support of its members and get elected. To the alliance's great disappointment, therefore, almost none of its legislative proposals were realized, either at the state level or in Congress.

The Populist Insurgency

Over the next two years, the Farmers' Alliance metamorphosed into the People's Party. The farmers' protest had contained two strands—the economic and cooperative as well as the legislative and political. As it became increasingly difficult to develop economic independence through cooperative ventures and the sub-treasury, the need to take political action became inescapable. When the legislators elected with Farmers' Alliance support in 1890 failed to secure the Democratic Party's support for alliance measures, the movement's future seemed to depend on the creation of a new party, whose candidates would be answerable to alliance instructions. The People's Party that emerged from this decision was not an exclusively southern institution but was national in scope like the Farmers' Alliance itself. Because farmers in the western plains were experiencing similar suffering and deprivation, they also joined the Farmers' Alliance and the People's Party.

In 1892, in Omaha, Nebraska, delegates representing western and southern farmers, along with other reformers, met to form the new party and choose its presidential nominee. The leading candidate was Leonidas L. Polk, a former Confederate officer who had been North Carolina's first agricultural commissioner in 1877. Founder and publisher of the influential journal *Progressive Farmer*, he had been elected president of the national Farmers' Alliance in 1889. By 1892, he was advocating the formation of a third party, telling the alliance convention in St. Louis:

> The time has arrived for the great West, the great South and the great Northwest, to link their hands and hearts together and march to the ballot box and take possession of the government . . . restore it to the principles of our fathers, and run it in the interest of the people. . . . We want relief from these unjust oppressions, and . . . we intend to have it if we have to wipe the two old parties from the face of the earth.[4]

The exhilarating prospect of redress through the formation of a new party of protest was matched by awareness of how radical and problematic this departure was bound to be, especially for the southerners. Joining the People's Party meant rejecting the Democratic Party, the political force that had redeemed the South from Reconstruction and that was the embodiment of respectability. As organizations memorializing the Confederacy, such as the United Confederate Veterans and the Daughters of the Confederacy, began to emerge in the late 1880s and early 1890s, Democrats identified themselves closely with "the Cult of the Lost Cause." Affiliation with the "third party" or "the Populites," as angry Democrats called the renegade organization, implied disloyalty to region as well as race, thereby jeopardizing the social status and reputation of those daring to vote for it. Thousands of desperate farmers faced this agonizing dilemma as they contemplated forsaking the Democratic Party.

For leaders in the agrarian movement, the personal and political consequences of affiliating with the Populists were serious. Milford W. Howard, a Populist congressman from Alabama, later recalled his own turmoil. "My father would not hear me speak," he remembered, "and said he would rather make my coffin with his own hands and bury me than to have me desert the Democratic party."[5] Another leading Populist, Frank Burkitt, a Democratic legislator and head of the Farmers' Alliance in Mississippi, took a long time to break with his party but eventually yielded in 1892 because he "was born a plebeian" and "every beat of my heart is in sympathy with the wealth producers of the land." Regrettably, "the Democratic party has ceased to hear the cry of [the laboring people of this country] and I cannot follow it further."[6]

Recent political developments had made the decision to desert the Democrats more difficult. In 1890–91, the southern Democrats had been threatened with passage of the Lodge bill, which would have increased the power of the federal government, then controlled by the Republicans under President Benjamin Harrison, to protect voters' rights in southern elections. The Democrats saw the bill as a direct attack on the region and the party and moved quickly to denounce it and rally the South's white people to repel what seemed like a second Reconstruction. If this was not enough to cause a wavering Democrat to stay where he was, southern Democrats' rush to embrace free silver as the 1892 campaign got under way made deserting to the Populists even less compelling. Yet the party's national convention in 1892 again chose Grover Cleveland of New York as its presidential nominee. Cleveland was well known for his ties to the banking interests and for his undeviating advocacy of "sound money" and the gold standard. After failing to head off his nomination, leading southern Democrats urged the region's state conventions to endorse the free coinage of silver as party policy in order to avert an otherwise certain electoral disaster. There was no resistance whatsoever. Democrats in every southern state realized that the free silver maneuver would offset the liability of Cleveland and probably stem defections to the Populists.

The second problem confronting potential Populists was directly related to the first. The Democratic Party's claim to be the only legitimate political organization in the South was based on its ability to guarantee white supremacy and solidarity. White men who were thinking of joining the Populists would have to turn their backs on the "white man's party." They would then have to grapple with the political reality that their newly adopted party had no chance of success without the support of African Americans. As they pondered this dilemma, the Populists could recall that a few years earlier the Farmers' Alliance was confronted by the same problem and had resolved it by deciding to exclude black farmers from participation and membership. As a result, blacks had formed the Colored Farmers' Alliance, which had grown to around 1 million members by the late 1880s. Although they had held their annual conventions in the same city and kept in touch with each other's proceedings, whites and blacks still met separately. Since a large number of Colored Farmers' Alliance members were tenants rather than landowners, they differed from the whites on economic grounds, not just on race.

These inauspicious precedents had to be overcome, however, if the People's Party were to be viable in the South. To a surprising degree, the Populists did reach out for African American support and, in doing so, broke with some aspects of the prevailing racial attitudes and practices. Most notable was the Populists' invitation to blacks to attend and participate in their meetings and, on occasion, to hold office in their party organization. Clubs were formed to draw African Americans into the party, instruct them about Populist policies, and train them as party organizers. They were invited to picnics and barbecues arranged by the party to win their support. Simultaneously, Populist officials met with black political leaders to encourage them to leave the Republican Party, in which the Lily White faction had become increasingly influential, to the detriment of blacks. Issues of concern to African Americans were included in Populist platforms, such as opposition to lynching and convict leasing, both of which victimized blacks in particular. The political rights of blacks were strenuously and repeatedly endorsed in platforms and in speeches, while the Democrats' interest in black voting for the sole purpose of bribing

Tom Watson. Perhaps the best-known southern Populist, Watson was forty-eight years old and the Populist candidate for president in 1904 when this formal portrait was taken. Southern Historical Collection, Wilson Library, University of North Carolina at Chapel Hill.

black voters and stealing their votes was denounced. Saying these things in public in the 1890s was both radical and risky, an indication of how far exasperated opponents of the region's status quo were prepared to go to break Democratic hegemony.

The Populists' racial position was perhaps best expressed by Tom Watson, the South's best-known Populist and, in his own estimation, "the worst abused, worst disparaged, worst 'cussed' man in Georgia."[7] In vitriolic speeches before massive crowds and in the pages of his *People's Party Paper*, Watson intoned over and over again his class-based antidote to racial politics. "Let it once appear plainly that it is to the interest of a colored man to vote with the white man, and he will do it." Believing that "self-interest always controls," Watson, like most thoughtful Populists, was convinced that race served to divide people who were in the same wretched condition and allowed their exploiters to take advantage of them. "You are kept apart," he warned, "that you may be separately fleeced of your earnings."[8] Although united by their class position, the poor were divided by race and more easily exploited. The People's Party would reunite the laboring class of blacks and whites in the South and the nation.

There were limits, however. Fraternization was possible in the political sphere and at the ballot box, but it could not apply to the realm of social relations. "It is best for your race and my race," Watson told blacks, "that we dwell apart in our private affairs," and he cited schools and churches as specific instances.[9] Accordingly, African Americans attended Populist gatherings, but they sat separately. Moreover, they could vote for the Populists, but the party would not run them as candidates. In this respect, the Populists were unwilling to follow the lead of the Readjusters in Virginia, one of whose leaders, Governor William E. Cameron, had appointed blacks to office and who had once commented privately that "we cannot expect to receive the means of victory from those people and monopolize the fruits."[10] Populists wanted black votes, but they were not prepared to give African Americans access to public office or to allow them much influence within their party.

Despite the Populists' economic and class-based appeals to African American voters, blacks themselves had other matters to consider when calculating their self-interest. The Republicans and Democrats also wanted their votes, and they both offered incentives, whether in the form of bribes or goodwill and public respect. At the same time, they could punish a black voter for betraying his race and the party of Lincoln or for defying his landlord's pressure to vote Democratic. And, of course, there was always the possibility of violence against those who asserted their political independence.[11] Beset by all these pressures, many blacks doubtless concluded that abstention was the wisest course, or they voted in whatever way seemed safest. By any measure, the safest way was certainly to not vote for the Populists. With election fraud widespread, any ballots they cast for the Populist candidate would probably be thrown out or end up somehow in the Democratic box. By the 1890s, the black voter was no longer voting freely. With few exceptions, his voting options and his actual vote were being manipulated by others.

While black supporters could not be counted on, the Populists were having some difficulty developing their white support too. In the Upper South, opposition to the Democrats was already being expressed through the highly competitive, well-established Republican Party in the mountains and foothills of Tennessee, Virginia, and North Carolina. In these predominantly white areas, there was no significant black vote for the Populists to capture, and the potential white vote was already beholden to the Republicans. Also unobtainable were the votes of whites in the Lower South's black belts. These whites were often tied to the economic operations of the large planters, and they were also surrounded by a majority of blacks. Consequently, they were readily enlisted for the defense of white solidarity and Democratic hegemony. Finally, in the black-majority state of South Carolina, the Populists were blocked out altogether because the Farmers' Association, led by the notorious agrarian leader Benjamin Tillman, had a lock on the suffering white farmers in the midland and upland sections and, with their support, had won control of the state in the early 1890s.

With its prospects in the white counties of the Upper South and in the black counties of the Lower South looking slim, the People's Party focused its attention elsewhere. Its chances looked promising in those parts of Texas, Arkansas, Georgia, Alabama, and even North Carolina where substantial numbers of suffering cotton farmers cultivated their own land and lived in areas with a white-majority population and a small but electorally pivotal black electorate, though not a significant Republican presence. These dissatisfied Democrats in the up-country could carry their states for the People's Party, with help from black voters bold enough to vote for the Populists.

The People's Party was formed in 1892, a presidential election year. In Leonidas Polk the new party possessed a candidate of almost Washingtonian stature. A commanding figure in both the Farmers' Alliance and in the new party, he gathered enthusiastic support from both the South and the West. But Polk died suddenly on the eve of the national convention, setting off a frantic search for an alternative standard-bearer. Unfortunately, the result was a decidedly inferior and unexciting ticket, consisting of James B. Weaver, a Union general from Iowa and perennial Greenback Party presidential aspirant, and James G. Field, a Confederate general from Virginia only marginally involved in the People's Party. This dull duo was thoroughly defeated in the South, receiving less than a quarter of the vote in every state, except in Alabama and Georgia. The ticket did better in the West, winning 22 electoral votes and carrying Kansas, Colorado, Nevada, and Idaho, where an alliance with the Democrats, who were the minority party in the West, made these victories possible.

In the South, the Populists did not do well enough to produce any electoral votes for the national ticket or to win any states. Nevertheless, many southern states experienced serious competitive elections for the first time since Reconstruction. Reuben Kolb (pronounced "Kobb"), Alabama's agricultural commissioner, who was running as an independent on the Jeffersonian Democratic ticket, should have won the governorship. He carried a majority of the white vote and eleven more counties than his opponent. But widespread intimidation, bribery, and ballot-box stuffing in the black belt denied him victory. Similar tactics defeated Tom Watson in Georgia's tenth congressional district around Augusta. In Texas, the Populist candidate for governor did well, winning more than 100,000 votes in a three-way race. But the Democratic incumbent, James Hogg, who had compiled a good record on issues of concern to the Populists, won reelection by drawing off large numbers of disgruntled farmers who would otherwise have supported the less charismatic Populist contender. And, of course, hundreds of Populists were elected to offices at the county level. All in all, the party had done well in its first election when, as Tom Watson reminded his disappointed supporters, "all the machinery in the state was against us; all the power of the 'ins'; all the force of old habit and old thought; all the unseen but terrible cohorts of ignorance and prejudice and sectionalism."[12]

Two years later, the Populists fared even better in the South. The depression that engulfed the nation for almost five years after the Panic of 1893 increased the suffering of the South's farmers. Rather than easing the depression, the actions of President Grover Cleveland exacerbated it when he tightened the money supply and returned the economy to the gold standard. His sympathy for the bankers and corporations rather than for the working people was further evident when he dispatched U.S. troops to put down the Pullman strike in 1894. As a result, hostility within the South toward the national Democratic administration and, by association, the party's southern branch intensified. Quickly seizing on the political possibilities, the region's Populists built up their party organization and held hundreds of large rallies at which their rabble-rousing, crowd-pleasing stump speakers, like "Cyclone" Davis in Texas and Tom Watson in Georgia, ridiculed the Democrats and President Cleveland and blamed them for the farmers' plight. Ben Tillman earned his nickname, "Pitchfork," when he told a cheering audience that the overweight Cleveland was "an old bag of beef and I am going to Washington with a pitchfork and prod him in his ribs."[13]

The possibility of actually winning in 1894 led the Populists into political arrangements that emphasized opportunism over principle, short-term gain at the expense of building the insurgent movement. They feared that losing another major contest to opponents, who flouted all the rules and simply stole elections, could prove fatal to their supporters' courage and tenacity. As Joseph C. Manning, a founder of the party in Alabama, observed, "We have got to get a new regime in office, new blood, new brains; got to change the whole system and whole spirit of the South. And the first step is to secure a free ballot and a fair count."[14] Since new election laws could not be passed unless the party gained power, winning became a prerequisite for more substantive reform. Marion Butler, the leading Populist in North Carolina, regarded fair elections as basic to "the very existence of our form of government and overtops and overshadows all others." In fact, "no other reform is possible till this thing is gained."[15] As had so often been the case when the Greenbackers and other independent parties had mounted challenges, the question of fair elections and opposition to the Democrats began once again to form the basis for coalitions with the Republicans. To this end, the more radical proposals in the party's Omaha platform of 1892 were downplayed in favor of free silver, which even southern Republicans were prepared to endorse in order to get elected.

The resulting electoral arrangements were called "fusion," an overused term in late-nineteenth-century southern politics that referred to Democratic schemes for supporting bolting Republicans during Reconstruction and for cutting deals with black Republicans to split the offices in black-majority counties in the 1880s. In 1894, the Populists experimented with fusion and worked out agreements with the Republicans in North Carolina, Alabama, Georgia, Louisiana, and Arkansas. In some cases, they were statewide, and in others they were confined to counties or congressional districts. But, in all instances, fusion was limited to electoral strategy and did not involve a merger of the two party organizations. Sometimes both parties agreed to support this Populist candidate in exchange for that Republican. On other occasions, one party would agree to withdraw a candidate in favor of the other party's choice. But, in all cases, the Republicans who fused were the party's Lily White faction, not the Black and Tan wing in the black belts. The Lily Whites could help make Populism seem less radical and so enable it to attract well-to-do Democrats temporarily angry at Cleveland.

With the Populists gaining support and the Democrats divided and unpopular, Fusion alliances raised the electoral stakes enormously. Fearing that they might actually lose, the Democrats in the Lower South resorted to violence and ballot-box skulduggery as never before. The Populists still did pretty well. In Alabama, Kolb was running for governor again and was ahead by 8,000 votes until the stuffed ballot boxes from the black belt were counted. The Fusion ticket of Jeffersonian Democrats and Populists increased its share of the gubernatorial vote to 44.5 percent. The regular Democratic majority dropped from 80,000 to 20,000, while five senators and forty-seven representatives were elected to the state assembly by the Fusionists. But the greatest success occurred in North Carolina where the Populists and Republicans fused statewide and won control of the legislature. As a result, Marion Butler was sent to the U.S. Senate, along with a Republican, Jeter Pritchard. The new legislature proceeded to enact a fair elections law and to repeal the county government act of 1876, which had given control over the appointment of local officials to the state legislature and thereby ensured Democratic control over the state. These critical changes in the state's electoral system and governance were followed by other Populist reforms, such as a limit on interest rates, increased funding for schools, and higher taxes on railroads and corporations.

The voters were sufficiently pleased with this record that, in 1896, they elected Daniel Russell, a Republican, as governor, thereby giving the Fusion alliance complete control of the state. In that same year, Fusion success in North Carolina was almost emulated in Louisiana, where the Populists' fusion with the Republicans in 1894 was considerably enhanced in 1896 by the support of the wealthy and powerful sugar growers. They had joined with the Republicans after the Cleveland administration had lowered the tariff duty on imported sugar and thereby deprived the state's industry of valuable tariff protection. The Populist-Republican Fusion lost only because it was counted out in the black-majority parishes by Louisiana's ever-resourceful Democratic election officials.

Everywhere else, 1896 was a terrible year for the Populists. They even suffered defeat in the West, although it was at the hands of the Republicans, who benefited more than the Populists from the ineptitude of the Democratic Cleveland administration. The Populist defeat in 1896 merely confirmed a decline that was already evident in the West in 1894. In the South, where Populism had been electorally successful in 1894, the election of 1896 also proved calamitous. The cause of the sudden collapse in the South was, however, neither the same nor so obvious as in the West. Southern Populism was not just beaten at the polls. It was eviscerated and destroyed by "the pattern of confusion" that was the southern political system of the post-Reconstruction era.[16]

In the 1896 presidential election, the national Democratic Party disavowed Cleveland and his obsession with the gold standard. Instead, the party's rallying cry became the free coinage of silver, and its nominee was thirty-six-year-old William Jennings Bryan, the "silver-tongued orator" from Nebraska, who captivated the party convention in Chicago with his denunciation of "the money power" for plotting to "crucify mankind on a cross of gold." To western Populists, who had already formed fusion agreements with the Democrats in 1892 and 1894 and who also considered Bryan, the westerner, to be one of their own, collaboration with the Democrats at the national level was unproblematic, even congenial. Some of the southern Populists, led by Marion Butler, saw a free-silver Democratic Party headed by a virtual Populist as a dependable ally against the Republicans, the party of the corporations and financiers of the Northeast. But Tom Watson and the more radical southern Populists rejected fusion because it required them to collaborate with their bitter foes, the southern Democrats. Instead, they insisted that the party retain its identity and its integrity by staying "in the middle of the road" between the two major parties. Rather than endorse the national Democratic ticket, they proposed a Populist ticket, with Bryan for president and Tom Watson for vice president.

The upshot was complete chaos. Southern Populists fused with Republicans at the state level, while allying with the hated Democrats in the presidential campaign. Meanwhile, negotiations for a Bryan-Watson ticket ran into resistance, not only from Democrats, as expected, but also from the Populists' fusionist leadership headed by Senator Butler. After months of stalling, Populist voters were left no alternative but to vote for the Democratic ticket. With so much electoral mayhem, Populist politicians in the South felt baffled and demoralized. William P. Guthrie, the party's candidate for governor in North Carolina, told Butler: "I confess that I myself am 'befogged' at present, hardly knowing where to go, what to say when I speak, or 'where I am at.' "[17] And the party's supporters were in the same quandary, as the thrust and momentum of their uprising dissolved into a desperate effort to form electoral combinations with incompatible and unsympathetic allies. Voting for Bryan, free silver, and fair elections made a good deal of political sense. But it fell far short of Populism's reform agenda. Consequently, large numbers of Populists just did not vote. Assessing the situation with accuracy, the "middle-of-the-roader," Tom Watson, acknowledged bitterly after the election: "Our party, as a party, does not exist any more. Fusion has well nigh killed it. The sentiment is there, but confidence is gone."[18]

Fusion did indeed prove fatal to the Populist movement, though it is far from certain that the party could have provided relief for farmers by keeping its integrity at the cost of remaining small and powerless. What killed the party in the South was not just fusion but the southern political system that made fusion necessary. The Democratic Party embodied the three R's, which made it hegemonic in southern politics in the late nineteenth century—respectability, redemption, and race. Possessing all three attributes and using them as political weapons to exclude and delegitimize any organized opposition, the Democrats were prepared to do anything necessary to maintain the economic and racial order. They managed the electoral system and manipulated the votes of their opponents to prevent them from winning, or even from becoming a serious threat. Organized opposition was illegitimate, and so were its voters. And they would be counted out, even if they managed to reach the polling place.

With the electoral deck stacked against them, it was no wonder that, as Tom Watson had observed, the Populists had "no confidence." Losing elections because they were rigged—and this had happened on three occasions by 1896—was enough to destroy the Populists' confidence in electoral politics and the efficacy of the ballot. So the Populists joined the Readjusters, the Greenbackers, the Republicans, and other lesser heretics who had fallen victim to the Democrats' ruthlessness ever since 1868, when African Americans first voted and cast their votes for the Republicans.

Disfranchisement*

While the dispirited Populists were coming to recognize that it was almost impossible to defeat the Democrats, the Democrats themselves were planning changes in the electoral system that would make it impossible even to oppose them in the future, let alone defeat them. Even before the People's Party was founded in 1892, a movement had commenced within the southern Democratic Party aimed at disfranchising the region's black voters. By this time, African Americans had been voting for a generation, and they provided the core constituency for the various coalitions and parties that, since Reconstruction, had opposed the Democrats.

Before the election of 1896, five southern states had revised or rewritten their constitutions so as to increase the requirements for voting in ways that would eliminate most black voters—Tennessee, Florida, Arkansas, Mississippi, and South Carolina. Over the next decade, the rest of the former Confederate states followed suit. The outcome was a vastly reduced electorate and the elimination of virtually all black voters, as well as hundreds of thousands of whites too. These changes in the South's suffrage qualifications wiped out the major source of electoral opposition to the Democrats.

*Although the word "disenfranchisement" is correct according to most dictionaries, it was never used once during this episode and is therefore anachronistic. In my view, "disfranchisement" is a shorter, more accurate, and therefore preferable, term. It is also accepted by most dictionaries.

Disfranchisement marked a decisive, qualitative change in the way the Democrats dealt with black voting. After they had driven the Republican Party from power in the mid-1870s, the Democrats refused to recognize the legitimacy and independence of the black voters who were its main supporters. So they tried to manipulate and control the black vote by intimidation, obstruction, bribery, and, most often and most systematically, fraud at the ballot box. Under disfranchisement, the manipulation of votes during elections was replaced by the elimination of these voters before the election even occurred by making them ineligible. Contemporary observers were scandalized by the audacity and deceit involved in depriving several million voters of their right to vote. An Alabamian named L. C. Coulson commented grimly about what was happening in his own state during the disfranchisement campaign in 1901: "Under the law as it now stands, white men steal the vote; if we adopt the new constitution, white men will steal the voter." The editor of an African American newspaper in Louisiana, the *Southwestern Christian Advocate*, employed a different analogy to describe how the Democrats viewed disfranchisement: "How can we perpetrate one big steal in favor of the Democratic party . . . so that we may have no more fraudulent work to do hereafter?"[19]

The switch from manipulating the black vote to eliminating it altogether was precipitated by two national developments. The first was the repeal, in 1893–94 during the Cleveland administration, of the Reconstruction-era federal election laws that enforced the right to vote guaranteed by the Fifteenth Amendment. With the federal government no longer able to supervise national elections in the South, the voting rights of blacks were in great jeopardy. The second was the remarkably sudden enthusiasm throughout the nation for the secret ballot. This new method of voting was adopted by thirty-two states between 1888 and 1892, many of them in the South. By introducing the secret ballot, southern states were supporting a widely approved reform of the balloting process. A voter would no longer ask for a party ballot and mark it in front of the judges but would do his voting in private. However, the voter now had to be able to read, and many in the South could not. In effect, the secret ballot made literacy a requirement for voting.

The removal of the federal government from the business of supervising elections and protecting the right to vote provided an opportunity, even an incentive, to impose ever-increasing restrictions on voting. But the fundamental reason for embarking on a campaign for even more extensive disfranchisement arose from a pressing need to solve what Senator James Z. George of Mississippi identified as "The Great Problem" confronting white southerners. In two long articles in the *Vicksburg Commercial Herald* on the eve of his state's constitutional convention in 1890, Senator George, who had been the leading advocate of the Mississippi plan to overthrow Reconstruction in 1875, explained what this "great problem" was. "Our situation is without parallel in human history," he announced, for "hitherto free government has succeeded nowhere, except among homogeneous peoples willing for and capable of harmonious political co-operation." But, in the South, with its democratic elections and universal male suffrage, one of the peoples (and in Mississippi this people was actually in the majority) was an "incapable race" devoid of "the slightest capacity to create, to operate, or to preserve constitutional institutions." Despite this inequality, "the men of both races are equal in political rights."[20]

In George's view, and in the opinion of the vast majority of whites, no doubt, a political system based on the assumption that two unequal races could possess equal rights was fundamentally unsound, contradictory, and bound to fail. Yet the South had been struggling to endure under such a system ever since African Americans had been invested with the right to vote by a hostile Congress, as part of its terms for southern readmission to the Union after the Civil War. A rising Democratic politician from Virginia's black-majority Southside, Walter Watson, described the predicament graphically when he observed of the black voter that, "at all times and in all places, he is separated—subordinated. It is only at the ballot box that he meets you face to face on terms of absolute equality."[21] For white politicians like Watson, it was humiliating to have to appeal to black voters for their support.

Relations between the races had been unclear and contested since emancipation. The freedmen had obtained equal rights, but, in practice, they had been denied equal treatment. By the 1880s and 1890s, southern whites intended to eliminate this discrepancy between equality under the law (de jure) and inequality in practice (de facto). To this end, they proceeded systematically, first ending the right to vote through disfranchisement and then removing civil and legal equality through segregation. Disfranchisement was therefore accompanied and supplemented by the system of segregation that emerged in the 1890s and spread throughout the region thereafter. Taken together, disfranchisement and segregation formalized black civil and political inequality by writing it into law.

Disfranchisement was a crucial element in a larger project during the final decade of the nineteenth century to reformulate southern race relations. And the disfranchisers themselves were fully aware of this. Alfred P.

Thom, a leading Democrat from Norfolk in Virginia's Tidewater, constantly reminded the delegates in the convention of 1901–2 that "there is something deeper and more far-reaching in what is before us than the mere question of whether we can carry an election. I see underneath it the fundamental problem of what is to be the relation of these two unequal races."[22] Senator George and countless other disfranchisers would have concurred.

If the reordering of race relations was the larger context in which disfranchisement took place, it was also intended to accomplish four immediate and essential objectives. First, disfranchisement would remove black voters from the body politic, so that the Democrats would no longer have to deal with a bloc of roughly 2 million votes that they could not win in a fair electoral contest. Second, the ending of black participation in southern elections would make it no longer necessary for white-led parties to court black voters. Before disfranchisement, the Democrats had had to control and neutralize the black vote, while their opponents—the Readjusters, Greenbackers, and Populists—had had to mobilize and win it. The black vote therefore became the fulcrum of southern politics. As a result, black voters acquired electoral leverage and power, which Democrats portrayed fearfully as "Negro domination."

The disfranchisers' third objective was eradication of fraud and corruption in southern elections. With no black voters to bribe or black votes to steal, corrupt activities of this kind would no longer be necessary. To many Democrats, the existing state of affairs had to be remedied before it became entrenched and considered normal. Perhaps the most dramatic depiction of the electoral practices that needed to be cleaned up came from Judge John B. Chrisman, at the very first disfranchising convention, Mississippi's, in 1890. "Sir, it is no secret," he informed the delegates, "that there has not been a full vote and a fair count in Mississippi since 1875—that we have been preserving the ascendancy of the white people by revolutionary methods. In plain words, we have been stuffing ballot-boxes, committing perjury[,] and here and there in the state carrying the elections by fraud and violence until the whole machinery for elections was about to rot down."[23] Fraudulent election methods like these had become, so Chrisman added, "a chronic ulcer on the body politic—and threatened to disintegrate the morals of the people."

By removing black voters, the temptation, or perhaps the need, for Democrats to resort to fraud would also be removed. But it was a perverse argument. Blacks had to be denied the vote, so that Democrats would not have to commit fraud. The Democrats saw the matter simply as one of expediency, not morality, for the problem they faced was merely technical—how best to prevent African Americans from voting against the Democrats.

The disfranchisers' fourth, and final, aim was not just the elimination of the black vote, but the elimination simultaneously of the electoral basis for any serious opposition party in the future, whether Republican or Populist or any other. Although the disfranchisers frequently promised that removal of the black vote would allow the whites to divide among themselves and debate substantive issues instead of being constrained by the need for white unity, this new political environment never had a chance to emerge. The political system the Democrats actually created in the process of disfranchising African Americans did not contemplate party competition and healthy political debate. Rather, the eradication of any opposition to the Democrats was the actual aim. That is certainly what they achieved. And they never expressed any regret about how things had turned out or tried to modify or reverse this outcome.

A remedy as drastic as disfranchisement could not be embarked upon carelessly, as it entailed considerable political risk. In the first place, the federal government would almost certainly object to the removal of African Americans' right to vote, a right provided by the Reconstruction Act and guaranteed by the Fifteenth Amendment. Second, changes in voting qualifications required the revision of a state's constitution. To accomplish this, the assembly had to pass legislation providing either for an election of delegates to a convention that would debate and draft a new constitution or for a statewide referendum to ratify an amendment to the state constitution that the legislature had already drafted and passed. At any point in this process of constitutional revision, the maneuver might be jeopardized or defeated by the emergence of opposition. A third problem was that the African Americans who were the target of this scheme were still eligible to vote and could rally to defeat their own disfranchisement. This real danger was usually averted by election laws, passed prior to the calling of a convention, that restricted black voting.

This legally questionable and quite extraordinary scheme to purge the southern electorate of its black voters and install the Democratic Party as the unchallenged political organization in the region was carried out over a twenty-year period, from 1888 to 1908. After three states—Tennessee, Arkansas, and Florida—had amended their constitutions in 1890–91 to require that a voter pay an annual poll tax to be eligible, Mississippi and South Carolina produced new constitutions in 1890 and 1895 that introduced a number of additional requirements for voting. Louisiana followed in 1898 with a constitutional convention and North Carolina in 1900 with a disfranchising amendment. Louisiana Democrats resorted to disfranchisement in order to thwart the Republican-Populist alliance, which would have won the state in 1896 but for the skulduggery of monumental ballot-box stuffing in the black-majority parishes. And North Carolina's Democrats moved on to disfranchisement after an avowed "White Supremacy" campaign in 1898 had ended the Fusion alliance and its control of the legislature since 1894. Having used race to regain the legislature, they capitalized on the momentum and enthusiasm they had unleashed, in order to eliminate black voting and also the Republican and Populist parties. In both states, disfranchisement was the device that destroyed the Populists. Other states met either before Populism became a significant political force or after it had become so weak that it no longer posed a threat to the Democrats.

In the last group of states, Populism was no longer much of a force. Constitutional conventions met in Alabama in 1901 and in Virginia for almost a year, from May 1901 to April 1902. In both cases, two factions were vying for control of the Democratic Party. One of them, the reform element, hoped to use disfranchisement and the ending of fraudulent election methods as a mechanism for gaining control over the party. But these maneuvers were actually foiled by the "old guard" that was based mainly in the black belt and that resisted the Progressive-style reforms advocated by its rivals. Both Texas from 1901 to 1905 and Georgia from 1906 to 1908 achieved disfranchisement by means of a constitutional amendment, in campaigns aimed at bringing the Populists back into the Democratic Party and pitting the Progressive-reform wing of the party against the establishment, rather like the alignment in Alabama and Virginia. In Georgia, Tom Watson forged an electoral alliance in the 1906 gubernatorial contest with the Democrat, Hoke Smith, who was running as a reformer. After Smith won with the crucial help of Watson's still-loyal Populist following, the new governor introduced and enacted the disfranchising amendment that he had promised as the quid pro quo of the deal. The process in Texas also involved an amendment, as well as a coalition of Progressive and former Populist reformers, which produced both a disfranchising amendment and several restrictive election laws.

The circumstances and the lineup of the contending Democratic factions differed from state to state, but the major features were common to them all. In every state, the campaign for disfranchisement was initiated and controlled by the Democrats. It was the brainchild and pet project of one party alone. Every convention was therefore overwhelmingly Demo-

"The Vampire That Hovers over North Carolina," *Raleigh News and Observer*, 27 September 1898. This was probably the most dramatic of the stream of powerful cartoons drawn by Norman Jewett that the *Raleigh News and Observer*, edited by Josephus Daniels, ran during the "white supremacy" legislative campaign in 1898. After ending Fusion (Republican-Populist) control of the North Carolina assembly, the Democrats proceeded to implement disfranchisement by constitutional amendment in 1900. North Carolina Collection, University of North Carolina at Chapel Hill.

cratic in composition. Only in Virginia and Alabama was there an opposition bloc of Republicans and Populists. Naturally, blacks were absent, except for one in Mississippi, Isaiah Montgomery of Bolivar County, and a bloc of five in South Carolina, several of them experienced Reconstruction politicians, such as Robert Smalls and William Whipper, who managed to raise some provocative and troubling questions in the debates about what was being perpetrated.

In every state, a similar package of disfranchising requirements was rolled out, consisting of residency in one place for one or two years; the payment of all taxes, usually six months before an election; a literacy test requiring a potential voter to read a section of the state or federal constitution; the secret ballot, which required that a voter be able to read the ballot; and a poll tax of one or two dollars per year, the taxes owed becoming cumulative in some states and therefore soon beyond the means of a voter to pay. All these devices were not overtly racial. But their intent was, of course, to ensure that blacks in particular would be unable to meet the qualifications.

Also common to all the states was a clause in their franchise plans that offered a loophole, or a "saving clause," as it was usually called, that enabled poor and illiterate voters who were white to keep their voting rights. The Democrats had campaigned for disfranchisement with the promise that no white man would lose the vote. After all, Democrats believed that whites were superior to blacks. And, besides, the support of all whites was needed to elect a convention or ratify an amendment. This loophole allowed illiterates to vote if they could explain what a particular clause in the state or federal constitution meant, even though they could not read it. This "understanding clause" gave registrars, inevitably Democrats, the power of decision over a person's right to vote. It was, of course, an invitation to fraud, as delegates and newspaper editors in Mississippi, the first state to propose such a loophole, were quick to point out. "We don't see where this would be any improvement on ballot-box stuffing," the Democratic *Brandon Republican* noted. The *Jackson Clarion* berated its fellow Democrats in the convention for "this most transparent fraud." The reaction among Mississippi Democratic papers in 1890 was repeated every time a subsequent convention introduced a "saving clause." Needless to say, Republican and Populist papers were appalled at this travesty.

Another loophole device, first introduced in South Carolina, proved more appealing in subsequent campaigns than the "understanding clause." This was the so-called grandfather clause, which bestowed the vote on descendants of voters who had been eligible prior to 1867, or alternatively to the descendants of Confederate soldiers. Again, these loopholes were not expressly racial. It just so happened that there were no black voters before 1867, the year of black enfranchisement under the Reconstruction Act, nor were there any blacks who had served in the Confederate army, naturally enough. Although not ostensibly fraudulent, the "voting grandfather" and the "fighting grandfather" exceptions were, of course, deceitful in intent. Despite the questionable morality of these loophole clauses and the outrage they provoked among Democrats themselves, one of the variants was adopted by each state as part of the franchise provisions in its amended or rewritten constitution.

When objections were raised, the Democrats simply shrugged them off. A Republican delegate in Virginia pointed out angrily that the proposed "understanding clause" could only be implemented "by fraud and discrimination." To this charge, Carter Glass, a Lynchburg editor who was later a U.S. senator and an architect of the Federal Reserve System, responded complacently: "By fraud, no; by discrimination, yes." It will be racial "discrimination within the letter of the law, and not in violation of the law. Discrimination! Why, that is exactly what we propose; that, exactly, is what this convention was called for." And just in case the Republican delegate still did not "get it," Glass explained that the convention intended to remove "every negro voter who can be gotten rid of, legally, without materially impairing the numerical strength of the white electorate."[24] The objective was to eliminate the black vote, and Glass was proud to acknowledge it.

Similarly unapologetic was Ernest B. Kruttschnitt, president of the Louisiana convention. In his closing remarks to the delegates, he proclaimed defiantly that the crazy quilt of tests they had thought up was just fine: "What care I whether the test which we have put be a new or an old one. What care I whether it be more or less ridiculous or not. Doesn't it let the white man vote, and doesn't it stop the negro from voting, and isn't that what we came here for?"[25] The convention's franchise provisions guaranteed that "those methods, which have prevailed in the elections of the state of Louisiana for the past twenty years [are] behind us." Instead, the delegates "have reared a perfectly clean structure" that will ensure "a clean electorate."[26]

A New Electoral System for the South

The Democrats' drive to eliminate the black electorate achieved its intended outcome within a few years, as African American participation plummeted in state after state. In Louisiana, for example, only 5,320 blacks were registered in 1900, whereas 130,344 had been registered in 1897. Black registration in Virginia, about 21,000 in 1903, was reduced by half a year later, yet those eligible in 1901 numbered about 146,000. And, in Mississippi, just 8,615 of the 147,205 black males over age 21 were registered after the new constitution went into operation in 1892. And many fewer of these eligible blacks actually voted. The massive decline in black registration and voting was predictable. Indeed, it was the purpose of the entire exercise. What was unexpected, however, was an accompanying steep decrease in white participation. Only a trickle of otherwise ineligible whites presented themselves for registration under the loophole clauses that were created especially for them. For example, 264,095 voters participated in the presidential election in Virginia in 1900, but four years later only 129,929 showed up to vote. The turnout had been cut in half, and this meant that only 28.8 percent of the adult males who were eligible actually voted. And a similar pattern of widespread nonparticipation by whites was repeated throughout the region.

Democrats expressed surprise at the decline in white voting, but they offered no convincing reason for why it occurred. In a speech in the House of Representatives in March 1902, John Sharp Williams of Mississippi presented what soon became the accepted explanation, namely, that "the white man who can not read or write feels that it is a humiliation for him to say so, and to ask for an understanding examination."[27] Even if their "understanding" was considered adequate and they were given a pass with a wink and a nod from the registrar, they still had to navigate the secret ballot at election time, which would expose them to further humiliation for their ignorance. These poor white men also had to go to the courthouse and pay their poll taxes as fees for the right to vote, and many of them may have found the cost prohibitive or else simply did not think it worth the trouble. What would voting achieve anyway? Better to spend the money on food for the children.

Meanwhile, Democrats, who often referred disparagingly in their disfranchisement debates to "ignorant" or "purchasable" voters, would not be too upset if poor illiterates were no longer voting. Nor would those like Judge Chrisman be, who believed that "no account" whites who might be disfranchised by the literacy test and poll tax should not "complain if it saves our civilization from barbarism."[28] If participation were restricted to the literate and propertied, in other words, the "better sorts," then so much the better. And this attitude was becoming widespread and not just in the South, since reformers in the North were seeking to "improve the quality" of their electorate through the secret ballot and literacy tests.

Disfranchisement transformed the electoral system in the South. As intended, the black vote had been eliminated. Accompanying it, a large segment of the white vote had vanished, overwhelmingly those who were poor and illiterate. With the disappearance of black voters, a reduction of fraud at the polls was almost certain, even though the fraud had just been removed from the ballot box, where it was rowdy and illegal, to the registration office, where the same goal was achieved inconspicuously and under cover of law. Elections became quieter and more orderly and were attended by far fewer people. The electorate had not merely been reduced. It had been decimated.

These drastic changes in the South's electoral system gave rise in turn to major changes in its party system as well. The removal of black and disadvantaged white voters eliminated the electoral base for the kinds of opposition parties the Democrats had encountered from the 1870s to the 1890s. Without support among the common people of the South, any opposition to the Democrats, who were the party of economic order and social status, was doomed. Consequently, their dominance of southern politics was now quite secure. Only if the party began to split because of unmanageable conflicts within its ranks or if new issues arose that generated different sources of opposition would the party be in any serious danger. And those perils might not emerge for many years.

But before the Democrats had to confront any possibility of a threat, another development elevated the party's recently obtained hegemony to long-term monopoly. The white primary arose as the mechanism to consolidate Democratic rule. Once disfranchisement had removed the black vote and, with it, the Republican Party, the general election was no longer very significant, since the nominee chosen by the Democrats would automatically be the winner. Josephus Daniels, a leading figure in the Democrats' "white supremacy" and disfranchisement campaigns in North Carolina, was quick to realize that "when the negro vote is eliminated, a nomination by the party of the white men is equivalent to election." The Democrats needed therefore to create a reliable method of selecting their candidates so as to ensure party unity. A well-managed procedure for uniting the party behind its nominee was, in Daniels's view, "a necessary adjunct" to disfranchisement.[29]

A direct election, in which registered party members voted to choose the party's candidates, was being advocated in the North at the turn of the century by Progressives like Robert La Follette of Wisconsin. He envisaged the direct primary as a method of challenging the machines and the insiders who controlled the nominating conventions and caucuses of the major parties. For these same reasons, reformers and factions that were out of power in the South saw a party primary as an effective mechanism for unseating their rivals. In Alabama's gubernatorial race of 1902, Joseph F. Johnston hoped to regain control of the Democratic Party through a primary election. Three years later, the reformers, who had lost out in Virginia's constitutional convention, convinced the legislature to pass a primary law. This statute required that Thomas S. Martin, the incumbent U.S. senator, who had created a personal machine that controlled the state Democratic Party, had to submit his claims for reelection to the approval of the Democratic voters.

During these experimental years, when primaries were being tested in the South, they proved to be more easily exploited by the insiders than by the reformist challengers, since Johnston lost and Martin was reelected. Alabama's primary was sanctioned and supervised by the Democratic state executive committee, as was Virginia's, an obvious indication that the insiders thought a primary might work to their benefit, at least this time. More often, however, primaries were created by the state legislature. For instance, Mississippi's primary in 1902 was created by statute, making it the first statewide primary election law in the nation, a year before Wisconsin's, in fact. The Mississippi law mandated an election throughout the state, on the same day, for all the party's nominees. Only those who had voted Democratic during the previous two years could participate.

A complete ban on African American participation in primaries followed. The requirement that all voters had to be white proved to be an essential feature in all subsequent primary laws and regulations in the South. This provision ensured that blacks could not participate. Because the disfranchisement provisions had specified that the new voting requirements applied only to general elections, African Americans might have grounds for claiming they were eligible to vote in party primaries. So the racial ban had to be imposed to prevent this possibility.

Besides this racial prohibition, the Democrats introduced another device, called the runoff. This mechanism ensured that the party's candidate would be the choice of the majority, because the two leading vote getters in the first primary (if the front-runner did not obtain an overall majority of the total votes cast in the first election) would be forced into a second contest, or "runoff." Under these conditions, no defeated aspirant would be likely to bolt the party and run as an independent, nor would he garner any support if he proved so willful and destructive as to even try. Only in the South were these two features added to the primary system, testifying to the distinctive southern compulsion for keeping the primaries white and making sure that they provided an ironclad guarantee of Democratic solidarity and unity.

By 1908, the effectiveness of the direct party primary was acknowledged throughout the South. As a conservative device that could unify the Democratic Party and also obliterate the Republican Party and any other organized opposition, it ensured the Democratic Party's uncontested hegemony in the region's political system. All the southern states except Louisiana and North Carolina had now adopted the primary as the crowning achievement of the new, postdisfranchisement order. As a result, the convoluted and utterly confusing electoral structure that the Democrats had manipulated so disastrously since the mid-1870s became a thing of the past. In its place, they had erected an undemocratic and rigid polity composed of a profoundly eviscerated electorate and a single, invincible political party. In this system, parties did not compete and most of the electorate did not vote. All the same, it was so firmly entrenched and protected by legal and institutional safeguards that it would endure for three generations, well into the second half of the twentieth century.

The "Solid South" had served as a rallying cry for Democratic and white unity in the 1880s and 1890s. By the turn of the century, it was no longer simply a slogan but a political reality. For the South was now solid indeed, and it would remain so until the 1970s, though not without constant vigilance and a few scares.

PART IV.

ONE-PARTY SYSTEM,

1901–1965

8

Democrats and Demagogues
in the Solid South

The disfranchisers' overriding goal was the elimination of the black vote. When their campaigns were over, they discovered, however, that disfranchisement had accomplished a good deal more. It had created a new political system. The distinguishing feature of this system was the disappearance of an opposition party. The southern states had, in effect, created a one-party system. With the region's politics now purged of organized party opposition, the South was unified around one party, the Democratic Party, and the proponents of this new system referred to it proudly as the "Solid South." And for most of the twentieth century, the South remained solid.

The Solid South as a Political System

The Solid South was a one-party *system*, not just a polity in which one party was in the majority and able to maintain its control without serious challenge. Throughout American history, regions of the country have been dominated by one political party, as, for instance, the Republicans in the Northeast in the late nineteenth century or the Jeffersonian Republicans in the South in the Early Republic. But these were not one-party *systems*. They were simply instances in a competitive, multiparty, or two-party, system of one party managing to attain superiority through its continuing ability to compile electoral majorities.

The South's one-party system was also quite unlike other kinds of one-party systems that emerged in other countries in the twentieth century. It was very different from the one-party states that invariably followed the rise to power of a revolutionary Communist party, as in the Soviet Union or China. It was also vastly different from the one-party systems that emerged in parts of Africa and Asia after movements for liberation from European colonial rule took power in the mid-twentieth century. Nor was the South's one-party system anything like the "dominant party" systems that ruled Japan and Italy after World War II or Mexico after its revolution in the 1920s.

These types of one-party polities took two general forms. Sometimes they were formally competitive party systems in which one party achieved and maintained a majority that was unassailable. Or they were one-party states, with the ruling party's monopoly recognized by varying degrees and kinds of formality. By comparison, the Solid South was a distinctive concoction, though probably not unique. The system in the South was sanctioned formally and legally, yet the single party that it established was extremely weak and bore no comparison whatsoever to the Communist or postcolonial parties in one-party nation-states. Indeed, the sole party in the South's one-party system was so constrained and diminished that it wielded less power and was less organized than political parties in the rest of the United States.

So what was this strange political plant that germinated in the swamps and bayous, the Delta and Tidewater, of the American South? The first of its features was an electorate purged of its poorest and most vulnerable members. Virtually all African American adult males were disfranchised by the residence, literacy, and poll tax requirements of the new state constitutions. They were joined by a large number of whites who were also unable to meet these prerequisites and who had failed to take advantage of the special loophole clauses that were made available to them for a limited time, usually a year or so after the constitutional revisions had been adopted. The southern electorate was therefore severely reduced and restricted to "the middling and better sorts," with most of the poor and disadvantaged excluded.

A second feature was the elimination of the opposition party, the Republicans, because they relied heavily on the support of precisely those African Americans and disadvantaged whites who had been disfranchised. The People's Party had already been shattered before disfranchisement began, but, in states like North Carolina and Louisiana where it was still viable, the disfranchisers' attack on its base of support proved devastating. Except in a few Upper South states where the Republicans remained operational but fell short of a majority, organized party opposition had become marginal. So the Democrats were dominant and virtually unchallenged, the only party in the one-party South.

The third, and final, element in the system was the white primary. The direct primary was a method of choosing a party's nominees, or candidates, by an election participated in by the party's members and supporters. In the South, the primary possessed two characteristics missing in the rest of the country. First, it took place in two steps. The first election reduced the field of aspirants to two, after which a second, or runoff, primary occurred to determine the nominee from among the final two candidates. This two-step sequence provided a cast-iron guarantee that the Democrats would be united around their undisputed nominee. After all, having survived two contests, his fitness and credentials could not be questioned, and neither could the rigorous winnowing process that selected him. The second distinctive feature of the South's primary system was its restriction of the participants. Only whites were allowed to vote in the Democratic Party's own, almost private, procedure to select its nominee. Without this party-imposed ban, African Americans who had been disfranchised from participating in general elections might have claimed they were eligible to vote in party elections, a supreme irony and a crushing blow to the Democrats that they could not possibly allow.

"The Democratic primary in the South is in reality the election," observed V. O. Key Jr., in *Southern Politics in State and Nation*, his classic analysis of the South's political system in the early twentieth century. Later in his study, he went a step further, announcing that "in a sense there are no elections in the South; the matter is settled when the Democratic party makes its nominations."[1] This contradiction arose because elections in the South were transformed into a contest for the support of voters within one particular party. And this was very different from other twentieth-century representative democracies in which elections were contests between two or more organized parties to win support from the voters. This shift in the meaning and understanding of widely used political terms would become characteristic of the South's one-party variant of the two-party system, its undemocratic system of modern democracy.

The Solid South rested, therefore, on an artificial tripod, consisting of a severely restricted electorate limited to qualified whites only; a marginalized, even nonexistent, opposition party, or parties; and a white primary for choosing the Democratic nominee, who would then be the predictable winner of the general election. And the sole aim and objective in the construction of this political edifice was the hegemony of the Democratic Party. Despite its undisputed dominance, the Democratic Party that resulted from this devious scheming was, ironically, a very feeble political institution. Indeed, it barely merited designation as a political party. Because the system was so rigged in their favor, the Democrats had little motivation to participate in the most basic activity of American political parties, the mobilizing of their supporters and the getting out of the vote.

Its electoral machinery atrophied, while the institutional organization that sustained it from one election campaign to the next virtually withered away.

Even though the nominating process took on greater significance, it did not stimulate much party activity, because the party organization was only minimally involved in arranging and supervising the nomination of candidates. The state primary law required that a direct primary be held. But candidates proceeded to announce, quite independently, that they intended to run. They themselves then financed and ran their own campaigns, producing their own literature and agendas, arranging their own events and activities, and organizing and mobilizing their own supporters to turn out on election day. As a result, the Democratic Party functioned essentially as an impartial administrator of the process, with even the appointment of election judges decentralized into the hands of party leaders at the county level. Primary elections were usually paid for by the party, while general elections were run and financed by state or local government. As Key saw it, the Democratic Party was little more than "an agency to administer elections, since it has to fight no campaigns."[2]

Under these circumstances, it is reasonable to conclude that the South was not a one-party system at all, but a no-party system. Admittedly, an entity called the Democratic Party did exist in all the southern states and it did perform some functions generally attributed to political parties. But such a feeble and tacit organization as this was merely a shell of a political party, as the term is generally understood in the rest of the United States and in most European representative democracies. Consequently, Key's observation that "the South has no parties" was quite plausible, even though provocative and counterintuitive.[3]

But the political environment in the South during the first half of the twentieth century was actually a little more complicated, as Key himself and political scientists since then have acknowledged. Rather than being one-party or no-party, the system had elements of both. In fact, Key argued that it operated on two levels and was "an institution with an odd dual personality." At the state level, he observed, "the Democratic party is no party at all, but a multiplicity of factions struggling for office."[4] In this context, the party acted as "a holding company for competing factions."[5] "In national politics, on the contrary, the party is the Solid South [and] it is, or at least has been, the instrument for the conduct of the 'foreign relations' of the South with the rest of the nation."[6]

These two analogies illustrate the dual functions of the new party system of the Solid South. The first describes a weakly organized, minimalist party throughout the states of the region. There was no coordination among the state Democratic parties and there was no cohesion within each of them—almost no party at all, just a "holding company" for office seekers and factions. By contrast, when it acted as the region's State Department, protecting the interests of its white inhabitants from external danger, the Democratic Party centralized its operations and spoke with one voice.

The foreign relations arm of the Solid South operated within two national arenas. The first was presidential politics, where the southern states' influence was coordinated through the selection in each state of delegates to the Democratic Party's national convention, which was usually channeled either through a state-level caucus of influential party leaders or through the state executive committee. Once the delegates were chosen, they were instructed to vote as a unit for a particular candidate, preventing a diffusion of state, and often regional, votes.

The other arena was Congress, where senators and representatives from the South acted together and dominated the Democratic caucuses in the two houses. They were able to exert a preponderant influence within the party caucus in each house, owing not only to their cohesion but also to their numerical strength as a region within the national party. In addition, they soon possessed greater experience in Congress than any other grouping. Because there was no opposition party in the South, Democrats, once elected, rarely faced serious challenges and were invariably reelected. As a result, they became long-term incumbents who were able to develop experience and considerable influence. Under the existing seniority system for determining promotion within congressional committees, the South's senators and representatives rose through the ranks, eventually becoming committee chairs and ranking members. When the Democrats were in the majority, these southern chairmen would be in charge of the drafting and scheduling of legislation, a power that could obviously be employed to benefit and protect the South.[7] The net result of southern organization, cohesion, and incumbency was an influence within the national Democratic Party and the national legislature far greater than the region otherwise warranted.

Meanwhile, within the South itself, the loosely organized, virtually party-less political world gave rise to a politics based primarily on faction. In sharp contrast with national politics, the party existed there only in name. Instead, faction prevailed and was the form that political activity assumed. Factions are loose coalitions or groupings within political parties that form for temporary purposes around matters of limited scope and significance, often little more than how to get or hold onto office. Within the ascendant but functionally minimal Democratic Party of the South, factions rose and fell, formed and dissolved. But this endemic factional politics was not altogether without pattern. It generally assumed one of three forms.

On rare occasions, there was just one dominant faction, such as Virginia experienced for most of the Solid South period. The statewide organization run by Senator Thomas S. Martin was preeminent from the 1890s to the 1910s, succeeded by the "Byrd machine" headed by Governor, and later Senator, Harry F. Byrd, which ran the state until the 1960s. More frequent, however, was a system of bifactionalism in which two relatively distinct factions arose and competed for temporary influence. The division might be based on geography, on socioeconomic or class differences, or on a rivalry between two political leaders. The third factional arrangement was multifactionalism, in which three or more groups emerged and then dissolved into different configurations. Very likely to produce a more volatile and disaggregated political environment than the other two variants, multifactionalism prevailed in about seven of the eleven former Confederate states in the early decades of the new system. By the 1930s, only Arkansas, South Carolina, Mississippi, and Florida remained multifactional, because the New Deal initiatives of President Franklin D. Roosevelt rearranged some of the others along bifactional lines, roughly as pro- and anti–New Deal groups.[8]

Another characteristic of the South's postdisfranchisement political system was the significance of personality in the region's politics. With the party itself taking a back seat in the process of selecting nominees, the task of testing and winnowing contenders for their suitability as candidates was no longer a responsibility or function of the party itself. Instead, the direct primary opened up the process of selection to the voters. With no party-approved candidate on the ballot, the whole field was wide open to anyone seeking the nomination. Any political aspirant could get on the ballot and try to appeal to voters through electrifying oratory or charisma, even though the candidate might lack a campaign organization and might have received no encouragement or support from the party leadership. Naturally enough, colorful and controversial personalities with little previous political experience or accomplishments emerged and were often successful. In an unstructured political environment in which party organizations and the platforms and issues they customarily generate were nonexistent, a politics of personality became increasingly appealing and appropriate.

This unstructured politics, with its reliance on factions and its fascination with personality, caused V. O. Key considerable dismay. "A disorganized politics" is how he characterized the southern system. At other times, he called the region's politics "individualistic" and "atomized." Becoming even more dismissive, he began to refer to it as "a pulverized politics," "a granulated political structure."[9] The factionalism and the politics of personality it spawned were proving extremely harmful to the South, he believed. In his book's opening sentence, Key contended that the system was so damaging to the region that "politics is the South's number one problem." This was a clever paraphrase of Franklin Roosevelt's provocative assertion in 1938 that "the South is the nation's number one economic problem."[10]

The destructive effect of the South's political system was then cataloged by Key. First of all, factions deprived the South of the political continuity and stability that parties usually provide. Despite the shortcomings of American political parties, the lack of them was far worse, in his view. After all, parties are institutions that intend to endure, so they create organizations and structures; they recruit, develop, and select candidates; they frame policies and issues in clear and distinguishable terms; and they appeal to and cultivate support among voters. As a result, the political arena is orderly and predictable and public discussion is comprehensible and rational, a sharp contrast with the disorganized politics created by shifting, transitory factions and their irresponsible, erratic leaders.

Second, the beneficiaries of the "disorganized politics" that factionalism generated were those who possessed economic and social power, the "haves." The "grand object of the haves is obstruction," because it is in their interest to keep things as they are and avoid having to redistribute resources to the "have-nots." A disorganized politics was valuable to these powerful interests because it impeded sustained action to develop policies that would benefit the disadvantaged. Tipping the scales further toward the "haves" was the disfranchisement of "substantial numbers of the 'have-nots,'" making their needs even less consequential to the region's politicians, who did not have to worry about their votes.[11]

Key's critique of the South's "disorganized politics" stemmed from his own views about the inadequacy of America's politics generally. He was one of an influential group of political scientists who, by the early 1950s, concluded that America's political parties were not performing well. They needed to be reformed so that they would function like parties in a parliamentary system like Britain's. Parliamentary parties

Jeff Davis of Arkansas addressing a crowd in Centre Point. In this undated photograph, Davis is standing, raised up on a dais or chair, to the left of the tree, which is filled with onlookers. Although Davis appealed to the white rural masses, those present at this stump speech seem to have been better off and also dressed up for the occasion. Nevertheless, the image shows how open-air electioneering looked in the rural South at the turn of the twentieth century. Picture Collection, number 2939, Special Collections, University of Arkansas Libraries, Fayetteville.

were stronger organizations. They stood for policies and issues that made them distinctive from each other. They campaigned with manifestoes and agendas that they put before the electorate. And they implemented these legislative programs once elected. These strong and coherent parties fostered "responsible government." A system of political parties in the parliamentary mold would, in Key's opinion, be a marked improvement over the existing polity of the United States.

These kinds of changes were far-reaching and so alien that they were unlikely to be viable and welcomed in the United States. The likelihood of such a transformation in the South, with its long-standing distaste for well-organized parties, was even more remote. In comparison with an idealized version of what American parties and government might become, southern politics was clearly not just insufficiently organized—it was actually disorganized. For Key, such a politics was so harmful that it could only be described as dysfunctional. The region's political system was its primary problem. Its "disorganized," "granulated," "atomized" politics was even worse than the flawed and inadequate national system of politics and government.

The Southern Demagogue

The political world of the Solid South was a strange place, devoid of competing parties but filled instead with loose factions. And it gave rise to some unusual political figures quite unlike any others in American history. What is more, they began to appear on the southern political scene in the immediate aftermath of disfranchisement. Most frequently categorized as "the Southern demagogue," these flamboyant, rabble-rousing, storytelling tribunes of the rural masses were a new type of southern politician. Because they were so colorful, these "fantastic creatures," as the journalist Gerald W. Johnson described them, have become some of the best known of the region's political figures. Often they are considered the typical and emblematic southern politician of the Solid South era.

Many of their names are familiar, and the nicknames they acquired reveal their unusual ability to connect with, and endear themselves to, their followers. The most notable were "The White Chief," James K. Vardaman of Mississippi; Jeff Davis of Arkansas, nicknamed "The Wild Ass of the Ozarks"; Coleman L. "Our Coley" Blease of South Carolina; Theodore G. "The Man" Bilbo of Mississippi, who was also called "Prince of the Peckerwoods"; Huey P. "The Kingfish" Long of Louisiana; Wilbert Lee O'Daniel of Texas, who was known affectionately as "Pass the Biscuits, Pappy," or just "Pappy"; Miriam "Ma" and James E. "Pa" Ferguson of

Senator James K. Vardaman of Mississippi (left) with Congressmen Tom Heflin of Alabama (center) and Ollie James of Kentucky (right). Vardaman and Heflin were two of the most racist and outrageous of the South's agrarian demagogues in the early twentieth century. This photograph was taken in Washington sometime between 1913 and 1920. Even while they were in Congress, both dressed in styles that were characteristically distinctive and ostentatious. Ollie James was a large but otherwise unremarkable congressman from Kentucky. Library of Congress, Prints and Photographs Division.

Texas; and Gene Talmadge of Georgia, known as "The Wild Man from Sugar Creek." All became governors of their states, and most of them, except the Fergusons and Talmadge, went on to the U.S. Senate. A few others, like Ellison D. "Cotton Ed" Smith of South Carolina or James Thomas "Tom Tom" Heflin of Alabama, spent their long careers entirely in Congress.

Although admired by their followers, these rabble-rousing politicians have very often been treated with contempt and offered as evidence of how low southern politics had sunk. H. L. Mencken, well known in the 1920s as one of the leading baiters of the South, used the term "Southern Demagogue" constantly as a way of denigrating these "yokel" politicians. He once defined demagoguery as "the trick of inflaming half-wits against their betters." And he predicted that "to get rid of its demagogues the South would have to wait until the white trash were themselves civilized," presumably a very long time.[12]

In the South itself, the political establishment and the social and economic elite were appalled, and often frightened, by the emergence of these skillful campaigners and orators who stirred up the emotions of the plain folk in the countryside. One of the most bitter and uninhibited depictions of a demagogue and the kinds of followers he appealed to was recorded by William Alexander Percy. In his autobiographical *Lanterns on the Levee*, which was a southern equivalent of *The Education of Henry Adams*, he described the contest between his father, LeRoy Percy, and James K. Vardaman in the Senate race of 1911. Vardaman, who had already served a term as governor of Mississippi from 1903 to 1907, went on to win by a wide margin. The author described his father's opponent as "a kindly, vain demagogue unable to think, and given to emotions he considered noble. He was a handsome, flamboyant figure of a man, immaculately overdressed, wearing his black hair long to the shoulders and crowned with a wide cowboy's hat. He looked like a top-notch medicine man."[13]

Strangely, Percy overlooked "The White Chief's" clothing on the campaign trail, which was all white—suit, shirt, tie, and even boots—no doubt intended to match his devotion to white supremacy. But it was Vardaman's supporters who elicited Percy's strongest reaction. Scorn mingled with fear as he described their behavior at a campaign rally: "I studied them as they milled about. They were the sort of people that lynch Negroes, that mistake hoodlumism for wit, and cunning for intelligence, that attend revivals and fight and fornicate in the bushes afterward. They were undiluted Anglo-Saxons. They were the sovereign voter. It was so horrible, it seemed unreal."[14]

Also critical of the new breed of agrarian politicians and their supporters was V. O. Key, who saw this phenomenon as a predictable outgrowth of the South's "disorganized politics." The experience of Texas in the 1920s and 1930s under the governorships of the Fergusons and O'Daniel exemplified this dysfunction. Key described "Pa" and "Pappy" as "rural demagogues." "Skilled in the arts of swaying the multitude," he wrote, "their electoral successes often depended on factors totally irrelevant to the welfare of the state or even their own supporters. Yet their victories had a veneer of logic in that they posed as the champions of the rustics, vaguely in the manner of Talmadge in Georgia."[15] Since the issues they campaigned on had little or no achievable policy content, their purpose was simply to dupe the voter by making him feel good, or angry, or both. But they offered no practical remedy for his actual deprivation or real worries. Similarly, Key excoriated Vardaman for his insistence, over several campaigns, on the repeal of the Fifteenth Amendment guaranteeing black suffrage. Key considered it "an utterly hopeless proposal, and for that reason an ideal campaign issue. It would last forever. The rednecks— and some delta planters—did not know that they were being humbugged and they loved it."[16]

Although it is impossible to tell whether their excited followers were aware that they were being duped or even whether they were being duped at all, these agrarian leaders understood something essential about the southern electorate after disfranchisement, and they stimulated as well as catered to it. But they were not the first to do so; there were precursors. In the 1890s, the farmers' revolt had generated several colorful and dynamic leaders, the best known of whom were Tom Watson of Georgia, "Fiddlin' Bob" Taylor of Tennessee, James Hogg of Texas, and, most notorious, the one-eyed "Pitchfork Ben" Tillman of South Carolina. All proclaimed themselves champions of the tillers of the soil. All used colorful language as invective against the city slickers and vested interests who were exploiting country folk. And all, Taylor and Tillman, in particular, made political campaigning into a spectacle and a drama. Taylor's hymn singing and violin playing transformed campaign stops into revival meetings, and Tillman's verbal threats against his political opponents, accompanied by the parading of his paramilitary Red Shirts, gave his rallies a menacing edge. These men were prototypes for a phenomenon that became a continuing feature of southern politics well into the twentieth century.

The one-party system arising at the turn of the century stimulated the emergence of politicians who claimed to be the champions of the people and who were skilled in the art of entertaining and mobilizing the masses. Because there was no longer a rival Populist Party or Republican Party or a menacing black vote, the dissident agrarians now led their protest against the established political and economic elite from within the Democratic Party. Not only was this a safer environment for opposition to flourish, but the recently introduced white primary provided a mechanism for legitimizing dissent while simultaneously weakening its

Jeff Davis, governor of Arkansas, 1901–6, and U.S. senator, 1907–13. This formal portrait was probably taken during Davis's three terms as governor, when he was in his early forties. Jeff Davis Papers, box 14:4, Special Collections, University of Arkansas Libraries, Fayetteville.

impact. Aspirants to office who were unacceptable to the leadership of the party were welcome to enter the primary and appeal directly to Democratic voters for their support. But the campaigns and organizations that the candidates created were identified with and attached to them personally; they were not endorsed by the party itself. These agrarian insurgents were therefore fostered and emboldened by the one-party system. But, menacing and unpredictable though they appeared, they were also contained and confined by it.

In many instances, the insurgent leader and his faction became a defining force within a state's politics for many years, causing a bifactionalism to form between him and his opponents. Notable instances were Vardaman in Mississippi between 1903 and 1910, Jeff Davis in Arkansas from 1901 to 1913, Blease in South Carolina in the 1910s, Theodore Bilbo in Mississippi in the 1910s and 1920s, Gene Talmadge in Georgia in the 1930s, Huey P. Long in Louisiana from the mid-1920s to the mid-1930s, and the Fergusons and O'Daniel in Texas in the 1920s and 1930s.

These factional divisions did not, however, endanger the Democratic Party, nor did they result in the creation of a rival party. The reason is not hard to find. None of these angry insurgents was prepared to subvert or overthrow the hegemonic Democratic Party, which guaranteed and protected white supremacy and perpetuated the exclusion of black voters from the region's politics. On the other hand, the one-party system of Democratic dominance allowed exploited farm dwellers to vent their frustrations and channel them through these heroic and iconoclastic champions without the reprisals that had been visited upon the Populists. Secure and unchallenged, the Democratic Party permitted their insurgency but also tamed it.

The one-party system imposed yet another constraint on the demagogues. The South's solidity enabled the region to exert an influence in Washington and within the national Democratic Party that was simply too valuable to be jeopardized. Even though their followers were not always aware of it, the leaders and their advisers knew better than to throw away the national power and respect that resulted from party loyalty and regional solidarity. And, besides, the primary system made a seat in the U.S. Senate quite accessible to the leader himself, and the most successful of them—Vardaman, Davis, Blease, Bilbo, Long, O'Daniel—sought and obtained this coveted position. The leaders, and to some extent their followers, acknowledged the gains provided by the South's one-party system, along with its restrictions.

Regardless of the political conditions that gave rise to the early twentieth-century "southern demagogue," his support came from a preexisting social group. These were the farmers and tenants who lived and worked in the still predominantly rural South. Because their economic conditions had not improved much since the unsuccessful efforts of the Farmers' Alliance and the Populists in the 1880s and 1890s, their deprivation and neglect were still real. And their hostility to the cities and their more prosperous residents was as virulent as ever, particularly since urban life and its modern amenities and attitudes seemed to be encroaching at a rapidly increasing rate on rural values and prospects. After Populism's defeat, the "revolt of the rednecks," as it has been described pejoratively, took on a new urgency, which popular leaders like Mississippi's Vardaman and Arkansas's Davis understood and quickly adapted to.

In his first race for governor, in 1900, Jeff Davis proudly identified his typical supporter as "the fellow who wears patched breeches and one gallus and lives up the forks of the creek, and don't pay anything but his poll tax."[17] Acknowledging his followers' poverty and distress, Davis nevertheless praised them for their hard work and endurance: "You know you can't make a cent—not a cent—and yet you work and toil and labor—the bravest men on earth. God bless them."[18] And he laced his compliments for their perseverance with a heavy dose of class resentment. In this same speech during the 1899 gubernatorial campaign, Davis proclaimed: "You have two classes. . . . Now, for years laws have been made in the interest of the wealth consuming class against the wealth producing class. . . . This wealth consuming class has got the money; they have cornered everything."[19] Having described the enemy, Davis proceeded to mock these wealth consumers, who were evidently "girlie-men," deserving only contempt from manly farmers. "If some of them high-collared, flyweight dudes of the East," Davis speculated mockingly, "had sense enough to sit down to a big dish of turnip greens, poke salad and hog jowl, they might sweat enough of that talcum powder off to look and smell like a man."[20]

Although they identified fervently with the masses they led, these agrarian politicians rarely came from their ranks. Instead, they were lawyers and newspaper editors, landowners and businessmen, who nevertheless spoke the language of the rural farmers, and, in the words of a more famous southern politician, they could "feel their pain." And they developed a public image that differentiated themselves from their one-gallused followers. Vardaman, for instance, was magnificent to behold. In the 1911 Senate race, at age fifty, he "still brushed his black hair straight back from his forehead and let it fall to his shoulders," and he "continued to wear only white." At one Fourth of July parade, he put on a spectacular show. "Behind marchers, mounted on a long, flat wagon pulled by eighty-six oxen, rode Vardaman," with onlookers pressing forward to touch the wagon and, if possible, the candidate.[21] Evidently, this showmanship had the desired effect, because John Sharp Williams, Mississippi's senior senator, felt compelled to acknowledge "a fanaticism about the fool performance that rather frightened me."[22] But the display of "the White Chief" was also meant to embolden his supporters and give them confidence that their leader was no ordinary politician but an exceptional and powerful figure who could threaten and intimidate their exploiters. For the same reason, Alabama's senator Tom Heflin always made himself look elegant by wearing "a Prince Albert coat, double-breasted vest, and flowing tie," while Gene Talmadge acted tough and menacing, once announcing at a press conference, "I'm just as mean as hell," and demonstrating in his two terms as governor of Georgia how ruthless and autocratic he could be.[23]

Their champions had to instill fear into the "high collared roosters," but they also had to show that they could protect their supporters from the "black menace." Although blacks had been disfranchised and segregated by law, race remained an ever-present concern, especially to those whose economic and social status was so precarious. Their leaders were therefore vigilant about reassuring them of the essential southernness and acceptability of white supremacy. This could be achieved overtly through race-baiting. The White Chief made the stoking of racial hostility and fear a mainstay of his political career. He used the most scurrilous and disgusting language to describe blacks and their behavior, always referring to them as "niggers" or "coons," in his incessant, unremitting denunciation of them. In one famous statement during his successful campaign for governor in 1903, he urged whites to lynch blacks, announcing, "If I were a private citizen I would head the mob to string the brute up, and I haven't much respect for a white man who wouldn't," a recommendation that was greeted with applause by his audience.[24] He was also famous for his oft-quoted observation that "to educate a negro is to spoil a good field-hand."[25] Similarly obsessed by race and forever indulging in graphic racial imagery were the likes of Tom Heflin and Theodore Bilbo, South Carolinians Cole Blease and "Cotton Ed" Smith, and Jeff Davis.

On the other hand, in Texas and Florida, where blacks were less numerous, agrarian leaders rarely indulged in race-baiting. There, they referred to race in ways similar to other, ostensibly more respectable, southern Democrats. Because the entire political system and social structure was built around white supremacy and the need to keep blacks "in their place," race could not be ignored. Mentioning it was more an affirmation of an understood and approved reality, an unspoken assumption, rather than an attempt to stir up racial hostility. Some of these leaders of the masses like Huey Long and Florida's Napoleon Broward barely mentioned it at all, because their focus was on issues of economic justice or railroad regulation. Injection of the issue of race would have served only as a distraction. For all but a few of these demagogues, however, racial antipathy was a stock-in-trade, whether it poured out in venomous ranting or was mentioned only as a way of reminding rural audiences of the need for whites to band together.

African Americans were not, of course, the primary threat, or enemy, of the region's impoverished rural masses. They were a scapegoat for the economic grievances that the Populists had addressed in the 1890s. The railroads, the insurance companies, the cotton marketing firms, all set prices and shaped the disadvantageous economic conditions that small farmers and tenants suffered from. Located in the region's larger towns and cities, or even out of state and faraway, these interests also embodied the forces of urbanization and modernization that were perceived as threats to the farming economy and the rural way of life. Unlike the Populists, who proposed policies for dealing with these problems and who tried to create broad, class-based, and even interracial alliances to promote these reforms, the rural rabble-rousers tended to present this ongoing conflict in social and cultural, rather than in economic and political, terms. Consequently, their protest became more an expression of cultural grievance than a reform movement driven by a program and an agenda. Employing the rhetoric of the Populists, they directed it at the "high-collared roosters" and the effete "wealth-consumers" in the cities who looked down their noses at the ignorant and grimy country dwellers. As Jeff Davis constantly reminded his listeners, he was fighting back, standing up for "the fellow who wears the britches," and demanding that he be treated better and shown some respect.

In the changed political environment of the early twentieth-century South, with its one-party system and white primary, another People's Party was impossible. Besides, the limitations of a party of protest had already been exposed and the party beaten back. The revolt of the rural masses was now channeled into cultural protest. And the flamboyant showmen who led and embodied it were supported enthusiastically because they ventilated their followers' complaints and did so with such bluster and braggadocio. As Huey Long's biographer, T. Harry Williams, once noted, they provided "psychological outlets that rural and poor people craved and needed." These country folk identified with orators who could express their own feelings of frustration and, on their behalf, "fling defiance at their enemies." "Because their chiefs were swaggering characters who told the mighty where to head in, they were pretty hell-for-leather fellows themselves."[26]

Agrarian protest became increasingly emotional and rhetorical as the demagogues took it over. Highly charged rhetoric and excitement assumed greater significance than practical remedies in the shape of legislation or administrative reforms. The agrarians' supporters were won over by the defiance and the showmanship, and they voted for their heroes in election after election. Jeff Davis, for instance, became beloved among the masses in Arkansas when, as attorney general in 1899, he filed dozens of antitrust suits against out-of-state fire insurance companies. Soon he was suing the tobacco, cotton oil, and express companies on behalf of the people they were exploiting. Although the courts usually decided against him, Davis had already won the affection of "the fellows at the forks of the creeks." In a succession of fights as governor against the interests that wanted to build a new statehouse and against convict leasing in the state prison system, he earned their enthusiasm and allegiance through three more election contests. Despite "the sound and the fury," "the tribune of the haybinders" actually accomplished very little. And this was the general pattern among the agrarian leaders.

There were exceptions to this poor record of accomplishment. James K. Vardaman was one agrarian leader who achieved a remarkable amount during his one term as governor of Mississippi, from 1903 to 1907. Among his many initiatives, he introduced a uniform textbook law, doubled the budget for public education, made major improvements in the state's charitable institutions, and reformed the prison system by ending convict leasing and protecting prisoners from abuse. For the most part, however, both the demagogues and their followers were less interested in legislative results than in the exhilaration of campaigning. As Raymond Arsenault once observed insightfully, their adherents "knew that good politics made them feel better, but they were not sure what good government would do for them."[27]

Relishing the campaign, with its barnstorming oratory of defiance and denunciation, rather than the less spectacular task of building coalitions capable of enacting and implementing public policy, the agrarian leaders accomplished little for their downtrodden disciples. After his brief and quite successful stint as governor, Vardaman spent the next six years trying to become senator. And the same was true of his apprentice, Theodore Bilbo, "the prince of the peckerwoods," who served an effective term as governor, 1915–19, but then returned to his first love, running for office. This failure to deliver has provoked considerable criticism from V. O. Key and many other historians. But these colorful agitators did, in fact, deliver what their followers wanted. They injected excitement and drama into the region's politics and into the dreary lives of poor white southerners. They acknowledged their needs, denounced their enemies, and restored their self-respect.

To have expected these men to attack the fundamental, structural causes of rural poverty—the crop-lien system, falling cotton prices, Jim Crow race relations, the underfunded schools—was even more unrealistic. All the same, it is hard to overlook their shortcomings as policy makers, no matter that they entertained and invigorated their followers when they ridiculed the well-heeled urbanites and denounced the economic interests that profited while the rural masses remained trapped in poverty. As Raymond Arsenault concluded, these agitators and performers "invariably forced their constituents (not to mention the mass of disfranchised blacks and poor whites) to pay a heavy price for what turned out to be ephemeral and self-defeating accomplishments."[28]

9

Reform and Reaction
in the Solid South

The unstructured one-party system that produced the rural agitator and demagogue also generated a very different kind of reform politician. Progressives were based in the region's cities and supported by the well-to-do and respectable classes, mainly businessmen and professionals. The issues they advocated and the way they promoted and accomplished them were quite different from those of the agrarian agitators. The Progressives were primarily concerned about the concentration of economic power in the hands of monopolies and trusts, which exerted a corrupt influence over state legislators and other public officials. Progressives were also aware of the region's social problems and deficiencies, especially its inadequate system of public education and its primitive public health facilities. To deal with each of these problems, Progressives were willing to call on the power of government. The result was a burst of legislative activity, with achievements far greater than their agrarian counterparts had accomplished, even though their scope and impact were still quite limited.

Southern Progressivism

Any semblance of Progressivism in the South during the first quarter of the twentieth century was for a long time dismissed, even denied, by historians. How could any movement that called itself "progressive" coexist with the "cracker messiahs" and "Dixie demagogues" who were springing up across the land? Was it possible that anything progressive could emerge from a region so backward and ignorant? Southern Progressivism seemed to be an oxymoron, a view that was prevalent even at the time. As late as 1912, Senator Robert La Follette of Wisconsin, the leading Progressive politician in the North, announced with assurance: "I don't know of any progressive sentiment or any progressive legislation in the South."[1] However, La Follette and subsequent historians were blinded by their prejudices and stereotypes. A Progressive movement very similar to its counterpart in the rest of the country did emerge in the South, and it was preoccupied with the same kinds of problems and proposed similar remedies as elsewhere. Progressive challenges and initiatives were pivotal in shaping the politics of the South, just as in the North.

Distinctions did exist, of course, but they were regional variations rather than fundamental differences. First of all, some reforms, such as the abolition of convict leasing and the campaign against child labor in the textile mills, targeted problems that were primarily southern. Other reforms, like the prohibition of alcohol, the creation of an adequate public school system, and public health campaigns against diseases arising from malnutrition, such as pellagra and hookworm, were of greater significance and generated more concern in the South than elsewhere.

Second, the South was less industrialized and urbanized than the Northeast and the Midwest. Consequently, city-dwelling Progressives were a smaller and less influential element in the population as a whole and they encountered considerable resistance from rural folk, with their traditional views about education, health and hygiene, gender roles, and race relations. Disdain for modernity and opposition to change was also prevalent among planters in the rural areas and merchants and bankers of the small market towns, further limiting southern Progressivism. Southern Progressives' views about urban and industrial development within their region also influenced their approach to reform. Most of them wanted the South to modernize and become transformed into a "New South," and they believed, like the New South boosters themselves, that this could be achieved by promoting investment capital and manufacturing in order to stimulate the economic development and prosperity that the region so urgently needed. Indeed, industrial development in the South was considered almost a public service in the early twentieth century. Progressive reforms requiring that corporations behave differently—for example, forcing them to be less monopolistic, to refrain from bribing legislators, and to pay and treat their employees decently—could not be allowed to discourage investment or hurt manufacturing firms. In a region so lacking in development, hostility toward corporations might do more harm than good. Such concern was far less in evidence among Progressives elsewhere.

A third regional variation was the political system within which southern Progressives had to operate. With an electorate that was exclusively white, the black one-third of the South's population was not likely to be a major beneficiary of these reforms. Indeed, in a memorable phrase, C. Vann Woodward described southern reform as "Progressivism—for whites only." This was strikingly evident in the public education campaigns. The illiteracy rate for blacks was an appalling 50 percent, compared to the whites' still-abysmal 25 percent. And black education was funded at very unfavorable ratios—such as North Carolina's 1:3 and South Carolina's shocking 1:12. Yet the campaigns were directed solely at improving white schools. The only consolation for blacks was the reformers' constant refrain that, if whites were educated and informed, they would be less prejudiced against them, a cruel apology for depriving them of decent schools. And the same racial exclusiveness applied to child labor and public health reforms.

Perversely, most southern Progressives regarded disfranchisement, which had produced the region's distorted political system, as a reform. Although it had not been introduced by reformers in the 1890s, disfranchisement eliminated the need for rampant electoral fraud and intimidation. Therefore, it cleaned up elections. It also "improved" the electorate by confining it to literate and tax-paying citizens, a change that northern Progressives also favored, although Eastern European immigrants rather than African Americans were their primary targets. Progressive electoral reform also included the secret ballot, compulsory registration, and even the direct primary, all of which the South had established for the purpose of eliminating the black vote and undermining the Republican Party. Identification with these electoral reforms enabled the Progressives to stimulate public interest in other reforms they proposed and to urge government to implement them.

But one reform that arose in the 1910s suffered directly as a result of disfranchisement. The movement for woman suffrage was severely hampered by the charge that if the campaign succeeded black women as well as white would obtain the vote. To the arguments raised elsewhere against the very idea of women voting, woman suffragists in the South had to contend with the pervasive fear that blacks would once again be voting, only a decade or so after the Democratic Party had finally removed them from the electorate. Even the suffragists' response that the votes of white women would be more numerous than those of their black counterparts failed to convince most southern whites, who believed that blacks as a race should be denied the vote and kept out of politics.

The issue was so potent that it split the suffragist movement in the South, resulting in the formation of the Southern States Woman Suffrage Conference, headed by Kate Gordon of Louisiana. The women of this

Equal Suffrage League of Richmond. In this undated photograph, a group of well-dressed and well-to-do members of the league, probably its leaders, sit in Richmond's Capitol Square. Library of Virginia.

organization seriously qualified their support of woman suffrage by insisting that the vote be confined to white women and by formulating their opposition to the proposed federal suffrage amendment as a matter of state rights. As Sophonisba Breckinridge, a leading suffragist in Kentucky, explained later, "The question of 'states' rights' in the decade 1910–1920, as in 1861, was really a question of the negro."[2] This objection contributed substantially to the defeat of the federal amendment throughout the South, except in Kentucky, Tennessee, Arkansas, and Texas. However, southern opposition was not enough to prevent ratification of the Nineteenth Amendment in 1920. The upshot was that many white women registered and managed to exert some degree of political leverage, but black women's attempts to participate were thwarted massively by the region's discriminatory voter registration practices and by all the means available for the enforcement of its system of white supremacy.

The one-party feature of the region's political system shaped its Progressivism. Without an organized opposition party, the reformers had to work through the only available party. The primary offered them relatively easy access to power, so that candidates for governor identifying themselves as reformers were able to get elected. Although they could not commit the Democrats to a reform agenda, they did manage to create a Progressive faction within the party and then enact reforms whenever they were in office. From about 1905 to World War I, when Progressivism was at its height, the Democratic Party in most states experienced a period of bifactionalism, with a reform faction lining up against a rival that was hostile to reform.

In Georgia, Governor Hoke Smith's reform faction battled Joseph M. Brown's probusiness forces between 1905 and 1915. In Alabama, Braxton B. Comer's administration, 1906–10, aligned the state's factional divisions around the issue of reform. A bifactional split emerged in three more states. In Mississippi, Governor Vardaman (1903–7) and Governor Bilbo (1915–19) headed the reform factions, even though they were agrarian leaders in that overwhelmingly agricultural state. Similarly, in Florida, agrarians Napoleon Broward (1904–8) and Park Trammell (1912–16) forged a reform faction. And in Texas, Governor Thomas M. Campbell (1906–10) led the reformers. However, in Virginia, North Carolina, and South Carolina, intraparty divisions were stifled because the conservative, probusiness forces that had gained control over the party decided to accommodate to the reformers and adopt some of their measures rather than confront and fight them.

The environment of the South, particularly its political system, may have given the region's Progressivism a form and tone that was distinctive, but the reforms themselves and the need for them were similar. The core target of the Progressive movement was economic monopoly, and the railroads were the primary and most visible offenders. In 1906 and 1907, mounting anger at the behavior of the railroads burst into the open in the South, with Governors Hoke Smith, Braxton B. Comer, Tom Campbell, and North Carolina's Robert B. Glenn leading the assault. Their state legislatures responded with measures to reduce freight rates and prohibit discriminatory rebates to favored shippers; to outlaw stock watering and other questionable financial practices; and to increase the powers of the state railroad commissions in overseeing and regulating the railroads. Progressives tried to restrict the railroads' ability to influence legislation by offering free passes on the trains to legislators and by sending paid lobbyists to influence them.

Out-of-state insurance companies were also targeted by these Progressive administrations because they charged excessive rates and siphoned off local capital to other states. Interestingly, New York had erupted in 1905–6 over revelations about the activities and practices of life insurance and utility companies, resulting in the creation of commissions and statutes to regulate these firms as well as railroads and other forms of transportation. Since many other states embarked on similar reform initiatives at the same time, the South's reformers were clearly in step with Progressives elsewhere.

The efforts of southern Progressives ran into obstacles because of the inherent conservatism of the governors who led these fights. Alabama's Braxton B. Comer was a case in point. Earlier in his life, he had managed to purchase cornmeal and flour mills and then acquire a Birmingham textile company called Avondale Mills. As a mill owner, he realized that the freight rates charged by Alabama's railroads were hurting his and others' businesses. So he became actively involved in efforts to reduce shipping rates and regulate the railroads, soon getting elected to the state's newly elective railroad commission in 1904. Two years later, he won the governorship in a campaign against the railroads that swept the state. Once in office, Comer's proposals for reducing freight and passenger rates, increasing the powers of the railroad commission, and expanding the state's authority over transportation and telegraph and telephone companies were passed by the legislature. But the Louisville and Nashville railroad refused to accede to these restrictions, resulting in a bitter public battle in the federal courts, which was not resolved until several years after Comer left office.

Like most Progressive governors, Comer was not a single-issue candidate. He doubled the state's budget for education. He increased tax revenues and made tax collection fairer and more accurate through a board of equalization to assess corporations and force them to pay more taxes. And he endorsed statewide prohibition, though he was rebuffed when he backed a move to strengthen it through a constitutional amendment. At the same time, he was decidedly lukewarm about legislation to combat the exploitation of child labor in textile mills such as his own. Eventually, he did endorse a measure raising the age for child workers from fourteen to sixteen and requiring that children attend school for at least eight weeks a year. He also supported a bill to improve the treatment of convict labor but was utterly opposed to abolishing the system. Finally, he mobilized the power of the state against a major strike in 1908 at Alabama's biggest coal mine operator, the Tennessee Coal, Iron, and Railroad Company, helping to break the strike and leaving the company with greater control over its labor force than before. Although Comer may have attacked the railroads, he was clearly an ally of Alabama's largest corporations and employers and very hostile to its poorly treated laborers.[3]

But these actions made him no less a Progressive. He espoused some of the movement's core issues—the regulation of railroads, the prohibition of alcohol, the improvement of public education, and the equalization of taxation. Like most Progressives, he was unwilling to interfere significantly on behalf of labor in its relations with capital, whether it be child, convict, or union labor. Progressives in the South, as elsewhere, sought to bring order to the emerging industrial and urban world, not to attack it or change it drastically. The drive to regulate railroads was the centerpiece of Progressive reform, especially in Alabama, Georgia, North Carolina, Florida, and Texas, where, in a wave of reform legislation between 1906 and 1909, railroad commissions were strengthened, rates for passengers and freight were lowered, and a uniform system of rates between the states was established. This regulatory impulse ramified into other areas, such as insurance, banking, futures trading, fertilizer manufacturing, and textbook publishing, as well as in oil and tobacco production.

Municipal reform was also a Progressive issue. The South contributed two innovations in urban governance aimed at removing it from elective politics and thus reducing the possibilities of corruption. An appointed commission was created in Galveston after the devastating tidal wave of 1900 and proved successful in rebuilding the city. Other Texas cities quickly adopted the "Galveston Plan." By 1913, it had spread across the region to most larger cities, among them Memphis, New Orleans, and Birmingham. Also southern in origin was the idea of an appointed, professional city manager, first introduced in Staunton (pronounced "Stanton"), Virginia, in 1908 and then adopted in many towns, though not in big cities, throughout the South and the nation.

Also bringing order to urban life in the South was racial segregation. Beginning with legislation in the 1890s to provide separate coaches, or separate sections within coaches, on passenger trains, the racial separation of public facilities spread throughout the region's transportation systems, in particular its passenger ferries and ships and its streetcars. It then moved into every facet of southern urban life—to public libraries and parks, to hospitals, hotels, restaurants, and water fountains, and on and on. By the 1920s, two separate racial worlds had become established, formally legalized by state statute or municipal ordinance, in the public institutions and spaces of the South's cities.

Another reform some might not consider progressive was the prohibition of alcohol. Although the origins of prohibition were rural, where it was advocated by the white, Protestant, respectable classes, it was nevertheless advocated by Progressives in the cities too, for drink generated the same kinds of social problems in the city as in the countryside and small towns. Moreover, saloons were ubiquitous in the city, as were the "lower orders," with their supposedly unquenchable thirsts, who frequented them. By 1909, Alexander McKelway, the Alabama child labor reformer, could observe proudly that "the crow can fly from Cape Hatteras in a straight line through North Carolina, Tennessee and Arkansas to the farthest boundary of Oklahoma, and return by way of Mississippi, Alabama and Georgia to the starting point, through prohibition territory."[4] This was possible because those seven states had enacted statewide prohibition over the previous two years.

The Progressives complemented their search for order with a concern for "the forgotten man" who had been left behind and ignored but who now needed desperately to be uplifted and improved. "There was, in truth," as C. Vann Woodward later observed, "enough to keep trainloads of philanthropists and battalions of uplifters busy in the South."[5] So the South's reformers took up the challenge by pressuring state governments to disburse funds and create agencies for improving the conditions of life for the region's disadvantaged and abused, provided of course that their skin was white. The education campaigns were the most public manifestations of the reform initiative. Usually organized by southern educational leaders associated with the northern philanthropic Southern Education Board and encouraged by "education governors" like Charles B. Aycock of North Carolina and Andrew J. Montague of Virginia, the campaigns mobilized citizen support to influence state legislators. And they produced a significant response. Between 1900 and 1915, per capita expenditure for southern public education doubled, the school term was lengthened considerably, and compulsory attendance laws were passed. As a result, the white illiteracy rate was reduced by half. But the higher black illiteracy rate was unaffected by this movement, for the simple reason that schooling for the children of segregated and disfranchised blacks was beyond the scope of these campaigns to educate the superior, and therefore more deserving, whites.

Related to the educational campaigns was the movement to protect those children who had little time or energy to go to school. The National Child Labor Committee, which was created in 1904 and headed by southerners, first Edgar Gardner Murphy, its founder, and then Alexander McKelway, generated pressure for legislation to raise the age limit and reduce the hours of child workers. By 1910, all the southern states mandated a minimum age requirement, though only four had reached the age of fourteen, not much of an improvement after all. Most states had also failed to reduce the long hours worked, during the day as well as at night, so children still labored for fifty or more hours a week. Despite the unrelenting efforts of the Progressive reformers, the decades-long campaign did not break down the intense resistance from the textile mill owners, who controlled the lives of their workers in the mill villages and claimed that their competitive advantage over northern textiles would be eliminated if their labor costs rose significantly. Not surprisingly, the four states with a minimum age limit of fourteen years were Kentucky, Tennessee, Oklahoma, and Louisiana, none of them centers of textile production.

Health was another area of southern life in desperate need of improvement, especially because of the frequency of epidemics of yellow fever, typhoid, smallpox, and malaria. The introduction of state boards of health in all the southern states was the most important development during these years of Progressive reform, because the boards could organize the distribution of vaccines and take preventive measures by ensuring healthy sanitation, disseminating health information, and enforcing food and drug laws. A campaign undertaken between 1909 and 1914 against a ubiquitous intestinal parasite called hookworm, which infected and debilitated 2 million southerners, was initiated and funded by the (John D.) Rockefeller Sanitary Commission for the Eradication of Hookworm. The hookworm campaign gave a boost to the idea of public health and to the state boards that administered the successful program. As a result, this initiative began to extend down to the county level, and state funding for public health increased.

The South in the Wilson Administration

The aim of Progressive reform was not to transform southern life but to organize and improve it. Within these more limited aims, it had accomplished a great deal during the opening decade or so of the new century. The election to the presidency in 1912 of a Progressive, who also happened to be southern born and a Democrat, raised hopes that the region's Progressive movement might acquire new momentum.

Although he had been president of Princeton University and governor of New Jersey, Woodrow Wilson still identified himself as a southerner. But he was not the only contender for the Democratic nomination in 1912 who had a claim on southern support. Even more southern than Wilson was Oscar W. Underwood of Alabama, the majority leader in the House and chair of its Ways and Means Committee. The intrasectional contest that ensued required forty-six ballots before the Progressive Wilson defeated the conservative Underwood. The Alabamian took all the delegates from four Lower South states (Alabama, Mississippi, Georgia, and Florida), and Wilson won Texas and South Carolina. The Upper South was split between the two front-runners. Then, in the presidential election, Wilson carried every southern state over his two major rivals, Theodore Roosevelt, the Bull Moose Progressive Party candidate, and William H. Taft, the incumbent president and the regular Republican nominee.

Outside the South, Wilson carried only one state, Arizona, by a majority, but he won forty states with a plurality and obtained 43 percent of the popular vote. Clearly a candidate with national appeal, Wilson's core support was nevertheless in the South. Not surprisingly, he brought many southerners into his cabinet. Josephus Daniels of North Carolina was secretary of the navy, David F. Houston of Texas was secretary of agriculture, and Albert Sidney Burleson of Texas was postmaster general. In addition, his treasury secretary, William G. McAdoo, and his attorney general, James C. Reynolds, were both transplanted southerners, from Georgia and Tennessee, respectively, although now living in New York. And Wilson's right-hand man was the experienced political operative from Texas, Colonel Edward M. House, who would become exceedingly influential in the Wilson White House.

At the other end of Pennsylvania Avenue, the Democrats' majorities were heavily southern, over half in the Senate and two-thirds in the House. Even more significant, southern Democrats were chairmen of all but two of the fourteen major standing committees in the Senate and all but two of the thirteen in the House. With the Democrats in control of both houses of Congress and the presidency, southerners appeared to have taken control of the national government. Surveying the Washington scene, political commentators observed ruefully that the South was "back in the saddle."

Unlike Cleveland in 1892, Wilson had not been elected by the South. But the region's visibility in Washington did cause Wilson to worry that "jealousies" might arise. He warned Oscar Underwood: "While I myself am deeply glad to be a Southern man and to have the South feel a sense of possession in me, we shall have to be careful not to make the impression that the South is seeking to keep the front of the stage and the possession of the administration."[6] This would be difficult to pull off, because the agenda for this anomalous Democratic, yet also Progressive, administration required passage of an array of measures that depended upon support from powerful committee chairmen, almost all of whom were southerners and mainly conservatives. Wilson had won the presidency, but the real victor was the "Solid South" strategy. By continually electing Democrats to Congress and then reelecting them once they became incumbents, these solid delegations from the South had gained a decisive influence, because of their seniority, within the Democrats' congressional caucus, as well as within the committee system. Not just the South, but the "Solid South," was "back in the saddle," and Wilson could not throw it off.

Nor did he particularly want to. For Wilson acquiesced in the ascendant southerners' drive to expand segregation, their new system of race relations, into the nation's capital. By segregating the national government, they hoped that the southern version of racial inequality and caste would become accepted and legitimate in the nation. At one of the first cabinet meetings, Postmaster General Burleson proposed separating white and black railway clerks so as to avoid friction between them. "Mr. Burleson thought the segregation would be a great thing as he had the highest regard for the negro and wished to help him in every way possible," reported Josephus Daniels, who had been one of the architects of North Carolina's "White Supremacy" campaign in 1898.[7] There followed a deluge of proposals for instituting southern race relations throughout the city and the government. And they were implemented, either through executive orders separating the races within the departments of government and in its facilities, like lunchrooms and restrooms, or through federal legislation to prevent racial intermarriage and to impose segregation on public transportation in the District.

President Wilson gave no general directive to segregate, but the process continued piecemeal, in the Post Office and the Treasury Department especially, as well as in most places where federal employees congregated. Because Wilson had appealed to northern blacks in the election campaign by offering them assurances that they would be treated fairly by a Democratic administration, he wanted to handle the issue "with the greatest possible patience and tact" rather than capitulate to the southerners' offensive.[8] All the same, he retained only eight of the thirty African Americans holding presidential appointments. And segregation spread throughout official Washington, even without the imprimatur of a presidential order. African American newspaper editors and interracial organizations, like the recently founded National Association for the Advancement of Colored People, protested vehemently against what they saw as Wilson's betrayal. But northern white sentiment acquiesced in the separation of the races, especially since much of it was not formalized in federal legislation.

The imprint of the triumphant South on the domestic agenda of Wilson's New Freedom, as it was called, was also indisputable. Every major piece of legislation was brought forward and steered to passage by southern congressmen, while receiving overwhelming support from the southern delegations. The heart of the president's Progressive plans consisted of measures relating to the tariff, banking and currency, and antitrust. Wilson's tariff bill, which introduced what George B. Tindall has called "the most drastic reduction since the Civil War," was driven through the House by Underwood, the chair of the Ways and Means Committee, who had been chairman of the campaign in 1901 to ratify Alabama's disfranchising constitution.[9] Meanwhile, the usually antireductionist Senate was handled by North Carolina's Furnifold Simmons, the Finance Committee chair, who had orchestrated his state's "White Supremacy" and disfranchisement campaigns as chairman of the state Democratic Party. Included in the measure was a federal income tax proposed by Cordell Hull, congressman from Tennessee and future secretary of state under Franklin D. Roosevelt, to which Senators Vardaman and John Nance Garner of Texas added a graduated surtax on large incomes.

Wilson's banking plan created the Federal Reserve System, the nation's first central bank since Andrew Jackson destroyed the Second Bank of the United States eighty years earlier. It was the brainchild of Representative and later Senator Carter Glass of Virginia, a leading figure in his state's disfranchising convention in 1901–2. Glass's insistence that there be twelve regional reserve banks was in accord with southern hostility to centralization, though Wilson still required a central board of governors to oversee the entire system. With Underwood and Simmons again moving the bill through both houses, it passed very easily in December 1913. Finally, antitrust legislation came in the form of the Federal Trade Commission Act and the Clayton Anti-Trust Act. Although Henry D. Clayton, who introduced one of the bills, was from Alabama, southerners played only a small role in shaping these laws. But they did vote solidly in support of them.

While the South's congressional leaders had ensured that Wilson's New Freedom legislation was enacted, they had not shaped it or obtained much from it for their own region. This was to change in the wake of the crisis that southern agriculture confronted when war broke out in Europe in 1914. The drying up of Britain's customary purchases of cotton, along with the wartime restrictions on its sale elsewhere in Europe, caused the staple's price to plummet. Aware that they were now influential players in Washington, southern politicians forgot their hostility to federal legislation and besieged Wilson and the Congress with proposals for relief, initially in the form of large federal purchases of cotton. In October 1914, Georgia's Hoke Smith led a filibuster to prevent the Senate from adjourning before aiding the stricken southern states. Some financial help did result, but the major outcome was a series of measures that provided stability and support for southern agriculture. Laws regulating cotton futures and providing federal licensing of warehouses where cotton was stored prior to sale were passed in 1914. While this legislation protected cotton producers from financial loss in the short run, the farmers' greater need was access to credit, which was eventually supplied through the Federal Farm Loan Act of 1916. It created twelve government-controlled and -financed banks to provide long-term loans to farmers, with their land as collateral. This act was accompanied by other southern-initiated measures, the Smith-Lever Act of 1914 and the Smith-Hughes Act of 1917, providing respectively for a federal agricultural extension program and for high school vocational education.

Southerners' support for farm owners did not extend to urban workers, however. Their congressional leaders endorsed neither the law giving workmen's compensation to federal employees nor the law protecting seafaring workers, the Furuseth Sailor Act. But, in 1916, they sponsored the Child Labor Act, which passed with a southern majority in favor, despite the vigorous opposition of the three or four southern textile states. That same year, southerners voted for the Adamson Act, named after William C. Adamson of Georgia, an opponent of the railroads and also chair of the House Interstate Commerce Committee. The law granted the eight-hour day to railroad workers as a result of the crippling railway strike that year and because of Wilson's great interest in preventing a further strike, as he prepared the country for war. With few exceptions, Woodrow Wilson's Progressive agenda was successfully implemented because of the organizational power and parliamentary experience of the southern Democratic leadership.

The South continued to be "in the saddle," as Wilson became increasingly involved in the European war. At first, the southerners were skeptical. When Wilson embarked on his military preparedness program in 1915, he encountered considerable opposition from the South because of its resentment of the British for their disruption of the cotton trade and their subsequent efforts to prevent America from trading with other European countries. Compounding this initial southern opposition was the traditional agrarian antipathy toward business and the suspicion that munitions makers and the financiers would be the primary beneficiaries from the preparedness measures and from any ensuing war. "I feel that it is big ammunition and war equipment interests that are trying to manufacture public sentiment into favoring a big naval and military propaganda," charged Claude Kitchen of North Carolina, the majority leader in the House in 1916, who played a major role in rallying opposition to defeat Wilson's initial program.[10] When the president submitted a reduced preparedness plan, it passed, although Kitchen managed to insert an income tax provision into the Revenue Act of 1916, which was intended to pay for preparedness. Kitchen also raised the surtax on profits to replace the regressive consumption and income taxes that Treasury Secretary McAdoo had sought.

After the German submarine campaign and the subsequent American entry into the war, however, the southerners' attitude changed. Their support for the declaration of war and for the measures to maintain the war effort was solid. Only five southern representatives, along with Senator Vardaman, voted against the war. On the eight principal measures for prosecuting the war that actually gave sweeping powers to the federal government, a mere 21 negative votes all told were cast by southern congressmen.[11] These votes did not mean that there was no opposition in the South to the war or to fighting in it. But they did indicate the extent of the support among southern congressmen for Wilson himself and for the national Democratic Party, as well as the degree to which the southerners had come to acquiesce in federal activism ever since they had become so involved in enacting most of Wilson's program.

After the war was over, Wilson urged the Senate to ratify the League of Nations treaty. The South again stood solidly behind him, supporting the league enthusiastically and insisting that the treaty be accepted unaltered and without reservations. When Wilson refused to approve the treaty after reservations were tacked on, only two southern senators opposed him. The twenty-three who supported him and the unamended treaty were all southerners. Loyalty to the president and the party were again evident in these votes, but the South's senators were also indicating their openness to international cooperation, unlike most of their colleagues from outside the South, who were either reluctant to join the League of Nations or were utterly opposed to it.

Business Progressivism and the "Benighted South"

During Wilson's second term, Washington's attention naturally turned toward preparing for war. Since almost all of Wilson's agenda for domestic reform had already been realized, Progressive issues began to fade away. In the South, however, the flurry of reform activity within the Democratic Party at the national level made Progressivism seem acceptable and even desirable. In the Lower South, governors were elected who proceeded to embark on reform programs that included most of the Progressive proposals. After years of enduring the turbulence caused by Governor Cole Blease and his followers among South Carolina's rural masses and textile workers, the state managed to elect Richard I. Manning to succeed him in 1914. Manning offered not calm but more activity, though in a more productive direction. He revised the tax system to make it more equitable and generate more revenue; he improved the schools and increased their funding; he established a highway commission; and he created a state board to supervise welfare and prisons. Most significant of all, he provided the protection so desperately needed by workers in the textile mills, both adult and juvenile, which Blease had failed to deliver even though he had claimed to be the mill hands' advocate.

In 1916, Arkansas swallowed a dose of Progressivism administered by Charles H. Brough, who like Wilson was a university professor, having actually studied with him at Johns Hopkins. Far more effective than Jeff Davis, though far less exciting, Brough equalized taxation and introduced most of the reforms in education, health, and agriculture that were important to Progressives. In Alabama, Thomas Kilby, who had been elected as a prohibitionist in 1918, surprised his state by proceeding to pick up Braxton B. Comer's Progressive mantle and embark on a program to reform the state's tax system, schools, prisons, and public health, as well as to build roads and pass a workmen's compensation law.

But most dramatic was the governorship of Theodore G. Bilbo in Mississippi from 1915 to 1919. A perennial figure in the state's politics for almost a decade, his scandalous reputation seemed to justify the verdict of the editor of the *Jackson Daily News* that, by electing Bilbo governor, the voters had decided that "they would rather wallow in filth than walk on clean ground."[12] Amazingly, Bilbo proceeded to compile a record of accomplishment, which rivaled that of his mentor, James K. Vardaman, and even exceeded Manning's in sheer volume and scope. This achievement would be sullied by his second four-year gubernatorial term in the late 1920s when he fought with the legislature and accomplished almost nothing. But, up to this time, Mississippi had been lucky with its two agrarian leaders who served as governor.

Less happy were the experiences of Florida and Texas, whose agrarian governors achieved very little. Sidney Catts injected prohibition and anti-Catholic prejudice into Florida's politics in his 1916 election campaign. After four years in office, he had disrupted the anticorporate focus of the state's Progressive faction and still left no record of reform. By contrast, James "Pa" Ferguson had at least offered the suffering tenant farmers of Texas a remedy in the form of fixed rental agreements, while also proposing better schools and a state-controlled warehouse system to keep the price of agricultural products from falling. But his provocative antiurban, antielite behavior produced a reaction that resulted in his impeachment in 1917 and a permanent ban on his holding office again. "Fergusonism," his appeal to the impoverished rural masses, survived his own political demise, however, because his wife, "Ma," would inherit the votes of his supporters, enabling her to win the governorship twice, serving from 1924 to 1926 and from 1932 to 1934.

Progressivism did not, in fact, die out, as historians used to believe, with the end of World War I and of the Wilson administration soon afterward. Instead, it metamorphosed into what George B. Tindall has called "business progressivism." The term is not the oxymoron it appears to be, because most southern Progressives had never opposed business in the first place. They looked to manufacturers and bankers as agents of southern development and prosperity but feared they were out of control and needed regulation. By the 1920s, the regulatory and antimonopolistic tendency in southern Progressivism had run its course and the behavior of corporations seemed no longer to be a matter of concern to the reformers.

Progressives now viewed the function of government rather differently. No more did state government need to be pushed and prodded into taking responsibility for solving the economic problems of the region and curing its social ills. Instead, so the Progressives deduced, government had to be streamlined and adequately funded, so that the tasks it had recently assumed could now be sustained and even broadened. For example, the departments of corrections and the public health agencies that had been created earlier had to be maintained and strengthened. To protect the reforms already achieved, a different kind of political leadership was called for. Rather than governors able to rally voters to demand reform, governors were needed who had bureaucratic experience and could make government reliable and efficient. Progressivism in the 1920s had therefore shifted into a new phase, from innovation to institutionalization, from creation to consolidation.

As might be expected, the governors who best exemplified this trend were gray, even colorless, compared to their predecessors, the theatrical agrarian reformers and the combative urban Progressives. Cameron Morrison in North Carolina, Bibb Graves in Alabama, Austin Peay in Tennessee, and Harry F. Byrd in Virginia gave their states cautious and constructive administrations that delivered the essential, but still insufficient, public services the Progressives had instituted. "Good government" was their primary concern, and so these governors reorganized the state bureaucracies, reducing the number of agencies and thereby cutting costs and making government more efficient. New sources of revenue were found from taxes on gasoline, tobacco, automobiles, and income (eight southern states had introduced an income tax by 1929), as well as more ingenious ways of taxing property and corporations. These savings and revenues enabled the states to fund their proliferating public health and public welfare responsibilities.

Despite these efforts to balance their budgets, the business progressives embarked on expansionist endeavors that generated large-scale indebtedness. Roads and schools were considered wise investments in infrastructure, sure to pay off in economic development and general prosperity. Between 60 percent and 70 percent of southern state expenditures in the 1920s went to highways and education, with the former usually consuming the greater portion. And the road building was impressive. Harry Byrd increased Virginia's paved roads by 5,000 miles by 1929, while North Carolina built over 7,000 miles of roads by 1928, almost 4,000 of them hard surfaced, for what was then a staggering sum of $153 million. By 1930, the South had acquired about 210,000 miles of paved rural roads, compared to 121,000 a decade earlier. These expensive programs of economic development meant that, in the end, debt eclipsed fiscal caution. The verdict of the editor of the *Montgomery Advertiser* on Governor "Bibb the Builder" Graves might apply to all of these efficiency-minded, but extravagant, business progressives. "Bibb Graves makes a good governor, but an expensive one."[13]

The political arena in the 1920s South was relatively calm, with respectable and reliable governors presiding over reputable and responsible administrations. Bilbo's disastrous second term as governor was probably the only real episode of buffoonery. Meanwhile, the factionalism generated by the one-party system settled into a less cantankerous mode very different from the earlier contestation between the dissidents, led by an agrarian leader or a Progressive, and the conservative party establishment. There were exceptions, however. In Texas, the rural-urban split represented by "Fergusonism" continued into "Ma" Ferguson's 1924–26 term, and a sharp, bifactional struggle emerged in Louisiana, as Huey P. Long mounted his challenge to the two-decades-old hegemony of the New Orleans ring, headed by Mayor Martin Behrman. Otherwise, factionalism was relatively fluid, which allowed for the emergence of colorless and respectable politicians like Morrison and Peay. Even in states like Virginia and North Carolina, where machines headed by Senators Thomas S. Martin and Furnifold Simmons were entrenched, they continued to be accommodationist and therefore able to adapt to business progressivism. This was a repeat of their earlier adaptation to the Progressivism of Montague and Aycock when they had run their own candidates, such as Claude Swanson who was governor of Virginia from 1906 to 1910 and Locke Craig in North Carolina who was governor from 1913 to 1917.

Beyond the arena of politics, however, the South was riddled with turmoil and conflict. In the early twentieth century, the values and practices of the modern, urban world had begun to penetrate the rural areas of the United States. Country dwellers and traditionalists lashed out and fought back. And the result was a "culture war" far more profound and acrimonious than its more recent incarnation in the 1990s and after. Nowhere was this reaction so visible or extreme as in the South. Indications first appeared in the crusade to eliminate alcohol throughout the nation, whose most enthusiastic advocates were Protestant, and often small-town and rural, southerners. Opposition was to be found predominantly within the nation's cities and among their immigrant populations. In 1915, a new version of the Ku Klux Klan was organized. Over the next decade, it spread throughout the southern states, broadening its scope from hatred of blacks to include Catholics and immigrants as its targets. Primarily a rural phenomenon with a southern identity, the Klan generated considerable support in the border states and even in the rural areas and small towns of the Midwest, especially Indiana. The Klan's fear of "the other" and the alien was also related to the South's publicly condoned practice of lynching, further evidence of the persistence of primitive attitudes and behavior in the region. Although the number of incidents had declined significantly after 1900, there were still about twenty to thirty lynchings each year in the 1920s.

Another dramatic example of the "benighted South" was the Scopes Trial in Dayton, Tennessee, in 1925. In this sensational public event, William Jennings Bryan, the Democratic nominee for president in 1896, 1900, and 1908, confronted Clarence Darrow, the well-known trial lawyer from Chicago. Bryan represented literal-minded, antiscientific, evangelical Protestantism, while Darrow defended the right of John T. Scopes to teach schoolchildren about Darwin's theory of evolution. The lineup of forces in the culture wars of the 1920s was dry, rural, Protestant, antiscientific nativism versus wet, urban, Catholic, cosmopolitan modernity. And the South became the embodiment of parochial, prejudiced traditionalism, a sectional scapegoat in the nation's showdown with its provincial and rural past.

In depicting the South as benighted and bigoted, the rest of the country seemed to have erased from its memory, or perhaps it had not even noticed, the region's recent espousal of Progressivism, as well as its pivotal role in Wilson's New Freedom and in his internationalism in the postwar creation of the League of Nations. But this amnesia was not entirely the North's fault. It was given a powerful boost by the behavior of the South's political class in the Democratic Party's national convention in 1924 and in the presidential election of 1928. Each time, the southern Democrats revealed how committed they were to rural, dry, nativist, Protestantism, when they struggled to prevent Governor Al Smith of New York from becoming the party's standard-bearer. Smith was an Irish Catholic from New York City who was opposed to prohibition and had earlier been a radical Progressive determined to obtain social justice and improve the conditions of workers and the poor.

In 1924, William G. McAdoo and Oscar W. Underwood were considered viable candidates whom the South could support against the totally unacceptable Smith. McAdoo, who had been Wilson's secretary of the treasury and was also his son-in-law, was considered the bearer of the Wilsonian mantle. Underwood was now Alabama's senior senator and a more conservative Democrat, who nevertheless opposed prohibition and wanted it repealed, while he also condemned the Klan as a secret and prejudiced organization. Senator Underwood and his supporters tried to insert a plank into the Democratic platform censuring the Klan. This maneuver was intended to wreck McAdoo's candidacy in the South. But McAdoo surprised everyone, including Underwood of course, when he refused to support the anti-Klan proposal. The only southern state to support the plank, which failed by just one vote, was Underwood's Alabama.

By his unanticipated refusal to censure the Klan, McAdoo kept his campaign alive and became the leading challenger to Smith. But the convention deadlocked over the choice of either Smith or McAdoo. After two weeks and 101 acrimonious ballots, the convention degenerated into what one reporter described as a "snarling, cursing, tedious, tenuous, suicidal, homicidal rough-house."[14] In a desperate attempt to end the impasse, the convention suspended the two-thirds rule, that century-old safeguard of the southern minority's ability to sway the party's choice of a nominee. With only a plurality needed to nominate, the divided convention reordered itself and selected a dark horse candidate, John W. Davis of West Virginia. Relieved that Smith had been eliminated, the South, with the exception of Kentucky, cast a solid and loyal vote in the general election for the Democratic Party's candidate, who was nevertheless soundly defeated by Calvin Coolidge.

Four years later, a replay of the disastrous 1924 convention seemed likely until McAdoo decided, "for the sake of party unity," to withdraw.[15] With only scattered opposition at the convention, Smith, the wet, Catholic, urban ethnic, became the Democrats' candidate. Even though the party's platform pledged to uphold the prohibition amendment and even though a dry, Protestant southerner, Senator Joseph T. Robinson of Arkansas, was selected as Smith's running mate, the South's powerful prohibitionist and Protestant forces rose up in anger against the New Yorker and vowed to mobilize the region's voters to defeat him. Southern voters and politicians now had to decide between the South's political identity and security within the Democratic Party and the cultural and religious values that had come to define the region in the 1920s.

Few Democratic leaders were prepared to forsake their party for Herbert Hoover. But millions of ordinary voters abandoned it. The border states of Kentucky and Tennessee, along with North Carolina and Virginia in the Upper South, went for Hoover, the Republican, and they were joined by Texas and Florida. Located around the edges of the South, these states have often been referred to as the Rim South or the Peripheral South. Also backing Hoover were a number of southern cities that perhaps considered themselves modern and Progressive—Houston, Dallas, Birmingham, Atlanta, and Chattanooga, to name a few. Ironically, the more rural and less modern parts of the South went for Smith, though he barely won Alabama. These Lower South states may have been more benighted and traditional, but they were the heartland of the South, where the Democratic Party was deeply entrenched and considered vital to the preservation of the racial and social order. So the wet, Catholic urbanite won the most rural, least developed, most provincial part of the South. A bizarre outcome, to say the least, it was explicable only by the powerful influence of the South's one-party system.

The 1928 election was ominous for the Solid South. The region had split decisively, with the more modern and developed parts abandoning the Democrats. Nationally, the Democratic Party was becoming quite unappealing to large numbers of southerners. Should it continue to be dominated by the forces behind the Smith candidacy in 1924 and 1928, the South might soon find itself politically isolated and vulnerable. But the Democratic Party itself was in trouble too. Deeply divided in both elections, it had just suffered an electoral debacle. Smith collected only 40.9 percent of the popular vote and won just eight states, six of them situated in the hostile soil of the Deep South and only two (Massachusetts and Rhode Island) located in the North. He failed even to carry his own state of New York or any of the more urban and industrialized states.

Divided and derided, the South was dependent on a rapidly declining national party, over which it was beginning to have very little influence and within which it was becoming increasingly anomalous and uncomfortable. In the 1920s, the Democrats were again the minority party. But, for the South, the situation looked even worse, since it was in danger of becoming a minority within that minority party.

10

The New Deal Challenge
to the Solid South

In 1928, Herbert Hoover was swept into the presidency with 83 percent of the electoral vote and 58.2 percent of the popular vote. Earlier that year, Huey P. Long became governor of Louisiana at the age of thirty-four with a convincing victory, carrying forty-seven of the state's sixty-four parishes. Four years later, however, Hoover was driven from the White House by an equally lopsided vote, his opponent, Franklin D. Roosevelt, winning with 89 percent of the electoral vote and 57 percent of the popular vote. That same year, Huey Long entered the U.S. Senate and was soon assailing the president he had helped nominate and elect.

The volatility of the national electorate between 1928 and 1932 can be explained by the intervening events of the stock market crash of 1929 and the onset of the Great Depression, and Hoover's inability to respond effectively to both of them. But Long's rapid rise and his bursting onto the national political scene when he was only thirty-eight years old was attributable not to the collapse of the national economy but, on a more limited scale, to the moribund state of Louisiana's politics and Long's own insatiable ambition and extraordinary showmanship.

Thunder from the South: Huey Long

Huey Long's rise to power in Louisiana was quite remarkable. After a few years as a traveling salesman peddling household products and patent medicines who, so it was claimed, could sell anything to anyone, he became a lawyer by passing a very unorthodox bar exam after taking a few courses as a noncredit student at Tulane's law school. Four years later, at the age of twenty-five, he was elected to the three-member state railroad commission as the representative of North Louisiana, where he had grown up in rural, predominantly white, Winn Parish. By 1922 he had become the commission's chairman. Two years later, at age thirty-one, he competed in a three-way race for the governorship and lost—but he ran again in 1928 and was easily elected. After four stormy years in office, he moved up once more, carrying all but eleven parishes to become U.S. senator.

"Huey," or "Kingfish," two names he liked to be called by, was the most spectacular, controversial, and best known of the South's twentieth-century agrarian agitators or demagogues. He made politics a spectacle and a performance, as did the other rabble-rousing politicians the region produced. And he employed the same colorful rhetoric, aiming it at the corporations and banks that were fleecing the people, as well as at the supercilious city slickers who looked down their noses at the simple and ignorant country folk. He also manipulated the region's unstructured primary system to build a massive personal following, which he mobilized to attack the dominant interests and the social elite. Despite the similarity of his political style to other "redneck messiahs" like Jeff Davis and Cole Blease, Huey Long brought to the role several qualities and characteristics that were distinctive and that actually produced quite different results. Although not entirely "sui generis," as his most distinguished biographer, T. Harry Williams, has claimed, his personal attributes and his state's politics turned him into an undisputable demagogue and his followers into an engine of political turbulence. He could not be dismissed merely as a clownish hell-raiser who provided a political outlet for the frustration of the masses.

Ever since the turn of the century, Louisiana's politics had been controlled by the reconstituted New Orleans machine, renamed the Choctaw Club and headed until 1920 by Martin Behrman. Closely allied with the state's major business interests such as the railroads and oil companies, the machine had managed to forestall significant Progressive reform throughout the state, except for the brief interlude of John M. Parker's governorship, 1920–24. Of course, a bevy of politicians who were attached to the ring and were supportive of the interests of the economic and social establishment held office, and still intended to, as the Choctaws began to reorganize once again after Behrman's electoral defeat in 1920. The state's pent-up and urgent need for reform of its basic infrastructure and public services meant that, as George B. Tindall observed so aptly, what was "accomplished with decorum in other states assumed the form of class struggle in Louisiana and provoked a vituperative hostility on both sides."[1] Because Louisiana politics was characterized by machine rule, a full-throated reform movement would require the

Senator Huey Long. This photograph shows "the Kingfish" in action, addressing the Louisiana state legislature with his characteristic gesture of raising his arms above his head to make his point. It was probably taken in 1934 when Long was in the Senate but was, at the same time, still running the state government. Library of Congress, Prints and Photographs Division.

replacement of the New Orleans Ring by an alternative organization also capable of dominating the state.

Louisiana needed a shake-up, and Huey was the man for the job. Unlike most of the agrarian agitators, who complicated their message by also lashing out at blacks, Long focused closely on the deprivation and disadvantages suffered by his country audiences. He was certainly not above using crude language to describe African Americans, but they were neither the central problem for the rural whites nor the cause of their poverty. Instead, their enemies were the whites who were economically powerful, along with their allies and agents among the old fogies and flunkies in the statehouse and legislature. And Long could explain very dramatically what the real issues were, as he did in an evocative and celebrated speech on the eve of his election as governor in 1928. Standing beside the "Evangeline Oak" in the Cajun town of St. Martinsville, the very same tree immortalized in Longfellow's poem about Evangeline waiting in vain for her lover to return, Huey asked:

> Where are the schools that you have waited for your children to have, that have never come? Where are the roads and highways that you sent your money to build, that are no nearer now than ever before? Where are the institutions to care for the sick and disabled? Evangeline wept bitter tears in disappointment, but it lasted through only one lifetime. Your tears in this county, around this oak, have lasted generations. Give me the chance to dry the eyes of those who still weep here.[2]

Eloquent and sentimental though he could be, Long's oratory nevertheless had a hard edge that distinguished him from other agrarian leaders. He hurled invective at his adversaries, whether it was Standard Oil and its managers or the politicians who did its bidding or anyone who found himself in opposition to Huey Long. In addition, he was personally abusive and contentious and seemed to go out of his way to get people's backs up. When he was in the Senate, Tennessee's Kenneth McKellar criticized Huey on the Senate floor for "his venom and the hatred and the malice toward anyone who disagrees with him."[3] Vitriol was used to fire up the resentment of the rural masses, denounce his political opponents, and scare state legislators and U.S. senators into getting out of his way or succumbing to his whims. One Democratic senator admitted, "Frankly, we are afraid of him. He is unscrupulous beyond belief. He might say anything about me, something entirely untrue, and it would ruin me in my state. . . . It's like challenging a buzz saw."[4]

Also distinctive about Long was his desire to control, to dominate. He certainly enjoyed running for office and the excitement and theater of the campaign, but he relished too the combat of governing, of bending people's will to his own agenda and goals. When he was elected governor, he was faced by a legislature of 139 members in which he had only 27 supporters. Rather than trying to influence and cajole both branches, he proceeded to take control by appointing his own Speaker of the House and president pro tem in the senate, and both then chose all the committees. Having organized the assembly, he rammed through his program for free school textbooks and for highway- and bridge-building, all of which required a bond issue that the electorate approved by a massive margin of 3 to 1. But his opponents rallied against the young governor's browbeating and manipulation, which he achieved mainly through personal threats and extensive use of the patronage, and they voted to impeach him. When that failed on a technicality, the legislators still refused to pass his bond bills. However, once he was elected to the Senate, his enemies realized he could no longer be stopped, so they relented and enacted his program for a new state capitol and for roads, bridges, and schools, while also repudiating the remaining impeachment charges. Nevertheless, Long's program remained quite similar to those of the business progressives (although the expenditures in Long's Louisiana were greater), since he, like them, did not provide much in the way of public welfare or social services.

Although he had been elected senator, Huey still managed the state through his surrogate, O. K. Allen, who was Long's choice to succeed him as governor. With the departments and the legislature now firmly under his thumb, he proceeded to gain almost total control over the governance of the state, that is, its administrative apparatus and its electoral system, down to the local level. He also extended his reach to the state's policing institutions, its taxing authorities, its newspapers, and its preeminent municipality, New Orleans. This unprecedented dominance was accomplished mainly through a series of five special sessions that were called by Governor Allen, with Huey in attendance and running the show. The legislators were summoned in 1934 and 1935. Each session lasted a week or less and passed dozens of bills, few of which were even read by the legislators who voted on them.

After these extraordinary legislative sessions, the influential journalist Raymond Gram Swing, who had earlier described Long as "the embodiment of the appetite for power," now dismissed him summarily as a "plain dictator."[5] Although many demonized him as a fascist, an inclination quite understandable in the mid-1930s, it is wise to put Long in perspective by recalling the astute assessment of Norman Thomas, the leader of the Socialist Party. Thomas decided that Louisiana's compliant officials seemed more like "circus-dogs jumping through hoops than [an] army . . . marching in goose-step."[6]

Long's ambition was not limited to the Pelican State. His purpose in getting elected to the U.S. Senate was to use his national position as a platform for his plans to develop a nationwide personal following and a movement, as a precursor to running for president, in 1940 perhaps. His potential and his prospects were not lost on Franklin Roosevelt. Soon after he had been nominated in 1932, Roosevelt received a phone call from Long complaining about his exclusion from the Democratic nominee's inner circle. After calming Huey down and ending the conversation, if such it could be called, Roosevelt explained to some staff members who witnessed the altercation: "It's all very well to laugh at Huey. But actually we have to remember that he really is one of the two most dangerous men in the country."[7] The other threat Roosevelt had in mind was General Douglas MacArthur, whose inordinate ambition President Truman would have to suppress later during the Korean War.

Long would be Roosevelt's own problem. And a real problem he soon turned out to be. For, in 1934, Huey embarked on his campaign to build a movement called Share Our Wealth, which would spread across the country through the creation of clubs and local organizations. With the Depression still devastating millions of people's lives, Long's plan to confiscate fortunes worth over $1 million and redistribute them, along with the excessive property and stocks owned by other rich people, possessed understandable appeal. Exactly how the redistribution was to be implemented and what effect it would have on personal incomes was unclear, although Long promised a guaranteed family income of $2,000 to $3,000 per year. Huey admitted that he had no idea but would "have to call in some great minds to help me."[8]

Nevertheless, huge numbers of people responded enthusiastically and hopefully to Huey's regular radio broadcasts, to his speeches to crowds all over the country, and to his self-promotional autobiography, *Every Man a King*. Meanwhile, his large staff of about fifty replied to letters, produced pamphlets, and organized Share Our Wealth clubs. By April 1935, they claimed that the clubs were located in all forty-eight states and numbered 27,431, with 7,682,768 members. Implausible as it sounds, Long's movement from the left against Roosevelt and his New Deal remedies, which the Kingfish deemed insufficient and unappealing, presented a real threat to the president's reelection prospects in 1936. Democratic Party polls estimated that perhaps 11 percent of the electorate favored Long over Roosevelt, which would enable him to exert considerable leverage if he himself mounted a third-party challenge, or at least supported one. In an attempt "to steal Huey's thunder," Roosevelt introduced a wealth tax in June 1935, which was intended "to soak the rich" by raising the tax rate sharply on the highest incomes. At first Long welcomed the initiative but then changed his mind and ended up opposing most of Roosevelt's Second New Deal proposals.

Huey's opposition did not cause Roosevelt lasting trouble because, on 8 September 1935, he was shot by an assassin in Baton Rouge. Four days later, he died, and a huge throng of approximately 175,000 people converged on the state's new capitol, which Huey had built, to witness his funeral. Long had won the affection of the common folk of his state with his theatrics, his bluster, and his ridicule. He gave them a feeling of empowerment and of hope, but he also compiled a record of achievement in Louisiana, beside which the performance of previous administrations paled. Furthermore, he had carried his campaign for wealth redistribution, as a remedy for the Great Depression and for the nation's underlying economic inequality, beyond the South and into the rest of the country. In this respect too, Long was breaking new ground. For here was a southern state-level politician appealing to northerners at the grass roots to challenge the powers that be and, quite surprisingly, discovering a favorable response. Thirty years or so later, another southern political agitator, a governor of Alabama, George C. Wallace, would attempt something similar.[9]

The South in the New Deal

While Huey Long opposed President Roosevelt's New Deal and ridiculed his upper-class origins by calling him "Franklin De-lah-no Rosy-felt" and "Prince Franklin," the rest of the South's congressional delegation, with but a few exceptions, supported the new Democratic president with the utmost enthusiasm. After two disastrous experiences with Al Smith, southern Democrats believed in 1932 that they had found a more palatable standard-bearer in Roosevelt.

A patrician from upstate New York, Roosevelt had cultivated a southern connection during his convalescence from polio when he often stayed in Warm Springs, Georgia. Although the veteran congressman from Texas, John Nance Garner, was a contender for the party's nomination in 1932, most of the South's congressional leadership rallied to Roosevelt's camp, at the instigation of Senator Cordell Hull of Tennessee. By the time of the Democratic convention, Roosevelt had won three southern primary elections and had gained the support of all but two delegations, Texas and Virginia, both of which were backing favorite sons. Garner, however, decided to throw his delegates to Roosevelt rather than risk a floor fight, for which he was rewarded with the vice presidential slot. The Democratic ticket proceeded to sweep all twelve southern states and the rest of the nation, except Pennsylvania and most of New England, which was all that Hoover could salvage from his own sweep four years earlier.

Once in office, however, Roosevelt's closest advisers included few southerners. His cabinet was decidedly less southern than Wilson's from twenty years earlier. Cordell Hull was secretary of state, Claude Swanson, a former governor and senator from Virginia, was secretary of the navy, and South Carolina's Daniel C. Roper was secretary of commerce. Among

Roosevelt's inner circle, his "Brain Trust" as it was called, only Senator James F. "Jimmy" Byrnes of South Carolina was a member.

Things looked very different on Capitol Hill, however. With the Democrats gaining control of both houses in 1932, Joseph T. Robinson of Arkansas, who had been the minority leader since 1923, was now majority leader, and he would be succeeded by Texas's Alban Barkley after Robinson's death in 1937. Meanwhile, the House Speakers during Roosevelt's four-term presidency were, in succession, Joseph Byrns of Tennessee, William B. Bankhead of Alabama, and Sam Rayburn of Texas. Southerners held the chairmanships of nine of the fourteen major committees in the Senate, Mississippi's Byron P. "Pat" Harrison on Finance being especially influential. In the House, they chaired twelve of the seventeen major standing committees, with Robert Lee "Muley Bob" Daughton of North Carolina at Ways and Means, Marvin Jones of Texas at Agriculture, and Henry Steagall of Alabama at Banking and Currency. Also, until 1937, Rayburn was at Commerce. Amazingly, the Texas delegation alone contained nine permanent committee chairmen.

By the time Roosevelt reached the White House, the committee system had become fully established, with the result that committee chairmen in 1932 wielded more power than their counterparts had when Wilson had been president. In that earlier era, the workings of Congress had been centralized under the control primarily of the dominant Republican leadership, Rhode Island's Nelson Aldrich in the Senate and Joseph Cannon of Illinois in the House. But a bipartisan progressive coalition had stripped them of their power in the late 1910s and transferred it to the standing committees and their chairs. Twenty years later, the committee system had become so fully established that the chair of each committee controlled its business, personally wielding the power to shape, schedule, and sometimes bottle up and withhold legislation under its purview. Situated "at the heart of legislative politics," the committees drafted legislation and discussed and controlled its flow, leaving little for the membership of either house to do besides endorse and enact the committees' handiwork.[10]

Since its members rarely left a committee once they had been assigned to it, they developed an expertise in the area it covered, such as finance or interstate and foreign commerce, and also considerable experience in the drafting and amending of bills. Together, these attributes amounted to a kind of professionalism and authority that few would dare challenge. In a legislative system conducted in this way, the ability to serve many successive terms would ensure greater expertise and experience and therefore a higher ranking within the committee. Because southern congressmen in the region's one-party system were rarely challenged for reelection, they naturally developed seniority. As time went on, it became apparent that this practice was extremely beneficial to the South since it guaranteed a steady and disproportionate influence for the region. The need to return incumbents also required that congressional districts be unchanged, and this resulted in an overrepresentation of the more rural areas in the region, whose proportion of the population was diminishing in relation to the growing towns and cities. Consequently, a part of the country that was already resistant to social and political change became even more solidly conservative because of its congressional delegation.

The Senate, however, was where the southerners' power was concentrated. The upper house had originally been conceived by the Framers of the Constitution as a bulwark, along with the Electoral College, against popular majorities. Composed of men possessing more than local eminence who were chosen by state legislatures, with each state having two senators whether the state was large or small in population, the Senate was supposed to act as a conservative force protective of outnumbered minorities. In the ensuing century and a half, the upper chamber had functioned exactly as intended, even after 1913, when the Seventeenth Amendment required senators to be "elected by the people" of their state rather than chosen by the legislature. The primary beneficiary during these years had, of course, been the nation's persistent and enduring minority, the South. By the 1950s, when William S. White published *The Citadel*, his analysis of the Senate's workings and history, he considered it to be, "to a most peculiar degree, a *Southern* Institution . . . growing at the heart of this ostensibly national assembly." The southern senators' "great home," it was "the only place in the country where the South did not lose the war." And, in a memorable phrase, White proclaimed that the U.S. Senate was "the South's unending revenge upon the North for Gettysburg."[11]

As in the House, southerners were continually reelected to the Senate, establishing continuity which could then be converted into seniority and power within the committee system. But the decorum and procedures of the Senate gave them added confidence and influence. Senators conducted themselves with personal dignity and treated each other with formality and respect. This public behavior accorded with southerners' views of themselves and their region's mores, and so they became the embodiments of senatorial courtesy. Protocol in the Senate was not confined to personal demeanor but extended to the rules governing the proceedings of the body. Accordingly, southerners learned the Senate's forty Standing Rules and the extensive regulations elaborating and explaining their meaning and operation. Their close study of Senate procedure gave them not just a knowledge of etiquette, but immense power, which they then employed to affect the course and outcome of the deliberative process. Since a seat in the Senate was the ultimate goal of the region's political class, the men who became senators from the South were some of its ablest leaders. And their ability, their parliamentary skill, and their seniority all combined to make the South's senatorial delegation an intimidating and almost invincible force.

Two other institutional devices contributed to the South's power and solidarity in the Senate. The first involved the parliamentary procedure for moving the previous question under debate and bringing it forward to an immediate vote. In 1806, the Senate voted to allow continuous debate, with only a unanimous vote capable of ending it. Called the "filibuster," this device was initially employed in 1817 by a southerner, John Randolph of Roanoke, and then from time to time by northerners as well (though most frequently by southerners). The procedure continued unaltered for more than a century, until 1917, when Rule 22 was adopted, which provided for termination of debate, or "cloture," on a "pending" measure when requested by sixteen senators and approved by two-thirds of those present and voting. At this point, each senator was to be allowed one hour to speak until the cloture vote was taken. Although this rule inadvertently made delay and evasion still possible, it actually contained a loophole that provided for its own undoing, for the rule had not prohibited unlimited debate on any motion to bring a bill to the floor and therefore make it "pending." This meant that the initial introduction of the measure could be filibustered. But the only way to prevent this outcome was to change Rule 22. And, of course, a rule change could also be subjected to endless debate. (Although the Senate's Rule 22 was a perfect example of a "Catch 22," it was not, in fact, the inspiration for Joseph Heller's neologism.) The ever-present threat of a loquacious logjam whenever a measure was introduced and known to be opposed by the South presented an obvious deterrent to taking any action in the first place. As both a deterrent and an instrument, the filibuster became an increasingly potent weapon in the South's institutional arsenal.

But, of course, the filibuster's viability depended on solidarity and unity among the region's senators. To accomplish this, southern senators formed the "Southern Caucus," initially to defeat the antilynching bills of 1935–37. Within the caucus, they met and decided on parliamentary strategies to protect their region's interests against hostile legislation or even to endorse measures considered beneficial. The existence of the Southern Caucus was of course known to the other senators, but they became very aware of its presence and power when its twenty-two members entered the Senate chamber together, as they often did after a caucus meeting as a tactic to overawe the rest of the assembled body. The result of these procedures and maneuvers was a general perception that the South was not just solid but also very powerful, well beyond its mere numbers. Although the Senate was the heart of the South's national operations, in effect its department of foreign affairs, the region's delegation in the House was also disproportionately powerful through its own caucus and its exploitation of seniority and the committee system. As Turner Catledge, who covered Congress for the *New York Times* in the 1930s, commented later in his autobiography, the southerners "knew they were a minority and could have strength only by unity. They differed on details, but on the great issues—race, and a generally conservative approach to social and economic issues—they usually spoke with one voice."[12]

The power of the South's committee chairmen and Democratic floor leaders was understood perfectly well by President Roosevelt. He relied upon their skill and cooperation as soon as he entered the White House and proceeded to act forcefully to deal with the Great Depression, which, after three years, was still devastating the economy of the nation and its people's morale. In his "First Hundred Days," March to June 1933, Roosevelt sent to Congress a stream of major plans and projects whose number and scope were then unprecedented in American history. In rapid succession, the relevant committees in Congress discussed and drafted them and then sent them on to passage. Although no doubt modified somewhat in the process, the legislation invariably proved acceptable to the president, who signed the measures into law. This outpouring of legislation was intended to stabilize the banking system (Emergency Banking Act, Glass-Steagall Act, Gold Repeal Joint Resolution); to provide relief and public works programs (Federal Emergency Relief Act, Civil Works Administration, Civilian Conservation Corps); to revive industry (National Industrial Recovery Act); to reorganize agriculture (Agricultural Adjustment Act); to provide funding to refinance farm and home mortgages (Home Owners' Loan Corporation); and, finally, to create a massive regional development program in the Upper South (Tennessee Valley Authority Act).

The southern congressional leadership facilitated the passage of Roosevelt's proposals because they were eager for his success and wanted to

President Franklin Roosevelt at Camp Fechner, the Civilian Conservation Corps camp in Big Meadows, Virginia, August 1933. Interestingly, the president's leg braces, which were rarely revealed in public, are clearly visible under the table. Seated at the far right is Assistant Secretary of Agriculture Rexford Tugwell, a close adviser to Roosevelt, and to Tugwell's right is Secretary of Agriculture Henry Wallace. On the other side of the table, third from the left, is Secretary of the Interior Harold Ickes, and to his left is Robert Fechner, director of the Civilian Conservation Corps. Library of Congress, Prints and Photographs Division.

play a critical role in a Democratic administration that they had worked enthusiastically to elect. Since the measures were aimed at economic recovery, the South was likely to benefit as much as, if not more than, any other part of the country. In particular, the infusion of funds and programs to provide relief for the suffering and work for the unemployed helped southerners. And so did the creation of the Tennessee Valley Authority, whose purpose was to control floods and irrigate farmland in the river valley itself, as well as to provide electricity to the states south of it. Also particularly beneficial was the intervention of the Agricultural Adjustment Act (AAA) into southern agriculture to reduce its chronic over-production, lack of diversification, and falling prices. Consequently, the New Deal was greeted with enthusiasm by the South. As late as 1936, Fred Sullens, editor of the *Jackson News* in Mississippi, reported that "the majority of the people are for it, stronger than horseradish."[13]

Such a large-scale response to the economic crisis was bound to provoke opposition. The growth of the federal government's role and the accompanying expansion of its agencies and institutions produced a predictable revulsion from some of the region's political leaders. Senators Carter Glass and Harry F. Byrd of Virginia and North Carolina's Josiah W. Bailey were instant adversaries of the New Deal. "Not only a mistake," declared Glass, "but a disgrace to the Nation."[14] The New Deal's intervention into the private economy as well as into the states was deemed offensive to these conservative southerners' laissez-faire and constitutional beliefs. But none of them broke with Roosevelt, since his programs were so popular among their constituents.

Even less likely to run such a risk were congressmen who objected to particular aspects of some New Deal programs. They opposed the national wage standard under the National Industrial Recovery Act because it would force southern employers to pay workers at national rates. The act's Section 7a, which recognized the right of collective bargaining and encouraged the formation of industry-wide unions, also produced resistance. The AAA's crop-limitation requirements were a source of complaints from planters and farmers, as were the consequences of leaving lands fallow and forcing laborers off cotton and tobacco farms, which angered tenants and sharecroppers as well as landlords. Even the work relief programs generated resistance because they were federal, not state, in origin and because they created national agencies that might compete for the loyalty and gratitude of the local recipients of jobs and aid. Within the South, the implementation of these federal programs was almost certain to provoke opposition, even though they brought relief and employment into the region in the short run and promised beneficial changes in the long run as well. To local merchants, bankers, planters, and politicians, the current or foreseeable benefits were outweighed by their recognition that, as George B. Tindall concluded, "the New Deal jeopardized [their] power that rested on the control of property, labor, credit, and local government."[15]

These murmurings of discontent came mainly from members of the local political and economic elite in the southern states and not from most of the region's voters. Elsewhere in the country, more important matters were coming to the president's attention, which required him to act, especially since he had to run for reelection in 1936. Although the Supreme Court had been hostile to some of his initiatives, particularly the National Recovery Administration's industrial codes, which it had declared unconstitutional, Roosevelt's main cause for concern came from the left flank of the New Deal. More radical third parties were emerging, in the form of Wisconsin's Progressive Party, Minnesota's Farmer-Labor Party, Upton Sinclair's End Poverty in California Party, and the popular front strategy of the Communist Party. The New Deal was also being attacked by Huey Long, who wanted a redistribution of wealth, and by Father Coughlin, "the radio priest," who wanted government to cut loose from its support of business. Both of these agitators merged left-leaning policies with right-wing, authoritarian instincts. But most important was the pressure for governmental action from the still unemployed as well as from the millions who had joined unions under the New Deal's provisions. Their demands for union recognition and better pay and conditions had been rejected by their employers, resulting in the eruption of over 2,000 strikes in 1934.

Roosevelt's response was another burst of legislative activity. The Second New Deal shifted the emphasis dramatically from recovery to reform. The aim of this new initiative was not, as had been the case for the First New Deal, to regulate and change the priorities of an economy that had collapsed primarily because of overproduction. Instead, the objective was to provide protection for workers and work programs for the unemployed. A related aim of the Second New Deal was to curb the rich and powerful and enable ordinary people to buy products and thus revive the economy through increased spending and consumption. To achieve these ends, significant and enduring legislation was enacted. Most important were the National Labor Relations Act, granting the right to join unions and bargain collectively; the Social Security Act, which provided unemployment insurance and old-age pensions; the Wealth Tax Act, which increased the tax rate on the wealthy and on corporations; and the Public Utilities Holding Company Act, breaking up monopolistic electric power companies. Legislation was also passed creating the Rural Electrification Administration, increasing relief by $5 billion through the Emergency Relief Appropriation Act, and setting up the Works Progress Administration to coordinate and expand the earlier relief programs. Absent from this list of successful legislation was a bill to establish national labor standards for wages and hours, which met with vigorous resistance, from the South in particular.

The four years of the Second New Deal presented the Solid South with its worst nightmare. The period 1935–38 was to be a moment of truth and a turning point for the region's political class. All of a sudden, after enjoying the immense power and exhilaration of enacting a Democratic president's initiatives, the political outlook turned ominous. The first warning sign appeared at the Democrats' national convention in 1936 when the delegates voted to eliminate the two-thirds rule. Ever since 1836, when it had been instituted at the behest of the southern delegates in return for their approval of the nomination of Martin Van Buren, this rule—or, more realistically, the threat that it might be invoked—had ensured that the South enjoyed a decisive influence over the party's choice of a presidential nominee. The end of the two-thirds rule meant that a Democratic convention would no longer need to avoid choosing a nominee unacceptable to its southern wing. Also ominous to the South was the presence at the convention of thirty African American delegates from twelve states. When a black minister appeared on the podium to open one of the sessions in prayer, Senator "Cotton Ed" Smith of South Carolina left the hall, exclaiming, "My God, he's black as melted midnight."[16] Then, in the election itself, FDR won by a landslide, winning all but two states, Maine and Vermont, and obtaining 61 percent of the popular vote. Even more alarming, he did not need to carry a single southern state to win the election. In his next two campaigns, 1940 and 1944, he would continue to win without needing even one electoral vote from the South. Actually, Roosevelt had won without the South in 1932 as well, but in the euphoria of regaining the presidency this danger signal went unnoticed by the region's political leaders.

Roosevelt's electoral base now lay outside the South. Instead, it was located in the northern cities and among their immigrant, African American, and working-class populations, not to mention the middle-class liberals who were also city dwellers. And this was evident from the tone of FDR's campaign, as he castigated the corporations as "economic royalists" who controlled "other people's lives" and turned his attention to the "Forgotten Man." The center of gravity in the Democratic Party had moved decisively into the urban North, and the thrust of party policy was in a reformist and liberal direction. The South's status and prospects had changed drastically. No longer a majority faction within the minority party, the South was fast becoming a minority faction within the majority party.

This political shift was certainly massive. Whether it was likely to be permanent and amount to a party realignment and a period of Democratic dominance was not obvious at this point. In the meantime, the South still benefited from being an influential segment of the ruling party. Also, the power of the region's committee chairmen and the South's strength within Congress was not diminished. But this was clutching at straws. The South's position had worsened significantly. The region was not only a self-conscious minority within the nation as a whole, a status the South had endured for the previous hundred years. But the region was now a minority within the Democratic Party, which it had managed to reign over during that same century since the party's formation in the Jacksonian era. Yet the Democratic Party was the rock upon which the Solid South had been built, the rock upon which the South's security and survival were assumed to depend.

Confirming this new political reality were the president's initiatives in the immediate aftermath of the election. Emboldened by his massive vindication at the polls, President Roosevelt, who was also the head of the national Democratic Party, proceeded to attack his opponents in the judicial branch and in the Senate in an attempt to rally all three branches of the federal government to the support of the reform agenda on which he had based his campaign for reelection—the Second New Deal. In February 1937, without informing congressional leaders, Roosevelt announced his intention to create fifty new federal judges and six additional Supreme Court justices. The reaction of Hatton W. Sumners of Texas was immediate. "Boys, here's where I cash in," he told some friends.[17] As chair of the House Judiciary Committee, he proceeded to denounce and obstruct Roosevelt's initiative. Senators Glass, Byrd, and Bailey were livid because of its infringement of the Constitution's separation of powers, and they were joined by several other southern senators. Still, fifteen of them supported the "court-packing plan," as its adversaries called it.

Even though the South was not about to break with him, Roosevelt continued his assault, targeting next several of the region's senators who were up for reelection in 1938. They were Walter F. George of Georgia, Cotton Ed Smith of South Carolina, and Millard E. Tydings of Maryland, along with John O'Connor of New York, who was chairman of the crucial House Rules Committee and a conservative opposed to the New Deal. The president urged voters to defeat them all. Nevertheless, George, who denounced the president's attempted "purge" as "a second march through Georgia," was reelected, as were Tydings and Smith, but ironically the northerner, O'Connor, was not.

To accompany his attack on the South's "Old Guard," the president issued the National Emergency Council's report, "Economic Conditions of the South." This document identified a set of structural obstacles that prevented the development of the region's economy and that the administration proposed to change. Roosevelt and the young southern policy makers who drafted the report intended to convince the South that lifting its economic burdens should be the region's primary objective.[18] But the report's assertion that the South was "the Nation's No. 1 Economic Problem" was perceived by the political and economic establishment not as an offer of help, but as an insult to the region and a threat to the status quo. The South's highly respected business journal, the *Manufacturers' Record*, responded defiantly that, far from being a problem, "the South represents the nation's greatest opportunity for economic development."[19]

Although the National Emergency Council report had little immediate effect, it provided impetus for the formation of the Southern Conference on Human Welfare, which, during the ensuing decade, would act as a forum and launching pad for reform and protest aimed primarily at the region's political system. Otherwise, the president's attempt to make the federal judiciary, the Senate, and the South safe for the Second New Deal and part of his expanding coalition was a disastrous failure. His Court plans were rebuffed, all but one of the targeted senators were reelected, and the South's economic priorities remained unaffected. More seriously, FDR's reputation as a skillful politician had been badly tarnished and his ability to overawe and outmaneuver his adversaries had been undermined. Nevertheless, southern congressmen had been served notice that they were no longer inside the Roosevelt tent, although he still needed their leadership in Congress to manage his legislation.

Naturally enough, southern support for the president and his proposals became less enthusiastic and less reliable after the 1936–38 confrontations. Some now broke with Roosevelt, though only a few inveterate anti–New Dealers, like Glass, Byrd, and Bailey, went so far as to contemplate an affiliation with Republican conservatives on the basis of the Conservative Manifesto that the bipartisan group issued in December 1937. Reasserting the principles of limited government and state rights, the manifesto called for a reduction in federal taxes, a balanced federal budget, and a greater role for state and local government and for private enterprise. But most southern Democrats continued to believe that party loyalty and the benefit to their constituents provided by federal largesse required them to vote for the administration's measures.

All the same, southerners balked over a number of issues in the late 1930s. On several, they were simply part of a growing bipartisan, conservative group within Congress that challenged the growth of the federal government and the continuing increase in its expenditures and programs. But on others, they played a conspicuous role. Southern Democrats were prominent in the successful opposition to the executive reorganization bill in 1938, which proposed to extend civil service coverage and give the president power to coordinate and centralize executive departments. And they also opposed the $1.5 billion relief measure, mainly funding the government's major public works project, the Works Progress Administration.

On two general issues, however, southerners organized into a solid bloc. The first was labor relations. Organized labor, and the protection it was demanding for workers, was clearly a major component of Roosevelt's New Deal coalition. Indeed, the president was responding very sympathetically to the concerns of the revitalized labor movement. His unwillingness to condemn the rash of sit-down strikes in northern industries in 1937 and 1938 and his introduction of two major labor bills in 1935 and 1937 provoked fear and opposition among southern congressmen. One of the bills required collective bargaining and a national labor relations board, while the other required fair and uniform national levels for wages and hours. On the labor relations bill, eventually the Wagner Act, southerners insisted successfully that agricultural and domestic labor, the kind of poorly paid work allotted to African Americans, be denied the protections offered under the bill. Despite these concessions, the leading southern senators, Joe Robinson and Pat Harrison, tried to postpone the measure, but they could not muster enough support to sustain their objections. Even after its passage, southern attempts to weaken the powers of the proposed labor relations board were so persistent that the act had to be amended in 1939. Exclusion of the same workers from the pending wages and hours bill was also demanded by the southerners. This insistence that agricultural and domestic workers, who were overwhelmingly African American, be denied protection was not unexpected because the region's congressmen had required it earlier in the Social Security Act, with agricultural workers also excluded from the National Industrial Recovery Act's coverage.

The minimum wages and maximum hours measure provoked immense opposition from the South. Charging that it would destroy the competitive advantage that its cheap labor gave to southern industries like textiles, lumber, and steel, southern congressmen mounted a furious resistance. They even claimed that the proposal was a plot by northern competitors, in the words of a former FDR adviser, Senator Jimmy Byrnes of South Carolina, "to stop the movement of industries into the South, and to cause some to return to New England."[20] The bill was kept bottled up in the House Rules Committee, headed by Howard W. Smith of Virginia and Eugene E. Cox of Georgia. A discharge petition requiring 218 votes was needed to bring the bill to the floor for a vote. When the vote was taken in late 1937, eighty-one of the ninety-nine southern Democrats voted nay, and it was defeated. A year later, the measure, now officially called the Fair Labor Standards Act, finally passed. After yet another discharge petition and a considerable amount of amendment that allowed for the regional, though actually racial, wage differentials, fifty-two of the fifty-six Democrats who were still opposed came from the South.[21]

The other issue that alarmed the South was the attempt on several occasions during the 1930s to enact a national law against lynching. An earlier effort in 1922, the Dyer antilynching bill, had been defeated by a filibuster in the Senate. But an increase in the ghastly practice during the Depression years, to a rate of around thirty incidents a year, prompted a renewed attack in which Senator Robert Wagner of New York, a leading New Deal liberal, played a central role. On two occasions, in the 1934–35 and the 1937–38 sessions, bills were introduced that would give federal authorities the power to arrest and try members of lynch mobs if the state failed to act and provide monetary damages to families of victims. Each time, they were defeated by a Senate filibuster, of six days' duration in 1935 and then six weeks' in 1938. In the second instance, the Wagner-Gavagan bill had passed the House, 277–120, and then gathered a majority in the Senate. But that was not enough for the two-thirds needed to cut off the endless talk about protecting southern womanhood, resisting federal coercion, administering swift punishment for a brutish crime, and— the real issue—preserving white supremacy. So, once again, the nation proved unable to establish jurisdiction over lynching cases, even though lynching was a barbaric crime.

Surprisingly, the executive branch refused to invest any of its considerable influence and prestige in support of this legislation. Why was that? A decade later, Walter White, the executive secretary of the National Association for the Advancement of Colored People (NAACP), reported Roosevelt's justification for his puzzling passivity. "The southerners by reason of the seniority rule in Congress are chairmen or occupy strategic places on most of the Senate and House committees," he once told White. "If I come out for the anti-lynching bill now, they will block every bill I ask Congress to pass to keep America from collapsing. I just cannot take that risk."[22] Roosevelt's political calculation was perhaps understandable. Less comprehensible was why southern congressmen invested so much energy to protect lynching, hardly a vital component, or one of the strongest defenses, of white supremacy and the region's racial order. Would they not have been better advised to cede lynching and conserve their political strength for the defense of the more essential aspects of their system of racial domination, such as disfranchisement?

Maybe so, but the strategy that the South's congressmen constructed for the defense of their segregated society seems to have been similar to the formula developed a century earlier when slavery was first attacked during the Missouri Crisis. On that occasion, it may be recalled, they took an unyielding stand at the margins of the system when they rejected any consideration whatsoever of gradual emancipation, even in Missouri, which was located on the periphery of the slaveholding areas. Likewise, by defending lynching, which a majority of southerners actually deplored, according to opinion polls taken at the time (though some respondents may have been unwilling to tell an interviewer they approved of lynching), they were taking a stand at the outermost limits of the system of white supremacy. And the position the congressmen took was solid and unequivocal. To allow the federal government any jurisdiction over any aspect of the southern system of race control was believed to be tantamount to surrender. The yielding of any control would, over time, result inexorably in the loss of all control. The defense of lynching was, therefore, not just symbolic or marginal. Politically, it was the heart of the matter.

The New Deal in the South

The president's agenda—for recovery through the First New Deal and for reform through the Second—required a massive increase in federal power and the dispersal throughout the country of enormous expenditures. Southerners wanted the programs and the funds but, like political leaders in other regions too, they pressed for as much control over their management and distribution as possible. In this demand, they actually met with little resistance from Washington, because the intention of FDR and his associates was, for the most part, to collaborate with state and local officials, not bypass or supplant them. Aware that they were expanding federal authority dramatically in order to deal with a national economic crisis, they sought to enlist the states in implementing the government's policies and programs.

Local authorities often perceived these initiatives as impositions that they themselves had not originated, and, over the years, the amount of federal activism did seem extensive if not excessive. But Roosevelt himself was, by temperament, a coalition builder, whose goal was to broaden his base of support and win over opponents rather than to challenge their political authority or force them to yield. The New Deal was therefore compatible with, and operated within, the existing local political structures. Liberal though its policies were, the New Deal was, in fact, politically and institutionally conservative.

Those southerners who came in contact with the New Deal's programs encountered them mainly through its agricultural and relief initiatives. The AAA and relief agencies like the Federal Emergency Relief Administration and the Works Progress Administration established an office in each state to initiate and supervise their programs there. But the funds and the projects were to be administered at the local level, where county agents would be chosen by the more established farmers, in cooperation with the Farm Bureau, and relief administrators were invariably either local Democratic officials or their appointees. Accordingly, both the AAA and the relief programs were to be operated with the concurrence of the dominant economic or political interests.

Under the AAA policy of reducing the amount of acreage under cultivation in order to restrict output and therefore raise prices, the planters were compensated for compliance. Yet their predominantly black tenants and sharecroppers, who became unemployed or were thrown off the land as a result, rarely received a share of the payment. In the provision of relief, administrators were often local Democratic officials who were allowed to run the programs according to local custom and interests. Payment and wages were set in the South at rates lower than in the rest of the country, and prevailing racial mores were observed by denying jobs or benefits to blacks or by maintaining differentials in wages and relief payments between the races. Rather than challenging or subverting local authorities, relief strengthened them, for they now had funds to disburse and favors to bestow, just like the county farm agents.

The South's one-party system and the factional arrangements within the states remained undisturbed by the political activity in Washington. The president's abortive attempt in the senatorial elections of 1938 to throw out some influential conservatives, and thus alter the course of southern politics, may actually have demonstrated how resilient the system was. Of course, state politicians could hardly be unaware of the New Deal, and many moved to align with it. Indeed, a number of gubernatorial candidates identified themselves as New Dealers and, once elected, collaborated actively with the New Deal programs and enacted legislative agendas that bore a close resemblance to those from Washington. South Carolina's governors from 1935 to 1939, Olin D. Johnston and Burnet R.

Maybank, followed this route, even though their own social origins and political rhetoric were quite different. Johnston was an up-country plebeian who was an advocate for laboring people, and Maybank was a patrician from Charleston more concerned about economic development. In one state, Georgia, a "Little New Deal" was undertaken by Governor Eurith D. "Ed" Rivers from 1936 to 1940. After defeating the demagogic governor, Gene Talmadge, who had opposed the New Deal from the right by denouncing its extravagance and its subversion of rugged individualism, Rivers attempted to satisfy the state's need for highways, education, and social services that Talmadge had thwarted.

In two other states, a bifactionalism emerged, but it was explained less by the New Deal than by the existence of one faction based on personality rather than on issues. In Texas, "Fergusonism" continued to dominate state politics when "Farmer Jim" Ferguson's wife once again became a surrogate governor, from 1932 to 1934. She was followed by an able reformer, James V. Allred, and then, from 1938 to 1942, by W. Lee "Pappy" O'Daniel, a maverick agrarian who promised Texans old-age pensions. A similar personal faction emerged in Louisiana, though not until the 1940s. After a half decade of corrupt government and plunder in the wake of Huey Long's demise, the Longites, now led by Huey's younger brother, Earl, consolidated into a coherent faction reasonably supportive of the New Deal. Their opponents, who consisted of a mix of conservatives and good government reformers, were nevertheless able to win control of the state, producing two quite effective governors, Sam Houston Jones and Jimmie H. Davis, from 1940 to 1948. By contrast, in the Upper South states of North Carolina, Tennessee, and Virginia, powerful statewide Democratic machines prevented an opposition faction from forming. O. Max Gardner and his successors in the "Shelby Dynasty," Edward H. Crump, the boss of Memphis, and the indomitable Harry Byrd from Virginia's Southside accommodated sufficiently to the New Deal's presence in their states that all of them, in various ways and in varying degrees, managed to prevent a rival faction from rallying around a New Deal agenda.

A liberal New Deal faction did not emerge and establish itself firmly in any of the southern states during the decade after Roosevelt became president. His New Deal policies poured programs and funds into the region but without noticeably altering the contours of state politics. They seemed to confirm factions rather than create them. Outside the South, a major political realignment occurred that altered both parties, the Democratic much more than the Republican, of course. But the South took no part in this realignment, even though the party that changed the most were the Democrats, the party from which the South derived its political identity and its security.

Amazingly, the course that the South's political leaders pursued over the following decade served to tie the region and its fate even more closely to the Democrats, who, everywhere but in the South, had changed beyond all recognition. The Conservative Manifesto of 1937 had suggested a basis for collaboration between conservative Democrats, most of whom would have been southerners, and conservative Republicans. Had this invitation led to the merging of the nation's conservatives within the Republican Party, it would have completed the realignment begun in 1936 by creating two parties that were sharply defined ideologically—a conservative Republican Party and a liberal Democratic Party. Alternatively, the South itself could have changed and become more liberal and therefore more compatible with the rest of the Democratic Party. But that avenue was not explored either. The South's apparent inability to change either its party affiliation or its political priorities would have enormous implications for the region itself—and also for the political development of the nation.

11

The Liberal Challenge
in the 1940s

At the very moment when the South's political class had to confront the reality that the region was an anomaly within the Democratic Party, the possibility of another large-scale European war began to loom on the horizon. To prepare for the eventuality that war might break out, President Roosevelt took measures to move the United States away from its recent commitment to strict neutrality and position it to influence developments in Europe and also in Asia.

To achieve this objective, he brought before Congress a number of measures dealing with neutrality and preparedness between 1939 and 1941, namely, revising America's neutrality laws, obtaining permission to sell arms to belligerents, requiring a peacetime draft, and providing lend-lease arrangements for the loan of arms to anti-German allies once war broke out in Europe. On all these urgent matters, southern Democrats voted overwhelmingly to support Roosevelt's requests. Only a very few southerners, like Senators Cotton Ed Smith of South Carolina and Bob Reynolds of North Carolina, favored noninvolvement. In fact, the major center of isolationism was in the West. As in its support for World War I and the League of Nations, the South was interventionist, even if its sentiments were not exactly internationalist. Furthermore, once America began to consider entry into the war, the South again provided solid votes in favor.

After backing his foreign policy so enthusiastically, southern Democrats were hardly likely to abandon Roosevelt when he decided to run for a third term in 1940, especially in this moment of national crisis with intervention in a worldwide war so imminent. They supported his nomination with near unanimity, as did the party's convention itself. When Roosevelt chose Henry A. Wallace as his vice president, however, the South dissented vociferously because he was a northern New Dealer whose public position on race was considered suspect. Instead, the region gave 193 of its 248 votes to the Speaker of the House, William B. Bankhead of Alabama, as a gesture of protest that did not actually alter the outcome. In the ensuing election, as in 1932 and 1936, the region voted overwhelmingly for the Democratic ticket, despite Wallace's presence on it, actually providing 300,000 more votes than in 1936.

The South and the Home Front

During the almost four years from December 1941 to September 1945 when the United States was at war in Europe and Asia, the South's economy underwent a remarkable change. Historians now regard these economic developments as pivotal in the creation of the New South. The term "New South" was first coined in the aftermath of the Civil War to suggest that the region was then embarking on a new economic course that moved it away from its prewar reliance on one-crop agriculture and its overwhelmingly rural existence toward a more diversified economy, with a significant manufacturing sector and a growing urban element. Cities and manufacturing were already emerging in the late nineteenth century, and they continued to grow in the first third of the twentieth century. These developments were greeted as evidence that the New South had arisen. But this new urban and industrial sector had not increased to a sufficient size and preponderance to signal the arrival of the New South until after World War II. At this point, the corner had been turned.

Corroboration for this interpretation, though not proof, can be found in the titles of the last three volumes of the distinguished and authoritative series, The History of the South. C. Vann Woodward's study of 1877–1913 is titled *Origins of the New South*; George B. Tindall's treatment of 1913–1945 is called *The Emergence of the New South*. Not until Numan V. "Bud" Bartley's volume covering the postwar years is the New South's arrival confirmed by the title, *The New South, 1945–1980*. This development was an evolving process, originating and emerging for almost a century. After World War II, the eagerly anticipated, yet prematurely announced, New South finally materialized.

The crucial ingredient in this economic transformation was the federal government's decision at the outset of involvement in the war to locate a very large number of its military installations in the southern states. The region's climate and readily available open spaces made it suitable for building training camps and airfields, but Roosevelt's avowed desire to give a boost to its economy also played a very large part. Quite consciously, he sought to address the Nation's No. 1 Economic Problem as well as involve the South more fully in the nation's life, through its participation in the war effort and in its encounter with military personnel who would flow into and out of the region. After a few years, government industrial plants whose production was war related were also steered into the region. Initially, this latter work was assigned to places outside the South where factories already existed capable of producing such war matériel as ordnance and motor vehicles. But soon these were operating at capacity, and so industrial plants for ordnance, petrochemicals, and aluminum, as well as aircraft assembly and shipbuilding, were located in the South. These, in turn, generated related economic activities in manufacturing and in extractive industries, some of it privately financed and owned. Nearly all of the industries and their physical plants and factories remained after the war, and they provided the infrastructure for an ongoing and developing industrial economy in the region.

The results of these war-induced investments and expenditures were astonishing. The government invested about $7 billion in military bases and industrial facilities and then spent additional money to run them, supply them, and pay their personnel and employees. One-quarter of the region's income payments, which rose 25 percent during the war years, came from the federal government. Spurred by these government initiatives, the region's industrial output increased by 40 percent during the war and the number of production workers almost doubled. With the growth of industries, there also came an increase in the number of urban areas and the size of their populations. By 1950, the number of urban dwellers had grown by 36 percent as people moved from the farm to the city to work in the new industries.

Meanwhile, around one million African Americans, most of them farm laborers, left southern farms for cities in the North. The resulting decline in farmworkers contributed to the process begun by the Agricultural Adjustment Act of limiting the acreage under cultivation and correspondingly reducing the need for laborers. As a result, farming became less labor-intensive, opening up the possibility for mechanization in the planting and picking of cotton and in the raising of other crops as well. Across the region, farm incomes and wages and even production rose, which meant that farmers enjoyed better times than they had experienced in years. These overall gains did not, of course, benefit everyone equally, since tens of thousands of agricultural laborers lost out and suffered deeply because of these changes. For instance, sharecroppers who were driven off the land faced similarly grim prospects once they reached a city where housing and a job would often be woefully inadequate or even impossible to find. Many of them, like the Joads in *The Grapes of Wrath*, left altogether in the forlorn hope of finding something in the Southwest, while others who were desperate, white as well as black, migrated to the North.

The economic benefits and changes that the war brought to the South provided the stimulus for the arrival of the long-awaited New South. That stimulus originated with the federal government, and southern congressmen had encouraged and welcomed it. When the Roosevelt administration created agencies to manage the wartime economy, such as the War Production Board and the Office of Price Administration, Congress approved them and rarely even attempted to restrict their powers. Indeed, the southern wing of the president's party participated fully in this massive expansion of the federal government's capacity to direct and, in many respects, control the nation's economy.

Postwar Repercussions and Dangers

At the same time as they encouraged wartime expansion of the nation-state, southern Democrats chipped away at those programs that they considered unrelated to the wartime emergency and therefore, in a sense, permanent, not merely temporary. New Deal agencies were subjected to intense scrutiny by investigating committees with odd names like the Joint Committee on Non-Essential Expenditures, headed by Senator Harry Byrd, and the Special Committee to Investigate Acts of Executive Agencies Beyond the Scope of Their Authority, presided over by Howard W. Smith, Byrd's protégé in the House.

In this campaign to shut the barn door after the horse had bolted, southerners were joined by conservative Republicans, who also vowed to impose restraints on government spending. In fact, some contemporaries as well as some historians discerned the emergence of a formally organized conservative coalition in the early war years. But all that transpired was an initiative to prevent further New Deal programs and curb existing agencies as far as possible, all in the name of retrenchment. This was primarily a broad conservative reaction, which, although led by southern Democrats, did not result in any formal coalition consisting of a unified southern component and an identifiable and persisting group of Republicans. A bloc of southern Democrats and conservative Republicans did emerge more distinctly in votes on measures to restrict organized labor later in the war and into the Truman administration. But, on a wider array of issues, it did not exist as an organized and consistent voting bloc.

The campaign for retrenchment still chalked up a number of successes. The Works Progress Administration, the Civilian Conservation Corps, and the National Youth Administration, all of them work-relief programs, were abolished in 1943. Funding for the Farm Security Administration, whose purpose was to attack rural poverty and provide loans to buy farms, was reduced by 30 percent in 1943 and finally abolished in 1946. The National Resources Planning Board, an early New Deal agency for planning how to meet the nation's social needs, was eliminated in 1943. Led by southern Democrats, this retrenchment campaign had succeeded in eliminating what they considered nonessential expenditures and ensuring that the New Deal, which they claimed was a response to an emergency that no longer existed, would not continue into the postwar era. To anyone who looked closely at the kinds of agencies that these men chose to eliminate, their unspoken agenda was pretty clear. They intended to kill those programs that gave aid to the poor and unemployed and that advocated social change.

On another issue that arose during the war, the South's congressmen acted and voted as a unit and in isolation. In the late 1930s, they had managed to parry several attempts to enact antilynching legislation. During the war, the problem of race and civil rights continued to make an appearance in Congress in several different forms, most of them related to voting. In each instance, southern Democrats moved in a united phalanx to repel the threat. The first was the demand for an end to discrimination in employment by firms under contract with the federal government, which emerged as a goal of the exclusively black March on Washington Movement mounted by A. Philip Randolph, head of the Brotherhood of Sleeping-Car Porters. Angered that black servicemen encountered pervasive discrimination and aware that America's impending involvement in World War II would expand the number of jobs created by the government, Randolph's movement threatened to march on the capital on 1 July 1941. To head off an embarrassing public protest on the eve of the United States' entry into the war, the president formed the Fair Employment Practices Committee (FEPC) to oversee his executive order No. 8802, prohibiting racial, ethnic, or religious discrimination in defense industries. Although the FEPC was hailed by black leaders as a victory, it did not have much impact on job discrimination, since its task was restricted to adjudicating individual complaints brought before it, and even then it could not enforce its own determinations.

But southern Democrats attacked the FEPC furiously. They investigated its operations and they tried to cut its funding. Although FDR never threw his weight behind the committee or tried to increase its limited authority, he did bring it under the control of the Office of the President in 1943, planning to make it permanent in 1945. At this point, southerners mobilized to defeat the move, after having cut its funds in half a year earlier. Despite the FEPC's obvious limitations, southern Democrats feared its very existence because it established a precedent of continuing federal interference in southern race relations. Mississippi's senator, Theodore Bilbo, was apoplectic about the FEPC, charging that it was "nothing but a plot to put niggers to work next to your daughters."[1] A stalwart New Dealer who had supported Roosevelt's reforms of the Second New Deal, as well as his wartime spending measures and his advocacy of the United Nations, Bilbo became the most ranting and virulent of race-baiters when confronted with the FEPC. After President Truman revived the idea of a permanent FEPC in 1945, Bilbo conducted a personal three-day filibuster against the legislation to fund it. He was not alone in his opposition, for his fellow southerners mounted another filibuster in January 1946 that lasted three weeks when a new bill for a permanent FEPC was introduced in the Senate.

The FEPC fight lasted throughout the war and beyond. And so did another civil rights issue, repeal of the poll tax. Payment of an annual poll, or head, tax had become probably the most effective device created by the South's disfranchising constitutions at the turn of the century. The poll tax disfranchised not just blacks but hundreds of thousands of impoverished and working-class whites too. Therefore, pressure for its abolition arose from labor unions such as the American Federation of Labor (AFL), the Congress of Industrial Organizations (CIO), and the National Farmers Union, as well as from black protest groups like the NAACP and from the League of Women Voters. In 1941, at the urging of the civil rights committee of the Southern Conference on Human Welfare, the National Committee to Abolish the Poll Tax was formed with the eager collaboration of Congressman Lee E. Geyer of California, who had already introduced an anti–poll tax bill in 1939, only to have it bottled up in Hatton Sumners's House Judiciary Committee. The newly formed organization exerted its influence by lobbying congressmen, who eventually produced the necessary 200-odd signatures for a successful discharge petition. In October 1941, the bill passed the House by a stunning 254–84 vote, despite solid opposition from all but nine of the southern members.

For the first time since the Lodge bill in 1890, Congress was debating voting restrictions in the South, and southern Democrats knew what was behind it all. "The direct object of this movement is to enfranchise the Negro in the South," charged Mississippi's William Colmer.[2] His colleagues in the Senate also understood that the Geyer bill, which ostensibly urged an end to the poll tax because it encouraged corruption among politicians who paid voters' taxes for them, was actually an entering wedge to dismantle the system of black disfranchisement. An eight-day filibuster greeted the bill when it arrived in the Senate. Only one southern senator, the liberal Claude Pepper of Florida, who was the bill's sponsor, voted to end debate. The body's only other liberal southerner was Lister Hill of Alabama, who, like Pepper, had first been elected in the "Senate purge" of 1938. But he voted with the majority to sustain the filibuster, arguing, "Once we start abolishing the poll tax we must admit that the federal government and the Congress have the power to get into the whole field of qualifications." Voting requirements, he added, were the "last existing cornerstone of states rights and local self-government," exactly what the race-baiting Theodore Bilbo was saying in his more lucid moments.[3]

The campaign to repeal the poll tax represented the ultimate threat to the Solid South. The federal government was claiming the authority to determine a state's voting requirements and therefore the form of its electoral system. Predictably, only three southern representatives voted for the bill when it was reintroduced in 1943. The Senate filibustered it to death a year later. In three consecutive Congresses, in 1945, 1947, and 1949, the measure would pass the House but then be kept from a vote in the Senate by southern-led obstruction in committee or by filibuster. Not until 1964, when a constitutional amendment was ratified that outlawed the poll tax in federal elections, was the device banned by federal action. Of course, states could end the poll tax in state elections, and several of them did so, mainly in the hope of increasing the white vote, as Huey Long had done in Louisiana in 1934 and Claude Pepper's faction managed to do in Florida in 1937. But when the federal government was behind the move, southerners feared they would lose control. So they resisted adamantly, managing to defer the dreaded outcome until the year before the Voting Rights Act of 1965 was passed.

This worry about federal intervention in southern election procedures had actually been provoked even before the first anti–poll tax bill. Immediately after the United States entered the war, a bill was introduced to provide men and women in the armed services with absentee ballots for federal elections. This caused some consternation because it would probably allow people who were disfranchised to vote. When an amendment was proposed in the Senate by Claude Pepper and Wayland Brooks of Illinois to waive the poll tax for the war's duration, the measure's import was undeniable. The bill would have been filibustered, had not southerners, like Walter George, suggested that opponents should avoid thwarting the right of soldiers on active duty to vote. The bill passed, 33–20. Because it was enacted just before the election and because its procedures proved very complicated, few were able to take advantage of the Soldiers' Voting Act in the 1942 elections.

Embarrassed by this contempt for the nation's soldiers, Roosevelt urged Congress to produce a new measure. The Green-Lucas bill provided for a U.S. War Ballot Commission to issue ballots and supervise elections at military camps and in combat areas. Despite assurances that this was temporary and not intended to alter the region's electoral system, southerners were outraged. An amendment proposed by three southern senators (James Eastland of Mississippi, Kenneth McKellar of Tennessee, and John McClellan of Arkansas) emasculated the bill by stipulating that the individual states should pass measures to enable their soldiers to vote in state and federal elections. The new bill passed, 42–37, but the president denounced it as "a fraud on the American people" and intervened to get the House to return to the original bill.[4] Feeling insulted, the southerners refused to comply, and they were joined by the Republicans who wanted to exploit the division among the Democrats. The resulting act that passed both houses was more like the Eastland amendment, so a frustrated Roosevelt let it become law without his signature. Because the final version left so much initiative to the states, it became a virtual dead letter in the South.

This episode revealed how determined the southern Democrats could be to block any perceived threat to their race-based electoral system, even when it was merely temporary or marginal and even if its defeat penalized the nation's soldiers during war. But the danger was clear. The party they had dominated for over a century had fallen into the hands of their enemies, the urban, liberal coalition of organized labor and African American protest. At one point in the Senate debate over the Eastland amendment, North Carolina's Josiah Bailey revealed how alienated, yet defiant, the southerners were. "If we cannot have a party in which we are respected, if we must be in a party in which we are scorned as southern Democrats," he acknowledged bitterly, then "we can form a southern Democratic party and vote as we please in the electoral college, and we will hold the balance of power in this country."[5] Hardly a declaration of secession from the Democratic Party, Bailey's professed feelings of humiliation and degradation were nevertheless similar to those of his predecessors on the eve of an earlier and ill-fated secession. Even though Bailey was just threatening some kind of disassociation from a political party, he was still admitting in public how cornered and desperate the South's conservative leadership felt.

Less than a year later, the southern Democrats' electoral system received a more severe shock than soldier voting or repeal of the poll tax could ever have inflicted. In *Smith v. Allwright*, the Supreme Court declared the white primary unconstitutional, rejecting the South's claim that the Democratic Party was a private organization and that its primary election to nominate its candidates was an internal administrative matter not subject to public authority. For over twenty years, despite three previous Supreme Court decisions (1927, 1932, 1935) questioning the white primary in Texas, African American plaintiffs and their lawyers had failed to overturn the procedure. Now the Court acknowledged that the primary was part of a public election process and therefore subject to the Fifteenth Amendment's protection of the right to vote from racial discrimination. Potential black voters, supported by national organizations like the NAACP and by local black societies and groups in cities and counties, mobilized quickly to take advantage of their new access to the primary, the real election in the South. By 1954, about one million African Americans had registered to vote, quadrupling the number from 1944.

At the same time, many southern states were devising ways to evade the Court's 1944 decision. South Carolina simply repealed its primary laws, and Alabama tightened its voting qualifications through a constitutional amendment. But both actions were soon invalidated by federal district courts. Other states, like Texas and Virginia, decided simply to accept what they believed to be inevitable. But, of course, the lack of official, formal alternatives for keeping blacks from voting did not mean that they were able to register unhindered. Democratic registrars still made the final decision about whether an African American "qualified," and Senator Bilbo's advice in his reelection campaign in 1946 was always available. As he had recommended in a public broadcast, "The way to keep the nigger from the polls is to see him the night before."[6]

External threats to the South's racial order generated a unity and solidity in which its congressmen stood alone. On another issue during the war they were again unified, but this time others joined them. This was the rapid growth of the labor movement in the South and the nation. During the 1930s, a political climate favorable to the formation of labor unions had been generated by several developments. Most important were New Deal legislation regulating labor practices and encouraging collective bargaining; President Roosevelt's conscious inclusion of labor in his governing coalition, which was changing the direction of the Democratic Party; and the emergence of industrial unionism and the CIO as a rival to the trade-based unions of the AFL. By 1941, organized labor had tripled its membership, to 8.4 million workers, with 23 percent of nonagricultural workers now unionized. In the South itself, growth was less spectacular but, given the obstacles, significant nonetheless, with 400,000 in AFL unions and another 150,000 organized in industries by the CIO. But the war stimulated even further growth of unions in the South. The number of people employed in industry almost doubled, to just under 3 million, while a tight labor market (because of the huge demand for workers in war-related industries) and the encouragement of union membership by the War Labor Board facilitated the unionization of this expanding workforce in manufacturing. With the southern industrial labor force growing and becoming more assertive and organized, the "docile" and "cheap" labor that the South's economic and political leaders had promised and praised since emancipation in the 1860s was endangered.

During the war years, southern Democrats' disillusionment with the New Deal had begun with their campaigns to retrench and eliminate agencies that provided relief and jobs or that engaged in centralized planning. This dissent crystallized into outright opposition on the two issues of race and labor. The administration's wartime labor initiatives proved difficult for the South's congressmen to counter, because almost all of them had been implemented by the administrative boards established to mobilize resources for the war effort rather than in the form of legislation. But an opportunity to take the offensive arose in 1943 in the wake of several strikes in major industries, namely mining, plastics, rubber, and railroads. Claiming that Roosevelt was unwilling to rein in the CIO leadership, even when it violated an agreed-upon no-strike pledge during wartime, conservatives in Congress, led by Representative Howard W. Smith and Senator Tom Connally of Texas, produced a bill to outlaw strikes in war industries. It provided for a thirty-day cooling-off period after a strike was called but before it went into effect; authorized the president to seize any factory engaged in war production that was threatened by a strike; and made labor leaders criminally liable for any strikes in plants taken over by the government. The War Labor Disputes Act (the Smith-Connally Act) was obviously an antiunion measure, and southern Democrats voted overwhelmingly in favor—all but five in the House and every senator. A similarly solid vote was cast to override the president's veto. In this move, which was successful, they were joined by the Republicans but not by northern Democrats, who were as solidly opposed to the measure as the South was in favor.

This sharp split within the Democratic Party on measures hostile to organized labor was evident after the war too, when employers and congressional conservatives mobilized their forces to clamp down on unions. In early 1946, they moved to repeal the Smith-Connally Act on the ground that the war emergency was now over. But the new bill they proposed went beyond mere repeal. It added further restraints on labor and undermined many of the protections provided for unions by the Labor Relations Act (Wagner Act) in 1935. The new measure, the Case bill (its sponsor was Francis Case of South Dakota), made unions liable to being sued for breach of contract if they called a strike during the period covered by a labor contract or if any property damage occurred. It also required a thirty-day cooling-off period. A Republican proposal, the bill was supported by 87 Democrats from the South (with only 9 voting no), along with most northern Republicans. In the Senate, only 2 southern Democrats, Lister Hill and Claude Pepper, opposed it. When Harry S. Truman, who had been elevated to the presidency after FDR's death in 1944, decided to veto the measure, it was sustained by 107 northern Democrats, 15 Republicans, and just 11 southern Democrats. The conservative coalition of Republicans and southern Democrats, which had been erratic during the war on most issues, except perhaps on retrenchment, clearly held firm on antiunion questions.

The coalition's antilabor animus was abundantly evident when the campaign to end the "closed shop," which the Wagner Act had recognized, reached its climax with the Taft-Hartley Act of 1947. Labor leaders protested that, without the requirement that all workers covered by a contract negotiated by the union had to become members, that is, a "closed shop," their ability to engage in collective bargaining would be fatally undermined. The "right to work," that is, permission to work in the plant and enjoy the benefits that the union had won for workers without actually joining it, was the counter-position demanded by employers. And they got what they wanted. For the language of the dispute, not just its outcome, favored the employers, as the pejorative term "closed shop" unlike the term "right to work" reveals so clearly. Taft-Hartley outlawed the union's right to speak for all the workers on whose behalf it had bargained, thereby rejecting the "closed shop." The law also prohibited secondary boycotts in sympathy with a strike in a related industry; imposed a sixty-day cooling-off period; made unions liable for breach of contract; and prohibited unions from engaging in political campaigns (targeted was the CIO's political action committee, CIO-PAC, which had been active in recent elections against candidates hostile to labor).

Although a ban on industry-wide collective bargaining, which would have virtually destroyed the CIO, was left out of the House's Hartley bill, the final version of the law still amounted to a devastating attack on labor and the recognition it had gained over the preceding decade as a legitimate and viable component of the American industrial system. And, once again, the Solid South threw its weight against labor and its unions. Only sixteen of the South's ninety-five House members voted against the stringent Hartley bill, and just three opposed the less repressive Taft bill in the Senate. All but nine southerners in the House and four in the Senate supported the successful override of Truman's angry veto of the Taft-Hartley bill.

Several other measures favorable to workers, which Truman proposed as part of his postwar reconversion agenda to sustain the momentum of the New Deal, were vigorously opposed by the southerners. In fall 1945, southern Democrats collaborated with Republicans on the House Ways and Means Committee to table indefinitely, and therefore to kill, Truman's unemployment compensation bill. A few months later, southern senators voted against the president's plan to expand and make permanent the U.S. Employment Service, because they wanted to restore control of the labor market to the localities. Finally, the South was instrumental, of course in alliance with conservative Republicans, in opposing and ultimately gutting Truman's bill to make the government responsible for ensuring full employment, once the war-induced demand for labor slackened. Only 6 of the 112 House cosponsors of the Wright Patman full-employment bill were southerners, while the Committee on Expenditures in the Executive Departments, chaired by Carter Manasco of Alabama, eviscerated Truman's bill. These two hostile moves ruled out the very idea of full employment as a desirable economic and social goal, as well as the government's role in achieving it.

The South's Widening Veto over Social Policy

The Solid South was still very much alive. Earlier, its vote had been cast preponderantly in support of Roosevelt's First New Deal and, with a few exceptions, for the Second too. Despite some weakening and diminution, it had endorsed his plans for war mobilization as well. But, with the ending of the war and the emergence of Truman's Fair Deal for maintaining the federal government's responsibility for economic stability and for its citizens' welfare, the conservative opposition counterattacked. Within that opposition a large number of southern Democrats were to be found, and their votes could be relied upon. But, on issues relating to labor and race, they were absolutely solid. The fight was nothing less than a pitched battle to protect the region's system of labor control characterized by low wages and unorganized workers, with its underpinning of racial discrimination and white dominance. These two aspects of labor control were integral to each other. It was not surprising that, on labor as well as on racial issues, the southern delegation acted as a virtual unit. Yet, because southern votes on labor matters were cast as part of a predominantly Republican majority, the solidity of the South was obscured and consequently overlooked. Unlike votes against the FEPC or black suffrage, which revealed the South acting alone, the votes on labor issues were combined with those of northern Republicans.[7]

Writing just a year or so after the imbroglio over the Taft-Hartley and War Labor Disputes Acts, V. O. Key was convinced that, "apart from the indubitably potent habit of voting Democratic, about all that remains to promote southern solidarity is the Negro."[8] Yet there was another component of the Solid South in the 1940s—the need to ensure that the southern labor system, of which blacks were an essential component, remained free from external influence and subversion. For the southern Democrats were protecting, not just their racial order consisting of political disfranchisement and social segregation, but also their economic order, with its labor market insulated from national wage levels and labor unions. A political wall was being built around the region's distinctive and interlocking system of labor and racial control.

A political wall was also being erected between the South's Democrats and the majority of Democrats from outside the region. As southern Democrats allied with members of the opposing party from the North, but not with their fellow Democrats from the North, their position became increasingly anomalous, even alien. Their primary political enemies were not Republicans but the majority of their own party, which, in fact, was in power nationally during the 1940s. The New Deal coalition, with its defining components of workers and African Americans, was the bête noire of the antilabor, white supremacist South. Disaffected though the southerners were, they were not powerless—perhaps not even marginalized. As the minority in the majority party, a status clearly less pleasant than their previous majority position within the minority party, southern Democrats still possessed considerable power. They were established figures within the party hierarchy because of the political experience and longevity of a large number within their ranks. They also held seniority within the committee system and were ranking members when the Republicans gained control of Congress in 1946.

Even when the Republicans increased their numbers during the wartime elections and the Democrats' ranks thinned as a result, the South continued to send a full complement of Democrats to Washington. Consequently, from 1933 to 1952, southern Democrats in Congress numbered between 115 and 118, a remarkable level of representation and an equally remarkable record of consistency, all the more significant because the rest of the party's numbers fell from 217 in 1937 to a mere 73 in 1947.[9] When this happened, the South became the dominant element in the party. This trend was very similar to the South's increasing majority within the Democratic Party in the decade before the Civil War when its northern wing collapsed after the Kansas-Nebraska Act, with many from the northern wing leaving to join the northern Republican Party. After 1942, when the Democratic edge in the House and the Senate fell to twenty and six, respectively, the influence within the party of its southern wing increased automatically.

In the 1944 presidential election, southerners became a major influence in the party's nomination process. Many of them preferred a candidate other than Roosevelt, so they ran Harry Byrd, who won a mere 89 delegate votes. But they had more success when they functioned as a unit in preventing Roosevelt from keeping his vice president, Henry Wallace, for another term. Instead, they agreed on Harry S. Truman, a border state senator from Missouri. Truman certainly owed his nomination to the South's Democrats, and, later, when he became president, they tried, though to little avail, to get him to show his gratitude to them.

Meanwhile, the South's power and reputation within the Democratic Party made it impossible to even consider leaving to join the Republicans. Besides, a sudden change of party by the bulk of the region's congressmen would have caused havoc among the state parties within the South itself. Indeed, Clark Clifford, one of Truman's closest advisers, could imagine no other possibility as he drafted his famous memorandum of 19 November 1947 outlining strategy for the 1948 presidential election. "As always," he predicted, "the South can be considered safely Democratic. And in formulating national policy, it can be safely ignored."[10]

The Truman administration could, and did, ignore the South "in formulating national policy," for the president proceeded to attack the South's racial sensibilities over the succeeding year. Unfortunately, Clifford seemed quite unaware that the South was a very potent element in

American government and had been influencing national policy fundamentally since the late 1930s. As a unified and powerful bloc within the Democratic Party, the South defined the limits of the government's liberal initiatives. The New Deal and the wartime planning boards provided the impetus for the Truman administration to pursue a program similar to those of the European nations after World War II. Such a program might have included a number of innovative social and economic policies. Among them were increased government responsibility for a stable economy with full employment; the incorporation of labor unions into the industrial system as acknowledged representatives of the labor force; public provision of health care and other features of a viable welfare state, with guaranteed protections and benefits; and elimination of structural discrimination on racial or religious grounds. These kinds of policies and plans were envisaged, and to a considerable degree implemented, in postwar Europe. Truman's twenty-one-point plan for reconversion and his Fair Deal included a number of them.

But what prospect did he have of getting his party to support policies like these when they had to run the gauntlet of the southern wing of the party, known in advance to be opposed to them? Advocates of these initiatives were therefore discouraged by prior knowledge of the southern Democrats' hostility. Even more important, they were deterred by the certainty of solid southern resistance. Accordingly, the Solid South exercised a decisive veto over the Democratic Party's pursuit of a social democratic agenda at a fluid and critical moment in recent American history.

The Solid South under Attack

WHITE DEFIANCE

Eighty years almost to the day after the sudden death by assassination of Abraham Lincoln, Franklin D. Roosevelt died, on 12 April 1945. Like Andrew Johnson, Lincoln's vice president, who became president on 14 April 1865, Vice President Harry S. Truman was a former senator from a border state who had not been part of the president's inner circle. His future course, like Johnson's, could not therefore be known right away, either by himself or by the public at large. Another similarity, and a source of great unease, was the timing of their gaining the presidency, for both men came to power as the two most massive wars in the country's history, the Civil War and World War II, were coming to a close and as critical policies for postwar settlement had to be devised. In Truman's case, the problems he faced were even greater, because, unlike the Confederacy, Germany and Japan had not yet surrendered.

And the response of each man to the circumstances in which they found themselves turned out to be unexpectedly similar, for they both surprised their initial supporters by the course they began to pursue. Andrew Johnson's wartime hostility to the South's political and economic elites and his denunciation of them as traitors who needed to be punished pleased the Republicans, especially the party's radical wing. But he soon adopted a conciliatory approach toward the former Confederates, which quickly degenerated into an attack on the radicals, and even on the Republican Party itself, over Reconstruction policy.

In a somewhat similar fashion, Harry Truman disappointed his backers from the South, who had engineered his nomination for the vice presidency over President Roosevelt's choice of Henry Wallace, the sitting vice president in 1944. Unlike Wallace, Truman was no committed New Dealer but a Missouri Democrat who concurred in his party's New Deal initiatives mainly for practical political reasons. He was equally pragmatic on matters of race. He once wrote a colleague from the South that, on an antilynching bill under consideration in the Senate, "all my sympathies are with you, but the Negro vote in Kansas City and St. Louis is too important."[1] Truman's racial attitudes were reassuring to South Carolina's senator Burnet R. Maybank, who acknowledged to a southern friend while traveling on the Roosevelt funeral train, "Everything's going to be all right—the new President knows how to handle the niggers."[2]

But Truman's stance on the New Deal and on race would soon change. For much of his first year in the White House, Truman was discovering how uncooperative conservative Republicans and southern Democrats were over his plans for postwar reconversion of the economy and protection of labor. At the same time, they gave the president little credit for his more conservative actions. Among these were his threat to draft strikers in the railroad strike of May 1946; his replacement of all of Roosevelt's senior New Deal officials by the end of 1946; and his hard line on foreign affairs with his detonating of two atomic bombs on Japan and his abrasive approach to the United States' wartime ally, the Soviet Union. Then, in the off-year elections of 1946, the Democrats lost control of both houses of Congress, forfeiting the dominance they had enjoyed since Roosevelt took office in 1932. Even more disconcerting to Truman was the suspicion and disapproval he received from the liberal New Deal majority within his own party. The extent of this estrangement became apparent during 1947 when Henry Wallace indicated his disaffection and pursued the possibility of a third-party challenge to Truman in the upcoming presidential election.

As his attempt to reassure the conservatives seemed only to upset the liberal wing of his own party, Truman reassessed his position and decided he had to keep the Democrats together for the presidential contest in 1948. The northern, urban, New Deal coalition, which was now at the heart of the realigned Democratic Party, had to be reassured and even strengthened. He had no alternative. In June 1947, he delivered a stinging veto of the Taft-Hartley bill. Nine days later, he appeared before a rally of about 1,000 people at the Lincoln Memorial organized by the NAACP's annual conference, which was meeting that year in Washington, the first time a sitting president had even considered addressing a civil rights organization. In October, the President's Committee on Civil Rights, which Truman had appointed a year earlier, published its report, *To Secure These Rights*, calling for federal action against racial discrimination in a number of specified areas of national life.[3]

In another precedent-setting move, Truman sent Congress a special message on 2 February 1948 containing proposals for legislative action on civil rights. His recommendations were less comprehensive and forceful than those of the report. But they were still groundbreaking because Truman asked for legislation to outlaw lynching, ban the poll tax, and create a permanent Fair Employment Practices Commission, a permanent commission on civil rights, and a civil rights division within the Justice Department. He also urged Congress to consider measures to protect the right to vote and to prohibit discrimination on interstate transportation.

The president expected the South to be dismayed by his message. On the morning he submitted it, he wrote in his diary: "They, no doubt, will receive it as coldly as they did the State of the Union Message. But it needs to be said."[4] The reaction of leading southern politicians must nevertheless have surprised Truman, because it was neither cold nor sullen but instead furious and scorching. Senator Tom Connally of Texas dared to call Truman's message "a lynching of the constitution" and vowed that "we will not take it lying down."[5] Congressman John Bell Williams of Mississippi wished to remind the president that "if it were not for southern Democrats, Henry Wallace would be in the White House today," so this civil rights assault was "a mighty poor way for him to evince his gratitude."[6]

And these outbursts of indignation and betrayal were just the beginning. The president's recent change of course demonstrated the power and importance of the urban, liberal coalition within the Democratic Party, and his unprecedented initiative of placing civil rights on the party's and the nation's agenda was ominous. The reaction of Mississippi's senior senator, James O. Eastland, revealed how threatening the new situation seemed to the party's southern wing. "The South we know," he exclaimed, "is being swept to its destruction. It is a real danger—it is an imminent danger." The region's political leaders felt they had to act in order to protect the South; they could not merely remonstrate.[7]

The Dixiecrat Revolt

But what effective political action could the angry and fearful southerners take? Some vowed to leave the Democratic Party altogether. Governor Fielding Wright of Mississippi led the way by organizing a rally in Jackson on 12 February and then calling for a national states' rights conference in May. But support for a movement to create a new party such as Wright envisaged generated little enthusiasm within the conference of southern governors, which met four days after Truman's civil rights message and soon became absorbed in devising an immediate course of action in defense of their region. The governors agreed that South Carolina's Strom Thurmond should head a delegation to see whether Truman would relent on his civil rights initiative. But the president refused to meet with them. Instead, the chairman of the Democratic National Committee announced that the president's position "remains unchanged" and added that he would accept a nomination from the party to run for the presidency.[8]

The southern governors had been snubbed, and their options had narrowed considerably. Besides, the prospect of leaving the Democratic Party—the foundation of the region's one-party system and the source of its political identity—was more than the governors could even consider. Also at risk if they abandoned the Democrats was the power they possessed in Congress through the South's accumulated experience and institutional dominance, that is, the seniority system. Therefore, these state governors were not about to overturn the structures that had provided security and influence for the region. Infuriated and worried though they were about the South's changed position within the party, they were fundamentally conservative state executives who were neither radical nor impulsive. They proposed, therefore, not to leave the Democratic Party or to subvert or dismantle it, but instead to take over the party machinery within the southern states in order to prevent Truman's election.

By the time Governor Wright's national states' rights conference met in May 1948, the governors had secured control over its proceedings and decisions.* The gathering set up a States' Rights Democratic campaign committee to oppose the nomination of Truman at the party's national convention in Philadelphia in July and demand that a state rights plank, not a civil rights one, be included in the party platform. If Truman were to be nominated on a civil rights platform, however, the States' Rights movement would meet in Birmingham to choose a presidential ticket and then the Democratic Party in each state would proceed to nominate the organization's choices for president and vice president as the Democratic candidates. But if the state parties refused to make these men the Democratic nominees, then they would have to run as independent, third-party candidates against Truman, or against whomever the party's convention chose.

---

*It is odd that the southerners used the term "states' rights," rather than "state's rights," because states do not have rights as a group. Surely, these rights refer to the sovereign rights of an individual state. Anyway, to avoid the whole problem, I prefer the neater and unproblematic usage "state rights" and have employed it in this book and elsewhere.

In that case, Democratic voters would have to vote against their party and cast their ballots for a non-Democratic ticket or abstain from voting altogether.

The States' Rights Democrats, who still, it should be noted, retained the name "Democrat," were not a real third party like Henry Wallace's Progressive Party, which also mounted a campaign in 1948 against the official Democratic nominee. Described at the time, and ever since, as the "Dixiecrats," the southerners saw themselves as a rebellious, insurgent faction within the party that was prepared to break, not with the party as a whole, but just with its presidential nominee. If they could not deny him nomination at the national convention through the approved mechanism of balloting by state delegation, they would substitute their own candidates at the state level and enable voters in the general election to vote for rival Democratic candidates. In effect, this unorthodox procedure would replace a presidential ticket chosen by the national convention with the choice made by the party's executive committee in each state. Only if the state party backed the official nominees would the Dixiecrat choices be running as non-Democrats and therefore as third-party candidates.

The Dixiecrats were anomalous in another way as well. They did not see themselves as an electoral organization whose purpose was to mobilize voters and generate mass support. The group of state governors who guided the movement did not run its campaign, but instead a campaign committee consisting of two members from each of the southern states handled it. And the campaign, such as it was, was aimed at the Democratic state executive committees, whose main official function, within the South's decentralized one-party system, was to prepare the ballots for primary and general elections. Since these committees could decide which candidates would be on the party's ballot, the Dixiecrats focused their attention on getting commitments to delay that decision until after the Democratic convention, so that the Dixiecrat candidates could be on the ballot rather than Truman, if he were the official nominee.

Consequently, the Dixiecrats' target was not the voters but the state Democratic committees and the leading Democrats in each state, such as the governor and other individuals of known influence in the party. As Numan V. Bartley has observed, the Dixiecrats' campaign committee "was first of all a lobbying body with the aim of garnering the support of party elites."[9] Naturally, the movement was not oblivious to the voters. Efforts were made to generate support and enthusiasm among the southern electorate through meetings and publicity and, in the general election, through speeches, rallies, and the other paraphernalia and activities of election campaigns. But the main focus was on the Democratic Party leadership and on obtaining a place on the ballot, rather than on appealing to and mobilizing voters. Evidently, the creation of an institutional structure and a mass base for a permanent political party was not part of the Dixiecrats' future plans.

The Dixiecrat revolt may not have produced a new party, but it did encourage disloyalty to the Democratic Party and undermine the electoral mechanisms that had maintained party unity in the South for decades. To protect their region's interests and present a united front, the Dixiecrats were prepared to repudiate the party's nominee and use the machinery of party unity to run a rival campaign and therefore divide the Democrats. Far less dangerous than forming a new party, the Dixiecrat maneuver nevertheless cannot be seen as anything but a bolt and an act of party disloyalty that could create a precedent for irregularity in the future. A further paradox in the Dixiecrat strategy lay in the confusion of ends and means. The purpose of the South's revolt was to reveal to the national leadership how important the southern Democrats were. Their allegiance to the party and their power within it could not be taken for granted. Yet, by acting independently and throwing their weight behind a rival presidential ticket, they were showing that these virtues and assets could not be relied upon either. Thurmond had threatened that "the present leadership of the Democratic party will soon realize that the South is no longer 'in the bag.' "[10] And the Alabama state chairman, Gessner T. McCorvey, predicted in October, "We are certainly going to let every citizen of America realize that we constitute a group to be reckoned with and that we are fighters and are not going to be kicked around anymore."[11]

The Dixiecrat strategy in 1948 was, therefore, to use the Electoral College to demonstrate the South's leverage. With the loss of both houses of Congress to the Republicans in 1946 and the splintering of the Democrats two years later because of the Progressive and Dixiecrat defections, Truman's reelection seemed unlikely. If he were defeated, the South would have contributed to his loss and would play a vital role in reviving the party in a conservative and Republican-controlled political environment. But, if the election were close, the 127 electoral votes of the States' Rights candidates would force the election into the House, where they could wield the region's eleven state votes (in the contingent House election, states voted as units) to pressure the Democrats into abandoning their party's civil rights plank.

Even more disheartening to them was the accuracy of Truman's calculation that his civil rights initiative was more likely to help him in the North than hurt him in the South. In the 1944 presidential election, ten northern states had been carried by Roosevelt by margins of 3 percent or less. By 1948, registered black voters constituted more than 3 percent of the electorate in sixteen northern states with 278 electoral votes, compared to the South's total of 127 electoral votes.[12] A forthright appeal to northern black voters made far more political sense, therefore. Just before polling day, Truman went to Harlem, where he addressed a huge audience of 65,000. But he made only a few appearances in the South— in Florida, Texas, and North Carolina, none of them with Dixiecrat electoral slates.

So the Dixiecrats' assumption that the South could exert leverage in the presidential election was dubious. Even more unsure was their expectation that the South would march in solid ranks behind the States' Rights banner. During the four months before the Democratic convention in July, the Dixiecrats urged state leaders to turn their party apparatus over to them in the event that the Democrats nominated Truman or anyone else on a civil rights platform. States were urged to defer their nominations for electors until after the Democratic convention and then, if need be, to choose a slate of electors for the Dixiecrat candidates. Mississippi agreed immediately, and soon after so did South Carolina.

But then the movement ran into difficulty, because Democratic leaders feared the consequences of a repudiation of the party's nominees. Even in Alabama, a Lower South state with a large black population, there was considerable opposition from loyalists, led by New Dealers, Governor Jim Folsom and Senators Lister Hill and John Sparkman, who worried about breaking with the party, despite being fearful of Truman's civil rights program. Eventually, the Folsom loyalists were defeated by the States' Righters, who were led by the state chairman, Gessner McCorvey, former governor Frank M. Dixon, and the rising Birmingham politician Eugene "Bull" Connor. All eleven presidential electors chosen in the May primary were pledged to vote against any nominee who favored the civil rights plank, and half of the state's delegates to the party convention agreed to walk out if such a candidate was nominated.

Of the remaining states, only Louisiana swung into line with the Dixiecrats, and even then only after a protracted struggle. Elsewhere, a combination of factors proved decisive in the victory of the party loyalists. In some instances, gubernatorial elections that year made candidates for reelection worry about leading a move to break with the national party. In Virginia, the Byrd machine, whose continued hegemony depended upon party regularity, considered the prospect of engaging in disloyalty to be unthinkable. Besides, in Virginia, as in Tennessee and North Carolina, the quite viable and competitive Republicans would be the only beneficiaries of a split among the Democrats, and this provided another disincentive for dissidence. Further contributing to the emergence of opposition in many states was the preexistence of rival factions, which naturally aligned around competing claims between States' Rights dissent and party loyalty.

There was also the practical question of whether the Dixiecrat strategy was likely to succeed. Was it worth investing political capital and prestige in a cause that might achieve little? This calculation seems to have been critical in Georgia. After an intense struggle for the governorship, in which the Dixiecrat issue had become a complicating factor, the winner of the Democratic primary, Herman Talmadge, who was running to succeed his father, Gene, decided he could not risk opposing Truman in pursuit of an initiative that might fail. So he maneuvered to have Georgia's electors uninstructed, a balancing act that disappointed the Dixiecrats, who had expected Georgia, as a Lower South state, to support the revolt.

The net result of the constant pressuring and lobbying of party officials in each state before and after the Democratic convention was that just four states agreed to consider the Dixiecrat candidates as the Democratic Party's official candidates—Mississippi, South Carolina, Alabama, and Louisiana. In the remaining seven, the States' Rights nominees were on the ballot as candidates of a separate party. In these cases, voters would be casting a ballot against the Democratic Party and not just for a different Democratic slate. Yet the Dixiecrats had conceived of their strategy of replacing Truman on the ballot as a maneuver that was carefully planned to avoid the stigma and risk of becoming an independent party. They had also intended that their movement would forge a united South, able to use its 127 electoral votes to force the national Democratic leadership to recant its civil rights heresy. Instead, a divided South had resulted, with a plurality of states resorting to the third-party strategy that the States' Rights leaders had determinedly opposed.

The predictions of the Dixiecrats about the outcome of the Democratic national convention were, however, far more accurate. Truman was in fact nominated without any difficulty. The sole source of opposition came from the South, which nominated Senator Richard B. Russell of Georgia, who received 263 votes. North Carolina was the only southern state to cast any of its votes for Truman, who received a grand total of 947½ votes. Russell might have received additional support if the Mississippi delegation and half of the Alabama delegation had not left the convention earlier after it had approved the civil rights plank. An alternative southern plank urged the party to return to its "fundamental principles" of state rights, by which the states "control and regulate local affairs and act in the exercise of police powers." This proposal was defeated, 925–309, with every southern delegate voting for it and with only 11 from outside the South joining them.

The civil rights plank that ended up in the platform was not, however, the vague and cautious statement approved by the platform committee and by the president. Instead, a far more forceful plank was proposed by Representative Andrew Biemiller of Wisconsin and Mayor Hubert Humphrey of Minneapolis, which commended Truman "for his courageous stand on the issue of civil rights" and urged Congress to support him in guaranteeing the rights of "full and equal political participation," "equal opportunity of employment," "security of person," and "equal treatment in the service and defense of our Nation."[13] Humphrey's speech proposing the plank closed with a pointed rebuke of the southerners, for he urged the Democratic Party "to get out of the shadow of states' rights and to walk forthrightly into the bright sunshine of human rights."[14] These words and the vigor of the plank itself galvanized the urban coalition into voting overwhelmingly in its favor, 651½–582½. The South's unanimity in opposition was supplemented by a group of western states and Kentucky and Maryland. A strong civil rights plank had been adopted and the South's enemies had triumphed. The Russell candidacy made the South's powerlessness even more visible, for the region's Democrats were now isolated.

The rebuffs they had received in Philadelphia did not stiffen the southerners' resistance or rally support for the beleaguered, conservative South. After the convention, the Dixiecrats held a rally in Birmingham and then a meeting in Houston at which they officially nominated Strom Thurmond and Fielding Wright, the governors of South Carolina and Mississippi, respectively, as their candidates. But these gatherings of the faithful did not lead to any noticeable upsurge in popular support. Nor did the interest of the all-important state committees and governors grow. Rather the opposite, for Georgia's Democrats backed away, under pressure from Herman Talmadge, as did the state executive committee in Texas and the governor, Buford Jester, who was running for reelection. As a result, the Dixiecrat nominees were the Democratic candidates in only four Lower South states, where the black population was a near majority and where no gubernatorial elections were being held in 1948. These were, therefore, states where race was an overriding issue but where party disloyalty during this election would not jeopardize the Democratic establishment.

Democratic officials were reluctant to take a political risk with the Dixiecrat revolt because they realized quite correctly that it was a single-issue movement with little else to offer the party or the voters. The purpose of the campaign was quite simple—to protect the South from the hostile plans of the ascendant wing of the Democratic Party. The movement was a defensive power play aimed at restoring southern influence in the Democratic Party. Devising a program of social reform or economic development was not its purpose at all. And, in any case, proposing plans and policies would merely distract the States' Rights bolters from their immediate goal of regaining influence within the national Democratic Party. As Thurmond once admitted to an adviser, developing a set of issues would be "pretty difficult," not to mention beside the point.[15]

Nevertheless, Thurmond himself was not happy about a purely race-based movement. In his political career prior to 1948, he had presented himself as a political moderate who stressed economic development as both the fundamental need of the region and the most effective way of improving the condition of whites as well as blacks. At the States' Rights meeting in Jackson in May, he had asserted that "economic underprivilege in the South has known no color line. Both races have suffered in the economic struggle to overcome artificial barriers to our recovery and growth imposed upon this part of the Nation from without."[16] Although "artificial barriers . . . imposed upon" the South retarded the region's economic development, the same artificial barriers imposed on southern blacks by southern whites like himself did not need to be challenged, it seemed. Rather these antiblack barriers had to be defended to the death. Indeed, this theme of external threat was further developed by Thurmond himself and many other Dixiecrats into an issue that did actually broaden their response beyond merely defending white supremacy. It was not northern economic interests but the federal government itself that posed the real threat to the South and therefore, by implication, to the states.

The Dixiecrats identified their struggle with the overthrow of Reconstruction and likened it to a renewed attempt by the federal government to intervene in local affairs. This time, however, the South was resisting federal interference in people's lives, with the way they related to each other, how they conducted elections, whom they could employ. In effect, the government was on a course to create "a police state." Aware of how salient was the fear of communism in postwar America, the Dixiecrats naturally associated this all-pervasive national government with communism and the communists, who had somehow infiltrated it and were exerting considerable influence over its policies. By broadening the scope of the South's campaign of resistance in this way, the Dixiecrats tried to move their concerns beyond race and region, so as to show how the fight against an intrusive national government was a matter of great concern to localities and individuals throughout the country. The struggle against an intrusive and alien central government was therefore a matter of national concern, and the South's problem was just one variation on a common theme. Although many of the party faithful may have actually believed this, the strategy was clearly manufactured for political purposes, and John Ed Peace of the *Louisville Courier-Journal* was quick to expose and ridicule it: "On the platform Mr. Thurmond and his fellow travelers shout of Americanism, our way of life, the right to choose one's associates, Communism, Reds. But they mean Nigger. Mr. Thurmond, of course, never says the word; he's not the type."[17]

When election day came, the attempt of the States' Rights Democrats to force the contest into the House of Representatives failed miserably. They won just those four states where they managed to install presidential electors who supported their ticket. Elsewhere, they had been forced to run as a third party and had only won between 8 and 13 percent of the vote, with more success in Georgia at 20.3 percent and Arkansas at 16.5 percent. Their 1.17 million popular votes had earned them 39 votes in the Electoral College, which was actually 39 more than Henry Wallace obtained with roughly the same number of popular votes. Despite the *Chicago Tribune*'s famously wrong headline, Truman defeated Dewey, winning 2 million more votes than the Republican and a clear majority of 114 in the Electoral College.

The fundamental reality of the Dixiecrat phenomenon was the inability of most southern Democrats to abandon "the party of the fathers," a party that had now become a great danger to their region. Although the Dixiecrats were willing to be disloyal, the South's Democratic leadership refused to go along. Meanwhile, all the region's Democrats, including the Dixiecrats, intended to remain in the haven of the Democratic Party, even though it was no longer an entirely safe one. In the short run, however, remaining with the Democrats proved not to be so bad after all. The great fear that Truman, once reelected, would inflict his civil rights agenda on the South turned out to be exaggerated. In his State of the Union address in January 1949, the president outlined his Fair Deal program, which included a commitment to take action on civil rights. But the legislation he introduced ran into strong opposition, ironically because the Democrats had regained control of both houses of Congress in the 1948 elections.

With the party in control again, southern Democrats automatically became chairmen of the crucial committees. For example, Senator Eastland now chaired Judiciary, and William Colmer, also from Mississippi, headed the House Rules Committee. As a result, Truman's civil rights proposals were bottled up in committee, while those that did make it through to a vote were defeated. This was the fate of his anti-poll tax, antilynching, voting rights, and permanent Fair Employment Practices Commission measures, the Senate as always performing the executioner's role. Moreover, an effort to undermine the filibuster, the weapon so frequently resorted to by the southerners, by reducing the number of votes required to end debate from a two-thirds vote to a plurality, failed completely. By June 1949, the president conceded defeat, until the next session, when once again his efforts would be frustrated, with not a single one of his bills emerging from committee in 1951. Staying in the Democratic Party was evidently a winning proposition as long as seniority and the committee system gave southerners the power to obstruct hostile legislation successfully.

But the presidency remained a problem. The South could not stay in the Democratic Party while refusing to vote for its nominee. Nevertheless, the experience of 1948 had opened the door for further, and more explicit, disloyalty. The sources of greatest support for Thurmond were located in the Lower South and particularly in the black belts, where African American population density was at its highest and where race relations were more traditional and paternalistic. With their bonds to the Democrats loosened, a large number of these black belt counties continued to vote over the next two decades for candidates running against the Democratic nominee.

In Mississippi, South Carolina, and Louisiana and sometimes in Alabama and Georgia, former Dixiecrats organized independent state campaigns and voted for the Republican nominee. In 1952, they supported Eisenhower. In 1956, they backed Senator Harry Byrd, who ran as a States' Rights candidate, while Louisiana voted for Eisenhower again. In 1960, they endorsed Richard Nixon, though he obtained only the electoral votes of Mississippi and half of Alabama's. In 1964, however, the entire Lower South was in the camp of the Republican nominee, Barry Goldwater. Then, four years later, Richard Nixon, the Republican candidate, and George C. Wallace, running as the candidate of the American Independent Party, together captured about 80 percent of the white southern vote, Wallace carrying every Lower South state except Thurmond's South Carolina and also Arkansas. In the 1964 and 1968 presidential contests, the region as a whole, not just the black belt sections, broke away from the Democrats. The South had become no longer reliably, let alone solidly, Democratic in presidential elections. And the Dixiecrat revolt was primarily responsible for this trend by first loosening the moorings.

A more important outcome of the Dixiecrat protest was perhaps its impact on the politics of race in the South. Because the movement had arisen from a fear that the region's race relations were threatened, V. O. Key had seen its failure to develop broad support as evidence that the issue of race could not arouse conservative feelings as it once had. "The Dixiecrats beat the drums of racial reaction in 1948 without impressive results," he suggested hopefully. "The Dixiecrat movement may turn out to have been the dying gasp of the Old South." Key discerned "a powerful strain of agrarian liberalism, now re-enforced by the growing [labor] unions of the cities" that was less visible than it warranted "because of the capacity of the one-party system to conceal factional differences."[18] Had he been writing a decade later, in 1958, such a hopeful comment would never have entered his mind. Rather than marking the end of race as the fundamental issue, the Dixiecrats actually prepared the way for the frenzied racial politics of the next fifteen years.

The attempt to frustrate the election of the official Democratic nominee in 1948 had failed. But the region's race relations still needed to be defended, and other ways of accomplishing this were available. In fact, one of them was already proving effective, as Congress and its southern-dominated committee system thwarted Truman's efforts to enact civil rights legislation. The Dixiecrats' failure could therefore be dismissed as a result of a misplaced focus on presidential politics. After all, the region's Democratic leadership did not disagree with the Dixiecrats' decision to oppose Truman's civil rights initiative. It was the Dixiecrats' decision to run a rival presidential candidate that was rejected as too risky.

Therefore, the Dixiecrat revolt's failure was not an indication that race was becoming less important. Rather the opposite, for their campaign had given the defense of white supremacy a salience and an urgency it did not possess before. After being just one ingredient in the mixture of southern reactions to the New Deal, with its centralizing tendencies and its sympathy for organized labor and the poor, race became the fundamental and overriding issue in the conservative South's resistance in 1948. The Dixiecrats made race central to their protest. The protection of southern racial institutions and practices was now acknowledged as a primary, and therefore legitimate, concern for the region as a whole. The only question was how best to defend the system. In the mid-1950s, another battleground would be selected and another weapon discovered for protecting the South's vaunted racial order.

"Massive Resistance"

For the Dixiecrats, the southern states' authority to select their presidential electors was the weapon and an alternative presidential campaign was the battlefield. The threat that provoked this outburst was a president's proposal of a civil rights agenda. In 1954, however, the threat was not a mere proposal but an imminent course of action by the federal government intended to undermine one of the bulwarks of the region's system of white supremacy, its racially segregated public schools. In *Brown v. Board of Education of Topeka, Kansas*, the U.S. Supreme Court declared the "separate but equal" doctrine unconstitutional because "separate educational facilities are inherently unequal." School districts with separate schools for blacks and whites were therefore put on notice to take measures to bring their systems into compliance with the Court's ruling. Once its public schools were desegregated, the wall of white supremacy would be breached and the South's racial order would be likely to collapse. The threat was therefore real and no longer imaginary.

Predictably, Senator Richard Russell denounced the decision as "a flagrant abuse of judicial power." His defiant reaction was endorsed immediately and publicly by Governors Herman Talmadge of Georgia, James Byrnes of South Carolina, and Fielding Wright of Mississippi. Also outspoken was the Upper South state of Virginia, whose governor, Thomas Stanley, proclaimed: "I shall use every legal means at my command to continue segregated schools in Virginia." Even North Carolina's moderate new governor, Luther Hodges, was adamant.[19] On the other hand, the *Louisville Courier-Journal* commented reassuringly that "the end of the world has not come for the South or for the nation. The Supreme Court's ruling is not itself a revolution."[20] And in Kentucky and other border states like Maryland, Missouri, and Oklahoma, preparations were made to comply with the decision. In fact, the decision itself had been expected for a year or so. In view of the Court's position on cases since the war challenging black exclusion from law schools in state universities, a verdict hostile to segregation in public schools was anticipated.

Nevertheless, a year of uncertainty and only minimal action followed, until the Court handed down its second *Brown* decision in May 1955 explaining how and when schools were to be desegregated. But these instructions produced even more uncertainty. According to the justices, the federal courts had to "require that the defendants [that is, segregated school districts] make a prompt and reasonable start toward full compliance" by proceeding to admit blacks to white schools "with all deliberate speed." No timetable or formula for achieving desegregation was specified, and responsibility for drawing up and initiating plans was left with the school districts themselves. Meanwhile, federal district courts presided over by southern judges were required to supervise the process once it began, and, of course, individual black students would be the ones to put themselves in harm's way as the human agents of integration. Under these vague and permissive conditions, it was highly unlikely that a governor or a school district would be willing to embark on so complicated and controversial a course of action.

At this critical moment, implementation of the Court's decision required the approval and support of the executive branch of the national government. President Eisenhower's response, however, was simply to do nothing and distance himself and his office from the entire matter. Before the *Brown* decision was announced, Eisenhower had once taken Chief Justice Earl Warren aside at a White House dinner and confided to him that southern whites "are not bad people. All they are concerned about is to see that their sweet little girls are not required to sit in school alongside some big overgrown Negro." Besides his sympathetic racial attitudes, his views about social change were also reassuring to most southern whites. For the former general was a conservative who did "not believe that prejudice . . . will succumb to compulsion" but could only change gradually and with the cooperation of those actually involved.[21]

Eisenhower later acknowledged privately, "I personally think that the decision was wrong." He was also "convinced" that it "set back progress in the South at least fifteen years."[22] His inner convictions about the imprudence of efforts to compel people to change their racial attitudes and behavior prevented him from making any public statement endorsing *Brown* and its charge to desegregate southern schools. Eisenhower was a popular president who commanded considerable respect among businessmen and city dwellers in the South. He had carried Florida, Tennessee, Texas, and Virginia in 1952 and had won almost 50 percent of the vote in the Deep South states of South Carolina, Louisiana, and Mississippi. Had he publicly approved the Court's decision and urged compliance, the course of events would almost certainly have been quite different.

Instead, his inaction and indifference contributed substantially to the disastrous power vacuum that arose in 1956. With no plan, no deadline, and no enforcement mechanism being proposed by Washington, out-and-out resistance, with every expectation of success, became the South's response. For a brief but vital phase from 1956 to 1958, the southern states would be unified, arrayed solidly together in defiance of the attempt to break down their system of racial subordination. Throughout the first half of the twentieth century, the South had tried, with considerable success, to function as a unit within the Democratic Party in Congress and in presidential elections. Now, when the South tried to achieve unity on a policy of resistance to desegregation, the state governments came together and adopted a common course of action. This was something the region had accomplished only once before, in the movement for secession of 1860–61, although even then four states had proven reluctant.

The policy of "massive resistance" did not emerge right away. In the year or so after the *Brown* decision in May 1954, a less radical policy was formulated, aimed at frustrating desegregation but not stopping it. Usually referred to as "local option," it was adopted in several states, such as Virginia, North Carolina, and Texas, as a method of minimal, or token, desegregation, with the initiative left in the hands of local school boards. Assuming some degree of desegregation was unavoidable, the "local option" policy aimed to keep its scope limited and to hand off responsibility to school boards, rather than commit state government to creating and implementing a statewide plan. To this end, the state legislature would pass a pupil assignment bill, providing for the placement of students in schools on a "nonracial" basis, such as their personal academic aptitude and their suitability to attend a particular school. And the school districts were then to implement pupil assignment however they wished.

By aiming the plan at individual children and permitting their parents to appeal any unwanted reassignment of their child, the system was purposefully lengthy and complicated. In addition, state compulsory attendance laws were modified and tuition grants were provided, so as to enable parents to withdraw a child from the public system and send him or her to a private school. Amendment to the state constitution was then required to allow state funds to be disbursed for private school tuition. This limited and reluctant acquiescence in the Court's decision appealed to moderates who nonetheless wanted to retain the essence of the existing segregated system. But their tentative approach was soon swept away by the realization in late 1955 that the federal initiative was so vague and feeble that it could actually be terminated if the South rallied solidly in opposition.

Sensing that escape from *Brown* was possible, Harry Byrd of Virginia and his newspaper organ, the *Richmond News Leader*, edited by James J. Kilpatrick, launched their campaign of so-called massive resistance, accompanied by a constitutional theory as justification. "State interposition" was a doctrine with origins in Jefferson's Kentucky Resolutions of 1798 and in the view of the federal union as a compact among equal states. According to this doctrine, a state could rightfully interpose itself between the federal government and its own citizens in order to protect them. Rather like Calhoun's doctrine of nullification, which was also based on theories of the union as a compact and on the doctrine of state sovereignty, interposition gave a state the right to take positive action on its own to protect its citizens from a federal threat.

Armed with this weapon and Kilpatrick's endless stream of editorials elucidating this implausible theory, Byrd and his machine went into high gear. First, they co-opted the constitutional convention that voters had called by a 2–1 majority for the purpose of approving private school tuition grants. The resisters claimed that the convention was an expression of, in Byrd's own phrase, the "opposition of the people to integration" and a vehicle for sanctioning interposition. Then, in August and September 1956, the Virginia assembly proceeded to enact legislation giving the state "direct responsibility for the control of any school . . . to which children of both races are assigned and enrolled" under court order and permitting it to close schools until segregation could be reestablished by the governor.[23] Since a state cannot be sued without its consent, segregated schools would be protected against legal challenge. Furthermore, a state board, not each school district, would determine pupil assignments, and any school that desegregated would be denied funding from the state.

Virginia's example was soon emulated by state legislatures elsewhere. By mid-1957, eight states had approved interposition and passed the necessary legislation for establishing state control over the public schools. Meanwhile, three others had endorsed interposition and were on the brink of passing laws to curtail token desegregation. Alabama, Georgia, Mississippi, and Florida had even gone so far as to declare the *Brown* decision null and void, a defiant reiteration of nullification. The rapid spread of massive resistance across the region had been stimulated by the South's congressional delegation in early 1956. Senators Byrd and Thurmond had circulated a Declaration of Constitutional Principles, subsequently referred to as the "Southern Manifesto." Although its original endorsement of interposition and its calling the *Brown* decision unconstitutional were removed at the request of more moderate congressmen, who were reluctant to sign a defiant segregationist appeal, the manifesto still accused the Court of a "clear abuse of judicial power" and considered *Brown* "contrary to the Constitution." It went on to commend the "motives of those States which have declared their intention to resist forced integration by any lawful means."[24] As Senator Byrd explained, the manifesto was "a part of the plan of massive resistance we've been working on and I hope and believe it will be an effective action."[25]

Nineteen of twenty-two senators signed the manifesto, including moderates like J. William Fulbright of Arkansas and Lister Hill and John Sparkman of Alabama, although not Tennessee's two moderates, Estes Kefauver and Albert Gore, both of whom had presidential ambitions in 1956. Texas's Lyndon B. Johnson, who was Senate majority leader and another southerner with hopes for a future presidential run, was not even asked to sign. Of the South's 106 representatives, 82 signed, with 17 of the 24 nonsigners coming from Texas, a state in which blacks constituted the smallest proportion of the population, just 13 percent. The remaining non-signers represented large urban centers in the Upper South or Florida. Sanctioned by the region's congressmen, the southern states dug in, bringing school desegregation to a standstill. During the decade after *Brown*, their legislatures would enact about 450 laws and resolutions maintaining segregation.

Faced by "the most serious crisis that has occurred since the War between the States," the Byrd machine and its mouthpiece, the *Richmond News Leader*, had ignited a movement that brought virtually all the region's public schools under state control and threatened to close any schools that took steps to integrate.[26] This "massive resistance"—the term was Byrd's—went beyond regional solidarity over school integration, however. Beleaguered, fearful, and atavistic, the South organized around the schools issue and forged an apparatus of enforcement and conformity that shut down, not just dissent and disagreement, but also moderation and reason. As Pat Watters of the Southern Regional Council recalled, "It was a frightening thing to go into a small city and to realize that not merely the semiliterate poor white gas attendant, but also the bankers, the mayor, the editor, even some of the preachers, all those who are personages in such a place support [massive resistance] fervently."[27] Just as the nullifiers in South Carolina over a century earlier had realized, a resistance movement required cohesion and conformity to be successful.

Even though nullification, like interposition, was a means of protecting a threatened minority, its exponents had little compunction about stamping out opposition from a minority within their minority.

The mechanisms for sustaining the united front against desegregation took a variety of forms. First were the Citizens' Councils, which emerged initially in Indianola, in the Mississippi Delta during the summer of 1954 but then spread to other states and even into the cities. By 1957, the organization was claiming a membership of 250,000, most of whom were small-town businessmen and political leaders, mainly from the black belt regions, who were determined that the local schools remained segregated. They deterred black parents from filing petitions for desegregation by threatening to fire them or by intimidating them, and they also made sure that whites toed the line and dropped all thoughts of social integration and racial change. Committed to defend local white folk culture and its racial mores and institutions, the Citizens' Councils therefore combined "the agenda of the Klan with the demeanor of the Rotary."[28]

To undermine the efforts of African Americans to force the issue of school integration, a second weapon was created when the state legislatures enacted hostile legislation aimed directly at the NAACP. The sponsor of almost all litigation challenging Jim Crow during the 1930s and 1940s and the only civil rights organization in the South with a large membership and experienced leadership, the NAACP became the target of laws intended to destroy its effectiveness. These laws required the association to register and provide the state with its membership lists; gave state attorneys general the power to investigate it for tax evasion or criminal law violations; used existing regulations governing foreign corporations to obstruct and harass the association; and compelled state employees to file a list of organizations they had joined, with NAACP membership becoming an excuse for harassment or even grounds for dismissal. By means of these statutes and their vigorous enforcement, the NAACP was investigated and forced to defend itself in court at considerable expense, its members were persecuted, and its ability to function as the only available legal agent for indigent blacks or litigator of anti–Jim Crow cases was severely curtailed.

The third device that the resistance forces resorted to was the investigating committee. The precedents for these bodies were the congressional committees that conducted investigations during the hysterical Cold War years of the late 1940s and early 1950s into the activities of groups and individuals deemed subversive and a threat to national security. Versions of the House Committee on Un-American Activities and the Senate Internal Security Subcommittee were created in eight southern states. They were given broad powers to conduct investigations, hold hearings, and issue subpoenas in order to harass and intimidate advocates of school integration, along with organizations like the NAACP, the American Civil Liberties Union, and labor unions, as well as teachers in schools and universities, who were charged with spreading liberal heresies about race. Once called by these committees, individuals were immediately discredited as traitors to their race and region, or more likely as communists, especially if they refused to testify. The atmosphere was chilling as these legislative committees and state sovereignty commissions proved very active in sniffing out and denouncing enemies of the state and its segregated racial order, with scant concern for due process of law. Although McCarthyism in Washington had been exposed in the early 1950s, something akin to it reemerged in the besieged and paranoid South later in the decade.

With these supporting measures and institutions in place, the social and political conformity needed for widespread and overwhelming resistance to school integration had been secured. In Little Rock, Arkansas, in September 1957, desegregation faced its first major test. Located in the Upper South and with a record on race that was moderate and reasonably enlightened, Arkansas had already desegregated its state university when the Little Rock school board decided in May 1955, after the second *Brown* decision, to introduce a phased plan of token integration of its four high schools, to begin at the start of the 1957 school year.

The governor of Arkansas, Orval Faubus, was also considered a moderate on race; he approved of segregation but was flexible enough to realize the need to adapt to *Brown*. Two other governors, Luther Hodges of North Carolina and LeRoy Collins of Florida, still paid lip service to local option, even though their legislatures had enacted the essentials of state control and massive resistance. Senator James O. Eastland, Mississippi's outspoken and defiant segregationist, was "ashamed we have three southern governors who howl that it is a local matter and feel no obligation to the people of their states."[29] But all three were strong advocates of economic development and good government and feared that, as Collins once put it, "nothing will turn investors away quicker than the prospect of finding communities . . . seething under the tension and turmoil of race hatred."[30]

But tension and turmoil seemed increasingly likely as Little Rock moved toward the day of decision when nine black students would enter Central High School. The school board had prepared carefully for this moment. But it had failed to include in its decision making those whites in the community most affected by integration, the parents and their children. Furthermore, white civic and business leaders did not want to be involved in the action, and blacks had, of course, not been consulted at all. Desegregation was treated merely "as a problem in school administration" for the board and Superintendent Virgil T. Blossom to take care of.[31] Governor Faubus himself feared becoming the instrument of integration through his official role of ensuring that the students were admitted safely. He hoped instead that the school board and its policy of local option could assume the responsibility.

But neither the mayor nor President Eisenhower, to both of whom Faubus appealed for help, would take responsibility for the admission of the nine black teenagers, which had now become, in essence, a matter of policing and the prevention of violence. Lacking support from any official quarters, Governor Faubus ordered the state National Guard to turn the students away and prevent the high school desegregation ordered by the federal district court. In response, the court issued an injunction requiring Faubus to stop impeding desegregation at Central High. The state troops were then withdrawn, and the nine students came to school protected from a large and threatening mob by just 100 city and state police. Later that day, the president decided finally to act by federalizing the Arkansas National Guard. Two days later, he ordered over a thousand U.S. Army soldiers in full battle gear to protect the students as they again walked to school. This time, they entered without incident. To protect them for the rest of the school year, National Guardsmen and police remained at Central High. Despite an estimated thirty fires and forty-three bomb scares, all but one of the courageous black students stayed there too.

The Little Rock drama was far from over, however. Toward the end of the turbulent academic year, the school board petitioned the U.S. Supreme Court for the restoration of segregation until 1960, so as to allow the racial disorder and animosity to die down. In August 1958, the Court rejected the appeal outright. In *Cooper v. Aaron*, it asserted that "the constitutional rights" of citizens cannot be "sacrificed to the violence and disorder which have followed upon the actions of the Governor and Legislature." To emphasize the seriousness of the decision, Chief Justice Earl Warren had each justice sign it individually. In the meantime, however, Faubus had become aware of the political advantage to be gained from "demagoguing" the issue and taking the lead in massive resistance. So he proceeded to announce the closure of all four of the city's public high schools, three of them white and one of them black. Fourteen new

The Little Rock crisis. Armed troops escort the "Little Rock Nine" students from Central High School in October 1957. During the first few months of the integration of Central High, the students had armed protection by U.S. soldiers when going to and from school. Library of Congress, Prints and Photographs Division.

segregation laws were immediately passed by the legislature, and a state-wide referendum was called to choose between closing all schools within a district or the alternative of integrating them all. By a 3–1 majority, the voters opted to close the schools. Concurrently, Virginia's governor, Lindsay Almond, was closing those white schools in Norfolk and Charlottesville that were under court order to desegregate. With opposition to integration solid in the Lower South states and with schools being closed in order to prevent integration in the Upper South states of Virginia and Arkansas, massive resistance seemed to have become unassailable by September 1958.

But the social reality of the policy of massive resistance told a different story. During the 1958–59 academic year, the closing of schools forced parents and students to scramble to find some alternative form of schooling. In Little Rock, almost all the whites managed to enroll in other districts or in private schools. But the black student population had neither of these options, and about half of them did not go to school at all that year. In Virginia, by contrast, only white schools were closed. So blacks stayed in school, and whites from closed schools had to find alternatives. However, in Norfolk, where six white schools were suddenly closed, alternatives were scarce, and most white parents could not come up with any. Although these Norfolk parents seemed willing to put up with the disruption for a year, white southerners throughout the region began to wonder whether massive resistance was worth it. Closed schools appeared to be considerably less attractive than schools with just a few blacks attending them as token agents of desegregation. Accordingly, organizations to save public schools with names and acronyms like Save Our Schools (SOS) or Help Our Public Education (HOPE) began to appear in several cities in the winter of 1958–59 and then spread across the region. The policy of local option and token desegregation began to regain acceptability.

Over the next year or so, the looming prospect of closed schools and continuing contestation and disorder enabled the moderate forces to reassert themselves. They were aided by Governor Almond's decision to reassess his state's position. He appointed a commission, which recommended token desegregation, with maximum "freedom of choice" for white students about which schools they would attend. Over the strenuous objections of the state's massive resisters, the legislature returned to local option, with its provisions for local pupil assignment and tuition grants. Teachers' associations began to disassociate themselves from complicity in school closings. And businessmen reasserted their moderate position on desegregation as a way of preventing the racial turmoil that would jeopardize the region's much-needed economic development and educational progress. Already businessmen were very aware of the harmful impact of the school crisis on investment and sales.

This shift was facilitated by two significant federal court decisions. In Virginia in January 1959, a lower federal court decided, in *James v. Almond*, that states could not close some schools and thereby deny some students an education while providing it to others whose schools remained open. This discriminatory treatment was a clear infringement of equal protection under the Fourteenth Amendment. *James v. Almond* and the Little Rock case of *Cooper v. Aaron* six months earlier made it clear that the federal courts had taken a firm stand against the closing of schools to avoid desegregation.

Although the threat to close schools rather than integrate them was the ultimate weapon of massive resistance, it proved in practice to be a stimulus for opposition from within the South as well as from the U.S. courts. For the united front of resistance was crumbling, as a number of cities—like Miami, Houston, and Atlanta—began to work on plans for gradual and token desegregation in 1959 and 1960. Little Rock was also moving in the same direction. Central High and Hall High each admitted three African American students in August 1959. When Governor Faubus tried to reinject the issue of school closings into the state's politics in 1960, desegregation advocates in the city campaigned vigorously against his proposed constitutional amendment allowing local communities to close their schools rather than integrate. Arkansas voters responded by defeating overwhelmingly his watered-down, local-option version of massive resistance. Faubus continued to be reelected governor biennially until 1966. But the movement to defeat integration, which he had joined belatedly and then had led to its climactic confrontation, was over.

Although massive resistance had failed to stop school desegregation altogether, it had certainly halted and delayed it. Throughout the 1960s, the process of desegregation continued, hesitantly and reluctantly, district by district, always minimal and token, beginning in the cities and then extending into the rural areas and ultimately into the Lower South's black belts. Particularly confrontational and prolonged was the experience of New Orleans, where the long-time mayor, deLesseps S. Morrison, led a vigorous resistance that resulted in boycotts during 1960–61 of two schools scheduled to be desegregated. The integration of two state universities, Alabama in June 1963 and Mississippi on 1 October 1962, brought to national attention once again the ongoing struggle in southern public education. In Alabama, Governor George C. Wallace took his "stand in the schoolhouse door," rather ineffectually as it happened. In the previous year, Mississippi's Governor Ross Barnett precipitated a particularly violent confrontation at the entrance to the campus in Oxford, resulting in two deaths and hundreds of injuries, including twenty-eight federal marshals who incurred bullet wounds, and also the dispatching of regular U.S. Army units to curb the segregationist mob.

By pressuring the South's white population to resist racial change by acts of outright defiance that required solidarity and even conformity, the champions of massive resistance had revealed the limits of the region's white solidarity. Just as the Dixiecrats had shown how unwilling most state Democratic parties were to participate in a revolt against the national party, so too the massive resisters discovered how unenthusiastic most white southerners were about going to the extreme of handing over control of their local schools to state officials who might then declare them closed for the school year. City dwellers, businessmen, and members of the respectable middle and upper classes saw little to gain from pitched battles to keep just a few African Americans out of white schools. More fearful about ending racial subordination were inhabitants of small towns and rural areas as well as working men and women whose children would be most affected by these experiments in integration. The struggle over massive resistance exposed a split within the region, which would become evident in the 1960s and 1970s when challenges were launched against the segregation of other southern institutions and public places.

Despite the hesitations and differences within the white South revealed by the experiment of massive resistance, the depth of commitment to the region's racial order was brought out into the open for all to see. When the Supreme Court and the president failed to take the initiative toward enforcing school desegregation, those few in the South who were prepared to accommodate and move forward were quickly and roughly swept aside. Under no pressure from Washington to comply but under immense pressure to conform to their region's mores, southern whites had no viable alternative policy to support and no good reason to go out on a limb.

13

The Solid South under Attack

BLACK GAINS

In the decade after the Supreme Court had declared in *Smith v. Allwright* (1944) that the white primary was in violation of blacks' right to vote, the number of African Americans in the South who registered to vote increased to around one million. With the Democratic primary, the real election in the South, now open to them, African Americans had an incentive to register. And in the presidential election of 1952, the small percentage of black votes (6 percent of the total vote in the South) that were cast for the Democrat, Adlai Stevenson, enabled him to carry Louisiana, South Carolina, Kentucky, and Arkansas by a hair's breadth.

This scintilla of political clout was offset by the reality that almost all of the registered blacks were residents of cities—Nashville, Memphis, Atlanta, and some of the mid-sized North Carolina towns such as Durham and Winston-Salem. And they were sufficiently numerous, and also organized, to make a difference in municipal contests. But still not enough blacks were registered to provide a critical electoral mass. Unfortunately, registration itself slowed down in the late 1950s during the racial turmoil of "massive resistance." Meanwhile, the Lower South states, as well as North Carolina and Virginia, still had literacy tests for voting, and five states continued to impose a poll tax requirement.

The Campaign for Civil Rights and the Vote

At the same time as whites were trying to keep blacks out of their schools, blacks opened up a new front. They demanded the ballot. At a protest in front of the Lincoln Memorial in Washington on 17 May 1957, the third anniversary of *Brown v. Board of Education*, the Reverend Martin Luther King Jr., who was now nationally known for his leadership of the Montgomery bus boycott in 1955 and 1956, addressed the crowd of 30,000. He called for federal legislation to guarantee the right to vote, which, he said, would lead the way to the other basic rights denied to blacks. Before King gave the speech, his adviser, Bayard Rustin, urged him to discard the phrase "Give us the ballot" and replace it with "We demand the ballot."[1] Even though King rejected this advice and asked for the ballot rather than demanded it, regaining the vote now became the primary issue for organized black protest. As King put it that day in May: "Give us the ballot and we will no longer have to worry the Federal government about our basic rights."[2]

In February 1958, King's newly formed Southern Christian Leadership Conference (SCLC) launched a campaign to register 3 million African American voters by 1960. Its Crusade for Citizenship was headed by Ella Baker, an experienced organizer with the NAACP, and it planned registration drives and training workshops in a number of southern cities. The longer-established NAACP, which had conducted most of the earlier registration efforts but was now facing hundreds of debilitating lawsuits aimed at crippling it, took action as well, with a goal of 3 million new voters by 1960. But insufficient funds and the heightened hostility of the late 1950s undermined the campaigns of both organizations, with the result that the SCLC drive registered only 160,000 blacks and the NAACP's returns were even more meager. When 1960 arrived, only 1.4 million southern blacks were registered, just under a third of those eligible.

The registration drives had petered out. But King's call for Congress to enact voting rights legislation had nevertheless produced a response in Washington. Prior to August 1957, the federal government had passed no legislation dealing with civil rights since the Civil Rights Act of 1875, during the last years of Reconstruction. Eighty-two years later, a strange confluence of political interests and ambitions produced a breakthrough. The initiator of this legislation was the Eisenhower administration. Although hard to believe from a later vantage point, the Republicans were reasonably confident that they could win a large portion of the potential black vote in the South. After all, the Democratic Party in the South was the party of white supremacy, and, from Reconstruction to the New Deal, blacks in both the North and the South had voted Republican. Later on, in the 1940s and 1950s, Republican presidential platforms had regularly included support for a Fair Employment Practices Commission and abolition of the poll tax and other civil rights issues. In 1952, Eisenhower had increased the Republicans' share of the black vote. Four years later, he carried a majority of the black vote in twelve southern cities, including Atlanta, New Orleans, and Richmond, while increasing his proportion by 5 percent in thirty-two pivotal districts in the North where blacks constituted over 10 percent of the population. Some serious and concrete action on civil rights could stimulate a trend toward black Republicanism, especially in the South.

Also pressing for congressional action were black protest organizations. Ever since Truman's far-reaching and dramatic civil rights initiative in 1948, which Congress had then scuttled, the national legislature had been unreliable, even obstructive, on the issue. But now, Roy Wilkins, head of the NAACP, announced, "Protection of the right to vote is the Number One item on the list for Congressional action."[3] Even more desperate for Congress to take action on civil rights was the liberal wing of the Democratic Party. Stymied by their southern Democratic colleagues on this increasingly important national question, liberals had come to the realization that they could not move forward to other parts of their reform agenda until this obstacle was removed. As Lyndon Johnson, the Senate majority leader in 1957, acknowledged, "it is a road-block to positive, constructive steps from which our party does gain advantages. . . . I hope we can find a just and equitable solution that will enable us to put an end to the present internecine warfare."[4]

Since he was a southern senator with avowed presidential ambitions, Lyndon B. Johnson was eager to take the lead in moving sympathetic northern Republicans and northern Democrats toward enactment of a historic civil rights law. A New Deal Democrat from the Texas hill country west of Austin, Johnson believed that the South's future depended on economic development that was thwarted by the region's preoccupation, even obsession, with race. The "angry defensiveness and parochialism" that its racial stand produced in southerners made the region a pariah within the nation.[5] Unfortunately, the need to be politically correct on race hobbled the more liberal of the region's politicians, like Johnson, Lister Hill, Frank P. Graham, and many others. But it also prevented them from gaining national stature and acceptance, something Johnson coveted, particularly after becoming majority leader in 1955. His closest confidant and mentor, Richard Russell, who led the Southern Caucus, had to admit in fall 1956 that "we can never make him President unless the Senate first disposes of civil rights."[6] The Eisenhower administration's determination to pass a civil rights law after the 1956 election gave Johnson the opportunity to crown his term as majority leader with a civil rights breakthrough that he himself could accomplish and take credit for.

Since the South could no longer rely on Republicans for support in blocking a civil rights bill and was thus *completely without allies*," as George Reedy, one of Johnson's closest advisers, pointed out, Johnson and Russell schemed to prevent the possibility of a ruinous southern filibuster of the bill the Eisenhower administration introduced early in 1957.[7] If they could remove those features of the bill that most upset the southerners, they might relent and enable it to pass. Title III of the bill increased the federal government's authority in integrating schools, and Title IV required a trial before a federal judge for anyone defying the provisions of the law. To conciliate the South, Russell and Johnson maneuvered, first, to eliminate Title III, which Russell castigated on the Senate floor as "the reimposition of post–Civil War Reconstruction."[8] After getting it removed, they then managed to emasculate Title IV by requiring a jury trial, which would consist of whites only in the South and thus guarantee a decision in favor of white defendants accused of depriving blacks of their civil rights.

With many liberal Democrats and administration Republicans worried that jury trials would deny effective legal redress to victims of civil rights violations, Johnson had to press relentlessly to win votes for the amended bill. Frequently, he stayed in his office overnight, and he worked constantly on those senators who could be persuaded by that personal "in your face" attention, known as "the Johnson treatment." Eventually, by a close vote of 51–41, the jury trial provision was adopted, and then the amended bill passed, 72–18. But House members of a joint House-Senate conference committee refused to accept the changes. When the bill returned to the Senate, senators were asked to accept a further alteration restricting the use of jury trials to serious cases carrying stiffer penalties and fines. At this point, Strom Thurmond mounted a lone filibuster that lasted twenty-four hours, breaking the record for a one-man "talkathon." But most southerners were incensed because Thurmond's stand put them to shame for not filibustering themselves. Also angry were those, like Richard Russell, who had agreed to vote nay but not actually defeat the bill with a filibuster, a strategy the South Carolinian's grandstanding might endanger. "Under the circumstances we faced, if I had undertaken a filibuster for personal aggrandizement," he complained, "I would forever have reproached myself for being guilty of a form of treason against the South."[9] As it was, only a few southern senators had supported the bill on the first vote, George Smathers of Florida, Albert Gore and Estes Kefauver of Tennessee, and Ralph Yarborough and Lyndon Johnson of Texas, a mere five of the region's twenty-two members.

Passage of the bill meant that Lyndon Johnson had achieved a personal triumph. Even though his region had not supported the measure, a civil rights bill had been enacted after years of successful obstruction against more limited threats to the South's racial order, such as the attempts to ban the poll tax and outlaw lynching. But the 1957 act was actually a very weak piece of legislation. Senator Paul Douglas of Illinois, who had led the fight against its emasculation, recalled one of Lincoln's more colorful phrases when he described the law as "soup from the shadow of a crow which had starved to death."[10] Most civil rights leaders dismissed it as worse than no bill at all, although Bayard Rustin felt that, despite its shortcomings, it "would establish a very important precedent."[11]

Rustin's assessment proved correct, although it did not seem so at first. The Civil Rights Act of 1957 had been stripped of its antidiscrimination features so that it was limited to political rights. In effect, it was a voting rights act, and a practically toothless one as well. Local registrars could prevent voters from registering, while others similarly inclined could later interfere with the ability of voters to vote at election time without fear of a federal response. With all its deficiencies, however, the law represented something of a political breakthrough, and Johnson himself was fully aware of this. In a speech just before the final vote on the bill, he recognized that, "out of debate has come something more important than legislation. This has been a debate which has opened closed minds." And he continued, "For the first time in my memory, this issue has been lifted from the field of partisan politics. It has been considered in terms of human beings and the effect of our laws upon them."[12] Although Johnson himself hoped quite genuinely that the legislation he had worked so hard to produce had changed the minds of senators, not just their votes, the extravagant praise of both Johnson and his law on the part of Robert Caro, Johnson's multivolume biographer, needs to be qualified. But for the continuing and growing pressure of civil rights activists outside Congress and the happenstance of a calamity that propelled Johnson himself into the presidency, the 1957 measure would have had little impact. Almost certainly, the civil rights legislation of 1964 and 1965 that dismantled the South's racial system would have been delayed even longer than the seven or eight more years.

The 1957 law confirmed the widespread sentiment that the right to vote was the preferred mechanism for dealing with the South's racial system. President Eisenhower was an inveterate gradualist who believed that the incremental expansion of the suffrage among African Americans would prevent resistance and confrontation and allow southerners of both races to adjust calmly to change. As he told Richard Russell, "With his right to vote assured, the Negro could use it to help secure his other rights."[13] Moreover, Eisenhower considered the right to vote different from those other more destabilizing rights, like equal access to education and housing, because it was an acknowledged and fundamental democratic right. He was thus satisfied that his initiative had produced, not a broad-ranging civil rights statute, but a limited voting rights law. The elimination of Title III had not bothered him at all, though he had objected to Johnson's jury trial amendment of Title IV because he believed, quite correctly, that it would weaken the bill. Voting rights legislation was so acceptable to the president and his cabinet that, three years later, they introduced another voting rights measure in response to findings by the Civil Rights Commission, created by Title I of the 1957 law, that a recent registration drive in Alabama's Macon County had been seriously obstructed. More federal action was obviously needed, especially since 1960 was an election year.

If it seemed that the congressional logjam on civil rights legislation had broken up, the Civil Rights Act of 1960 suggested otherwise because it was actually more timid than the 1957 measure. While the Civil Rights Commission had urged the dispatch of federal registrars to districts where a pattern of obstruction was detected, the law itself provided merely that court-appointed referees could look into the allegations and observe the process of registration. Hardly a reassurance that a new day had dawned in Congress, this feeble proposal indicated that minimalism and delay were all that could be expected. Indeed, progress on the new front of voting rights may actually have slowed since the act's passage, while the civil rights division of the Justice Department, another creation of the 1957 act, had initiated only nine cases in three years.[14]

Like the 1957 act, its successor in 1960 was symbolic. But its symbolism represented, not the hope that more could now be accomplished, but a mere gesture to satisfy blacks that the Republicans had done something about voting rights. At the same time, the expectations of the SCLC and the NAACP that voting rights was the next phase of the movement's campaign began to dissipate as their registration drives foundered. Even the few hundred thousand voters they did register were offset by the purging of registration lists by worried and hostile officials in the midst of the school integration crisis.

Prior to this new emphasis on voting and registration, the bus boycott in Montgomery had been the focus of the movement to end segregation. The boycott had lasted two years and generated a new group of black leaders around Rev. Martin Luther King Jr. and the young Christian ministers who formed SCLC. The Montgomery boycott was a success that also sparked similar actions in many other southern cities. Nevertheless, its tactic of boycott, that is, the refusal of passengers to use the buses and thereby deprive the white-run bus company of the fares it needed to operate, did not confront and destabilize the racial system and its institutions. The boycotters removed themselves from the buses and withheld their fares, but they did not stop the buses from running. They joined together collectively and exerted group pressure, but their only remedy was to wait for their opponents to back down. The limitations of this kind of protest led the historian Steven F. Lawson to conclude that "civil rights proponents needed additional techniques that would actively engage blacks in directly confronting white racist practices. Through such encounters they would dramatically expose the source of their oppression, bring the evil to the surface, and exert moral pressure to eradicate it. In the process, people would have to break laws they considered unjust and go to jail for their convictions."[15]

Like the bus boycott, voter registration also precluded confrontational encounters with the South's racial system, since potential voters sought inclusion in the electoral system. Admittedly, they had to act collectively and organize drives and, as individuals, take the initiative and muster the courage to approach the registrars. But this tactic did not expose the corruption and discrimination at the heart of disfranchisement, because the registrants simply asked to be allowed in. For this reason, gradualists and moderates of all kinds, from President Eisenhower and the Republicans on down, seized on voting rights as a more congenial and controllable route, because it limited the scope and impact of protest by channeling it into voter registration and the courts.

The calming effect of this strategy was shattered on 1 February 1960 when four students at North Carolina Agricultural and Technical College staged a sit-in at the Woolworth's lunch counter in Greensboro. Within two months, similar actions took place in over sixty southern cities involving thousands of high school and college students, and they expanded to several hundred more over the course of the year. Because of this dramatic stimulus, civil rights protest moved into a new phase in 1960—direct action and civil disobedience. In the "Second Wave" of the movement, organized direct action took the form initially of sit-ins at lunch counters, and these were followed by the Freedom Rides of summer 1961, aimed at desegregating interstate bus travel. During the next few years, citywide campaigns organized around street demonstrations were initiated by King's SCLC in conjunction with local black organizations, most notably in Albany, Georgia, in 1962 and in Birmingham, Alabama, in 1963.

Throughout these actions, protesters—the leaders as well as the rank and file—trespassed into public spaces reserved for whites and defied the laws of racial segregation, with both actions resulting in arrests and jail terms. Over the next five years, the pace of protest quickened and the pressure intensified until the legal structure of segregation and disfranchisement was formally dismantled by the passage of the federal Civil Rights and Voting Rights Acts of 1964 and 1965. This outcome was not achieved easily, however. Dozens of protesters died during these years. Violence was ever present when protesters found themselves confronted by the force and power of the entrenched white South and its police. And the setbacks, disappointments, and frustrations were frequent.

Throughout this second phase of the civil rights movement, the campaign for the vote continued, although it took two different paths. The first was the already familiar route of voter registration favored by the Eisenhower administration and then, after his election in 1960, by President John F. Kennedy and his brother, Robert, the attorney general. The Kennedys wanted to avoid racial confrontations in the South. To their dismay, however, the Freedom Rides in 1961 presented a situation similar to Little Rock, which necessitated federal intervention, this time to protect protesters traveling on interstate buses from white mobs in Alabama and Mississippi. The Kennedy administration finessed this crisis by sending federal marshals to ensure the safety of the riders in Alabama and by working out an agreement in Mississippi with Governor Ross Barnett, permitting him to arrest the riders as long as he protected them physically.

In the aftermath of the Freedom Rides, the president and his brother maneuvered to redirect civil rights into the safer channel of voter registration. Not only would registration be nonconfrontational and nonviolent, so the Kennedys assumed, but it would also generate voters who would be likely to vote Democratic out of gratitude. Accordingly, they established the Voter Education Project as a tax-exempt organization, not a government-funded program, whose purpose was to promote and support registration drives. Although the civil rights organizations knew perfectly well what the administration was trying to do, all of them, even the newly formed and more radical direct-action organization, the Student Nonviolent Coordinating Committee (SNCC), decided to get involved. They all still considered voting rights to be a crucial goal, and they also wanted to encourage federal interest in civil rights.

Although the Kennedys failed to supply the amount of funds they had promised and they reneged completely on their pledge to ensure the safety of the workers on the southern voting rights battlefield, the project was moderately successful. Between 1962 and 1964, black registration rose from just under 30 percent to 43.1 percent, about half of which was attributable to the Voter Education Project, roughly 287,000. In addition, the civil rights division of the Justice Department was active in challenging the denial or obstruction of voting rights. About fifty suits were filed during these years, a drop in the bucket but better by far than any previous administration.

The second route toward the acquisition of the vote was pursued by SNCC organizers in Mississippi during 1963 and 1964. Although getting blacks registered to vote was still the objective, SNCC's Mississippi campaign was utterly different from all previous suffrage drives. First of all, it moved away from the cities, where previous registration efforts had taken place, and into the rural areas, where racial control was more personal and oppressive, and even into the most recalcitrant part of the South, the Mississippi Delta. Second, the demand for the vote was conceived by SNCC, not in moderate and gradualist terms, but as a radicalizing and decisive experience for the poor rural blacks who had lived so long in fear of asserting their rights. The very act of joining with others to march to the courthouse and demand to be registered could, so SNCC activists believed, break the thrall of deference and passivity. Registering to vote could be as mobilizing and confrontational an experience as street demonstrations and protest marches.

But there was a third feature of the Mississippi campaign that distinguished it even more sharply from other registration campaigns. Unimaginable to SNCC organizers in 1963 when they started focusing their activity on the Delta, the Mississippi registration drive became transformed into a mechanism for creating a political structure in the state capable of challenging the regular Democrats. SNCC organizers encountered such massive opposition and violence in places like Greenwood that they managed to register very few voters. Confronted by this reality, Bob Moses, the thirty-year-old African American from New York who was the coordinator of the campaign, decided to hold an informal "freedom vote" alongside the official state election to choose a governor in 1963. Before the vote, Moses predicted that "the freedom ballot will show that if the Negroes had the right to vote without fear of physical or economic reprisal, they would do so." All adult blacks were eligible to vote, and 80,000 African Americans participated in this unofficial election to select a governor who was black and a lieutenant governor who was white. The turnout in the election was four times the number of blacks actually registered in the state. Moses's confidence was amply confirmed.[16]

Fannie Lou Hamer. A resident of Ruleville in the Mississippi Delta, Hamer came to typify the suffering and struggle of poor black Mississippians. She was the most outspoken and charismatic member of the Mississippi Freedom Democratic Party's delegation that went to the Democratic National Convention in August 1964, hoping to challenge and unseat the official Democratic delegates. Library of Congress, Prints and Photographs Division.

Armed with this evidence of a profound desire for the vote and a willingness to wield it, the SNCC leader next planned a concerted, statewide drive for the summer of 1964. "Freedom Summer" it was to be called. Its aim was to register blacks and create a rival party organization, the Mississippi Freedom Democratic Party, to challenge the regular delegation to the Democratic national convention to be held later in the summer of 1964, a presidential election year. A thousand or so mostly white college students went to Mississippi to join black residents in the state and help staff the campaign. Their efforts were thwarted constantly by the registrars themselves, as well as by the local white inhabitants. And the level of violence encountered by all who were involved in Freedom Summer as well as by the potential voters themselves was enormous. That summer, six murders, thirty-five shootings, and eighty beatings were inflicted on civil rights workers and those they were helping to register, along with the burning of thirty-five black churches.[17]

Despite these incredible obstacles, the election took place and the Mississippi Freedom Democratic Party delegation was chosen. Its members traveled to Atlantic City and demanded to be seated at the Democratic Party's convention, but they were brushed aside with just two at-large votes and the right to attend as nonvoting guests, a dismissive gesture intended to assuage the distress of the state's regular Democrats at the effrontery of a biracial, unofficial delegation claiming to represent the state of Mississippi. To the local activists and SNCC volunteers who had struggled and taken such personal risks in Mississippi, such an insulting and heartless rejection rankled bitterly, and they derided it as "the back-of-the-bus proposal."[18] Nevertheless, the SNCC approach had transformed voter registration from a cautious and restricted device into a weapon for community organizing and direct action. Through politically imaginative maneuvering, the campaign brought Mississippi's new voters and their new party into the national spotlight, albeit briefly.

The day after the 1964 election, which Lyndon Johnson won by the biggest landslide thus far in American history, Martin Luther King Jr. announced that he planned to call for demonstrations "based around the right to vote."[19] The campaign would be aimed at either Alabama or Mississippi, where only 21 percent and 6 percent of the eligible voters respectively were registered. In Dallas County in the Alabama black belt just west of Montgomery, a mere 156 of the more than 15,000 adult blacks had been registered by 1963. Calculating shrewdly, SCLC selected the county's main town of Selma as the principal location for the planned action. Selma was chosen, not just because of its scandalously low registration, but also because SNCC had already been active there. The county authorities, led by sheriff Jim Clark, had constantly attacked civil rights organizers and blacks attempting to register in Selma and, at one time or another, had arrested several thousand of them. By concentrating on one town only, the organizers hoped that the new drive would focus public attention and might well provide dramatic evidence of the obstacles barring the way to the enfranchisement of African Americans.

The strategy worked. Several months of demonstrations, arrests, and fruitless efforts to register voters followed, prompting King to call for a march to the state capital of Montgomery to protest what was happening in Selma. The violent attacks that Sheriff Clark and his deputies unleashed on the marchers as they crossed the Edmund Pettus Bridge gave President Johnson the opportunity to consolidate his earlier triumph with the passage of the Civil Rights Act, in July 1964, by pressuring Congress to pass comprehensive legislation to secure the right to vote as well. In his remarkable address to a joint session of Congress, on 15 March 1965, Johnson identified the federal government with the cause of equal rights when he promised, "And we *shall* overcome." He also admonished white southerners: "It is wrong—deadly wrong—to deny any of your fellow

Americans the right to vote in this country."[20] By August, the voting rights legislation he had promised in March had become law. The formal, legal structure of disfranchisement had been dismantled. The Solid South was in its death throes.

Securing the Right to Vote

The 1964 election had been lopsided and unusual, not merely because of Lyndon Johnson's massive national vote but also because of his huge loss in the Deep South. His Republican opponent, Senator Barry Goldwater of Arizona, carried Mississippi, Alabama, Louisiana, Georgia, and South Carolina and won them by large majorities—87.1 percent in Mississippi and 69.5 percent in Alabama, with the others ranging between 50 percent and 60 percent. Mississippi's rush into the Republican column was so abrupt and so fulsome that a bemused onlooker commented that "Mississippi believes in the two-party system; it just believes in having them one at a time."[21] The hesitancy among the Dixiecrats about breaking with the Democrats in 1948 had vanished in the Deep South sixteen years later, as both political leaders and the rank and file, who had always voted Democratic, changed course dramatically.

The year 1964 marked a decisive change for the national Republican Party, not just for Deep South Democrats. In the presidential elections of the 1950s, the Republicans had been doing quite well by winning southern states outside the Deep South. Eisenhower carried Texas, Virginia, Tennessee, and Florida in 1952 and the same four, plus Louisiana in the Lower South, in 1956, although Nixon won only Florida, Tennessee, and Virginia in 1960. The Republican presidential presence on the southern rim (an arc around the northern edge of the South from Texas to Virginia and also including Florida) did not, however, translate into any significant party growth at the state level. The party's support in presidential elections in the Rim South consisted, for the most part, of well-off urban and suburban dwellers. By contrast, those voters in the Deep South who rallied to Goldwater lived in rural areas and small towns, most of them in locations heavily populated by blacks. The disparity with the Republicans' most recent supporters in the Rim South where blacks were a small part of the population could not have been sharper.

Since Goldwater had voted consciously and purposely against cloture and against the Civil Rights Act, he had made clear his intentions of targeting angry whites in the South and making the region the base of what he hoped would become a new Republican majority. As early as 1961, well before he had even obtained the nomination, he had told a press conference in Atlanta: "We're not going to get the Negro vote as a bloc in 1964 or 1966, so we ought to go hunting where the ducks are."[22] Goldwater's strident racial and political conservatism was quite different from the somewhat moderate, and certainly less ideological, racial and political views of the Eisenhower Republicans on the region's periphery. In the 1964 election, the Rim South supported Johnson, the Democrat, who actually won a slim majority of the vote throughout the entire region, while Goldwater swept the Solid South's heartland. But his coattails were not sufficiently strong to carry with him more than a few congressional and state-level candidates. The South therefore remained heavily Democratic, although the attractiveness to southern whites of a racially conservative Republican Party was duly noted by the party's national leadership.

Goldwater's successful incursion shattered the Deep South's tradition of voting solidly and unhesitatingly Democratic, except for the Dixiecrat revolt in 1948. Also shattering was the passage of the Voting Rights Act nine months later. This law served notice that the vehement resistance to the very idea of blacks ever again exercising the right to vote had to cease. It required that African Americans obtain full access to the ballot, and its provisions were surprisingly forceful and stringent. Exactly a century after African Americans had first acquired the vote, in 1867, they had finally regained it in 1965 through a remedy with teeth.

The bill that Lyndon Johnson signed into law was very close in content to the proposal initially presented by his administration. Most important, it rejected two possible courses of action that would have weakened and delayed a remedy to the constant harassment of blacks in their effort to register as voters. The first was a constitutional amendment, which would have taken many months, even years, to pass and ratify. The second was the continuation of the time-consuming process of bringing voting rights cases before the courts, which would have meant endless delay and obstruction. Robert Kennedy's successor as attorney general, Nicholas Katzenbach, declared that the government was finally ready to take stronger measures than "the tortuous, often ineffective, pace of litigation."[23] Instead, voting rights were to be obtained and secured by statute; the act's provisions were to take effect immediately; and the enforcement of voting rights was to be placed under continual supervision, so as to ensure that efforts to obstruct or subvert them were countered. Unlike previous attempts under Eisenhower, and even Kennedy, this legislation involved the federal government directly in the process of registration and it ended the timid, gradualist approach of incremental black registration.

After four months of discussion and with only minor alteration, the bill was presented for debate on the Senate floor, the decisive point at which civil rights measures could be derailed. But Johnson knew he had the votes, and, after twenty-four hours, cloture was voted by a 70–30 margin, most of the nay votes coming from southern Democrats. The bill passed by 79–18 in the Senate and 328–74 in the House. The Voting Rights Act consisted of three basic elements. First, literacy tests and other disqualifying "devices" were suspended for five years in states and counties where less than half of the eligible voters had participated in the 1964 election. This automatic "triggering mechanism" affected the five Deep South states and also Virginia and parts of North Carolina. Second, federal registrars, not just monitors or observers, as had often happened in the past, could be sent to these "covered" states when requested by twenty citizens, once the attorney general deemed it necessary. Third, states had to submit any new voting requirements for approval, or "preclearance," by the civil rights division of the Justice Department. A fourth provision that would have banned the poll tax in state elections (it had already been outlawed in federal elections by a constitutional amendment in 1964) was watered down to a requirement that the Justice Department investigate whether legislation to this effect could be drawn up later. Within a year, a federal law was passed banning the poll tax in the four states that still required it.

Originally conceived as an emergency measure, the act had a limited life span of five years, but the reenfranchisement of several million people and the need to prevent new obstructions have made renewal of the law necessary. It was first renewed in 1970, then again in 1975 and 1982. In 2007, twenty-five years after its third iteration, Congress would have had to consider whether it needed to be continued. But the matter was moved up a year, and, after some resistance from southern states protesting that they were still being singled out for special oversight, the law was renewed once again in 2006 for another twenty-five years.

The early years after the act's passage witnessed a remarkable surge in the registration of African Americans. Since they knew that local registrars were under legal constraint to enroll voters and that federal registrars were being sent into counties where the authorities were still recalcitrant, prospective voters felt sufficiently encouraged to go out and register. By 1969, black registration in the former Confederate states had increased from 35.5 percent of those eligible in 1964 to 64.8 percent. In the six states "covered" by the act, registration more than doubled, soaring from 24.4 percent to 60.7 percent. By the end of the decade, about a million more blacks had registered to vote under the 1965 act. In sheer numbers, 3.4

The signing of the Voting Rights Act, 6 August 1965. President Lyndon Johnson hands Martin Luther King Jr. one of the pens he used to sign the bill into law. To King's right, slightly obscured, is Rev. Ralph Abernethy, who would succeed King as head of the Southern Christian Leadership Conference. In the center is Congressman Claude Pepper of Florida, a southern liberal with a long record of opposition to segregation. Library of Congress, Prints and Photographs Division.

million blacks were registered by 1970, compared to 1.5 million in 1960. Black voters had become a political factor, especially in the black belt areas of the Deep South where they had been barely visible as registered voters before the Voting Rights Act. Across the region, these 3.4 million black voters, who would increase further to 5.6 million by 1984, now played a conspicuous role in the South's changed political universe.

Dramatic though it was in terms both symbolic and actual, this change was accompanied by two developments that soon began to limit its impact. The first was a simultaneous increase in white registration. Hundreds of thousands of poor and ill-educated whites had been disfranchised by the poll tax and literacy requirements imposed by the disfranchisers a half century earlier, and they also took advantage of the expanded access to registration in the late 1960s. Of the increased registration of around 6 million during the decade, 70 percent were whites. This meant that 4 million additional whites registered during the 1960s, compared to 2 million more blacks. Registration among eligible blacks rose from 35.5 to 64.8 percent from 1964 to 1969, but the proportion among whites increased from 73.4 percent to 83.5 percent. In the 1970s and 1980s, this discrepancy grew even greater because of the influx of whites, who moved from the North to the South in large numbers, usually locating in the prospering and growing metropolitan areas of the region. Thus the dramatic gains recorded by blacks were more than offset by the increase of whites. In 1984, 5.6 million black registered voters were out-numbered by 28 million registered whites. Blacks had finally regained the vote, but the number of black voters was now a smaller proportion of a considerably enlarged electorate.[24]

The second development arose out of the Voting Rights Act itself, although it had not been anticipated by it. The drafters of the law had included, in its section 5, a "pre-clearance" clause, requiring that states obtain federal approval of any changes in their voting laws, because they feared that the southern states might reintroduce schemes to restrict the right to vote or to make registration more difficult. And their fears were borne out. In the 1970s, these states were creating laws that changed the method of representation and apportionment so as to limit, or "dilute," the impact and influence of the votes cast by African Americans. In this way, they were not endangering the right to vote but were instead reducing the value of the vote once it was cast.

A number of possible mechanisms could achieve this end, and all were pursued. Legislative districts could be redrawn in ways that gave blacks fewer representatives. Districts that chose one member (single-member districts) could be changed to multimember districts, and small districts could be altered to at-large districts. Offices previously elective could be made appointive. These devices began to come under the purview of the "pre-clearance" clause, because they were changes in state election laws. And since states reapportioned the congressional districts within their borders, congressional redistricting was also involved. But the effect of these devices on state as well as congressional elections was to weaken and "dilute" the impact of the black vote, even though blacks were not actually being prevented from voting.

These continuing attempts to restrict or contain black voting have necessitated periodic renewal of the Voting Rights Act beyond its initial five years, and they have resulted in a rash of court cases, many going as far as the Supreme Court. Almost all of them have involved redistricting, and the Court has had to determine whether the redrawing of a district's boundaries was driven by an intent to discriminate on racial grounds. If so, the redrawing or reapportioning of districts would be in defiance of the Fifteenth Amendment's prohibition of the denial of the right to vote for racial reasons and the Fourteenth Amendment's "equal protection of the laws" provision. Admittedly, other reasons for redistricting could apply, the most obvious being simply a change in the size or composition of the district's population, in which case the action would be acceptable. Since intention is difficult to discern, the courts have introduced a litmus test, which goes beyond intent and examines "the totality of circumstances" to see if the context and outcome of the action indicate an implicit intention to discriminate.

In effect, the struggle to regain the right to vote has not ended but has moved to a different arena or level, where the outcome of voting, not just the act of voting, is at stake. Will black votes count as much as the votes of others or will the structure of representation be manipulated or rigged to deny blacks the kind and number of representatives and officials that their votes indicate they want and are entitled to? The old struggle over equal suffrage has become a new struggle to obtain equal representation.

PART V.

FROM ONE PARTY TO TWO, 1965–1994

14

Old Responses and
New Directions, 1965–1980

At the end of his rambling inaugural address in January 1963, the new governor of Alabama, George C. Wallace, hit on a phrase that was as memorable as it was menacing. "Segregation now . . . segregation tomorrow . . . segregation forever" was the battle cry he proclaimed on the steps of the state capitol in Montgomery where, a century earlier, Jefferson Davis had delivered his inaugural as the provisional president of the Confederacy. Over the next three years, Wallace would play a leading role in the dramatic confrontation between the civil rights movement and its foes, the defenders of segregation. Wallace's nemesis in this struggle was Martin Luther King Jr., who had been pastor of the Dexter Street Baptist Church a few blocks from the state capitol in Montgomery and had risen to prominence as the leader of the bus boycott in the city in the mid-1950s.

In May 1963, Birmingham, the largest city in Alabama, was engulfed in massive street demonstrations that lasted over a month, culminating in a police rampage against the protestors. Governor Wallace was deeply involved, urging the city government to stand firm against the demonstrators and not to negotiate with them.

A month later, in June, when the University of Alabama was under court order to admit several African American students, Governor Wallace took his "stand in the schoolhouse door," as he defied Deputy U.S. Attorney General Nicholas Katzenbach before a battery of national television cameras. A few hours later, the students entered the university under a prearranged agreement between Wallace and the Justice Department. Therefore Wallace's theatrical public "stand" masked the reality of his capitulation and defeat. On that very evening, President Kennedy went on television to announce that he intended to introduce a civil rights bill. A year later, that bill became the historic Civil Rights Act of 1964, although Kennedy was no longer alive to witness it.

Governor George C. Wallace "standing in the schoolhouse door." On 11 June 1963, Wallace decided to take a public stand against the integration of the University of Alabama at Tuscaloosa, staging a confrontation with Deputy Attorney General Nicholas Katzenbach, with photographers and policemen on hand to observe and report the scene. Library of Congress, Prints and Photographs Division.

In 1965, Wallace was again confronting civil rights activists when the campaign to register African Americans in Selma was launched. The governor threatened to stop the march from Selma to Montgomery, and he took no action to prevent the state troopers from attacking the marchers on the Edmund Pettus Bridge. Like the use of fire hoses and dogs against the demonstrators in Birmingham and the face-off at the schoolhouse door in Tuscaloosa, this melee was captured live on national television. A week later, Lyndon Johnson appeared on television before a joint session of Congress and delivered his dramatic speech, expressing his sympathy for the protestors and vowing to pass a voting rights law.

Wallace's "stand in the schoolhouse door" and his refusal to protect the Selma to Montgomery march led directly to public commitments by Presidents Kennedy and Johnson to enact landmark civil rights legislation. Yet, curiously, these decisive defeats for the cause of segregation served only to build Wallace's reputation as its leading defender. His public defiance was applauded, even though it hastened the demise of the very thing he was defending. Remarkably, this record of conspicuous failure projected him onto the stage of national politics, where he became a fixture for almost a decade, running for the presidency no less and doing so for four elections in a row—1964, 1968, 1972, and briefly 1976.

Stoking the White Backlash: George Wallace

George Corley Wallace grew up in the small town of Clio, in Barbour County, southeast of Montgomery, where most of the population were farmers and six in ten were black. The feisty and diminutive young Wallace became a success as a two-time state Golden Gloves champion in the bantamweight division. But his sights were set on a career in politics. After service in the air force during World War II, which ended with his flying in B-29 raids on Japanese cities and getting himself discharged for a nervous condition, he ran for the legislature and won.

In the late 1940s and early 1950s, Alabama's politics was dominated by James E. Folsom, who served two four-year terms as governor. Folsom was a populist from north Alabama, whose instincts and speeches, and sometimes even his policies, favored the disadvantaged and the common folk. The tall and large Folsom was described affectionately as "the little man's big friend," and even his racial attitudes were expansive and tolerant. Sharing "Big Jim's" feelings of ease and empathy with ordinary people and resenting the powerful economic interests, Wallace attached himself to Folsom, becoming his campaign manager in south Alabama in 1954 and fully expecting that this would help him to realize his ambition of becoming governor. By 1958, Wallace had decided to run for the state's highest office, but he miscalculated badly because "massive resistance" was then at its peak and Folsom and his iconoclastic populism had been repudiated. Wallace's opponent was the young attorney general of Alabama, John Patterson. Playing up his own segregationist credentials and his support from the Klan, Patterson defeated Wallace handily. "Well, boys," a bitter Wallace is supposed to have told his campaign staff as he went in to give his concession speech, "no other son-of-a-bitch will ever out-nigger me again."[1]

Until this point in his political career, Wallace resembled Huey Long. Both grew up in rural small towns and both discovered early on that they loved to talk and were able to use words so well that they could readily charm or convince others. And both were extroverted and aggressively ambitious, vowing before they even entered politics that they would become governors of their states. In fact, their ambition soon climbed higher, even as high as the presidency, or at least campaigning for it, which was much more feasible and enjoyable. Also common to both men was a populism that gave them a feeling of familiarity with and responsibility for the masses and a hostility toward the rich and powerful. Each of them realized his ambition of becoming governor, though Long's tenure was brief whereas Wallace served as governor for almost twenty years. He was continually reelected with massive pluralities, and he held the state of Alabama in the palm of his hand. Unlike Long, however, who relished the power of the office and exerted near-dictatorial control over Louisiana, Wallace never enjoyed governing and accomplished little for his state. Instead, he loved the excitement of campaigning and firing up audiences with his vitriolic, ranting speeches. And they had one more experience in common. Both were felled by assassins' bullets. Wallace survived, but he was severely crippled and his national political career effectively ended. His physical disabilities never stopped him from completing his gubernatorial term in 1974, or from entering the Democratic presidential primaries briefly in 1976 and being reelected governor twice, in 1978 and 1982.

The essence of Wallace's appeal and the trajectory of his career once he became governor were very different, however, from Long's. Huey's gubernatorial ambitions were shaped by Louisiana's economic backwardness and its domination by a powerful and corrupt political machine, and the Depression had generated his national "Share Our Wealth" campaign. By contrast, Wallace's Alabama had developed a dissenting tradition based on up-country north Alabama's running battle with the black belt oligarchy and on the support of the state's working class in industrial Birmingham. As a result, it could boast two liberal-leaning senators, John Sparkman and Lister Hill, as well as Jim Folsom's brand of populism. Wallace started his political career within an established politics of dissent—he did not have to create it, as Long did. But when he ran for governor in 1962 and in his subsequent state and national campaigns, race was the driving and pervasive issue, not class and privilege. In this respect, too, Wallace diverged from Long. And, finally, it was the climactic phase of the civil rights movement, not a nationwide depression, that provided Wallace with the opportunity to campaign beyond the borders of his provincial Deep South state and become involved in national politics unceasingly for almost a decade.

As he had supposedly vowed in 1958, Wallace seized hold of the race issue in his second campaign for governor four years later. Invigorated by the attention he had received by refusing to hand over the registration records of Bullock County and Baker County demanded by the Civil Rights Commission in 1959, George Wallace, the circuit judge for the district, announced for governor in 1962. Armed with his slogan of "Vote right—vote white—vote for the Fighting Judge" and with his pledge to "stand in the schoolhouse door" to prevent school integration, Wallace promised to protect white Alabamians from the "lousy, federal court system" that was "destroying our schools, our government, our unions, our very way of life."[2]

During his first year as governor, Wallace used his position to stage a series of public confrontations with federal officials in Tuscaloosa and Birmingham that put him in the national spotlight as the leader of the South's last stand in defense of segregation. As he was becoming better known, he arranged lecture tours into the North in late 1963 and early 1964 that were immensely successful, bringing him even more publicity and demonstrating that he could draw audiences, even among those who were openly unsympathetic, like students at Harvard and at the University of Wisconsin in Madison. The thinking behind this strategy was hard to refute. If he was greeted with hostility, it would play well back in Alabama where Wallace would be seen as a courageous fighter against the enemies of white southerners. But if he was received with approval and some degree of respect, it would be an indication that the cause of southern whites had resonance and support beyond the region and that Wallace was a trustworthy and effective spokesman for them. It seemed to be a "win-win situation." After these two tours had tested the political waters and with a civil rights bill moving through Congress, Wallace decided, in March 1964, to enter some of the remaining Democratic primaries for the party's presidential nomination.

To the amazement and dismay of most political observers, this "anachronistic Southern demagogue," as the *New York Times* described Wallace, did very well. The candidate himself had already recognized that "you don't have to win a majority of voters to win" when the purpose of the campaign was purely to protest and express anger.[3] Despite his limited expectations, Wallace nevertheless won more than a third of the 780,000 ballots cast in Wisconsin's Democratic primary. A month later, in May, 30 percent of the Democrats in Indiana voted for Wallace, and by as much as 53 percent in the two industrial counties of Lake and Porter, which contained the steel towns of Gary and Hammond, neither of which the Alabama governor had even visited. And then he almost won Maryland, carrying the white vote on the Eastern Shore overwhelmingly, for a total of sixteen out of the state's twenty-three counties. If not for a massive turnout by African Americans, who polled at twice their usual rate in primaries, Wallace would have won, and he knew it. "If it hadn't been for the nigger bloc vote, we'd have won it all."[4] But there was irony in this observation that even the candidate himself did not perceive. Had apprehensive whites not conceived of blacks as an undifferentiated group, or bloc, Wallace's popularity in the South and his impressive foray into the North would have had no basis at all.

The appeal of George Wallace to so many voters in both regions was based on four elements. The first and fundamental ingredient was his realization that fear of blacks and their aspirations for inclusion and equal treatment was deep-seated in many, if not most, whites, whether from the South or not. Race was an American, not just a southern, preoccupation. And it could well become the central issue of national politics, as school integration, equal access to public accommodations, and open housing began to challenge long-standing practices of racial discrimination in the North. To ensure that race did become the major issue, Wallace intended to acknowledge these fears and then fire them up and channel them into political action.

The blame for these upsetting and destructive developments that threatened white Americans' values and way of life lay with the federal government, the second feature of Wallace's appeal. The interference of the federal courts and an assortment of federal bureaucrats in faraway Washington was the cause of all the instability and the menace to established ways. Since the federal government posed such a threat to the values and practices of ordinary Americans, Wallace proceeded to explain that it was full of communists, atheists, and other un-American types who were the stock-in-trades of the frenzied and paranoid rhetoric of the Cold War that Joe McCarthy had manipulated a decade before in the early 1950s.

The third element in Wallace's diagnosis of the ills afflicting America followed naturally from this assertion. The liberal and permissive policies favored by the federal government gave aid and comfort to other enemies such as beatniks, hippies, antiwar protesters, welfare recipients, and criminals on the streets. And the list grew as the 1960s saw the emergence of increasing numbers of alienated and countercultural social groups. As Wallace's portrait of the evils afflicting America enlarged beyond the initial racial threat, the feelings of anger and outrage among the audiences who thronged to his rallies were amplified by a sense of helplessness and victimization in the face of these threats instigated and encouraged by an all-powerful and alien federal government.

And this led to the fourth weapon in Wallace's armory. Cornered and under attack, white Americans, who were being described increasingly as "Middle America" and "the silent majority," needed to find their voice and fight back. Depicted as the middle, they were beset, on one side, by the federal government and the liberals who ran it and, on the other, by assertive blacks, young protesters, and all sorts of countercultural dissidents. Pressured from above by the liberal government and from below by demanding minorities and disrespectful youth, the victimized people in the middle saw themselves as the mainstream and the upholders of traditional values, which were under attack. Wallace offered himself as their protector and spokesman. He understood them, and he invited and incited them to lash out and give vent to their anger and rage.

This swirling brew of racial prejudice, class resentment, group victimization, and individual anger gave Wallace's appeal compelling force among ordinary Americans who felt threatened and dispossessed during the turmoil of the 1960s. The Alabama governor played on their fears and presented them with a set of increasingly familiar stereotypes and villains to resent and blame. And they flocked to his meetings and rallies in the thousands to hear him express their hatred and denounce their enemies. As Dan Carter, his biographer, has observed, he was "the perfect mimetic orator, probing his audience's deepest fears and passions and articulating those emotions in a language and style they could understand. On paper his speeches were stunningly disconnected, at times incoherent, and always repetitious. But Wallace's followers reveled in the *performance*; they never tired of hearing the same lines again and again."[5]

The bantamweight Alabama segregationist with the slicked-down hair and mean look connected with his huge audiences. There were 7,000 of them on Boston Common and 20,000 in Madison Square Garden who rallied to his cause during the last weeks of the 1968 campaign. Electricity and energy were palpable as the crowd responded to his vitriol, his ridicule, and his coarse humor. To some in the audience, like "T. R. B." of the *New Republic*, this spectacle was simply alarming and even dangerous.

"There is menace in the blood shout of the crowd," he wrote of the reaction produced by the "ablest demagogue of our time, with a bugle voice of venom and a gut knowledge of the low-income class."[6]

Wallace was a master of the rabble-rousing techniques of the twentieth-century southern agitator, reaching back to Vardaman and Heflin. Performing on the national political stage at a moment of political crisis and turbulence, George Wallace was stirring passions and discord to a degree that made the earlier southern demagogues appear quaint and rustic. As Martin Luther King Jr. told Dan Rather of CBS News after "the stand in the schoolhouse door" in 1963, "Wallaceism is bigger than Wallace." Paraphrasing FDR's comment about Huey Long, he proceeded to describe the Alabama governor as "perhaps the most dangerous racist in America today." The decisive and destructive role Wallace was to play in American politics over the next decade confirmed King's insight.[7]

Before he could advance his national political ambitions after his unexpected success in 1964 in the three Democratic primaries, Wallace had to make sure he kept control of the Alabama governorship in 1966, despite the state's prohibition against a governor succeeding himself. His solution was to run his wife, Lurleen, for the position. Knowing Wallace would continue in power, yet admiring the inexperienced but public-spirited and willing Lurleen, an outpouring of support greeted George, accompanied by his wife, as he "moved through the state like a tribal chieftain." On election day, Lurleen beat the Republican candidate by a 2-to-1 margin.[8] With his Alabama base secured for another four years, Wallace could now concentrate on the 1968 presidential contest.

By 1968, Wallace's prospects had brightened considerably because of the black uprisings in the northern ghettoes of Watts, Newark, and Detroit, and then, after Martin Luther King Jr.'s assassination in June 1968, in Chicago and Washington and in a number of other northern cities as well. With the "white backlash" growing stronger and Wallace's prophecies about the results of racial integration seeming to be vindicated, he managed to get on the ballot in all fifty states as the candidate of a third party, the American Independent Party. Despite its name, it was not a political party but simply a vehicle for promoting George Wallace. His electoral strategy was to carry the Upper and Lower South as well as Ohio and Indiana. These victories, it was hoped, would throw the election into the House. But what would he try to achieve there? Bargain for the presidency? Create mayhem as a spoiler? No one knew what his objective was, probably not Wallace himself. Certainly his independent candidacy caused the Republican nominee, Richard Nixon, a great deal of unease, because Wallace was certain to win a number of southern states and, in a close election, might even deprive him of several in the North.

Nixon considered a strategy to undercut Wallace's support in the South, a "southern strategy," in effect. But he did not need to pursue it very far because the Alabamian's campaign began to lose momentum in the last month of the contest. His choice as his vice president was General Curtis LeMay, who was advocating the use of nuclear weapons in Vietnam. Wallace now seemed even more dangerous and was likened to Goldwater in 1964, who had enthusiastically embraced the nuclear option. He was also ridiculed for his choice of LeMay by the Democratic nominee, Hubert Humphrey, who referred to them both as "the Bombsey twins." Furthermore, Humphrey's campaign picked up steam after he distanced himself from Lyndon Johnson and the Vietnam War, and so the contest became much tighter, making a vote for Wallace a vote denied to the mainstream conservative, Nixon.

In the end, Wallace carried four Deep South states (Alabama, Georgia, Mississippi, and Louisiana) and also Arkansas, and he lost North Carolina and Tennessee by the slimmest of margins. In the popular vote, he won 8 percent outside the South and just under 14 percent of the national total. A switch of less than 1 percent of the vote in New Jersey and Ohio to Humphrey would have given the Democrat those two states and forced the election into the House. After Walter Cronkite of CBS News had announced derisively that Wallace had "gone down to ignominious defeat," the Alabama governor reminded his assembled staff that he had captured 10 million votes. "A deep Southerner getting that many votes is not ignominious," he crowed.[9]

President Nixon was quite aware of the extent of Wallace's support and the danger he would pose in 1972, should he run again as an independent. By 1970, as he prepared for his reelection campaign, Nixon pursued a two-pronged strategy to deal with the "Wallace factor," as he called it. The first tactic was to attack Wallace personally and politically in Alabama, by backing Wallace's opponent for governor in 1970, Albert Brewer, and providing him with considerable financial and political help. But Wallace won the runoff primary by resorting to his instinctive stratagem of race-baiting. Next, Nixon ordered an Internal Revenue Service investigation of the tax returns of Wallace's brother, Gerald, as well as of the dealings of Wallace supporters with the state of Alabama to see if there was any evidence of corruption that could be prosecuted.

The second maneuver was Nixon's southern strategy, the purpose of which was to undercut Wallace's appeal in the region and, at the same time, build up the Republican Party in the South by drawing whites away from the Democrats. First, the administration tried, though unsuccessfully, to eviscerate the Voting Rights Act when it came up for renewal in 1970. This attempt was accompanied by a passive policy toward African Americans that came to be described by its proud proponents as "benign neglect." Then, to further convince white southerners that he was sympathetic to their concerns, Nixon nominated a southern conservative to the Supreme Court in 1970. After Clement Haynesworth was rejected, he sent up an even less-qualified conservative southerner, Harold Carswell, who in turn was rejected. Although both were less than illustrious choices, Nixon berated the Democratic-controlled Senate for being unfair and antisouthern. Wallace's claim to the loyalty of southern whites was also challenged by Nixon's attempt to deprive him of the emotive and increasingly critical issue of busing. The president urged Congress to impose a moratorium on court-ordered busing to achieve school integration and later endorsed the idea of a constitutional amendment prohibiting busing, which Wallace had been promoting with considerable success.

Nixon's preoccupation with the South had both a long-term and a more immediate purpose. Since the southern electorate was undergoing a massive transformation in the late 1960s and 1970s, it was critically important for the Republican Party to establish its identity and electoral base by becoming the party of the region's whites, leaving the Democrats with a remnant of party loyalists and a majority of blacks. If successful, this strategy would realign the parties in the region and create an enduring base for the Republicans nationally. In the short term, Nixon could not allow Wallace a monopoly on the social issues of school busing, disorder and crime in the streets, and the permissive and drug-ridden counterculture that so worried and angered the "silent majority" in the South and in the nation as a whole. He and Wallace were both conservatives who appealed to the same conservative portion of the electorate, Middle America. But the president would always be playing catch-up to Wallace's irresponsible rabble-rousing and be constantly exposed to the Alabamian's sneering taunt that Nixon came down "forthrightly on both sides of most questions."[10] Even more worrisome to Nixon was the prospect of Wallace running again as an independent, because he would take millions of conservative votes from Nixon and his Republican Party. Having failed to destroy Wallace in Alabama, he had to prevent him from pursuing the third-party route.

Nixon's great fear was removed on 13 January 1972 when Wallace revealed his intention of seeking the Democratic nomination for president rather than running as the candidate of an independent third party. The day before, the Justice Department had announced without fanfare that it was terminating the Internal Revenue Service investigation of his brother and dismissing the grand jury that had spent eighteen months looking into the records of Alabama's state contracts. This sequence of events more than hints that a deal was struck with George Wallace. But Dan Carter, his extremely careful biographer, has found no evidence that such an arrangement was worked out between the two men. Perhaps Nixon hoped that Wallace would understand that his cancellation of the two probes was a reprieve, for which Wallace should provide, on his own initiative, a quid pro quo by abandoning all thought of an independent campaign.

In any case, Wallace did what Nixon hoped for and was soon creating havoc among Nixon's Democratic opponents by entering the spring primaries in eight states, most of them in the North. Focusing on the busing issue, which he continued to blame on out-of-touch bureaucrats in Washington, Wallace told his audiences to "send them a message." Voters could let out a cry of frustration and defiance without actually having to address the more problematic question of whether Wallace was their choice for president. As a spoiler, therefore, he could raise issues the other Democratic candidates could not mention without the risk of losing touch with the party's liberal base. Among the Democratic contenders, Wallace alone could appeal to and identify with the conservative "white backlash."

The results of the primaries were extraordinary. Wallace romped to victory in Florida, winning 42 percent of the vote in a ten-candidate primary. He won the Tennessee, Alabama, and North Carolina primaries and finished second in Wisconsin, Indiana, and Pennsylvania. On 15 May, he won in Michigan and Maryland. He now had three and a half million votes, well ahead of Hubert Humphrey and George McGovern, his nearest challengers, each of whom had a million fewer votes than Wallace.[11] But his campaign came to an end that same day when he was paralyzed from the waist down by an assassin's bullet in his spine at a rally in Laurel, Maryland.

George Wallace's three campaigns for the presidency—and he even tried yet again briefly in 1976—made him a continuing, perhaps looming, presence in American politics during the tumultuous 1960s. He had very little organization, no cadre of experienced political operatives and advisers to run his campaigns, and no structure at the local level to get out the vote. Wallace's operation was simply a one-man show, dependent on the candidate's ability to draw throngs of people to his rallies and then fire them up. Yet the candidate himself, who pulled in these very large and enthusiastic audiences, was just a "poor man's segregationist" who had played a principal role in the collapse of the southern racial order. Rather than disqualifying him in the eyes of whites, his defiant and completely ineffective role in defending an anachronistic racist institution seemed actually to make him credible and attractive. Wallace had first-hand experience dealing with what he considered the "unreasonable" demands for equality of African Americans, and he too was a victim of the similarly "unreasonable," and also unrealistic, plans of Washington bureaucrats to change the racial system, not just in the South but in the North as well.

Wallace was a fellow sufferer who had already been through it all and who therefore sympathized with the anxiety and frustration of ordinary white people in both regions. What was more, he seemed to be as angry about it as they were. By voting for him, they could "send a message" to those "briefcase-carrying bureaucrats who are trying to run your lives" but "can't park their bicycles straight."[12] This improbable empathy between a stereotypical southern segregationist and northern working people was made possible by Wallace's ability to fire up the "white backlash." But it was also cemented by the southern brand of populism that turned the deprivation and resentment of disadvantaged whites against those beneath them socially, that is, blacks. Furthermore, African Americans now had influential allies and advocates who supported their aspirations to equality, and these liberals, with their access to and positions inside the national government, were also to be treated as enemies and derided and ridiculed. This racist and reactionary populism resonated deeply with Middle America. And it functioned as a conservative, rather than a progressive, force in American politics.

Wallace had sensed and tapped into a deep-seated instinctive conservatism among ordinary working people in both regions. Nixon knew that conservatives had to attract this constituency, but, unlike Wallace, he was too stolid and aloof to be able to reach it. Because of his own limitations, his only recourse was to call on Spiro Agnew, his less-uptight vice president, to poke fun at liberals and make a laughingstock of them as "nattering nabobs of negativism." But the president's worries evaporated when Wallace was removed by his assassin's bullet. In the election, three of every four voters who had supported the Alabamian in 1968 switched to Nixon as the alternative conservative candidate four years later. The Republicans managed to appeal to working people and obtained a large share of the vote of Middle America by endorsing Wallace's depiction of the social crisis the country faced.

According to Wallace's portrayal, liberals were elitists; the federal government was the enemy; the very poor, especially blacks, were a menace and a threat; and social change was unsettling and dangerous. Through its appropriation of much of Wallace's rhetoric and insight, the Republican Party had become, by the 1980s, a party with which working people could ally, even though the liberals in the Democratic Party just happened to be the people responsible for the New Deal, the Great Society, and other similar federal programs that were intended to, and did in fact, benefit and protect working people and the disadvantaged. "Law and order" and the "traditional values" of family, and later religion, seemed more emotive and important than substantive programs and government benefits. This reorientation of American conservatism meant that the traditional party of the rich and powerful and the "country club set" was becoming an ally of working people and "the silent majority" in a contest in which the Democratic Party was depicted as elitist and out of touch.

These strange bedfellows, who were now together within the changing Republican Party, had been brought together initially by George Wallace. Quite a remarkable legacy for "a deep Southerner," especially one whose ill-advised actions and posturing had contributed to the ending of segregation and who, through his presidential campaigns, had hastened the disintegration of the Solid South.

Southern Democrats in the Carter Decade

In anticipation of another run for the presidency, George Wallace was crisscrossing the country in early 1972, inciting racial passions and stirring up fears about social disorder. Within Wallace's own turbulent region, however, a very different and unexpected political development was occurring. On 31 May 1971, the front cover of *Time* magazine carried a picture of Jimmy Carter, the newly elected governor of Georgia, and its feature story rhapsodized about "A New Day A'Coming in the South." From the ruins of the Solid South, there sprang a group of young moderates, almost all Democrats, who won governorships and a few Senate seats, as the 1970s began. Instead of pursuing the politics of rancor and resentment that had characterized the region's initial response to the collapse of the old order, these attractive and articulate moderates seemed to offer an alternative direction for southern politics.

Besides Carter, this cadre of new political leaders included Reubin Askew of Florida, Dale Bumpers of Arkansas, and John West of South

Carolina. All of them were elected governor, often defeating well-known opponents, either in the Democratic primary or in the general election. Actually, Bumpers did both, for he outpolled Arkansas's former governor, Orval Faubus, in the primary and the current governor, Winthrop Rockefeller, a Republican, in the general election. But the representative figure in this new wave was Georgia's Jimmy Carter, who defeated a popular former governor, Carl Sanders, in the Democratic primary. In his inaugural address, in January 1972, he announced: "I say to you quite frankly that the time for racial discrimination is over. Our people have already made this major and difficult decision."[13] The inaugurals of Bumpers, Askew, and the others contained similarly dramatic announcements that segregation was a relic of the past and that the region's future progress depended on its repudiation.

Nevertheless, all four governors had carefully avoided the highly contentious issue of busing during their campaigns. By 1970, the busing of students had become the most feasible way of achieving the desegregation of public schools in the South and in the rest of the nation. To have taken a position for or against busing would have embroiled their candidacies in a polarizing and possibly fatal dispute. Evasive though it certainly was, such a course was essential, not only to their own electability, but also to their hopes of moving beyond segregation and race as the defining elements in the region's politics. After all, Carter and this "new wave" were self-proclaimed moderates. And they were trying to unite their party by positioning themselves between its traditional segregationist supporters and its new African American backers. At the same time, they hoped to calm racial tensions by pursuing a middle course that adapted to the desired outcome of desegregation without advocating any specific means for attaining it.[14]

In other ways too, these men represented moderation. They ran as allies and friends of the common people, folksy and unpretentious, and as outsiders who had no ties to the political establishment. Jimmy Carter was, after all, just a peanut farmer, and he castigated Sanders as "Cufflinks Carl" because of his connections to the political and social elite. Simultaneously, Carter distanced himself from the large corporations and powerful institutions, which he believed threatened the general public interest. This kind of populism was vastly different from the incendiary appeal to the masses by the Solid South's demagogues, George Wallace in particular. Moreover, unlike Wallace and many of his predecessors, Carter and the other moderates were serious about governing once elected. Not just a farmer, Carter was actually a businessman who ran a successful and profitable agricultural enterprise, and he had also been an engineer while in the navy.

Once in office, Carter acted forcefully to make state government more efficient by reducing the number of agencies and centralizing their operation, and he also improved the public services that government provided. Like his "new wave" colleagues, Carter actively promoted economic and industrial development within his state, an initiative that required him to collaborate with the corporations he had once impugned. Although the new governors employed populist rhetoric to get elected, they were more like the business progressives of the 1920s who wanted to make state government more effective and their state's economy more prosperous. Their efforts to expand government services, however, ran into the South's traditional reluctance to raise taxes and increase expenditures, a pattern that left most of the region's states still collecting the least taxes per capita in the nation.[15]

The efforts of these moderates to capture the middle ground and pull the southern states away from the polarization of the civil rights era and its immediate aftermath were also aimed at holding the Democratic Party together, now that its regional hegemony was being contested and now that its base of support included over 3 million African American voters. In effect, the "white man's party" was being compromised, if not subverted, by an influx of black supporters. The difficulties facing southern Democrats at the state and local levels were compounded by their party's woeful record in presidential elections. In 1968, the Democratic nominee, Hubert Humphrey, had won just a single state, Texas, in the party's southern bastion. Humphrey had split the region's popular vote pretty evenly with Richard Nixon, the Republican, and George Wallace and his American Independent party. But Wallace had captured four Deep South states plus Arkansas, and Nixon had won the four Rim South states of Tennessee, Virginia, North Carolina, and Florida and also South Carolina, which Strom Thurmond delivered to him. Four years later, when Nixon was reelected and the South's new moderates resided in most of the region's executive mansions, the Democrats, led by George McGovern, won not a single state in the region—or anywhere for that matter, except Massachusetts and the District of Columbia. McGovern's popular vote in the South dropped to 28.9 percent from Humphrey's 31 percent in 1968, a precipitous decline, considering that there were no longer three major candidates to divide up the vote in 1972.

Four years later, however, something remarkable occurred in the presidential contest. A southern Democrat secured the party's nomination and went on to win the presidency. Unlike Woodrow Wilson of New Jersey and Lyndon Johnson of Texas, Jimmy Carter had spent his whole life in the Deep South, and he had no previous national political experience and so was barely known outside the region. Moreover, he proudly emphasized his southernness by declaring that "come November we are going to have a President in the White House who doesn't speak with an accent." Carter also pointed to his rural southern roots as the source of his own honesty, spirituality, and authenticity.[16] In the wake of the forced resignations of President Nixon and Vice President Agnew, a candidate's character and trustworthiness was the crucial ingredient. Pledging "I'll never lie to you" and promising a government "as good as its people," Jimmy Carter campaigned as an upright and incorruptible outsider who could be trusted to "clean up the mess in Washington." Responding well to the public mood and faced by an opponent, President Gerald Ford, who had become complicit in the Watergate scandal through his overeager pardon of the disgraced Richard Nixon, Carter won the election. But, with only a 2 percent lead in the popular vote and just 60 more electoral votes than Ford, he squeaked through in the closest presidential election since 1916.

Carter's election as president was enormously significant because it acknowledged a growing convergence between the South and the rest of the country. A quintessential and unapologetic southerner, from the Deep South no less, had been accepted and considered suitable to hold the highest public office in the land, the first time since Zachary Taylor in 1848, whose credentials as a southerner were actually far less impressive and credible than the Georgia farmer from Plains. Perhaps even more important, Jimmy Carter showed the nation that the same rural, small-town southern origins that had spawned snarling segregationists like George Wallace, Gene Talmadge, and Ben Tillman could also produce political leaders who felt optimistic and confident about their region, especially now that it had given up Jim Crow.

Carter's success was also greeted with pleasure by the national Democratic Party, whose prospects were suddenly brightening after the debacles of 1968 and 1972. The congressional elections of 1974, in the aftermath of the Watergate scandal, and now the presidential election in 1976 had dramatically reversed the party's decline. Nowhere was this revival more welcome than among the South's Democrats. The party had done well in congressional and gubernatorial races, and Carter had carried all the southern states except Virginia. Offsetting this apparent triumph, however, was a less encouraging electoral reality. Carter won less than half of the white vote (46 percent) in the region, which meant that the white majority could not be relied on even when the Democratic presidential candidate was an unabashed southerner. The whites who voted for Carter tended to be lower class, while the better off identified with the Republicans. Also worrisome, the rate of turnout by less-educated and poorer whites was lower. These trends had to be headed off if the Democrats were to remain viable in the South, at the presidential level certainly, but also at the state level.[17]

So how did Carter manage to win in 1976? African American voters in the South and in the nation as a whole made the difference. They responded to his efforts to reach out to them by going to the polls in greater numbers than in the previous two national elections and providing him with 5.2 million votes, three times his margin of victory. Delighted at the contribution from blacks, Andrew Young, a close aide to Martin Luther King Jr. and now congressman from Atlanta, announced: "I knew that the hands that picked the cotton finally picked the President."[18] Even more remarkable was the realization that African Americans had enabled a white southern Democrat to carry the South. Although it had seemed unlikely that blacks, newly enfranchised by the Voting Rights Act, would vote Republican, they now found themselves inside the traditional party of white supremacy. Indeed, blacks were becoming as solidly and reliably Democratic as whites had once been before 1965.

The South's 3.4 million registered black voters in 1970, increasing to 4.3 million by 1980, created a constituency sufficiently large that it could elect African Americans to office, particularly in those districts where they constituted a majority, or close to one. And they managed to do so. Compared to a mere 72 black officeholders throughout the South in 1965, and none at all in a state like Mississippi, their numbers grew to around 700 by the end of the decade and then shot up to 1,847 in 1976 and 2,457 four years later.[19] Initially, many of the candidates had been activists in the civil rights movement, but soon a new kind of black leader emerged who possessed different attributes, such as the ability to build and sustain an electoral organization and the financial security necessary for personal involvement in a lengthy campaign. Accordingly, they came increasingly from the ranks of the better off and the better educated, who already possessed the confidence that stems from success in the business or professional world. Once elected, they needed the savvy to negotiate and bargain with other politicians, almost all of whom would be whites with greater experience and contacts. Others who were elected to executive offices—mayors of small towns like Johnny Ford of Tuskegee or of big cities like Maynard Jackson of Atlanta or Richard Arrington of Birmingham—had to form governing coalitions as well as show they could run a municipality and even a metropolis.

For the black voters who elected them, political victories like these demonstrated that they could do more than just participate in elections; they could actually win them. This sense of empowerment was supplemented by a growing awareness among black southerners that they had access to public officials. They expected these officials to be responsive to the needs of blacks, as individuals and as a group, and these needs required urgent attention because they had been neglected for so long. In towns where African Americans were mayors or council members, they could provide municipal services that blacks had previously been denied or they might be able to upgrade them if they were already available but inadequate. These officials might also be able to open up jobs in city government to blacks. Less tangible was the ability of black officials to represent and promote what were believed to be the interests of their constituents within the town's governmental system. But there were severe limits to what they could do. They rarely had the numbers or the influence to obtain what their black constituents needed. And, besides, the needs of these long-neglected black communities were invariably so great that the local government's resources were quite inadequate to meet them. As Richard Arrington discovered in Birmingham, he had to deal with "the expectations of the black community that expects you to do more than you can do."[20]

Despite the evident sense of accomplishment and the feeling of empowerment that the growing numbers of black officials conveyed to 4 million black voters in the South, these officials were still very few in number and they inhabited an unfriendly white world. There were just 127 state legislators in 1982, a mere 7 percent, in a region where African Americans made up 20 percent of the population. Moreover, most of the 2,601 elective offices that blacks held in 1982 were minor, such as aldermen in municipal councils, members of school boards, or county commissioners. Of course, some were mayors—236 of them in fact. But, overwhelmingly, they were in small towns, unlike the five black mayors in large cities such as New Orleans and Atlanta. The 2,601 officials in 1982 represented a mere 2.3 per county among the South's 1,147 counties and parishes. This meant that just over one-third of the region's counties contained no black official at all, and only one-fifth had five or more.[21]

Like so much else in the South's changing political world, the increase in black officeholding could be judged either as inadequate or as quite remarkable. Similarly ambiguous was the meaning of the growth in black voter registration. Over 5 million were registered in 1984, yet this vast increase in more than twenty-five years amounted to just 17 percent of the voting population. Since the remaining 83 percent was white, blacks' chances of getting elected depended on either the existence of districts with a black majority or near majority or on the willingness of large numbers of whites to vote for a black candidate. Although this latter course seemed unlikely, it might remain a possibility if the Democratic Party could persist as a viable biracial electoral organization. And, in the 1970s, this was the fundamental question in southern politics. With African Americans identifying overwhelmingly with the Democrats, would whites—most of whom had been segregationists—continue to remain in the party and keep it biracial? The answer was not obvious.

The presidential elections of 1968 and 1972 seemed to indicate that a rapid decline and disintegration was the likely future for the Democrats. And the Republicans sensed this. After his election in 1968, Nixon developed his southern strategy, aimed at winning whites over to the Republican Party. His strategy "rested, finally, on a calculated appeal to white segregationist sentiment," according to Reg Murphy and Hal Gulliver of the *Atlanta Constitution*: "It was anti-black, not with passion but with a cool, clear-eyed political cynicism."[22] Surprisingly, this calculated policy of conciliating southern white voters ran into practical difficulties. Nixon's Supreme Court nominees were not confirmed. His efforts to stall school desegregation in the South were circumvented by Supreme Court decisions upholding the policy of busing. And his attempt to weaken black voting rights was countered by the federal courts and by the lawyers in the Justice Department, most of whom were civil service appointees who had been working there since the years of civil rights protest. As a result, the policy of "benign neglect" that underpinned Nixon's southern strategy foundered badly.[23] Even so, the signals of support and empathy that Nixon transmitted to the South were understood by its intended beneficiaries, who had little difficulty voting for Nixon in 1972. He gained three out of four of Wallace's 1968 voters and carried 79 percent of the regionwide white vote.

But the Watergate crisis and Nixon's impeachment and resignation gave the Democrats a boost four years later. With Jimmy Carter as president, a rather different southern strategy replaced Nixon's. Blacks were appointed in significant numbers to high-level positions, and the administration's stance on desegregation and civil rights was supportive rather than obstructionist. The Republicans' determined campaign to draw off southern whites from their traditional allegiance to the Democratic

Party seemed to have stalled. A survey in 1976 suggested instead that the South's white voters were divided into three groupings, not just two: 46 percent still identified with the Democrats, and a mere 21 percent saw themselves as Republicans, but a third of the voters considered themselves independents.[24] The ambivalence and hesitance of these independents suggested to the political scientist Paul A. Beck that, rather than realigning, the parties were actually in a state of "dealignment." This term described a shifting, middle position, moving away from the former one-party system but not yet toward a new configuration, with two distinctive parties based on different constituencies and different identities.[25]

After all, there were many reasons for southern voters, and also politicians, to stay with the Democratic Party. First, the Democrats continued to command the loyalty and affection of many whites. Carter himself was convinced in 1973 that there still existed "a very detectable reservoir of Democratic party allegiance," and he believed that, even though many had strayed to vote for Nixon or Wallace, they "had now come back to the Democratic Party as their permanent home."[26] A second disincentive against deserting the Democrats was the widely held perception of the Republican Party as a moderate party associated with Eisenhower and even Nixon. It was neither recognizably conservative nor reliable on the issues that wavering Wallace followers felt deeply about.

A third consideration was the continuing institutional power of the Democratic Party. Democrats controlled almost all of the governor's mansions and every statehouse in the South and, of course, they still had an entrenched presence in the county and local government of the region. Not least, the party's delegation was well established in Congress through the seniority of its incumbents and the institutional control and influence it wielded. That dominance in Washington was, however, under siege and about to be destroyed. Nevertheless, the Democrats contained within their ranks a preponderance of the South's experienced and influential politicians. They constituted a large pool of ambitious and seasoned operatives who would be candidates for office over the coming years, perhaps for decades. It was one thing to vote for Nixon for president or to send a message by attending a rally and marking a ballot for Wallace, but quite another to abandon the party that was the source of the region's political identity and power at the national level and that still controlled its political life at the state and local levels.

Fourth, and finally, the inflammation of racial tensions in the 1960s that had initially provoked many southern Democrats into voting Republican, or independent, had diminished considerably during the 1970s.

Offsetting these gains among whites was the Republicans' evident loss of the black vote, which, even at just 17 percent of the electorate, could mean the difference between winning or losing a contest. Moreover, in the Deep South states, black population majorities in a large number of electoral districts ensured that they would remain in the hands of the Democrats. Compounding the Republicans' difficulty was the cadre of moderate Democratic candidates who had put race behind them and who offered governmental efficiency and economic development as attractive policies to win broad support, especially among independent, former Democrats, who had been toying with the idea of leaving the party for good. With but few exceptions, such as the election of Jesse Helms to the Senate from North Carolina in 1972, politicians in the South shied away from using race as an issue in the 1970s. In this calmer atmosphere, the Republicans had to set aside, for the time being at least, their earlier resort to race as the defining characteristic of their party in their attempt to win over disaffected, white Democrats.

By the late 1970s, a two-party system was therefore in the process of formation in the South. But its contours and components were unclear. The elements were in flux, with the parties in an unstable condition of "dealignment." This instability would end, however, once those voters who described themselves as independents and who made up a third of the electorate decided to align themselves with a party. If they continued to move away from the Democrats, or if they split evenly, the Republicans would become a competitive force in the region. But if they all decided to drift back to the Democrats, who were currently trying to hold together a coalition of African Americans, racial moderates like Carter, and rural disadvantaged whites, then the Democrats would have the lion's share of the electorate and a system of competitive parties would not arise.

But this uncertainty did not last long. As a Mississippi Republican acknowledged gratefully during the 1980 presidential campaign, "God has given the country a second chance to elect Barry Goldwater."[27] With Ronald Reagan's capture of the presidency, the independents were not likely to remain undecided for much longer. Perhaps the flux and instability in southern party politics was about to end.

The End of the Solid South in Congress
Just when the Democrats were jettisoning their reputation and identity within the South as the party of conservatism and white supremacy, they also lost the enormous power they had wielded nationally inside Congress as the instrument, the embodiment, of the Solid South.

The Solid South was a political structure that rested on four pillars. Two were located in the South. The other two were situated within two national institutions, the Democratic Party and the U.S. Congress. By the end of the 1960s, three of these four pillars had been dismantled or overthrown. Within the South, the pillars were the exclusion of African Americans from the electoral process and the Democrats' monopoly of the region's party system. They were being replaced by a growing black electorate and an emerging Republican opposition. Outside the South, the abolition in 1936 of the two-thirds rule in the Democrats' national convention had eliminated the South's minority veto over the party's presidential choice. That left just one pillar of the structure standing, the South's entrenched position within the committee system of Congress. With the dismantling of the committee system itself in 1975, the Solid South was finally destroyed.

The movement for congressional reform that eventually triumphed in the mid-1970s arose in the postwar years when Truman's Fair Deal and his civil rights initiative ran into strong opposition in Congress, particularly from the southern wing of the president's own party. In 1948, the year of the Dixiecrat revolt, Eugene McCarthy of Minnesota, Richard Bolling of Missouri, and Paul Douglas of Illinois were elected to the House, and Hubert Humphrey of Minnesota was elected to the Senate. They began to assemble a cadre of liberal Democrats with the aim of pressuring their party to take action against the southerners who were at odds with the majority of Democrats. Even more than labor legislation, civil rights was the critical issue, so they believed, that faced the nation and the party in the emerging Cold War contest with the Soviet Union, when it seemed prudent for the United States to remove some of the obvious defects in its purportedly egalitarian and democratic society. Yet inveterate opponents of civil rights were permitted to use their influence within the Democratic Party itself, and also the enormous power of the committee system, to thwart progress toward full and inclusive democracy in America.

The progress of the campaign for reform was neither direct nor rapid, because Congress's committee system proved remarkably resistant to change. Although the Humphrey-Douglas group was expanded considerably after the Democratic landslide in 1958—which added even more liberals, such as John Brademas and Shirley Chisholm in the House and Eugene McCarthy and Walter Mondale in the Senate—very little change resulted. The Democratic Study Group that they formed to advance their agenda produced a report showing that conservative House Democrats were siding with the Republicans on 80 percent of the roll-call votes in the

1959–60 session. In addition, the twelve Democratic committee chairs from the South voted 86 percent of the time with the opposition party.[28]

When the liberals challenged the South's power at two of its key points, the filibuster in the Senate and the Rules Committee in the House, they made little headway. The attempt in 1960 to reduce the majority needed for cloture was defeated. A year later, they obtained some changes in the Rules Committee aimed at curbing the power of its chair, the truculent and obstructionist Howard W. Smith of Virginia, who single-handedly controlled the movement of legislation to the House floor for debate and a vote. But the impact of these changes was minimal. Even though the Democrats held a 130-seat majority, they barely managed to pass a minor measure to expand the size of the committee by adding two Democrats and a Republican. These votes might cramp "Judge" Smith's style, but they hardly challenged his power.

Ten years later, however, the prospects for success had increased greatly, although the committee system was still very much intact. Two changes in particular had brought this about. First, the composition of Congress, especially in the House, was considerably different as a result of the redistricting required after the Supreme Court's critical "one man, one vote" decision in *Baker v. Carr* (1962). By 1972, the number of congressional districts with overrepresented rural population majorities had declined from 214 in 1964 to just 130. As a result, men and women who were less conservative and less wedded to the old ways entered the House. This reapportionment had also taken into consideration the presence of millions of previously disfranchised African Americans, resulting in a considerable loss for the southern Democrats of their rural, white bastions.

In a second development, the drive for reform of Congress shifted away from its connection to civil rights and southern domination toward an emphasis on reform for its own sake. Electoral changes within the South were already undermining the region's Solid South delegations, and Howard W. Smith had been one of the first victims, after his northern Virginia stronghold had been redistricted prior to the 1966 election. Besides, civil rights legislation was being enacted in any case, as the 1964 and 1965 acts and the Fair Housing Act of 1968 demonstrated. Furthermore, congressional reform was now backed by a growing coalition of interests and organizations. The first component was the group of newly elected members of Congress from previously underrepresented suburban districts who wanted their constituents' interests to be recognized. They were joined by a new cohort of members who were shaped by the iconoclasm of the 1960s and who wanted no part of a hierarchical structure that reduced members of Congress to puppets of all-powerful committee chairmen. Also pressing for reform were print and even television journalists, who, during the 1960s, had become much more critical of the nation's institutions. Now they were not merely reporting the news but probing and investigating below the surface of day-to-day events, thereby generating what was being welcomed as "investigative journalism." Not least was the emergence of citizens' advocacy organizations, like Common Cause, founded in 1970, and Ralph Nader's Congress Watch, which were dedicated to reforming Congress. This broad coalition brought to a climax the campaign to reform the committee system.

The final phase began in 1970 with the passage of the Legislative Reorganization Act after the rather mild recommendations of the newly formed Joint Committee on the Organization of Congress had been prevented from coming to a vote in the House Rules Committee in 1967. Under this new law, committee hearings were to be open to the public and could be covered by radio and television, while votes in the House on amendments to bills were to be recorded. Both of these provisions undermined the power of chairmen to run their committees in secret and get legislation enacted without further input or opposition.

After the 1972 elections, when congressional reform had been a major issue, the growing body of reformers in Congress maneuvered to involve the parties and their leadership in the legislative process, so as to counter the committee chairs and make legislation a party matter and not merely the prerogative of a dozen or so powerful chairmen. The Democratic caucus required that these chairmen be voted on at the beginning of each session (though a secret ballot was required if 20 percent of the caucus wanted it, a slight concession to the chairs). Also, the Democratic leadership (Speaker, majority leader, and whip) was to serve on the pivotal Ways and Means Committee, which had functioned traditionally as a committee on committees, appointing the members and chairs of the standing committees. A "Subcommittee Bill of Rights" followed, giving subcommittees a degree of autonomy and influence over the standing committees, from which they had been formed and to which they had previously been entirely subordinate. And, finally, the House itself voted in March 1973 to make all committee meetings, not just hearings, open to the media and the public, unless a majority of its members were opposed.

Less successful were the reformers' attempts to overhaul the committee system itself by changing both how committees operated and what matters each of them was responsible for. The proposals presented by Richard Bolling, one of the original members of the Democratic Study Group and now chair of the House Select Committee on Committees, tried to overcome the power of the committee chairs. His committee recommended, first, to grant the Speaker the authority to send a bill to more than one committee, a process he called the "referral mechanism," and, second, to confine members of Congress to one committee, rather than allowing them to be dispersed to a number of them, a practice that resulted in their being inexpert and uninfluential. But these procedural changes, which would have centralized committee operations in the party leadership, were gutted by the Democratic caucus, along with Bolling's efforts to reorganize the committees and reassign their responsibilities. As a result, a weaker measure was passed by the House in October 1973. Although a disappointing outcome for the cause of congressional reform, the diluted remedies were still a setback for the committee system and its powerful chairmen.

But these minor changes were merely precursors of the system's ultimate demise, for the showdown came a year or so later, after the 1974 midterm elections. These elections were influenced decisively by two Washington scandals. The more important was the Watergate crisis of 1972–74, but the strange saga of Arkansas's Wilbur Mills, the powerful chairman of Ways and Means, the keystone of the committee system, also contributed. The Mills scandal and the Watergate crisis, coupled with the resignation and subsequent pardon of Richard Nixon, handed the Democrats a major victory in 1974. They increased their majority in the House by 43, for a total of 291, and in the Senate by 3, for a total of 61.

Young, politically inexperienced, suburban, and angered by the revelations of how the political establishment ran Washington, the new members of Congress had no ties to the existing system and vowed to change it. Their distaste for Washington and its ways was confirmed on the eve of the election when Wilbur Mills was discovered to be having an affair with a strip club performer and also to be suffering from alcoholism. Then, two days before the House Democratic caucus was to meet, Mills appeared on stage at the club of the stripper, Fanne Fox, and later announced defiantly, "This won't ruin me . . . nothing can ruin me."[29] With the graphic example of Mills fresh in their minds, the Democratic caucus voted to deprive Ways and Means of its power to appoint committee members, transferring that authority to the steering and policy committees of the caucus, which had already been given considerable input into committee assignments in 1973. Meanwhile, the Speaker was empowered to appoint all members of the Rules Committee, though subject to caucus approval. The increasingly powerful Speaker, Carl Albert, then asked Mills to resign from Congress, which he did.

Sensing that they possessed a mandate for reform, the seventy-five freshmen in the House formed a "new members' caucus" and embarked on several initiatives of their own. First, they called the committee chairs before them and insisted on interviewing them behind closed doors to decide whether they deserved reappointment. Since there were 75 votes at stake, the chairmen had no alternative but to attend and be subjected to a grilling from the young upstarts—"boys and girls," as Louisiana's Edward Hebert of the Armed Services Committee referred to them. He himself, as well as W. R. Poage of Agriculture and Wright Patman of Banking, Currency, and Housing, all made bad impressions and all were southerners. Subsequently, both the steering and policy committees and the caucus voted to remove them from their chairmanships. So unprecedented was this sequence of events that it marked a decisive shift of power away from the chairmen. Their era of domination was effectively over. As the *Washington Post* proclaimed, "The seniority system as the rigid, inviolable operating framework of the House has been destroyed."[30]

And the same could be said for the Senate. Although a very different kind of legislative body from the House, the Senate too had undergone a gradual change over the previous decades that had given individual senators greater influence and more independence from the committee chairmen, a process that the political scientist Barbara Sinclair has called "the transformation of the Senate."[31] Evolutionary and nonconfrontational as it had been by comparison with the experience of reform in the House, the finale in the overthrow of the committee system was, however, quite similar, and it occurred concurrently.

As the senators assembled after the pivotal 1974 election, three major changes were introduced and adopted. The Democratic majority decided, at the urging of Dick Clark of Iowa, that its caucus should vote by secret ballot for committee chairs, a fundamental change. A Senate resolution was passed guaranteeing junior senators a staff of three, thereby removing the allocation of staffers from the committee chair's control. And the caucuses of both parties agreed to open most committee and conference meetings to the public. Although most of the Senate's reform of its committees had occurred earlier than in the House, it had lagged behind on the question of making its proceedings public and of submitting chairs to election. Next, the Senate embarked on its final campaign against the filibuster.

Like the new House members' insistence on interviewing the committee chairmen, the Senate's concurrent decision in early 1975 to challenge its cloture rule once again, after several failures in the 1960s, marked the culmination of the reformers' campaign in the upper chamber. At this point, however, reform of cloture was more symbolic than real. Cloture had become less important to reformers because the filibuster's effectiveness as the ultimate weapon of southern conservatives had diminished by the late 1960s, after the civil rights and voting rights measures had become law. In fact, despite the availability of an actual or threatened filibuster on the part of conservative southern Democrats, Lyndon Johnson's Great Society legislation had been enacted. Ironically, the filibuster was now being wielded by liberals themselves as a way of countering measures from President Nixon and President Ford, and it was being invoked more frequently than before and on a variety of issues unrelated to civil rights.

Nevertheless, reformers in the Senate still considered the filibuster and its ability to paralyze the Senate an undesirable and antimajoritarian device that needed to be curbed, if not eliminated. A debate ensued in the new session that had all the drama of a showdown, ending on 5 March 1975, when the vote required for cloture was reduced from two-thirds to three-fifths, that is, from 67 to 60. Although the complete eradication of the practice by requiring a simple majority to end debate had proven to be more than the Senate could swallow, the easing of the required supermajority was still a victory and a breakthrough.[32] Since fewer votes were needed to shut off debate, the filibuster became less of an obstacle to the passage of legislation and the smooth functioning of the Senate. And since the southerners no longer needed it to obstruct civil rights initiatives, the device lost all of its menace.

With the collapse of the last of the four pillars of the Solid South, southern politics, not just Congress, had been reformed, even transformed. For the Democratic Party's claim to be the protector of the South and the embodiment of its interests and identity could not be invalidated until the southern Democrats' power base in the committee system of Congress had been demolished. Now that the party had been deprived of its ability to wield disproportionate power through the committee structure and of its capacity to function as a unit through the Southern Caucus and the Senate filibuster, the Democrats' Solid South simply evaporated.

But if southern Democrats could no longer wield power in Congress by the late 1970s, what could they offer instead? How could they persuade the party's white voters—who were experimenting with voting independent or defecting outright to the Republicans—to remain loyal to a political party that had once been considered vital to the South but was no longer indispensable?

15

The Emergence of a
Two-Party South since 1980

Increased Democratic majorities in Congress and the consequent dismantling of the committee system were not the only outcomes of the Watergate scandals and the resulting constitutional crisis. The 1976 presidential contest resulted in a Democratic victory with the election of Jimmy Carter, who ran against Washington as a fresh and untainted outsider. At the very moment when the congressional power of the southern Democrats had finally been destroyed and the Solid South dissolved, the first southerner from the Deep South since Zachary Taylor in 1848 entered the White House. Andrew Johnson came from Tennessee. Woodrow Wilson had been born in the South but ran from New Jersey where he had lived most of his life. Harry Truman hailed from Missouri. And Lyndon Johnson was from Texas. All of these presidents with a southern patina came from the Rim South or had spent most of their adult lives outside the region. But Jimmy Carter was a farmer from Plains, Georgia, who had never even held national office.

The irony was not hard to miss. But it was explained by the extraordinary events of the Watergate saga and the resignation of Richard Nixon, followed by the hasty and questionable pardon granted him by his successor. Public disgust at the corruption of Washington insiders continued into the next presidential election, when a conservative California Republican, who had served two terms as governor of his state and twice sought the Republican nomination, finally won it and then went on to defeat Carter, whom he now depicted as another failed Washington insider. Ronald Reagan was reelected in 1984, and his two terms in the presidency proved to be decisive for the ensuing transformation of the South's political system.

In 1980, when Reagan sent Carter back to Georgia, southern politics was in the midst of major changes as the region struggled to replace its previous system of one-party domination. That there would be a replacement was already evident; in fact, it was unavoidable. But exactly what form it might take was far from clear. Ever since the passage of the Voting Rights Act, the Democrats had been in the process of reconstituting themselves, as they sought to attract and absorb millions of new black voters. For the party of the Solid South, the party of white supremacy, it was no easy matter to become biracial. At the same time, the Republican Party was also reconstituting itself. Prior to the 1970s, its base of support had been confined to the Rim South states of the Upper South and Texas, where it was a more moderate alternative to the overwhelmingly conservative and segregationist Democrats. Republicans also did well in presidential elections, but they proved unable to penetrate down to the congressional and state levels. They needed, not only to appeal to traditional Democrats, but also to build and grow as an organization. Both parties needed, in effect, to reconstitute themselves by developing a different kind of agenda and appealing for support from unfamiliar sources.

By 1980, these developments were under way, although the eventual outcome was far from obvious. Two possibilities presented themselves. In the first scenario, the region would be dominated once again by one or the other of the existing major parties. The Democrats might keep their existing supporters and add the extra voters so as to remain preeminent. Alternatively, the Republicans might manage to win over traditional Democrats in such numbers that the Democratic Party would be left with little more than a restricted base of African American supporters.

The second possible outcome was a competitive party system, in which the Democrats lost much of their previous support to a more conservative Republican Party but nevertheless retained enough former Democrats, along with the recently enfranchised black voters, to make the party competitive but not dominant. In this case, neither party would be in the ascendancy, and a two-party system, with the parties well balanced, would arise instead. Neither party would become a permanent majority, but each would see itself as a minority trying to win majorities, election by election.

The reorganization of southern politics was therefore a complicated process whose outcome was by no means assured. Was one-party dominance an unchanging and impermeable feature of southern politics that would continue, although in a different form? Or was the region about to enter a new and unfamiliar era of competitive party politics, fostering, in effect, a two-party system? By 1980, after spending fifteen years dismantling the Solid South, the region's politics had gone through a process of dealignment, in which the previous alignment, or relationship, between the parties had broken up or dissolved. This was the destructive part of the transition. What followed next was the constructive part, the realignment of the parties on a different basis. And it had not yet begun when Reagan assumed the presidency in 1980. In other words, the parties were not what they were before. But what would they become? How would they realign? The answer was as yet unknown.

The source of this indeterminacy was the problem the Democrats faced in trying to hold together the two basic components of their fragile coalition—the white supporters, who had formed the backbone of the party when it was the instrument of white supremacy and southern solidarity, and the reenfranchised black voters. The party had succeeded during the 1970s in its attempt to offset its previous but now-dwindling core constituency of whites by running candidates at the state level, like Carter and Askew, who were flexible and moderate on race and able simultaneously to promote economic development and provide competent, efficient government. At the congressional level, too, Democrats had to walk a tightrope. Increasingly reliant on black votes, they also had to retain the support of white working people and businessmen. To do this, they had to "straddle" on the issues and policies of the day. As David Bowen, a successful six-term Democrat from the Mississippi Delta, explained in 1982, "I never did anything to alienate the black support that I had. I never did anything to alienate the business support that I had." But he acknowledged that this "was not a very doctrinaire sort of pattern. . . . No one could really stamp me as a liberal or a conservative."[1]

The task of these nondoctrinaire Democratic moderates was not as impossible as it seemed because the most conservative and most racist Democrats had already left the party. They had either switched to the Republicans permanently when Goldwater and Nixon were the party's presidential candidates between 1964 and 1972, or they had backed Wallace's third-party campaigns in 1968 and 1972, calling themselves independents because they no longer considered themselves Democrats but were not ready to cast their lot with the still unproven and somewhat alien Republicans. Nevertheless, the Democrats' task was beset with difficulties. How long could they hold together such a discordant coalition by straddling the issues and walking a political tightrope? Besides, what was the future for a party cobbled together so opportunistically and lacking an agenda and firmly held beliefs? Yet if they failed to keep a substantial portion of their former white and moderate-to-conservative constituency, the party would become a permanent minority. In that case, southern politics would realign along racial lines, with Republican domination the almost certain result.

The possibility that the Democrats might be reduced to a marginalized minority was countered by a stubborn political reality. The Democratic Party was a well-established political institution in the South. It had, after all, been the only political party of any consequence for more than fifty years. It still possessed influence and experience and it could still count on the allegiance of many southerners as the region's traditional protector. Its Republican rival had done well in the South at the presidential level in the 1960s and 1970s. But the party had made little progress in congressional races. By contrast, the fact that the Democrats controlled Congress almost continuously from the 1960s through the 1980s meant that continuing to elect Democrats made political sense. Because the party held power and controlled the committees, southerners had a good chance of wielding influence on those committees and getting their constituents' interests met. So why send a Republican to Washington and relinquish the access and influence enjoyed by a Democratic member of Congress?

Besides the disincentive to replace a Democrat with a Republican, there was also the problem of defeating the Democrat in the first place. Democrats held all but a few of the South's seats in the House and almost all of them in the Senate in the 1960s and 1970s. They were incumbents, and a candidate running for reelection enjoys many advantages—name recognition and status; greater ability to raise funds; and appreciation and gratitude from individuals and interests in his or her district who have benefited from favors and influence. During these two decades, incumbent Democrats were involved in two-thirds of all southern congressional elections, and they won 97 percent of them. With the Democrats still ensconced, voters were strongly inclined to reelect them. Equally important, the still-entrenched Democrats could count on a continuing supply of candidates who would know in advance that the party offered assurances of support and experience in running an effective campaign, not to mention an odds-on likelihood of victory. Consequently, the pool of qualified candidates was large and showed little signs of drying up, even into the 1980s. The Democratic Party was still "the only game in town," and anybody with ambition for public office and a political career was bound to gravitate toward the region's traditional party and seek its endorsement. The sibling political scientists, Earl and Merle Black, who are the acknowledged authorities on modern southern politics, have called this "the Democratic Smother" because it stifled the Republicans' ability to develop and grow.

The Republicans, by contrast, lacked these institutional assets of the Democrats. They presented an electoral alternative but had little to show for it. They had made serious inroads at the presidential level, a phenomenon that political scientists began to label a "split-level realignment." But outside a few Rim South states, little progress had been made by the end of the 1970s in undermining the Democrats' domination of the region's congressional delegation and its state governments.

A decade or so later, however, the South's political landscape had been transformed. The critical element in this change was the shift in party affiliation by most conservative whites and many moderates during the twelve years in which Reagan controlled the presidency for two terms and then George H. W. Bush for one. Reagan was an avowed conservative, and an unusually sunny and upbeat one, who identified the Republican Party nationally with conservatism. And those southerners who were of a conservative disposition, and there were large numbers of them, found him and his political inclinations and beliefs particularly attractive. In 1980, only 40 percent of southern white conservatives identified themselves as Republicans, yet eight years later 60 percent did so.[2] Meanwhile, 84 percent of conservative whites as well as 59 percent of those who called themselves moderates, together making up over 80 percent of the southern white electorate, voted for Reagan and Bush in the three presidential elections of the 1980s. Knowing how important a viable presence in the South was for the creation of Republican national majorities, Reagan often recalled to southern audiences that he knew "what it's like to pull that Republican lever for the first time because I used to be a Democrat myself. But I can tell you—it only hurts for a minute."[3] Evidently, millions of southern voters were able to pluck up their courage and make the switch.

Reagan's conservatism was well known before he became the Republican nominee, and so were his racial views. At the outset of his 1980 campaign, he made it clear to conservative white southerners that they could rely on him to be sympathetic on racial issues. It was significant that he kicked off his campaign as the nominee with a rally in Mississippi at the Neshoba County fair in Philadelphia, the small town where local officials had been involved in the notorious slaying of three civil rights workers during Freedom Summer in 1964. Ten thousand whites greeted the Republican candidate with "thunderous applause," especially when

Ronald Reagan delivering a speech while president. Reagan's presidency, 1980–88, provided the catalyst for the rise of the Republican Party to a position in southern politics where it was competitive with the Democrats. Library of Congress, Prints and Photographs Division.

he told them: "I believe in states' rights. I believe in people doing as much as they can at the private level." If elected, he would "restore to states and local governments the power that properly belongs to them."[4] Code words like "states' rights" and "local control," accompanied by Reagan's always genial and avuncular manner of expressing views that were far from innocent or kindly, made clear where he stood on an issue that was still fundamental to the region's life and politics.

Reagan's proclivities on the other traditional ingredients of late twentieth-century American conservatism were made abundantly clear, and often quite memorable, by the Republican candidate, both in the campaign and once he was elected. His knee-jerk contempt for the national government was indicated by his oft-quoted pledge to "take the lead in getting the government off the backs of the people of the United States and turning you loose." And he harped constantly on the refrain about government being "the problem, not the solution." To curb and diminish the federal government, he invoked the conservative mantra of cutting taxes and government spending and programs. And, as expected, he paid homage to a stronger military, soon calling the Soviet Union "the evil empire" and implementing a massive arms buildup by the middle of the decade. This was "red meat" for southerners, who had a long-established tradition of support for the military and who stood to gain considerably from greater arms purchases since the region's economy had become increasingly involved in weapons production during the Cold War.

What was different about Republican conservatism under Reagan was his endorsement of the so-called Religious Right, which had surged in the 1970s and was becoming a political force through its opposition to abortion, its demands to "bring prayer back into the schools," and later its aversion to gays and lesbians and the recognition of their rights. Unlike Jimmy Carter, who was a born-again Christian, Reagan never even went to church. Yet the Moral Majority, the Christian Coalition, and other large and highly politicized evangelical organizations threw their energies into Reagan's campaign in 1980 and again in 1984. This shift of allegiance increased the Republican vote considerably in the South, where evangelical Christianity had long been a feature of its life and identity and was growing stronger in the widespread reaction to the permissive 1960s and 1970s.

The religious and cultural issues of the Religious Right also cut across the lines of class and occupation, giving the Republicans access to ordinary people who might otherwise have felt uneasy about affiliating with a party of the conservative and the well-to-do, in effect the "country club set." By defining these issues broadly as "family values" and "cultural values," the Republicans secured a conservative ally among working-class as well as middle-class people, an ally that was vital for the party in the South, and also in the nation, during the 1980s. Since then, the influence of this constituency has become even greater within the Republican Party.

During the Reagan-Bush years, the Republicans were succeeding in their campaign to replace the Democrats as the repository of southern conservatism and whiteness. These two ingredients had defined the Democratic Party of the Solid South. If the Republicans could persuade southern voters that they were the party of whites and conservatives (and the party's conservatism was now not only antigovernment but also religious and cultural), they would have established their credentials as a respectable and reliable southern party. And they might even be able to marginalize the Democrats by reducing them to a remnant consisting of blacks and liberals.

The realignment of conservative whites as Republicans was not accomplished on purely racial grounds, however. There were other developments in the South that facilitated this rearrangement of southern voters and parties. In February 1976, the *New York Times* ran a series of four front-page articles on the dramatic social and economic changes occurring in the region that warranted renaming the South, along with the Southwest, the "Sunbelt." While the civil rights movement was capturing the headlines in the 1960s, a little-noticed transformation was taking place as the southern economy and population grew and diversified. In 1980, 40 percent of the Defense Department's budget was spent in the South, and new industries were moving into the region. One of them was the space program, also funded by the federal government. Its five centers were located in such places as Houston in Texas, Huntsville in Alabama, and Cape Canaveral in Florida, and much of the research it required was allocated to southern universities. After the oil crisis of 1973, greater reliance was placed on domestic production, which was heavily concentrated in Texas, Louisiana, and Oklahoma. And other industries followed, such as chemicals and aircraft building. They were lured to relocate by a business-friendly and warmer environment where trade unions were scarce and state governments offered incentives such as tax breaks, land to build on, and publicly financed social programs and facilities. Banking and insurance and numerous other service-based industries established operations in the South during these years, soon to be joined by information technology. By comparison with the deindustrializing North, especially the Midwest and Great Lakes regions, which were being derided as the "Rustbelt" and the "Snowbelt," the South began to seem like a new land of warmth and opportunity.

This southward movement involved people too. The region's population grew from 56 million in 1970 to 68 million a decade later and 84 million by 2000. Much of this growth came from in-migration, from the North as well as from Mexico and Cuba and other parts of the Caribbean and Latin America. For the first time since the early nineteenth century, the South gained more migrants than it lost. Even African Americans began to move south. Soon more arrived each year than left. Moreover, the character of this migration was different, as younger, better-educated people, mainly from the North in this case, moved in. They were business executives and managers, salesmen, office workers, and professionals employed in the service and technological industries proliferating throughout the changing South. And they tended overwhelmingly to live in the metropolitan areas, particularly in the new and expanding suburbs. This ambitious and confident new population was not encumbered by historic loyalty to the Democratic Party, and they did not need Ronald Reagan to reassure them about pulling the Republican lever. They were upwardly mobile suburbanites, and they voted Republican for the same reasons as their counterparts outside the South.

Although the Republicans controlled the executive branch in the 1980s, they proved unable to convert this advantage into a similar run of successes in congressional elections or in state contests in the South. They were still very much a minority in southern politics and government. In 1980, Republicans controlled 45 percent of the region's combined 22 Senate seats and 11 governorships. Twelve years later, in 1992, the numbers were pretty much the same. Similarly, in the House of Representatives, the Republicans won 39 of the South's 116 seats in 1980, and the number was exactly the same in 1990. They had not been able to capitalize on their considerable increase in 1980 when the Republican Party had seemed to achieve a breakthrough in the Senate and governors' races to accompany their capture of the White House. Furthermore, only 416 of the 1,782 southern state legislators were Republican in 1988, a mere 23 percent.[5]

Even though the GOP had not increased its share of the offices, it had nevertheless become an established presence within the southern political world. Its portion of between a quarter and a third of the offices in Congress and the states was therefore unlikely to decline. The question was whether it would increase. And the answer was not long in coming, as the Republicans made dramatic increases by the mid-1990s. In fact, the off-year election of 1994 proved to be a defining, a critical, election, not just in southern political history but in the nation's as well.

Two years earlier, in 1992, a Democrat from the South, Bill Clinton of Arkansas, won the presidency with just 43 percent of the popular vote. A third party, organized around the candidacy of Ross Perot, a maverick Texas businessman, whose primary issue was a drastic reduction of the federal deficit, had captured almost 19 percent of the popular vote, much of it in the South. Although his 20 million votes earned Perot not a single vote in the Electoral College, they did cut into the first George Bush's support, certainly in the South but nationwide as well. A minority president from the start, Clinton stumbled badly in his first two years, mainly on account of his ambitious but poorly managed attempt to reform the nation's inadequate system of private medical insurance. With Clinton weakened and unpopular, the Republican whip, Newt Gingrich, sensed an opportunity in the upcoming 1994 election to increase the GOP's strength in the House, possibly giving it a majority of seats and therefore control.

Since becoming the second most powerful Republican in the House when he became whip in 1989, Gingrich, who hailed from a well-heeled suburban district outside Atlanta, had campaigned tirelessly to build the party in the lower chamber. By 1994, he was ready to initiate and coordinate a national campaign to win control. It was organized around a list of promises that he called the "Contract with America," which contained a number of familiar conservative priorities and shibboleths. Signers of the contract promised, if they won control of Congress, to end "government that is too big, too intrusive, and too easy with the people's money" and to become "a Congress that respects the values and shares the faith of the American family." To achieve this aim, they pledged, within the first hundred days, to enact a series of laws, the most important of which would cut taxes and spending, protect the family, cut welfare benefits and force recipients to work after two years, impose term limits on members of Congress, and increase the military budget.

Although his opponents ridiculed it as "a contract on America," Gingrich's idea of a programmatic, nationally coordinated party campaign for Congress was unprecedented in American political history. Traditionally, presidential nominees run on platforms, but the hundreds of congressional candidates shape their own campaign agendas around the needs of their district. Gingrich's plan envisaged "something completely different."

The campaign itself was unprecedented, and so were its results. The Democrats were trounced. They lost 55 seats, allowing their opponents to win control of the House, 230–204, for the first time since 1954. Republicans also regained the Senate, which they had held from 1980 to 1986 during most of Reagan's presidency. A crucial part of Gingrich's formula for the election was a concerted effort to break the Democrats' hold on the South. And here again, the Republican gains were astonishing. In the 1992 election, the party had gained 9 seats and reduced the Democrats' 77–39 advantage to a level where their majority was vulnerable. In 1994, they defeated 16 more Democratic incumbents, which meant that they now controlled the region's House delegation, 64–61, or 51 percent. Not since their comeback in 1874, a century earlier during Reconstruction, had the Democrats been reduced to less than a majority in the South's delegation in the House. Nevertheless, in 1996, they slipped even further

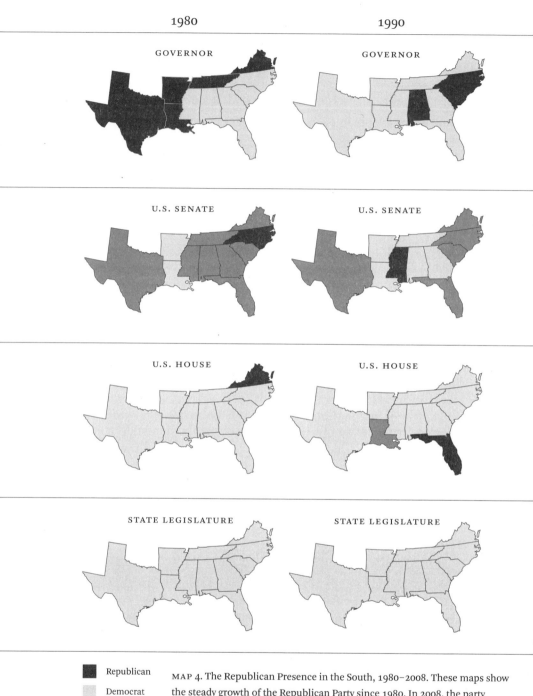

1980

1990

GOVERNOR

GOVERNOR

U.S. SENATE

U.S. SENATE

U.S. HOUSE

U.S. HOUSE

STATE LEGISLATURE

STATE LEGISLATURE

■ Republican

Democrat

▨ Split

MAP 4. The Republican Presence in the South, 1980–2008. These maps show the steady growth of the Republican Party since 1980. In 2008, the party suffered a setback, losing three states in the presidential election (Virginia, North Carolina, and Florida) that curbed its previously upward trajectory. The maps reflect the outcome of the November elections in each year.

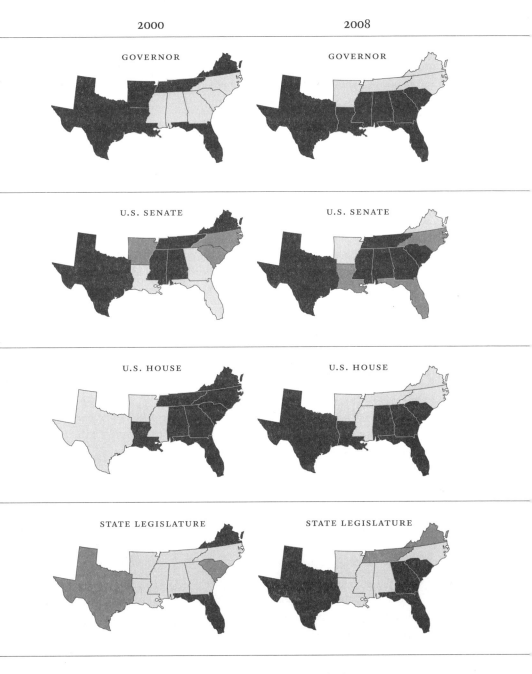

2000   **2008**

GOVERNOR   GOVERNOR

U.S. SENATE   U.S. SENATE

U.S. HOUSE   U.S. HOUSE

STATE LEGISLATURE   STATE LEGISLATURE

SOURCES: *Almanac of American Politics*, 1982, 1992, and 2002, for data on 1980, 1990, and 2000; National Conference of State Legislatures for data on state legislative and gubernatorial elections of 1980, 1990, 2000, and 2008; and U.S. Senate and House websites for data on 2008.

behind, as the Republican Party increased its lead to 71–54, even though it dropped a few seats elsewhere in the nation. Ever since 1933, Democrats in the North had relied on a heavy majority from the South to enable them to control Congress, provided they themselves won about a third of the seats in the rest of the country. Alarmingly, that cushion was no longer available to them.[6]

The off-year election of 1994 marked a breakthrough for the Republicans. In the South, their victory was even more significant, nothing less than a watershed in southern political history. The Democrats no longer controlled the region's delegation in the House or the Senate, nor even its governorships, since they now held just five of the eleven in the former Confederacy. How had this astonishing reversal happened? Certainly, Gingrich's "Republican Contract with America" campaign had been a triumph, attributable to the enormous energy and organizational skill that infused it. But several elements in the political situation came together to make it possible, and all were successfully exploited.

By the 1990s, a near majority of southern voters identified themselves as Republicans in the wake of the dozen years of the Reagan and Bush administrations. The party had not managed to capitalize on this realignment among the voters by producing a corresponding increase in election successes that could give them a majority of the offices and therefore political power. But the party's prospects were obviously improving. There was a growing sense that the Republicans were on the rise and that the political momentum was running in their favor. As a result, financial backing for Republican campaigns was proving easier to obtain, and in sufficient amounts, so that Republicans were outspending the Democrats by the early 1990s. With funding available and with better prospects of winning, far more people were prepared to run for office, and so the party's candidate pool grew considerably. The cumulative effect of these developments was to give Republicans a competitive edge that they had never even approximated previously.

A crucial ingredient in the GOP surge during the 1990s was the reapportionment of congressional districts after the 1990 census. Because the region's population had grown by yet another 10 million during the 1980s, it gained an extra nine seats. Obviously, these were new, and therefore open, seats. With no incumbent to deal with, Republicans could well win them. In addition, the redrawing of district lines that occurred simultaneously had resulted in the carving out of one district, maybe two, in each state, except Arkansas, that contained a black majority. A district like this was certain to return a Democrat. More important, he or she was likely to be an African American, thereby ensuring that the number of black representatives would grow. In the 1970s, there were just two blacks in Congress, Andrew Young of Georgia and Barbara Jordan of Texas. By 1990, that number had increased to five, although still a mere 4 percent of the South's representation, hardly a fair share. Creating black-majority districts might make it possible for more blacks to be elected. At the same time, the concentrating of black voters in one or two districts meant that, in most states, the rest of the black population would be dispersed across the remaining districts, leaving them in a minority that had just been reduced in size. In that case, those districts could well be easier for the Republicans to win. The end result was likely to be that black Democrats could win one district, two if they were lucky, in each state. And the Republicans would take the rest.

The post-1990 reapportionment rearranged most congressional districts. In fact, it was the most disruptive redistricting since the 1960s, when every southern district had to be redrawn in the wake of the Voting Rights Act and the Supreme Court's *Baker v. Carr* decision of 1962, which struck down malapportioned electoral districts. The destabilization caused by the extensive redrawing of district lines, the creation of nine new districts, and the diminution of the black presence in most white-majority districts, all presented opportunities for the Republicans to achieve a breakthrough.

The potential for the Republicans was further evident to party strategists when they realized that a large number of districts already existed that their party should be able to carry. These were the districts that had given landslide victories of over 60 percent to the elder Bush when he was the Republican presidential candidate in 1988. In effect, Democratic members of Congress were sitting in seats that should be Republican. If a Republican presidential candidate could sweep these districts, why not a Republican candidate for Congress? In 1988, 53 of the South's 116 congressional seats were carried by George H. W. Bush with landslide majorities. Yet the party carried only 30 of these in the 1990 elections for Congress. After redistricting, however, Bush won landslides two years later in 65 of the South's congressional districts that now numbered 125. By specifically targeting these winnable seats in 1994, the Republicans managed to take 55 of the 65. Over the course of two elections, 1992 and 1994, the Republicans had increased their victories in presidential landslide districts from 30 in 1990 to 55 in 1994. And this focusing of their attention and resources contributed significantly to their breakthrough in 1994.[7]

This Republican breakthrough turned out to be decisive and not just a temporary outcome of an unusual election organized around an unprecedented campaign plan. During the rest of the decade, the GOP continued its ascent. Despite losing seats here and there in ensuing congressional and gubernatorial elections, the party won 71 of the South's 125 House seats in 2000, retaining its slight majority in the region over the previous three elections. In the 2000 elections for Senate and governor, the Republicans held 19 of the 33 positions, or almost 58 percent, the same percentage as in 1994. Meanwhile, their share of the state legislatures stood at 43 percent, not yet a majority but more than 1994 (37 percent) and substantially more than their 18 percent of state senates and 24 percent of state lower houses in 1986.[8]

During the 1990s, the realignment of southern politics was completed. A slim majority of southern voters now identified themselves as Republicans, and the party controlled a majority, in the mid-50 percent range, of the region's major national and statewide offices. Ironically, this fundamental political change resulted in the newly emergent party acquiring the defining characteristics of the old Democratic Party. In a region that was widely understood to be conservative, the Republicans were clearly the conservative party in the realigned political order of the 1990s. It was of course not a replica of the Democratic Party of the Solid South, because its conservatism was more ideological in tone and it included the Religious Right, which had not come into existence as a self-conscious and organized political force before the late 1970s, at the earliest. The Republican Party was also the party of whites. Although the organization was not "the white man's party" or the party of white supremacy, the GOP vote was overwhelmingly white, at least 90 percent of it in fact. Moreover, the origins of the late twentieth-century version of southern Republicanism lay in the anti–civil rights candidacy of Barry Goldwater in 1964 and in the attractiveness of the Republicans as the alternative in the 1970s, once blacks identified solidly with the Democrats. And the various "southern strategies" of the national party, first under Nixon and then under Reagan and Bush, were aimed at encouraging southern whites to repudiate the Democrats and join the more congenial Republicans.

All the same, the reasons why these whites voted Republican were not entirely attributable to racial prejudice. Several other incentives for supporting the party played a role. For example, its conservative economic outlook might have had a strong appeal and so might its position on religious and family values, or perhaps its social status as the party of middle-class suburbanites. And the Republicans' constituency was far more diverse and differentiated than had been its Democratic predecessor. It contained ethnic elements—the Spanish-speaking population, primarily Cubans in Florida and Mexicans in Texas. And its support from the white-collar middle class that had arisen in the South since the 1960s to become around 46 percent of the region's population by 1996 made the Republican Party a very different political entity than the heavily rural and small-town Democratic Party of the mid-twentieth century and before.[9]

Nevertheless, even though race has become less salient in southern politics since the 1960s and no longer defines the two parties in indelible terms, it is still a major factor. When party candidates and strategists calculate what they need to do to win a campaign, race automatically becomes a crucial element in their planning. Because the black vote is almost certain to be polled for the Democratic candidate, each party has to base its electoral strategy on an estimation of how much of the white vote it will need in order to obtain a majority. Depending on the size of the black population, each party will require a particular proportion of the white vote. Even in black-majority districts, Democratic candidates will have to win some of the white vote, both as a safety net and as evidence that the party is biracial in its identity and support. This stubborn electoral reality keeps alive the racial component of southern politics, even though race as a primary campaign issue or as a determinant of party identity has abated during the three decades of party realignment.

Race was, of course, conspicuous in the creation of black-majority congressional districts (the awkward and confusing term "majority-minority district" is sometimes used to describe them). Despite regaining the vote, African Americans had elected only a few candidates of their own out of a total southern delegation in the House of 116, a woefully inadequate representation. The upshot was an attempt to form districts that had a good chance of electing an African American to Congress. With black Democrats and civil rights organizations taking the initiative, efforts were made in state redistricting commissions to ensure that one district at least would be able to elect a member who was especially preferred by blacks or was black. In this project, they were joined by the Justice Department's voting rights division, claiming that such districts would prevent the dilution of the black vote and ensure the rights of blacks as voters to a fair representation. Also supportive were Republicans, who recognized the considerable advantage for their party in concentrating the black vote in one district and dispersing the rest in the other districts at levels below 30 percent. Rather cynically, Republicans anticipated that their own party would benefit from further identification of the Democratic Party with African Americans if there were a dozen members of Congress who were black. The result was an alliance of strange bedfellows, black Democrats and white Republicans, for the purpose of creating black-majority districts that could elect black Democrats.

The redrawn congressional maps produced twelve new black-majority districts. All of them were won by black Democrats in the very next election in 1992. At the same time, however, the Republicans gained nine seats overall, and then another sixteen in 1994. This result has led some observers like Earl and Merle Black to conclude that the compressing of black voters into a few districts "radically reduced the number of black voters in many other districts." As a result, "Many Republicans could now run for Congress without having to attract such overwhelming percentages of the white vote." Since 46 percent of southern districts contained black populations of less than 15 percent in 1992, compared to 60 percent with a black minority greater than 15 percent in the 1980s, Republicans running in white-majority districts now had an electoral advantage that was significant.[10]

On the other hand, Bernard Grofman, a leading expert on voting rights and redistricting, has countered that the Republicans' ability to amass votes was so invincible in 1994 and in subsequent congressional elections that they would have won most of those black-minority districts anyway and thus gained control of the southern delegation and of the entire House. So the contribution of the black-majority districts to the Democrats' losses in the early to mid-1990s is perhaps not clear.[11] But, even if it can be shown that they were detrimental, the Democrats cannot undo the change, nor would they want to. The vote of the overwhelming majority of southern African Americans is currently committed to the Democratic Party, and their understandable need to have blacks in Congress to represent them has to be respected and met.

The rise of the Republicans to majority status in the South during the 1990s presents the Democrats with a dilemma that is not exactly unfamiliar—how to hold together its biracial coalition without losing its moderate whites to the Republicans. This was the difficulty it faced in the late 1970s before the Reagan years. Until the 1990s, the party had shown how skillful its leaders were in managing a strange and unknown phenomenon in southern political history—a biracial party. Democratic incumbency within the southern states and the party's lengthy experience in grooming candidates and running elections had protected the experiment with biracial politics and given it breathing room in the 1970s and 1980s.

In the 1990s, however, that institutional advantage—"the Democratic

Smother"—evaporated. Republicans became the incumbents and their party a generally accepted feature of the region's political scene. Deprived of the asset of incumbency, their Democratic opponents have had to struggle to keep their party competitive, in spite of its biracial foundations and its liberal-to-moderate outlook. Sadly, this biracial party has not been hailed as a long-awaited breakthrough in southern politics and race relations, an innovation as welcome and essential to the region as the emergence of competitive two-party politics. Instead, the newly constituted Democratic Party may well find it difficult to remain influential in a region that is still more consistently conservative than most of the non-South.

But that remains to be seen. The Democrats did manage to stay competitive with their Republican opponents throughout most of the region into the new century. And, even after a decade of Republican superiority, the election of 2008 showed that several southern states, such as Virginia, North Carolina, and Florida, could be taken by the Democrats at the presidential level as well as in statewide contests for governor and senator. Quite possibly, the South's new two-party system could become more closely competitive in the future.

CONCLUSION

The South has undergone a thorough transformation over the past century. Fundamental change came first to the region's economy. After the initial stimulus of federal military expenditures during and after World War II, the southern economy took off, resulting in the emergence of the "New South," which had been anticipated so desperately ever since the Civil War. This renovated South contained manufacturing firms and industrial enterprises, as well as considerably expanded commercial and banking operations. From the 1940s to the 1970s, the region metamorphosed from the "Cotton Belt" into the "Sunbelt." Meanwhile, cities grew and suburbs sprawled, in order to provide housing for southerners who were moving away from small towns and villages, as well as for employees of national corporations who were transferring into the region in order to establish branch offices and manage new plants.

Economic development of this scope can occur without parallel changes in the social and political order. Contemporary China is an obvious example. But this was not the case in the South. Mainly through pressure inside the region on the part of black southerners, who struggled to bring their exclusion and oppression to an end, the region's system of racial domination was overthrown. Aided by liberal allies, white as well as black, from outside the South, national legislation in the form of the Civil Rights and Voting Rights Acts to prohibit formal and legal discrimination was passed. And these acts of Congress were supplemented by a series of Supreme Court decisions that confirmed and elaborated the new laws. With African Americans regaining the vote, the South's political structure, which had been created to sustain and protect the region's reactionary racial order, was no longer necessary. As a result, it too collapsed, though not all at once.

The enfranchisement of millions of voters (and there were many whites among them, not just blacks) expanded massively the restricted electorate imposed on the region at the turn of the century. This outcome made possible the emergence of organized political opposition. The presence of an opposing party to challenge the southern Democrats' one-hundred-year monopoly meant that the Solid South was no longer viable, or even appropriate. In its place, a system of two or more parties was almost certain to arise.

During the 1970s and 1980s, as we saw in chapters 14 and 15, this was precisely what happened. The Republicans saw an opportunity in the South after the Voting Rights Act and proceeded to shake up the Democrats with a dose of unfamiliar electoral competition. Although not unexpected, the ensuing contest nevertheless took a strange turn. Instead of finding themselves challenged from the left, as V. O. Key and others had anticipated in the 1940s and 1950s, the Democratic establishment was attacked from the right, from a party that was conservative rather than liberal or progressive. Because the Democratic Party at the national level had become increasingly liberal after the New Deal, the South's newly enfranchised black voters gravitated naturally toward the Democrats, even though the party in the South had been the bastion of white supremacy. Knowing that they could not win the support of black voters, the Republicans proceeded to court the whites already in the Democratic Party, that is, the former segregationists and traditional supporters of the region's economic and social order, who might feel more comfortable in a conservative party.

In the electoral struggle that resulted, the Republicans had to attract a following almost from scratch, and the Democrats had to retain their existing source of support and try to reconcile it with their new allies among African American voters. Both parties would, in actuality, become new and unfamiliar features of the southern political scene. But they would arise and develop along quite different lines. The Republicans had to create and build a party, whereas the Democrats had to hold what they already had and fuse it with their recently acquired base of support among African Americans. Put another way, the Republicans had to create a new party organization, while the Democrats had to forge a new biracial party.

This complicated political process was taking place within the South, of course, but its implications were not confined to the region. Because it had a crucial national bearing as well, the leadership of both parties could not stand by and just watch events in the South unfold. For decades, the South had been solidly Democratic, but now the region was in play and could well slip out of the Democrats' control and into the hands of their Republican rivals. If that happened, the Republicans would receive an enormous boost, which might even lead to their challenging the Democratic domination of Congress since the 1950s. Consequently, each party had, in effect, to adopt a "southern strategy" during the 1970s and

1980s in order to influence the partisan reorganization and realignment occurring in the South. And each party's approach to the South was undertaken in the context of the ongoing interparty contest at the national level, either to maintain their traditional advantage, which was the Democrats' objective, or to change the balance of forces, as the Republicans hoped to do.

As chapter 15 explained, the outcome of the struggle within the South was not just the creation of a Republican Party, but its rise and ascendancy thirty years later. After some notable success at the presidential level in the 1970s and 1980s, the party became increasingly competitive in congressional and state elections by the 1990s. As a result, the South's Republican delegation expanded in the 1990s, enabling it to contribute substantially to the party's brief dominance in Washington during much of the second Bush administration when it held the presidency as well as both houses of Congress.

The rise of the Republicans in the South shifted the balance of power in Washington in the national party's favor, and it also contributed to the sharpening of the differences between the two major parties that was occurring at the same time. The Republican Party's capture of the conservative wing of the southern Democratic Party strengthened its own conservative credentials and identity, and it forced the Democrats to redefine themselves in increasingly liberal terms. The Democrats' core constituency soon became, not the segregationist whites of earlier days, but liberal blacks, and the upshot has been the emergence of divergent parties in the South. For the Democrats, this has been problematic because they have had to restrict and confine their liberalism or else lose the support of moderate whites. As a result, the southern wing of the party has adopted a moderate, centrist strategy to keep it from becoming identified as overly liberal.

This trend toward defining the parties more sharply as conservative or liberal has, however, been proceeding a good deal more rapidly at the national level. Earlier in the twentieth century, when the Democratic Party had contained within its folds the conservative, Solid South Democrats, its ability to move decisively in a liberal-to-progressive direction was always checked, as was evident from Harry Truman's presidency in the 1940s until Lyndon Johnson's in the 1960s. In this context, the national Republican Party was also pulled to the center, since its traditional conservative wing was never able to dominate the moderate Eisenhower–Nelson Rockefeller faction. With the factions within the two parties offsetting each other, the parties were kept in equipoise and drawn to the center. The result was two national parties that were not dramatically different from each other in terms of ideology and identity.

But the reconstitution of the South's parties in the 1970s and 1980s has meant that the national Democrats and Republicans were destabilized. In this fluid situation, the parties began to realign along more clearly divergent tracks, moving away from the center to become conservative or liberal. Now that they have become more ideologically consistent and coherent and party lines have become more rigid, the major parties are less able to collaborate. Naturally, a polarized, and far less cordial, politics is the result as the twenty-first century begins.

The recent emergence of a two-party system within the South, containing branches of the Republican and Democratic parties that are similar to and compatible with their counterparts in the rest of the country, has ended the incongruity of the region's politics. As we have seen, the South's political experience for most of America's history was as a region overwhelmingly committed to, and organized within, one of the country's major political parties. At first, the region was solidly in the camp of the Jeffersonian Republicans. Thereafter, the South was aligned with the Democratic Party for 150 years, from its inception under Jackson and Van Buren, with only a brief two-party phase in the 1830s and 1840s, which ended when the northern Whigs proved unreliable as allies. This exclusive affiliation with one of the national parties became habitual, because keeping the South politically united in the face of opposition to its system of racial domination was deemed essential, both within the South and in Washington.

Within the South itself, the slaveholders, who were a minority of the population, had to ensure that opposition to the institution of slavery itself as well as to the elite that benefited from the ownership of slaves did not assume organized political shape. Once slavery was abolished, the emergence of opposition parties (the Republicans during Reconstruction, the Greenbackers and other independents like the Virginia Readjusters in the 1880s, and the Populists in the 1890s) had to be countered vigorously by all means necessary, including fraud and violence. Eventually, opposition was eliminated altogether by law with the disfranchisement of virtually all African Americans around 1900 and the creation of a formal one-party system soon afterward. This draconian system organized all whites, except those who could not pay the required poll taxes or pass the compulsory literacy tests, into the Democratic Party in defense of white supremacy.

Outside the region as well, the South's vital interest had to be defended within a national polity that was often unsympathetic and, on occasion, quite hostile. The region's politicians had to find ways to operate effectively through the nation's political institutions. Because the South was part of the larger national political system, it could not simply retreat within its own borders and hope for the best. Instead, the South decided that it had to assert itself and act forcefully to protect what it considered its interests, and this is what it did for almost two hundred years.

The structure and institutions of the national government presented the South with opportunities to direct and expand its influence as long as it managed to coordinate its efforts and keep its members united. Without cohesion, its influence would naturally be dissipated. The first arena that offered the South leverage was the divided jurisdiction of the federal system between the central government and the states. Since states possessed sovereignty over all areas not assigned to the national government, these extensive state rights could be invoked to protect interests that were local. And this the South proceeded to do, pushing the scope of state jurisdiction and authority to the farthest extent possible, especially during the slavery era. This tactic did not, however, preclude the region's leaders from claiming in the 1850s that since slavery was an institution that was protected by the Constitution the federal government had to act on its behalf, particularly in the western territories prior to statehood.

Supplementing the constitutional structure of the federal system were the institutions of the federal government. And these also proved very useful to the South as it waged its struggle to protect itself. Most important, of course, was the national Democratic Party. Within the Democrats' organization in Congress, the southern delegation found itself in a majority from the years of Andrew Jackson until the 1930s. The southerners constituted the majority faction within the majority party before the Civil War. When the Democrats declined to a minority within Congress for the bulk of the period between Reconstruction and the New Deal, the southern Democrats continued to be the majority within it almost all the time. During this long spell of majority status, the South exerted its numerical influence within the party caucus to press for support of measures of importance to the region or to reject those that were considered inimical. Provided their ranks were cohesive, this numerical majority could wield enormous influence over the Democratic Party.

Their superior numbers within the Democratic Party also translated into institutional power through Congress's committee system. In the antebellum years, when the party controlled Congress almost all the time, southern Democrats were heavily represented on the major committees and were frequently the chairmen. But even when the party was in the minority, as in the early twentieth century, southerners had acquired so much seniority and experience because they were continually reelected that they dominated the committees and therefore the business of Congress. Ever since the reforms of the first decade of the century that had decentralized power from one or two bosses who had run each house in the 1880s and 1890s, the committees and their chairmen had become the drivers of Congress's legislative activity. And southerners moved aggressively and successfully to acquire seniority and expertise and thereby exert influence within the Democratic Party organization. When the Democrats controlled Congress, as they did on occasion, such as during the administrations of Woodrow Wilson and Franklin Roosevelt, they were strategically placed as committee chairmen to determine the course and the fate of the administration's legislative agenda.

Operating as a self-conscious minority, the South also made sure that it took advantage of whatever weapons of institutional obstruction were available to prevent undesirable political outcomes. Two devices proved particularly effective. The first was the two-thirds rule in the Democratic Party's presidential nominating conventions. In return for acquiescing in the nomination of Martin Van Buren in 1836, the southerners had insisted that, thereafter, a two-thirds majority would be required to endorse a nominee. This supermajority gave a dissatisfied minority of only one-third of the delegates the power to reject a possible nominee. Rarely did the southerners have to wield this veto, however, since the mere threat of it was sufficient to cause the convention to pass over a choice known to be unfavorable to the South. Over an entire century, from 1836 until 1936, this provision gave the southern delegates veto power over the selection of the Democrats' candidates.

Another mechanism that enabled an organized minority to veto or obstruct was the Senate's practice of filibuster. Arising from the Senate's coveted tradition of "unlimited debate," a supermajority of two-thirds, or more recently three-fifths (60 percent), has been required to shut off debate and bring a measure to a vote. Like the two-thirds rule for Democratic nominees, the mere threat of a filibuster has usually sufficed to ensure that a measure unpalatable to the South was not enacted, or even introduced in the first place. This device was frequently used from the 1930s to the 1960s, however, when the South's system of segregation and disfranchisement came under increasing attack. The availability of minority devices like the filibuster and the two-thirds rule enabled a bloc of adequate size and cohesion like the southern Democrats to manipulate and obstruct in order to protect its vital interests.

But all this has changed over the past forty years. Possessing two competitive parties and with no endangered interest or institution to protect, the South has no occasion and no need for the mechanisms and strategies it employed so relentlessly in the past. Since the South does not need to pursue unity, it is no longer an anomalous one-party region within a two-party nation. In other words, peculiar institutions, whether of the racial or the political kind, do not exist any more in the South. Yet, without these anomalous institutions that contributed so fundamentally to the distinctiveness, even the existence, of a particular region called the South, the question has to be raised: Is there still a South? Does the South still exist? This is a perplexing matter that contemporary residents and observers of the region have been pondering and weighing over the past thirty years. After this journey through the South's political history, the appropriate answer would seem to be, probably not. And, of course, if "the South" has ceased to exist, then so too has "the North."

NOTES

Chapter One

1 Sharp, *American Politics in the Early Republic*, 221.
2 For the Republicans' economic views, see McCoy, *Elusive Republic*, chaps. 6 and 7.
3 Broussard, *Southern Federalists*, 83.
4 Ibid., 80.
5 Mercer on mass education and suffrage, in Egerton, *Charles Fenton Mercer*, 125.
6 Cunningham, *Jeffersonian Republicans in Power*, 176.
7 William Brockenbrough to Joseph C. Cabell, 18 June 1801, in ibid., 278.
8 Risjord, *Old Republicans*, 161–74.
9 Banner, *To the Hartford Convention*, 340.
10 Hamilton, *Writings of James Monroe*, 6:3.
11 Jefferson to Philip Mazzei, 24 April 1796, in Koch and Peden, *Writings of Thomas Jefferson*, 537.
12 Moore, *Missouri Controversy*, 53n56.
13 Fehrenbacher, *Sectional Crisis and Southern Constitutionalism*, 19.
14 *Richmond Enquirer*, in ibid.
15 Jefferson to John Holmes, in Koch and Peden, *Writings of Thomas Jefferson*, 698.
16 Ibid.

Chapter Two

1 *Baton Rouge Gazette*, 25 October 1828, in Sydnor, *Development of Southern Sectionalism*, 193.
2 In 1828, the southern states were ten in number—Virginia, North Carolina, South Carolina, Georgia, Alabama, Mississippi, Louisiana, Kentucky, Tennessee, and Maryland. South Carolina did not record a popular vote because the state legislature still chose its presidential electors.
3 The 1828 election is assessed in Sydnor, *Development of Southern Sectionalism*, 193–94.
4 Ibid., 205–6.
5 Van Buren to Ritchie, 13 January 1827, in Remini, *Martin Van Buren and the Making of the Democratic Party*, 130–33.
6 Clay's speech in the Senate, 14 April 1834, in Remini, *Henry Clay, Statesman for the Union*, 459.
7 Philip Hone diary entry, quoted in ibid., 553.
8 Sydnor, *Development of Southern Sectionalism*, 316.
9 McCormick, *Second American Party System*, 14, 353.
10 Ibid., 14.
11 Ibid., 14, 353.

12 For more on the sources of Whig strength in the South, see Holt, *Rise and Fall of the American Whig Party*, 115–17, 214, table 20; and McCormick, *Second American Party System*, chaps. 5 and 6.

13 For Louisiana, see Sacher, *A Perfect War of Politics*, chaps. 1 and 2.

14 Quoted in Ford, "Inventing the Concurrent Majority," 50.

15 Ibid.

16 Ford, "Prophet with Posthumous Honor," 5.

17 *New Orleans Bee* and Thomas Ritchie, quoted in Cooper, *South and the Politics of Slavery*, 103, 111.

18 Henry Clay speech in the Senate, 1 September 1841, quoted in Remini, *Henry Clay, Statesman for the Union*, 595.

19 Brady and Martineau, quoted in Meredith, *Lincoln's Cameraman*, 24; and Wiltse, *John C. Calhoun: Sectionalist*, 308.

20 See Ford, "Prophet with Posthumous Honor," 3–25.

21 Calhoun's role as secretary of state in the Texas annexation issue is examined in Holt, *Rise and Fall of the American Whig Party*, 220–22.

22 For the origins of South Carolina's unusual governmental system, see Klein, *Unification of a Slave State*, 1–32.

Chapter Three

1 Alexander H. Stephens, quoted in Carey, *Parties, Slavery, and the Union in Antebellum Georgia*, 83.

2 Holt, *Rise and Fall of the American Whig Party*, 460n2.

3 John C. Calhoun, quoted in Sinha, *Counterrevolution of Slavery*, 83.

4 Thomas Hart Benton, quoted in Peterson, *Great Triumvirate*, 467.

5 Quotes in Kruman, *Parties and Politics in North Carolina*, 78, 81.

6 Sacher, *A Perfect War of Politics*, 163–68.

7 Kruman, *Parties and Politics in North Carolina*, 48–50.

8 For Alabama and Georgia, see ibid.

9 Ibid.; Carey, *Parties, Slavery, and the Union in Antebellum Georgia*, 125–26. See also Sacher, *A Perfect War of Politics*, 209–11, for Louisiana.

10 Kruman, *Parties and Politics in North Carolina*, 119.

11 Cantrell, *Kenneth and John B. Rayner*, 116.

12 Alexander H. Stephens to W. W. Burwell, 26 June 1854, in Carey, *Parties, Slavery, and the Union in Antebellum Georgia*, 186.

13 Stephens speech, April 1855, quoted in Schott, *Alexander H. Stephens of Georgia*, 184.

14 Carey, *Parties, Slavery, and the Union in Antebellum Georgia*, 207–10, 216–17.

15 Sacher, *A Perfect War of Politics*, 259–78.

16 Kruman, *Parties and Politics in North Carolina*, 180.

17 Link, *Roots of Secession*, 37, table 1.3.

18 Kruman, *Parties and Politics in North Carolina*, 181–96.

19 Potter, *Impending Crisis*, 326; see also 174–76, 238–40.

20 Bonham at a public meeting in Columbia, S.C., in Freehling, *Road to Disunion*, 398.

21 Brown, Message to Georgia Assembly, 7 November 1860, in ibid., 439.

22 Report in *New York Herald*, 11 October 1860, in Walther, *William Lowndes Yancey*, 262.

23 Edmund Ruffin, quoted in Sinha, *Counterrevolution of Slavery*, 237.

24 Memminger to John Rutherfoord, 27 November 1860, in Potter, *Impending Crisis*, 50.

25 A. F. Pugh diary entry, 8 January 1861, quoted in Sacher, *A Perfect War of Politics*, 297.

Chapter Four

1 Quoted in Fehrenbacher, *Sectional Crisis and Southern Constitutionalism*, 142.

2 Alexander H. Stephens, quoted in Rable, *Confederate Republic*, 57.

3 Davis inaugural address, cited in ibid., 122.

4 Howell Cobb to Provisional Congress, 17 February 1862, in Perman, *Major Problems in the Civil War and Reconstruction*, 239.

5 Stephens, "Cornerstone" speech, 21 March 1861, in ibid., 281.

6 Davis to Harris, 17 July 1861, in Cooper, *Jefferson Davis, American*, 389.

7 Thomas R. R. Cobb, quoted in Rable, *Confederate Republic*, 74.

8 *Richmond Whig*, 19 November 1861, in ibid., 98.

9 Ibid., 100.

10 Eugenius Nisbet to Stephens, 6 February 1862, in ibid., 112.

11 Alexander and Beringer, *Anatomy of the Confederate Congress*, 332.

12 Cooper, *Jefferson Davis, American*, 499.

13 Rable, *Confederate Republic*, 69.

14 Laurence M. Keitt to James H. Hammond, 14 June 1862, quoted in ibid., 148.

15 Stephens, quoted in ibid., 259.

16 Wigfall, quoted in ibid., 148.

17 Ibid., 262.

18 McPherson, *Battle Cry of Freedom*, 69.

Chapter Five

1 Douglass, "The Work of the Future," November 1862, in Philip S. Foner, ed., *Writings of Frederick Douglass*, 3:292–93.

2 Cited in Perman, *Reunion without Compromise*, 70.

3 Thaddeus Stevens, quoted in Foner, *Reconstruction*, 236.

4 Andrew Johnson, quoted in Perman, *Reunion without Compromise*, 107.

5 *Augusta Constitutionalist*, 22 January 1867, in ibid., 246.

6 James L. Orr to Herschel V. Johnson, 11 November 1866, in ibid., 241.

7 Jonathan Worth to Benjamin S. Hedrick, 10 October and 4 July 1866, in ibid., 238.

8 Benjamin F. Perry to *New York Herald*, late September 1866, in ibid., 242.

9 *Raleigh Sentinel*, 8 March 1869.

10 Quoted in Franklin, *Reconstruction: After the Civil War*, 105.

11 *Charleston Mercury*, 12 December 1867, in Perman, *Reunion without Compromise*, 339.

12 Tunis Campbell to Benjamin Conley, 22 February 1872, in Perman, *Road to Redemption*, 22.

13 Quoted in ibid., 32.

14 *Jackson Weekly Pilot*, 11 May 1871, in ibid., 34.

15 *Savannah Morning News*, 19 August 1973, in Foner, *Reconstruction*, 425.

16 Ibid.

17 Cited in Hahn, *A Nation under Our Feet*, 276.

18 These details on violence in 1868 are in ibid., 286; and Foner, *Reconstruction*, 342–43.

19 John Winsmith, quoted in Foner, *Reconstruction*, 443.

20 John B. Hubbard's report is in Zuczek, *State of Rebellion*, 81.

21 Quoted in Foner, *Reconstruction*, 442.

22 Quoted in ibid., 457.

23 See Williams, *Great South Carolina Ku Klux Klan Trials*.

24 *Charleston Daily News*, 18 April 1873, in Perman, *Road to Redemption*, 151.

25 Nathaniel B. Meade to Philip Dandridge, 28 April 1873, in ibid., 155.

26 Walter L. Bragg to E. D. Moren, 15 August 1874, in ibid., 149.

27 Adelbert Ames, quoted in Foner, *Reconstruction*, 561.

Chapter Six

1 Wade Hampton, quoted in Perman, *Emancipation and Reconstruction*, 116.

2 Cited in Woodward, *Origins of the New South*, 105–6.

3 Ibid., 58.

4 This boast was taken at face value by most historians of the post-Reconstruction South until Woodward's *Origins of the New South* exposed its emptiness and fraudulence in 1951. Historians since then have found Woodward's assessment to be accurate.

5 Cited in Ayers, *Promise of the New South*, 44.

6 William L. Royall, quoted in Woodward, *Origins of the New South*, 105.

7 Kousser, *Shaping of Southern Politics*, 91.

8 George C. McKee to the secretary of the navy, William E. Chandler, 6 July 1883, in Woodward, *Origins of the New South*, 103.

9 Cited in ibid., 80–81.

10 Dailey, *Before Jim Crow*, 36.

11 Chester A. Arthur, quoted in Tindall, *Disruption of the Solid South*, 13.

12 James L. Kemper, quoted in Dailey, *Before Jim Crow*, 30.

13 William Mahone to Harrison H. Riddleberger, 31 August 1877, quoted in ibid., 41.

14 William F. Cameron inaugural address, 1882, quoted in ibid., 84.

15 Ibid., 73–76.

16 Both quotes are in ibid., 150, 145.

Chapter Seven

1 Cited in Woodward, *Origins of the New South*, 191.

2 Quoted in Ayers, *Promise of the New South*, 220–21.

3 Ibid., 266.

4 Leonidas L. Polk speech, quoted in ibid., 259.

5 Milford W. Howard, quoted in McMath, *American Populism*, 165.

6 Frank Burkitt letter, 21 July 1892, quoted in Ayers, *Promise of the New South*, 268–89.

7 Tom Watson, quoted in ibid., 271.

8 Watson, "The Negro Question in the South," *Arena*, 1892, in Woodward, *Origins of the New South*, 257.

9   Tom Watson speech at Sparta, 25 August 1892, in Ayers, *Promise of the New South*, 273.
10 Cameron to H. H. Riddleberger, 22 March 1881, in Dailey, *Before Jim Crow*, 66.
11 The pressure on black voters is well analyzed in Ayers, *Promise of the New South*, 278–80.
12 Watson, *People's Party Paper*, 9 December 1892, quoted in Woodward, *Tom Watson*, 242.
13 Benjamin Tillman, quoted in Woodward, *Origins of the New South*, 279–80.
14 Joseph C. Manning, in *New York Tribune*, 19 March 1895, quoted in Ayers, *Promise of the New South*, 285.
15 Ibid., 291.
16 The term was coined by Woodward in *Origins of the New South*, 289.
17 Guthrie to Butler, 26 September 1896, in ibid., 288.
18 Tom Watson in his *People's Party Paper*, 13 November 1896, in ibid., 289.
19 Both quotes can be found in Perman, *Struggle for Mastery*, 15.
20 Ibid., 22.
21 Walter Watson speaking at the Virginia constitutional convention, quoted in ibid., 35.
22 Ibid., 9.
23 Reported in the *Jackson Clarion*, 9 September 1890.
24 Carter Glass speech to the Virginia convention, 4 April 1902, in Perman, *Struggle for Mastery*, 221.
25 Ernest B. Kruttshnitt speech to the Louisiana convention, 13 May 1898, in ibid., 147.
26 Ibid.
27 John Sharp Williams statement, in ibid., 315.
28 Chrisman speech, in *Jackson Clarion*, 9 September 1890.
29 Daniels's editorials on the need for a Democratic primary appeared in his paper, the *Raleigh News and Observer*, and appear in Perman, *Struggle for Mastery*, 302–4.

Chapter Eight
1   Key, *Southern Politics*, 407, 491.
2   Ibid., 447.
3   Ibid., 299, 385.
4   Ibid., 315.
5   Ibid., 346.
6   Ibid., 315.
7   Rae, *Southern Democrats*, 35–39.
8   Grantham, *Life and Death of the Solid South*, chaps. 2 and 4.
9   Key, *Southern Politics*, 304, 307n9.
10 Ibid., 3.
11 Ibid., 307, 308.
12 H. L. Mencken, quoted in Arsenault, *Wild Ass of the Ozarks*, 5.
13 Percy, *Lanterns on the Levee*, 143.
14 Ibid., 149.
15 Key, *Southern Politics*, 263–64.

16 Ibid., 232.

17 Jeff Davis, quoted in Arsenault, *Wild Ass of the Ozarks*, 97.

18 Jeff Davis speech at Conway, Arkansas, 13 June 1899, in ibid., 81.

19 Davis, quoted in ibid., 81.

20 Davis, quoted in ibid., 14.

21 Holmes, *White Chief*, 251–53.

22 John Sharp Williams, quoted in ibid., 253.

23 Arsenault, "Folklore of Southern Demagoguery," 83, 85.

24 Vardaman, quoted in Holmes, *White Chief*, 109.

25 Vardaman, quoted in ibid., 56.

26 T. Harry Williams, quoted in Arsenault, *Wild Ass of the Ozarks*, 15.

27 Ibid., 16.

28 Arsenault, "Folklore of Southern Demagoguery," 132.

Chapter Nine

1 Robert La Follette, quoted in Woodward, *Origins of the New South*, 371.

2 Sophonisba Breckinridge, quoted in Green, *Southern Strategies*, 149.

3 For Comer's career, see Harris, "Braxton Bragg Comer," 150–55.

4 Alexander McKelway, quoted in Grantham, *Southern Progressivism*, 161.

5 Woodward, *Origins of the New South*, 397.

6 Wilson to Underwood, 21 January 1913, in Grantham, *South in Modern America*, 65.

7 Josephus Daniels diary entry, quoted in Tindall, *Emergence of the New South*, 143–44.

8 Wilson to Oswald Garrison Villard, 21 August 1913, quoted in Grantham, *South in Modern America*, 68–69.

9 Tindall, *Emergence of the New South*, 11.

10 Claude Kitchen to Clyde Tavener, 3 August 1915, quoted in Grantham, *South in Modern America*, 76.

11 Tindall, *Emergence of the New South*, 48.

12 Fred Sullens, in *Jackson Daily News*, 8 August 1915, quoted in ibid., 24.

13 Grover C. Hall, quoted in ibid., 228.

14 Quoted in Grantham, *South in Modern America*, 106.

15 William G. McAdoo, quoted in Tindall, *Emergence of the New South*, 245.

Chapter Ten

1 Tindall, *Emergence of the New South*, 237.

2 Huey P. Long, quoted in Hair, *Kingfish and His Realm*, 159.

3 Kenneth McKellar, quoted in ibid., 309.

4 Quoted in Williams, *Huey Long*, 714.

5 Raymond Gram Swing, quoted in Hair, *Kingfish and His Realm*, 276, 297.

6 Norman Thomas, quoted in ibid., 296.

7 Franklin D. Roosevelt, quoted in ibid., 246.

8 Huey P. Long, quoted in ibid., 270.

9 Prior to Long, a precedent had been set in the first decade of the century by Senator Ben Tillman, who lectured and campaigned extensively in the northern states on behalf of white supremacy. Tillman had not created a national movement or party, however. See Kantrowitz, *Ben Tillman*, 268–86.

10 Zelizer, *On Capitol Hill*, 17.

11 William S. White, quoted in Caro, *Years of Lyndon Johnson: Master of the Senate*, xxiii, 94.

12 Turner Catledge, quoted in Grantham, *South in Modern America*, 123.

13 Fred Sullens, quoted in Tindall, *Emergence of the New South*, 608.

14 Carter Glass, quoted in ibid., 612.

15 Ibid., 618.

16 "Cotton Ed" Smith, quoted in ibid., 556.

17 Hatton W. Sumners, quoted in ibid., 620.

18 The details of this initiative are recounted in Sullivan, *Days of Hope*, 61–67.

19 *Manufacturers' Record*, quoted in Tindall, *Emergence of the New South*, 599.

20 Jimmy Byrnes, quoted in Grantham, *South in Modern America*, 133.

21 Patterson, *Congressional Conservatism and the New Deal*, 193–96, 244–46.

22 Walter White, quoted in Grantham, *South in Modern America*, 129.

Chapter Eleven

1 Theodore Bilbo, quoted in Grantham, *South in Modern America*, 195.

2 William Colmer, quoted in Sullivan, *Days of Hope*, 117.

3 Lister Hill, quoted in ibid., 119–20.

4 Garson, *Democratic Party and the Politics of Sectionalism*, 49.

5 Josiah Bailey Senate speech, 7 December 1943, quoted in ibid., 48.

6 Bilbo, quoted in Grantham, *South in Modern America*, 196.

7 See Katznelson, Geiger, and Kryder, "Limiting Liberalism," 283–306; and Katznelson, *When Affirmative Action Was White*.

8 Key, *Southern Politics*, 315.

9 Katznelson, Geiger, and Kryder, "Limiting Liberalism," 285.

10 Clark Clifford, quoted in Garson, *Democratic Party and the Politics of Sectionalism*, 231.

Chapter Twelve

1 Harry S. Truman, quoted in Lawson, *Running for Freedom*, 32–33.

2 Burnet R. Maybank, quoted in Donovan, *Conflict and Crisis*, 33.

3 "To secure these rights" is a phrase in the Declaration of Independence, and the rights to be secured were those specified in the Declaration's third sentence, namely, "life, liberty and the pursuit of happiness."

4 Harry S. Truman diary entry, quoted in Donovan, *Conflict and Crisis*, 353.

5 Tom Connally, quoted in ibid., 354.

6 John Bell Williams, quoted in Garson, *Democratic Party and the Politics of Sectionalism*, 235.

7 James O. Eastland, quoted in ibid., 233.

8 Donovan, *Conflict and Crisis*, 356.

9 Bartley, *New South*, 87.

10 Strom Thurmond, quoted in Garson, *Democratic Party and the Politics of Sectionalism*, 239.

11 Gessner McCorvey, quoted in ibid., 289.

12 Bloom, *Class, Race, and the Civil Rights Movement*, 76.

13 The plank is in Frederickson, *Dixiecrat Revolt*, 264n57.

14 Hubert Humphrey, quoted in Garson, *Democratic Party and the Politics of Sectionalism*, 278.

15 Strom Thurmond, quoted in Frederickson, *Dixiecrat Revolt*, 171.

16 Strom Thurmond, quoted in ibid., 105.

17 *Louisville Courier-Journal*, 18 October 1948, in ibid., 143.

18 Key, *Southern Politics*, 670–71.

19 Richard Russell and Thomas Stanley, quoted in Patterson, *Brown v. Board of Education*, 78–79.

20 *Louisville Courier-Journal*, quoted in Grantham, *South in Modern America*, 205–6.

21 Both of Eisenhower's comments are in Patterson, *Brown v. Board of Education*, 81.

22 Eisenhower, quoted in Bartley, *New South*, 231.

23 Ibid., 192–93; quote on 194.

24 Southern Manifesto, quoted in Patterson, *Brown v. Board of Education*, 98–99.

25 Byrd to *Richmond News Leader*, 12 March 1956, quoted in Bartley, *Rise of Massive Resistance*, 117.

26 Harry F. Byrd, quoted in ibid., 10.

27 Pat Watters, quoted in Grantham, *South in Modern America*, 212.

28 A comment by historian Charles Payne, quoted in Patterson, *Brown v. Board of Education*, 96.

29 James O. Eastland, in *Jackson Daily News*, 5 October 1955, quoted in Bartley, *New South*, 213.

30 LeRoy Collins, in *Miami Herald*, 8 February 1956, quoted in ibid., 217.

31 Ibid., 225.

Chapter Thirteen

1 Branch, *Parting the Waters*, 317.

2 Lawson, *Black Ballots*, 175.

3 Reported in *Chicago Defender*, 12 January 1957, in Lawson, *Black Ballots*, 166.

4 Lyndon B. Johnson to Arthur Schlesinger Jr., 21 June 1957, in Dallek, *Lone Star Rising*, 518–19.

5 Harry McPherson, a longtime aide of Johnson, in ibid., 519.

6 Russell to George Reedy, in ibid., 518.

7 George Reedy, quoted in ibid., 518.

8 Richard Russell, quoted in ibid., 522.

9 Richard Russell, quoted in Caro, *Years of Lyndon Johnson: Master of the Senate*, 1007.

10 Paul Douglas, quoted in ibid., 1007.

11 Bayard Rustin, quoted in Dallek, *Lone Star Rising*, 527.

12 Speech in the Senate, 7 August 1957, in Caro, *Years of Lyndon Johnson: Master of the Senate*, 1010.

13 Eisenhower, quoted in Lawson, *Black Ballots*, 179.

14 Ibid., 249.

15 Lawson, *Running for Freedom*, 72.

16 Bob Moses, quoted in Lawson, *Black Ballots*, 191.

17 This list was compiled by Pat Watters and Reese Cleghorn, in their book, *Climbing Jacob's Ladder*, cited in Bartley, *New South*, 347.

18 Lawson, *Black Ballots*, 306.

19 Martin Luther King Jr., quoted in Branch, *Pillar of Fire*, 523.

20 Lyndon Johnson speech to joint session of Congress, 15 March 1965, quoted in Lawson, *Black Ballots*, 312.

21 Quoted in Bartley, *New South*, 388.

22 Barry Goldwater, quoted in ibid., 385.

23 Nicholas Katzenbach, quoted in Lawson, *Black Ballots*, 313.

24 Data on registration by race cited in this note can be found in ibid., 331, table 3; Black and Black, *Politics and Society in the South*, 134–51; and Grantham, *South in Modern America*, 287.

Chapter Fourteen

1 George C. Wallace, quoted in Carter, *Politics of Rage*, 96. As Carter indicates, there is some uncertainty about when Wallace made this remark, or even whether he said it at all. But the ugly phrase stuck with him throughout his career.

2 Wallace, quoted in ibid., 106.

3 *New York Times*, quoted in ibid., 208; Wallace, quoted in ibid., 194.

4 Wallace, quoted in ibid., 215.

5 Ibid., 346.

6 "T.R.B.," quoted in ibid., 367.

7 Martin Luther King Jr. interview with Dan Rather, CBS News, June 1963, in ibid., 156.

8 Ibid., 291.

9 Wallace, quoted in ibid., 367.

10 Wallace, quoted in Bartley, *New South*, 411.

11 Despite carrying these states, Wallace obtained few delegates because he failed to pick them and put them on the ballot, a typical oversight on the part of a Wallace campaign organization. But Wallace was simply campaigning and stirring up his supporters rather than actually seeking the nomination or wanting to be president.

12 Wallace, quoted in Carter, *Politics of Rage*, 432, 472.

13 Jimmy Carter inaugural address, quoted in Bartley, *New South*, 400.

14 These tactics are analyzed in Sanders, *Mighty Peculiar Elections*.

15 See Bartley, *New South*, 398–404; and McMath, "Constructing Southern Lives," 180–88.

16 Jimmy Carter, quoted in Lamis, *Two-Party South*, 39.

17 Ibid., 37–38; Black and Black, *Politics and Society in the South*, chap. 8.

18 Andrew Young, quoted in Lawson, *Running for Freedom*, 194.

19 Ibid., 126, 157; Black and Black, *Politics and Society*, 148.

20 Richard Arrington, quoted in Lawson, *Running for Freedom*, 159.

21 Black and Black, *Politics and Society*, 147–48.

22 Quote from Murphy and Gulliver's *Southern Strategy*, in Lamis, *Two-Party South*, 30.

23 Lawson, *Running for Freedom*, 139.

24 Lamis, *Two-Party South*, 35–36, table 3.4.

25 Beck, "Partisan Dealignment in the Post-War South," 477–96.

26 Jimmy Carter interview, 20 November 1973, in Lamis, *Two-Party South*, 35.

27 A Mississippi Republican, quoted in ibid., 40.

28 Zelizer, *On Capitol Hill*, 54.

29 Wilbur Mills, quoted in ibid., 165.

30 *Washington Post* editorial, quoted in ibid., 167.

31 See Sinclair, *Transformation of the U.S. Senate*.

32 The debate and its outcome are analyzed in Zelizer, *On Capitol Hill*, 172–75.

Chapter Fifteen

1 Interview with Representative David R. Bowen, 28 July 1982, in Lamis, *Two-Party South*, 230.

2 Black and Black, *Rise of Southern Republicans*, 222.

3 Ronald Reagan, quoted in ibid., 212.

4 *Washington Post*, 4 August 1980, in ibid., 216.

5 Lamis, *Two-Party South*, 39; Black and Black, *Rise of Southern Republicans*, 328; Grantham, *South in Modern America*, 302.

6 Black and Black, *Rise of Southern Republicans*, 328–29.

7 Ibid., 328–43.

8 Lamis, "The Emergence of a Two-Party System," 237–40; Bullock, "Creeping Realignment in the South," 232.

9 Black and Black, *Rise of Southern Republicans*, 261.

10 Ibid., 334–35.

11 Grofman and Handley, "Estimating the Impact of Voting-Rights-Related Districting," 51–65.

BIBLIOGRAPHY

The books, articles, and essays listed here include those works cited in the notes as well as a selection of items that readers might find useful in pursuing topics discussed in a particular chapter. Of course, this short list is far from definitive or thorough, since the historical literature on southern political history is enormous.

Southern history has been covered in nine of a planned ten volumes in the series, A History of the South, published by Louisiana State University Press in Baton Rouge. Of these, four in particular have been consulted for this book about the political history of the South. They will not be listed in the bibliography below, though they are sometimes cited in the notes. The relevant volumes are the following: Charles S. Sydnor, *The Development of Southern Sectionalism, 1819–1848* (1948); C. Vann Woodward, *Origins of the New South, 1877–1913* (1951); George B. Tindall, *The Emergence of the New South, 1913–1945* (1967); and Numan V. Bartley, *The New South, 1945–1980* (1995). Two volumes by Dewey W. Grantham, which cover extended periods of southern history in the twentieth century, will be mentioned here; each will appear just once in the list that follows, although they are cited more often in the notes. They are *The Life and Death of the Solid South: A Political History* (Lexington: University Press of Kentucky, 1988); and *The South in Modern America: A Region at Odds* (New York: Harper and Row, 1994), a volume in the New American Nation series. Finally, a college textbook, William J. Cooper Jr. and Thomas E. Terrill, *The American South: A History*, 4th ed. (New York: Rowman and Littlefield, 2008), provides a useful general history.

1. A One-Party South: Republican Ascendancy

Ambler, Charles H. *Thomas Ritchie: A Study in Virginia Politics*. Richmond: Ball Book and Stationery, 1913.

Banner, James M., Jr. *To the Hartford Convention: The Federalists and the Origins of Party Politics in Massachusetts, 1789–1815*. New York: Alfred A. Knopf, 1969.

Broussard, James H. *The Southern Federalists, 1800–1816*. Baton Rouge: Louisiana State University Press, 1978.

Cunningham, Noble E. *The Jeffersonian Republicans in Power: Party Operations, 1801–1809*. Chapel Hill: University of North Carolina Press, 1963.

Egerton, Douglas R. *Charles Fenton Mercer and the Trial of National Conservatism*. Jackson: University Press of Mississippi, 1989.

Ellis, Joseph J. *American Sphinx: The Character of Thomas Jefferson*. New York: Knopf, 1996.

Fehrenbacher, Don E. *Sectional Crisis and Southern Constitutionalism*. Baton Rouge: Louisiana State University Press, 1995, 9–23.

Forbes, Robert Pierce. *The Missouri Compromise and Its Aftermath: Slavery and the Meaning of America*. Chapel Hill: University of North Carolina Press, 2007.

Hamilton, Stanislaus Murray, ed. *The Writings of James Monroe*. Vol. 6. New York: Putnam's, 1902.

Koch, Adrienne, and William Peden, eds. *The Life and Selected Writings of Thomas Jefferson*. New York: Modern Library, 1944.

McCormick, Richard P. *The Presidential Game: The Origins of American Presidential Politics*. New York: Oxford University Press, 1982.

McCoy, Drew R. *The Elusive Republic: Political Economy in Jeffersonian America*. Chapel Hill: University of North Carolina Press, 1980.

Moore, Glover. *The Missouri Controversy, 1819–1821*. Lexington: University Press of Kentucky, 1953.

Risjord, Norman K. *The Old Republicans: Southern Conservatism in the Age of Jefferson*. New York: Columbia University Press, 1965.

Sharp, James Roger. *American Politics in the Early Republic: The New Nation in Crisis*. New Haven: Yale University Press, 1993.

2. A Two-Party South: Whigs and Democrats

Cooper, William J., Jr. *The South and the Politics of Slavery, 1828–1856*. Baton Rouge: Louisiana State University Press, 1978.

Fehrenbacher, Don E. *Sectional Crisis and Southern Constitutionalism*. Baton Rouge: Louisiana State University Press, 1995, 81–112.

Ford, Lacy K., Jr. "Inventing the Concurrent Majority: Madison, Calhoun, and the Problem of Majoritarianism in American Political Thought." *Journal of Southern History* 60 (February 1994): 19–58.

———. "Prophet with Posthumous Honor: John C. Calhoun and the Southern Political Tradition." In *Is There a Southern Political Tradition?*, edited by Charles W. Eagles. Jackson: University Press of Mississippi, 1996.

Holt, Michael F. *Political Parties and American Political Development from the Age of Jackson to the Age of Lincoln*. Baton Rouge: Louisiana State University Press, 1992, 151–91.

———. *The Rise and Fall of the American Whig Party: Jacksonian Politics and the Onset of the Civil War*. New York: Oxford University Press, 1999.

Klein, Rachel N. *Unification of a Slave State: The Rise of the Planter Class in the South Carolina Backcountry, 1760–1808*. Chapel Hill: University of North Carolina Press, 1990.

McCormick, Richard P. *The Second Party System: Party Formation in the Jacksonian Era*. Chapel Hill: University of North Carolina Press, 1966.

Meredith, Roy. *Mr. Lincoln's Cameraman: Mathew Brady*. 2nd rev. ed. New York: Dover, 1974.

Niven, John. *John C. Calhoun and the Price of Union*. Baton Rouge: Louisiana State University Press, 1988.

Remini, Robert V. *Henry Clay, Statesman for the Union*. New York: W. W. Norton, 1991.

———. *Martin Van Buren and the Making of the Democratic Party*. New York: Columbia University Press, 1959.

Sacher, John M. *A Perfect War of Politics: Parties, Politicians, and Democracy in Louisiana, 1824–1861*. Baton Rouge: Louisiana State University Press, 2003.

Watson, Harry. *Liberty and Power: The Politics of Jacksonian America*. New York: Hill and Wang, 1990.

Wiltse, Charles M. *John C. Calhoun: Sectionalist, 1840–1850*. Indianapolis: Bobbs Merrill, 1951.

3. A One-Party South Again: Democratic Ascendancy

Cantrell, Gregg. *Kenneth and John B. Rayner and the Limits of Southern Dissent*. Urbana: University of Illinois Press, 1993.

Carey, Anthony Gene. *Parties, Slavery, and the Union in Antebellum Georgia*. Athens: University of Georgia Press, 1997.

Cooper, William J., Jr. *Liberty and Slavery: Southern Politics to 1860*. New York: Alfred A. Knopf, 1983.

Crofts, Daniel W. *Reluctant Confederates: Upper South Unionists in the Secession Crisis*. Chapel Hill: University of North Carolina Press, 1989.

Dew, Charles B. *Apostles of Disunion: Southern Secession Commissioners and the Causes of the Civil War*. Charlottesville: University Press of Virginia, 2001.

Faust, Drew Gilpin. *James Henry Hammond and the Old South: A Design for Mastery*. Baton Rouge: Louisiana State University Press, 1982.

Fehrenbacher, Don E. *The Dred Scott Case: Its Significance in American Law and Politics*. New York: Oxford University Press, 1978.

Freehling, William W. *The Road to Disunion: Secessionists Triumphant, 1854–1861*. New York: Oxford University Press, 2007.

Kruman, Marc W. *Parties and Politics in North Carolina, 1836–1865*. Baton Rouge: Louisiana State University Press, 1983.

Link, William A. *The Roots of Secession: Slavery and Politics in Antebellum Virginia*. Chapel Hill: University of North Carolina Press, 2003.

Peterson, Merrill D. *The Great Triumvirate: Webster, Clay, and Calhoun*. New York: Oxford University Press, 1987.

Potter, David M. *The Impending Crisis, 1848–1861*. New York: Harper and Row, 1976.

Sacher, John M. *A Perfect War of Politics: Parties, Politicians, and Democracy in Louisiana, 1824–1861*. Baton Rouge: Louisiana State University Press, 2003.

Schott, Thomas E. *Alexander H. Stephens of Georgia: A Biography*. Baton Rouge: Louisiana State University Press, 1987.

Sinha, Manisha. *The Counterrevolution of Slavery: Politics and Ideology in Antebellum South Carolina*. Chapel Hill: University of North Carolina Press, 2000.

Thornton, J. Mills, III. *Politics and Power in a Slave Society: Alabama, 1800–1860*. Baton Rouge: Louisiana State University Press, 1978.

Walther, Eric H. *The Fire-Eaters*. Baton Rouge: Louisiana State University Press, 1992.

——. *William Lowndes Yancey and the Coming of the Civil War*. Chapel Hill: University of North Carolina Press, 2006.

4. Politics without Parties: The Confederacy

Alexander, Thomas B., and Richard E. Beringer. *Anatomy of the Confederate Congress*. Nashville: Vanderbilt University Press, 1972.

Bensel, Richard Franklin. *Yankee Leviathan: The Origins of Central State Authority in America, 1859–1877*. New York: Cambridge University Press, 1990.

Cooper, William J., Jr. *Jefferson Davis, American*. New York: Alfred A. Knopf, 2000.

——. *Jefferson Davis and the Civil War Era*. Baton Rouge: Louisiana State University Press, 2008.

Escott, Paul. *After Secession: Jefferson Davis and the Failure of Confederate Nationalism.* Baton Rouge: Louisiana State University Press, 1978.

Faust, Drew Gilpin. *The Creation of Confederate Nationalism: Ideology and Identity in the Civil War South.* Baton Rouge: Louisiana State University Press, 1988.

Fehrenbacher, Don E. *Sectional Crisis and Southern Constitutionalism.* Baton Rouge: Louisiana State University Press, 1995, 137–61.

McPherson, James M. *Battle Cry of Freedom: The Civil War Era.* New York: Oxford University Press, 1988.

Nieman, Donald. "Republicanism, the Confederate Constitution, and the American Constitutional Tradition." In Kermit L. Hall and James W. Ely, eds. *An Uncertain Tradition: Constitutionalism in the History of the South.* Athens: University of Georgia Press, 1989.

Perman, Michael, ed. *Major Problems in the Civil War and Reconstruction.* 1st ed. Lexington, Mass.: D.C. Heath, 1991.

Rable, George C. *The Confederate Republic: A Revolution against Politics.* Chapel Hill: University of North Carolina Press, 1994.

Yearns, Wilfred Buck. *The Confederate Congress.* Athens: University of Georgia Press, 1960.

5. Party Politics under Assault: Reconstruction

Fitzgerald, Michael W. *Splendid Failure: Postwar Reconstruction in the American South.* Chicago: Ivan R. Dee, 2007.

Foner, Eric. *Nothing but Freedom: Emancipation and Its Legacy.* Baton Rouge: Louisiana State University, 1983.

———. *Reconstruction: America's Unfinished Revolution, 1863–1877.* New York: Harper and Row, 1988.

Foner, Philip S., ed. *The Life and Writings of Frederick Douglass.* Vol. 3. New York: International Publishers, 1952.

Franklin, John Hope. *Reconstruction: After the Civil War.* Chicago: University of Chicago Press, 1961.

Hahn, Steven. *A Nation under Our Feet: Black Political Struggles in the Rural South, from Slavery to the Great Migration.* Cambridge: Harvard University Press, 2003.

Holt, Thomas C. *Black over White: Negro Political Leadership in South Carolina during Reconstruction.* Urbana: University of Illinois Press, 1977.

Perman, Michael. *Reunion without Compromise: The South and Reconstruction, 1865–1868.* New York: Cambridge University Press, 1973.

———. *The Road to Redemption: Southern Politics, 1869–1879.* Chapel Hill: University of North Carolina Press, 1984.

Rable, George C. *But There Was No Peace: The Role of Violence in the Politics of Reconstruction.* Athens: University of Georgia Press, 1984.

Tunnell, Ted. *War, Radicalism, and Race in Louisiana, 1862–1877.* Baton Rouge: Louisiana State University Press, 1984.

Williams, Lou Falkner. *The Great South Carolina Ku Klux Klan Trials, 1871–1872.* Athens: University of Georgia Press, 1996.

Zuczek, Richard. *State of Rebellion: Reconstruction in South Carolina.* Columbia: University of South Carolina Press, 1996.

6. Achieving Democratic Hegemony: The 1880s

Anderson, Eric. *Race and Politics in North Carolina, 1872–1901: The Black Second.* Baton Rouge: Louisiana State University Press, 1981.

Ayers, Edward L. *The Promise of the New South: Life after Reconstruction.* New York: Oxford University Press, 1992.

Dailey, Jane. *Before Jim Crow: The Politics of Race in Postemancipation Virginia.* Chapel Hill: University of North Carolina Press, 2000.

Hair, William Ivy. *Bourbonism and Agrarian Protest: Louisiana Politics, 1877–1890.* Baton Rouge: Louisiana State University Press, 1969.

Kantrowitz, Stephen. *Ben Tillman and the Reconstruction of White Supremacy.* Chapel Hill: University of North Carolina Press, 2000.

Kirwan, Albert D. *Revolt of the Rednecks: Mississippi Politics, 1876–1925.* Lexington: University Press of Kentucky, 1951.

Moore, James Tice. "The Redeemers Reconsidered: Change and Continuity in the Democratic South, 1870–1900." *Journal of Southern History* 44 (August 1978): 357–78.

Perman, Michael. *Emancipation and Reconstruction.* Wheeling, Ill.: Harlan Davidson, 2003.

Rabinowitz, Howard N. *Race Relations in the Urban South, 1865–1900.* New York: Oxford University Press, 1978.

Tindall, George Brown. *The Disruption of the Solid South.* Athens: University of Georgia Press, 1972.

7. Eliminating the Opposition: The 1890s

Gilmore, Glenda Elizabeth. *Gender and Jim Crow: Women and the Politics of White Supremacy in North Carolina, 1896–1920.* Chapel Hill: University of North Carolina Press, 1996.

Kazin, Michael. *Godly Hero: The Life of William Jennings Bryan.* New York: Alfred A. Knopf, 2006.

Kousser, J. Morgan. *The Shaping of Southern Politics: Suffrage Restriction and the Establishment of the One-Party South, 1880–1910.* New Haven: Yale University Press, 1974.

McMath, Robert C., Jr. *American Populism: A Social History, 1877–1898.* New York: Hill and Wang, 1993.

Perman, Michael. *Struggle for Mastery: Disfranchisement in the South, 1888–1908.* Chapel Hill: University of North Carolina Press, 2001.

Shaw, Barton C. *The Wool-Hat Boys: Georgia's Populist Party.* Baton Rouge: Louisiana State University Press, 1984.

Woodward, C. Vann. *Tom Watson, Agrarian Rebel.* New York: Macmillan, 1938.

8. Democrats and Demagogues in the Solid South

Arsenault, Raymond. "The Folklore of Southern Demagoguery." In *Is There a Southern Political Tradition?*, edited by Charles W. Eagles. Jackson: University Press of Mississippi, 1996.

——.*The Wild Ass of the Ozarks: Jeff Davis and the Social Bases of Southern Politics.* Philadelphia: Temple University Press, 1984.

Grantham, Dewey W. *The Life and Death of the Solid South: A Political History*. Lexington: University Press of Kentucky, 1988.

Holmes, William F. *The White Chief: James Kimble Vardaman*. Baton Rouge: Louisiana State University Press, 1970.

Key, V. O., Jr. *Southern Politics in State and Nation*. New York: Alfred A. Knopf, 1949.

Michie, Allan, and Frank Rhylick. *Dixie Demagogues*. New York: Vanguard Press, 1939.

Morgan, Chester M. *Redneck Liberal: Theodore G. Bilbo and the New Deal*. Baton Rouge: Louisiana State University Press, 1985.

Percy, William Alexander. *Lanterns on the Levee: Recollections of a Planter's Son*. New York: Alfred A. Knopf, 1941.

Rae, Nicol C. *Southern Democrats*. New York: Oxford University Press, 1994.

Webb, Samuel L. *Two-Party Politics in the One-Party South: Alabama's Hill Country, 1874–1920*. Tuscaloosa: University of Alabama Press, 1997.

9. Reform and Reaction in the Solid South

Burner, David. *The Politics of Provincialism: The Democratic Party in Transition, 1918–1932*. New York: Alfred A. Knopf, 1967.

Gould, Lewis L. *Progressives and Prohibitionists: Texas Democrats in the Wilson Era*. Austin: University of Texas Press, 1973.

Grantham, Dewey W. *Southern Progressivism: The Reconciliation of Progress and Tradition*. Knoxville: University of Tennessee Press, 1983.

——. *The South in Modern America: A Region at Odds*. New York: Harper and Row, 1994.

Green, Elna. *Southern Strategies: Southern Women and the Woman Suffrage Question*. Chapel Hill: University of North Carolina Press, 1997.

Harris, David Alan. "Braxton Bragg Comer, 1907–1911." In *Alabama's Governors*, edited by Samuel L. Webb and Margaret Armbruster. Tuscaloosa: University of Alabama Press, 2001.

Link, William A. *The Paradox of Southern Progressivism, 1880–1930*. Chapel Hill: University of North Carolina Press, 1992.

Sanders, Elizabeth. *Roots of Reform: Farmers, Workers, and the American State, 1877–1917*. Chicago: University of Chicago Press, 1999.

Sarasohn, David. *The Party of Reform: Democrats in the Progressive Era*. Jackson: University Press of Mississippi, 1989.

Tindall, George B. "The Benighted South: Origins of a Modern Image." *Virginia Quarterly Review* 40 (1964): 281–94.

Wheeler, Marjorie Spruill. *New Women of the New South: The Leaders of the Woman Suffrage Movement in the Southern States*. New York: Oxford University Press, 1993.

10. The New Deal Challenge to the Solid South

Badger, Anthony J. *The New Deal: The Depression Years, 1933–1940*. New York: Hill and Wang, 1989.

Biles, Roger. *The South and the New Deal*. Lexington: University Press of Kentucky, 1994.

Brinkley, Alan. "The New Deal and Southern Politics." In *The New Deal and the South*, edited by James C. Cobb and Michael V. Namorato. Jackson: University Press of Mississippi, 1984.

Caro, Robert A. *The Years of Lyndon Johnson: Master of the Senate.* New York: Alfred A. Knopf, 2002.

Grantham, Dewey W. *The South in Modern America: A Region at Odds.* New York: Harper and Row, 1994.

Hair, William I. *The Kingfish and His Realm: The Life and Times of Huey P. Long.* Baton Rouge: Louisiana State University Press, 1991.

Leuchtenburg, William E. *The White House Looks South.* Baton Rouge: Louisiana State University Press, 2005, chaps. 1–4 on Franklin D. Roosevelt.

Patterson, James T. *Congressional Conservatism and the New Deal.* Lexington: University Press of Kentucky, 1967.

Sullivan, Patricia. *Days of Hope: Race and Democracy in the New Deal Era.* Chapel Hill: University of North Carolina Press, 1996.

Williams, T. Harry. *Huey Long.* New York: Alfred A. Knopf, 1969.

Zangrando, Robert L. *The NAACP Crusade against Lynching, 1909–1950.* Philadelphia: Temple University Press, 1980.

Zelizer, Julian E. *On Capitol Hill: The Struggle to Reform Congress and Its Consequences, 1948–2000.* New York: Cambridge University Press, 2004.

11. The Liberal Challenge in the 1940s

Garson, Robert A. *The Democratic Party and the Politics of Sectionalism, 1941–1948.* Baton Rouge: Louisiana State University Press, 1974.

Katznelson, Ira. *When Affirmative Action Was White: An Untold Story of Racial Inequality in Twentieth-Century America.* New York: W. W. Norton, 2005.

Katznelson, Ira, Kim Geiger, and Daniel Kryder. "Limiting Liberalism: The Southern Veto in Congress, 1933–1950." *Political Science Quarterly* 108 (Summer 1993): 283–306.

Leuchtenburg, William E. *The White House Looks South.* Baton Rouge: Louisiana State University Press, 2005, chaps. 5–7 on Harry S. Truman.

McMillen, Neil R., ed. *Remaking Dixie: The Impact of World War Two on the American South.* Jackson: University Press of Mississippi, 1997.

Schulman, Bruce J. *From Cotton Belt to Sunbelt: Federal Policy, Economic Development, and the Transformation of the South, 1938–1980.* New York: Oxford University Press, 1991.

12. The Solid South under Attack: White Defiance

Barnard, William D. *Dixiecrats and Democrats: Alabama Politics, 1942–1950.* Tuscaloosa: University of Alabama Press, 1974.

Bartley, Numan V. *The Rise of Massive Resistance: Race and Politics in the South during the 1950s.* Baton Rouge: Louisiana State University Press, 1969.

Bloom, Jack M. *Class, Race, and the Civil Rights Movement.* Bloomington: Indiana University Press, 1987.

Cohodas, Nadine. *Strom Thurmond and the Politics of Southern Change.* New York: Simon and Schuster, 1993.

Donovan, Robert J. *Conflict and Crisis: The Presidency of Harry S. Truman, 1945–1948.* New York: W. W. Norton, 1977.

Frederickson, Kari. *The Dixiecrat Revolt and the End of the Solid South, 1932–1968.* Chapel Hill: University of North Carolina Press, 2001.

Freyer, Tony. *Little Rock on Trial: Cooper v. Aaron and School Desegregation.* Lawrence: University Press of Kansas, 2007.

Lassiter, Matthew D. *The Silent Majority: Suburban Politics in the Sunbelt South.* Princeton: Princeton University Press, 2006.

Lassiter, Matthew D., and Andrew B. Lewis, eds. *The Moderates' Dilemma: Massive Resistance to School Desegregation in Virginia.* Charlottesville: University Press of Virginia, 1998.

Patterson, James T. *Brown v. Board of Education: A Civil Rights Milestone and Its Troubled Legacy.* New York: Oxford University Press, 2001.

Tushnet, Mark V. *The NAACP's Legal Strategy against Segregated Education, 1925–1950.* Chapel Hill: University of North Carolina Press, 1987.

Webb, Clive, ed. *Massive Resistance: Southern Opposition to the Second Reconstruction.* New York: Oxford University Press, 2005.

13. The Solid South under Attack: Black Gains

Branch, Taylor. *Parting the Waters: America in the King Years, 1954–1963.* New York: Simon and Schuster, 1988.

———. *Pillar of Fire: America in the King Years, 1963–1965.* New York: Simon and Schuster, 1998.

Caro, Robert A. *The Years of Lyndon Johnson: Master of the Senate.* New York: Alfred A. Knopf, 2002.

Dallek, Robert. *Lone Star Rising: Lyndon Johnson and His Times, 1908–1960.* New York: Oxford University Press, 1991.

Garrow, David J. *Protest at Selma: Martin Luther King, Jr., and the Voting Rights Act of 1965.* New Haven: Yale University Press, 1978.

Keyssar, Alexander. *The Right to Vote: The Contested History of Democracy in the United States.* New York: Basic Books, 2000.

Lawson, Steven F. *Black Ballots: Voting Rights in the South, 1944–1969.* New Haven: Yale University Press, 1978.

———. *Running for Freedom: Civil Rights and Black Politics in America since 1941.* New York: McGraw Hill, 1991.

Leuchtenburg, William E. *The White House Looks South.* Baton Rouge: Louisiana State University Press, 2005, chaps. 8–11 on Lyndon B. Johnson.

Polsby, Nelson W., ed. *Reapportionment in the 1970s.* Berkeley: University of California Press, 1971.

14. Old Responses and New Directions, 1965–1980

Beck, Paul A. "Partisan Dealignment in the Post-War South." *American Political Science Review* 71 (July 1977): 477–96.

Black, Earl, and Merle Black. *Politics and Society in the South.* Cambridge: Harvard University Press, 1987.

Carter, Dan T. *The Politics of Rage: George Wallace, the Origins of the New Conservatism, and the Transformation of American Politics.* Baton Rouge: Louisiana State University Press, 1995.

Lamis, Alexander P. *The Two-Party South.* New York: Oxford University Press, 1984.

Lawson, Steven F. *In Pursuit of Power: Southern Blacks and Electoral Politics, 1965–1982.* New York: Columbia University Press, 1985.

McMath, Robert C., Jr. "Constructing Southern Lives: Jimmy Carter, Bill Clinton and the Art of Political Biography." In *Is There a Southern Political Tradition?*, edited by Charles W. Eagles. Jackson: University Press of Mississippi, 1996.

Sanders, Randy. *Mighty Peculiar Elections: The New South Gubernatorial Campaigns of 1970 and the Changing Politics of Race*. Gainesville: University of Florida Press, 2002.

Sinclair, Barbara. *The Transformation of the U.S. Senate*. Baltimore: Johns Hopkins University Press, 1989.

Zelizer, Julian E. *On Capitol Hill: The Struggle to Reform Congress and Its Consequences, 1948–2000*. New York: Cambridge University Press, 2004.

15. The Emergence of a Two-Party South since 1980

Black, Earl, and Merle Black. *The Rise of Southern Republicans*. Cambridge: Harvard University Press, 2002.

Bullock, Charles, III. "Creeping Realignment in the South." In *The South's New Politics: Realignment and Dealignment*, edited by Robert H. Swansbrough and David M. Brodsky. Columbia: University of South Carolina Press, 1988.

Carter, Dan T. *From George Wallace to Newt Gingrich: Race in the Conservative Counterrevolution, 1963–1994*. Baton Rouge: Louisiana State University Press, 1996.

Davidson, Chandler, and Bernard Grofman, eds. *Quiet Revolution in the South: The Impact of the Voting Rights Act, 1965–1990*. Princeton: Princeton University Press, 1994.

Grofman, Bernard, and Lisa Handley. "Estimating the Impact of Voting-Rights-Related Districting on Democratic Strength in the U.S. House of Representatives." In *Race and Redistricting in the 1990s*, edited by Bernard Grofman. Bronx: Agathon Press, 1998.

Lamis, Alexander P. "The Emergence of a Two-Party System." In *The American South in the Twentieth Century*, edited by Craig S. Pascoe, Karen Trahan Leathem, and Andy Ambrose. Athens: University of Georgia Press, 2005.

——, ed. *Southern Politics in the 1990s*. Baton Rouge: Louisiana State University Press, 1999.

Rae, Nicol C. *Southern Democrats*. New York: Oxford University Press, 1994.